Hodding Carter

Also by Ann Waldron

Close Connections: Caroline Gordon and the Southern Renaissance

FOR CHILDREN

The House on Pendleton Block

The Integration of Mary-Larkin Thornhill

The Luckie Star

Scaredy Cat

The French Detection

The Blueberry Collection

True or False? The Detection of Art Forgeries

Monet

Goya

Hodding Carter

The Reconstruction of a Racist

Ann Waldron

Algonquin Books of Chapel Hill

1993

Published by
Algonquin Books of Chapel Hill
Post Office Box 2225
Chapel Hill, North Carolina 27515-2225

a division of
Workman Publishing Company, Inc.
708 Broadway
New York, New York 10003

Library of Congress Cataloging-in-Publication Data
Waldron, Ann.
    Hodding Carter / Ann Waldron.
        p.   cm.
    Includes bibliographical references and index.
    ISBN 0-945575-38-6
    1. Carter, Hodding, 1907–1972.   2. Newspaper editors—
Mississippi—Biography.   3. Civil rights movements—Mississippi
—History—20th century.   I. Title.
PN4874.C27W35   1993
070'.92—dc20
[B]   92-42416 CIP

10 9 8 7 6 5 4 3 2 1

First Printing

To the memory of Martin Waldron, newspaperman

Contents

[Greenville was] the most urbane and progressive city in Mississippi . . . an oasis in the racial strife and obsession that smothered the rest of Mississippi. Strict segregation prevailed, but there was an atmosphere of harmony and respect for basic rights that did not exist elsewhere. It was a main ingredient of the economic progress of the town. The moving force behind the spirit of Greenville was Hodding Carter, and his newspaper the *Delta Democrat-Times*.

—Frank Smith, *Congressman from Mississippi*

Introduction

When I said I wanted to write a book about a southern white liberal during the civil rights revolution, more than one person asked me, "Were there any?"

Indeed there were white liberals in those years from 1954 through 1964, when the South was the battleground for diehard white segregationists on one side and frustrated African-Americans at last demanding basic rights on the other. To defend their "way of life," a squalid, outmoded, totally reprehensible dehumanization of a whole race, segregationists used every weapon they could muster, from lunatic legal schemes such as interposition, to bombs. Backed up by the "law of the land," including the 1954 ruling of the United States Supreme Court in *Brown vs. Board of Education* that outlawed segregation in the public schools, black and northern white civil rights leaders battled on. Caught in the middle were southern white liberals. They were reviled by their white neighbors, scorned by northern liberals, and abandoned by the black activists who took over the civil rights movement.

Some of them paid personally a heavy price for their liberalism. LeRoy Collins, a former governor of Florida who headed the U.S. Office of Civil Rights under Lyndon Johnson, was present at the 1965 Selma march; he was defeated afterward when he ran for the U.S. Senate. Clifford and Virginia Durr, of Montgomery, Alabama, were exiled from the white society in whose highest echelons they had grown up, and they faced real financial hardship when Durr lost all of his white legal clients. Charles Morgan, who spoke out against a church bombing in Birmingham, was forced out of town and went to work for the American Civil Liberties Union in Washington, D.C. The handful of southern newspaper editors who took a moderate, or reasonable, stand on civil rights faced threats and endured the hostility of their neighbors, only to have the next generation turn on them for having been too slow.

I knew this much, but I learned much more as I researched the life of William Hodding Carter, Jr., editor and publisher of the *Delta Democrat-Times* in Greenville, Mississippi, who died in 1972. I marveled at Carter's long, spectacular journey from his childhood in a segregated Louisiana to the lonely place where he was almost the only voice of reason in Mississippi during the early days of the racial revolution and eventually the South's most celebrated spokesman for racial justice. I could hardly believe the day-to-day horror of his life—threats, ridicule, insults, boycotts—as he conscientiously goaded fellow Mississippians on racial matters and they, in turn, tried to isolate him socially and run his newspaper out of business, and even threatened to kill him.

To understand the depth of his courage it is necessary to examine the context in which he acted. One might ask: What was so great about running a picture of Jesse Owens in a newspaper in the thirties? It was great because in the thirties *no* southern newspaper (and not all northern newspapers) ran pictures of black people—it was one of the ways in which white society kept blacks invisible. What was so brave about editorializing, on the day the Supreme Court ruled against segregation in the public schools, that it was the only decent thing the Court could do? It was brave because almost all white Mississippians vowed that blood would flow before they would integrate their public schools, and detested anyone who dared suggest that integration was even thinkable. Why make a fuss about a man who editorially supported President Eisenhower when he sent federal troops to Little Rock to guarantee the safety of black students attending formerly all-white schools? Such a man deserves a fuss, because he incurred the wrath of his neighbors for supporting this kind of law and order. So he attacked White Citizens' Councils—didn't everyone? Not at all. Many Mississippi newspapers supported them, and legislators, doctors, lawyers, and mayors of towns and cities joined them. Hodding Carter came out in favor of integration in colleges and universities in a place where and at a time when it was dangerous to hold such views. He was as brave as a kamikaze warrior, year after year writing articles and editorials that attacked racism and discrimination.

Yet he was honestly afraid that another civil war would erupt if Mississippi had to integrate its public schools in the 1960s. He was proved wrong on that count, but he was right about everything else. He displayed enormous courage when it probably would have been prudent to be less outspoken. *Prudence* is a word that was not in his vocabulary, and his imprudence is another name for sheer bravery under fire. He provided leadership and a rallying point for the younger people of Mississippi who were beginning to see the light and to realize that Mississippi had to join the United States in spirit as well as in fact. He was an example and an inspiration to newspaper men and women across the South who could look to Mississippi— of all places—and see a newspaper publisher who could be liberal and still live. While it is true that outside forces integrated the state against its will, those outside forces who brought the victory would have had an even tougher time—and might not have succeeded— without Hodding Carter's solitary voice of reason.

I. 1923–1927

"I Said I Was Prejudiced"

William Hodding Carter, Jr., was a racist when he entered Bowdoin College in Brunswick, Maine, in the fall of 1923. When he graduated four years later, he was still a bigot, but he had received what he called "some healthy jolts" that challenged for the first time the received wisdom of his childhood, "the folklore, mores, inherited certainties" of the South.[1]

Sixteen years old, bright, charming, and handsome, with dark eyes and black curly hair, the quintessential young southern gentleman, Hodding had grown up in the little town of Hammond, Louisiana. He was one of only two southerners in the freshman class of 181 young men, and was at Bowdoin because his first cousin, Hamilton Hall, a junior from Camden, Maine, whom Hodding regarded as a man of the world, had talked him out of going to the University of Virginia.

In May 1923, the principal of Hammond High School had sent Hodding's transcript to Bowdoin with a letter stating that Hodding was "the best, the top boy in every sense, in the Class of 1923."[2] Hodding was admitted, in spite of a deficiency in Latin, and four months later he could write to his high school friend Maxine Carr, "My college life has *begun!*"

He arrived early to try out for freshman football—he weighed 157 pounds and was still growing—and Ham Hall took him into Port-

1

land to buy new clothes. "I got some swell stuff," his letter to Maxine Carr continued, "but it's not what one sees in 'dear old Louisiana'"; instead he found knickers and sports sweaters and clothes "strictly English in style." His roommate was Julius "Joe" Kohler, a good-looking six-foot, 165-pound blond from Newton, Massachusetts, who played varsity football. "I can see awful arguments on the Civil War!" Hodding said.[3]

Hodding and Joe Kohler could hardly have been more different. Kohler was a Yankee with a Boston accent, a Republican from a family he described as "far from affluent." He had never met a Southerner before, and here was Hodding, not just a Southerner with a drawl, but obviously the product of a family of position and some means. Furthermore, he was what Kohler called a "damned Democrat," the only one on campus as far as Kohler could tell. Hodding was literary and Kohler was not. Hodding was three years younger, but to Kohler he seemed sophisticated and cosmopolitan. "I learned more from Hodding than he learned from me," Kohler said some sixty years later.[4]

As Hodding had predicted, the two did argue about the Civil War. Both Hodding's grandfathers had fought for the Confederacy, and he had been brought up to believe in the justice of the South's Lost Cause. His maternal grandmother had filled his head with stories about how after the Civil War the Ku Klux Klan had saved southern womanhood and the southern ballot, and how she had sewn his grand-father's Klan robes with her own hands. Hodding and Kohler argued also about race. Kohler was baffled by his roommate, who spoke with affection of his black nurse but thought that slaves should not have been freed and that the South should have won the Civil War.

Ham Hall made sure that Hodding joined Alpha Delta Phi, the oldest fraternity at Bowdoin. Ham was embarrassed by Hodding's actions toward Bowdoin's only black student, a sophomore named Lincoln Johnson. Hodding refused to speak to Link Johnson and would leave the room if Johnson entered. He tried not to use a toilet that he thought Johnson had used. Hall tried to set his cousin straight, without much success; years later he said that he had started Hodding Carter on the road to liberalism.[5] Others would make the same claim.

Hodding and Kohler shared a bedroom and study at 19 North Winthrop Hall, a hundred-year-old Georgian brick building where Henry Wadsworth Longfellow had lived. Their rooms were on the first floor of North Winthrop, just across from Bowdoin's only canteen, which could be fairly noisy at night. When Kohler came back to Bowdoin after Christmas vacation, he found their room in North Winthrop empty: all his possessions, as well as Hodding's, had disappeared. He finally learned that Hodding had moved everything to a room on the top floor of South Hyde, the newest and most expensive dormitory at Bowdoin.

"I can't afford this," Kohler told Hodding.

"Don't worry about it," Hodding said.

And so Kohler didn't, he later remembered.[6]

Hodding had gone to the trouble—and expense—of changing rooms because Link Johnson lived in South Winthrop Hall. South Winthrop was separated from North Winthrop by a brick fire wall—there was no way to get from one to the other without going outside—but Hodding felt he could not remain under the same roof with what he then called a Negro. He explained to the dean that he wanted to move because of the noise from the canteen. And when basketball season started, Hodding refused to play for the Alpha Delta Phis in an intramural tournament because Johnson played—he was the star—on the independent team.[7]

Hodding's friends were appalled by his behavior. He had a fistfight with one of them, Albert Dekker, his freshman year, when he was very much "the old-fashioned Southern Bourbon." According to Dekker's later account, they both lost.[8] To defend his racial views, Hodding turned from fists to the pen and wrote an article, "Prejudices," that appeared in the literary magazine *The Bowdoin Quill* in December 1924. His first intention, he said in this silly piece, had been to deliver an impassioned defense of the Ku Klux Klan and become a martyr, but better judgment intervened. A good thing, he wrote, or he probably would have been killed. He went on to discuss prejudice in a general way, saying that everyone was prejudiced. His definition of prejudice: a person's "own pet, little dislike or biased opinion." Where would we be if Columbus, after a few drinks, had not become prejudiced in his belief that the world was round? he asked.

"I said I was prejudiced," he wrote. "Somebody else told me the same thing, only he said I was a narrow-minded lyncher. Is that fair . . . ?" He might be narrow-minded, he continued, "but I do get rather riled when my state is subjected to a governmental appointment of the grandson of a probable slave of my grandfather's, sold to him by a Yankee skipper, and only sixty years removed from the jungle . . . when I see some utter fool from Cape Cod fraternizing with a descendant of his blackbirding ancestor's source of income."

In grammar school, Hodding said, he had read that a man could do as his conscience dictated, if it did not interfere with the lawful pursuits of others, and when "a man can't plant a burning cross on his own ground . . . without being attacked by a small army of American citizens of celtic and French-Indian origin, I feel like doing a little attacking myself."

As a matter of "self protection," he defied anyone to interpret his article as a defense of the Ku Klux Klan. "Save for my introduction, I have not named it. But if some son of Erin, or offspring of Uncle Remus objects to my utterances, when I become Grand Kleagle I'll excommunicate him." He was not yet eighteen, a long way from home, and obviously struggling to find some kind of logic in the deeply racist philosophy that permeated his life.

While Hodding's classmates and fraternity brothers were amused and troubled by his southern prejudices, they could not resist his charm and the pleasure he took in everything around him. "I'll never forget the day we had the first snowstorm," recalled Joe Kohler. "My God, you'd think it was gold. He went out and scooped it up and ate it. Rolled around in it."[9]

When spring came, Hodding's father sent a crate of fresh strawberries that delighted his friends, as did the chicory coffee his parents

4

sent up from the New Orleans French Market. Classmate after class-mate, years later, would speak of Hodding's deplorable attitude re-garding race, but inevitably mention as well his popularity, his good spirits, his practical jokes, his flair for the dramatic, and his literary talents, using such words as "intelligence," "brilliance," "flamboy-ance," "unpredictability."

Hodding's classmates remembered also that he worked hard for Alpha Delta Phi to pledge Bill Murphy, an Irish Catholic, and finally succeeded in his senior year. When Bowdoin men charged him with prejudice, he replied that worse things happened in the North than in the South and that while Southerners might be prejudiced against Negroes, Northerners were prejudiced against Jews and Catholics. These were to be recurring themes when he became an ambassador from the South to the North, lecturing widely about southern difficul-ties and telling Northerners they should clean up their own backyard and be patient and let the South work out its problems.

As a Southerner, Hodding felt in many ways an alien in the self-righteous New England atmosphere. Harriet Beecher Stowe—not one of the South's favorite authors—had written *Uncle Tom's Cabin* in Brunswick, while her husband taught at Bowdoin. Hodding was somewhat cheered to discover the name of a Confederate cavalry-man from Louisiana in the school's Memorial Hall, among the names of the alumni who were Civil War veterans, all of the others being Union soldiers and officers.[10] He was pleased to learn that Bowdoin had conferred an honorary degree on Jefferson Davis, a United States senator from Mississippi and secretary of war, who used to vacation in Maine. When the Civil War broke out and Davis became president of the Confederate States of America, there was a great deal of pres-sure on Bowdoin to rescind the degree. The president of the college refused.

Bowdoin's own history in racial matters was not exemplary. While John Brown Russwurm of the Bowdoin class of 1826 was one of the first blacks to graduate from an American college (he went on to co-found the nation's first black newspaper, *Freedom's Journal*, in 1827),

5

the school did not produce another black alumnus until 1910.[11] From 1820 until 1859, Bowdoin had one black student, Middlebury two, and Amherst one. Harvard, Wesleyan, Yale, Trinity, and Dartmouth had none. In 1849, Harvard students threatened to boycott classes if black students were enrolled. From 1820 until 1899, northeastern colleges graduated a total of fifty black students. (Before the Civil War, Brunswick had many abolitionists, but there were few who could even conceive of full integration.)

Certainly the few black students at Bowdoin had not been integrated into the student body. Herman Dreer of the Class of 1911 chose to live a half-mile from campus until another black, Arthur Madison, was admitted and they could room together. In 1913, when the college found out that David Lane was black, after he had already been admitted, an official wrote to him that Bowdoin was very "conservative" and suggested he might prefer to go elsewhere. Lane insisted on going to Bowdoin, where he roomed in Winthrop, and he remembered for the rest of his life that the student proctor did not speak to him once. He enjoyed his membership in the Bowdoin Club, an eating club founded by the college for non–fraternity men, but the members voted him out when they wanted to join a national fraternity.

Fraternities, which were far more than just social organizations, were crucial in the life of Bowdoin men. Because the college provided no dining hall, students, to eat, almost had to belong to a fraternity. Non–fraternity men ate at scattered boardinghouses or in restaurants. The college made official announcements through the fraternities, according to an article in the student newspaper in 1926,[12] and nonmembers did not always know, for instance, how to try out for publication staffs or dramatic groups. Since none of the fraternities admitted blacks, Irish Catholics, or Jews, these students were doomed to a certain amount of isolation. (Two Chinese students, one the son of the Chinese ambassador to Mexico, were admitted to Delta Sigma.)

Hodding seldom went home while he was at Bowdoin—he worked one summer in a lumber camp in Maine—and he came to like the place, and even the Maine winters, when his wet-combed hair froze on his bare head as he went to compulsory chapel at eight in the morning. He liked it that Nathaniel Hawthorne and Henry Wadsworth Longfellow had gone to Bowdoin. He enjoyed having coffee and tea at the homes of professors in the afternoons and evenings. It was at one such visit that he began to think seriously about the Bill of Rights.[13] At the Saturday-night student bull sessions, as the only Democrat in the group, he had to defend the Democratic Party as well as the Old Confederacy. It was here that he first encountered "that tough, town-meeting mind of New England" and discovered that "a man who differs with you—in ideas, in race, in politics, in creed—is not necessarily or even likely to be a scoundrel."[14] In the masculine atmosphere of the fraternity house, he learned that a campus editor, or in fact a poet, could rank with a football captain. There was great camaraderie at the fraternity house, but little drinking. Bowdoin was a place of pastoral simplicity, or at least alumni from that time later remembered it that way. The college was so small that the president and the dean shared an office in Massachusetts Hall and sat at opposite ends of a big table. If one of them had a confidential interview, the other would tactfully leave the room.[15]

High points of the social year were fraternity house party weekends. The boys moved out of the fraternity houses and the girls who came up for the dances, along with their chaperons, moved in. Hodding knew no one to invite to the first dance, the Christmas dance, and Joe Kohler took him home to Newton to meet a friend of his own girlfriend's so Hodding could ask her. They all danced in Brunswick's Eagle Hotel, under the eyes of chaperons. After that Hodding was able to get his own dates. Rita Brent, a Hammond girl who was studying dance in Washington, D.C., went up, and so did Anna Boatner, Hodding's cousin from New Orleans.

In 1925 he met Rita's roommate in Washington, Theodosia Shalor, from New York, who was studying drama at the King-Smith Studio School. Theodosia went to Bowdoin for the spring dance and on to Camden with Hodding and some other friends to spend a long weekend with his aunt and grandmother at Undercliff, a big house on Penobscot Bay. (Hodding's friends always recalled his Aunt Cora, known as Toto, her hospitable family, and the house full of young people.) Theodosia was the same age as Hodding, small with dark hair and dark eyes. She was fascinated with the idealistic southern boy who had a "flair" and wanted to write. She was aware how much he was learning at Bowdoin, not from classes, but from life outside the South. Soon Theodosia was wearing his fraternity pin, and Hodding was going to Washington to see her as often as he could.

As important to him as his social life was his literary work. By January 1925, when he was still a sophomore, Hodding was on the board of the *Quill*; eventually he would be editor.

During his sophomore and junior years he roomed with his fraternity brother, Alden Sawyer, who was working his way through college. Sawyer liked to do his studying early and go to bed early. Not Hodding. Sometimes the two met as Hodding was going to bed and Sawyer was getting up. During his senior year, Hodding moved in with more literary friends, Joe Darlington and Horace Robbins, Ham Hall's half brother. Sawyer became business manager of the *Quill*, and Darlington and Robbins joined Hodding on the editorial board.

He made his first contribution to the magazine in April 1924, with a short story, "Maurepas," about two brothers, Achille and Raymond, who are trappers and fishermen on Lake Pontchartrain in Louisiana. The brothers are familiar with the tale of a fratricide on the lake. Achille kills Raymond and, haunted by the ghost of the other man who had killed his brother, dives over the side of the boat to join Raymond. Hodding continued to mine his regional heritage in the magazine, using language that was not considered particularly racist at the time, with a poem, "Quatrain":

> Tiny pickaninnies playing as their mothers croon
> Lullabies of Hoodoo folklore, neath the April moon.
> Rollin over mid the litter on the cabin floor
> While the Mississippi rumbles by the open door.[16]

In the same issue he had a humorous essay on fingernails.

Hodding published an enormous amount of poetry in the *Quill*, much of it with southern motifs: "Mardi Gras," "Hymn to the Gulf Wind" ("the breeze / Caresses languidly the river town / Bienville loved, New Orleans"), and the insensitive "Flood Song" ("All the white folks run away / But the Delta niggers stay. / No place to go so they might as well pray— / An' there ain't no niggers when it comes next day. / Ole Mississipp was rollin' last night"), which was published the year before the disastrous Mississippi flood of 1927.

Various faculty members reviewed each issue of the *Quill* in the college newspaper, and Hodding's work usually won high praise. Richard Hallett said that in his poem "A Question of Ethics," Hodding "turned a smoking car yarn into a tuneful ditty." His "Aphrodite," Hallett said, had freshness and delicacy, and his "Five Above Zero" the vehemence and menace of Carl Sandburg. (Sandburg made a strong impression on Hodding when he came to lecture during his sophomore year; Hodding tried to sing for him a Louisiana version of "Bill Bailey."[17]) The faculty reviewer of another issue of the *Quill*, Professor C. H. Gray, said in November 1926 that four of Hodding's poems set a high standard for the year's poetry. They were so nearly perfect that there was nothing to be said about them. "Whether it is grief or love that moves him, within a few lines he can create unerringly a quick deep passion," Gray wrote. Other students "could learn from Mr. Carter a fine sense of form."

Hodding's fiction in college foreshadowed his later journalism. It was sentimental, moralistic, often deeply passionate, sometimes very witty, just as nearly everything he would write later in life would be. He wrote short plays, one of them, published in the spring of 1926, set in New Orleans and featuring the pirate Jean Lafitte and Alisette, the governor's daughter.

When he became editor of the *Quill*, in March 1926, his work again gave a hint of the qualities he would bring to future editorial jobs. The magazine took on a lighter tone and ran shorter, less serious articles. He dropped criticism and historical essays.

Like many of the *Quill*'s contributors, Hodding also worked on the humor magazine, the *Bear Skin*. A contributing editor, he even furnished drawings for a number of issues. By his junior year, the masthead listed H. Lincoln Houghton, '26, as "Big Noise" and Hodding Carter, '27, as "Bigger Noise."

Hodding also edited the yearbook, the *Bugle*, which carried a paragraph about each student in each fraternity. "William Hodding Carter, Junior," reads his own entry, "the very, very youthful genius . . . from the swamps of the extreme South . . . is known as a poet, but he isn't; as a radical, he can't quite make it; as a K.K.K. they wouldn't pledge him. . . . But he will spend long hours in telling tales of how the white man rules."

His classes and his professors seemed to have made little impact on Hodding—he seldom if ever mentioned them in later writing—but his extracurricular activities were many and varied. He wrote the libretto (and a classmate, Charles DeBlois, the music) for a musical comedy, a satirical version of *Faust*, for the Ivy Revue, part of the festivities of spring house parties their junior year. He was on the fencing team and became president of Pi Delta Epsilon, the journalism fraternity. He won the Class of 1868 Prize for public speaking. Although his friends often referred to Hodding as brilliant, his grades were not outstanding and he did not make Phi Beta Kappa. He did demonstrate his writing skills, however, and became class poet—reading at Class Day in 1927 his long, romantic tale of a troubadour—and he won the Forbes Rickard Poetry Prize.

His parents did not go up for commencement, but sent him a watch. He wrote them that his poem had created quite a stir. Several aunts and cousins had come to Class Day exercises to hear him read the poem, but he felt lonely on Commencement Day.[18] He left Brunswick for Camden, then went on to Portland, Boston, and New York, where he boarded a ship for Europe. He left, downcast because Theodosia Shalor was going to marry somebody else, Hubert Davis, an older, more sure-of-himself Bowdoin alumnus.

2. 1907–1923

"Un Jeune Homme de Bonne Famille"

Hodding Carter always made his Louisiana childhood sound bliss-
ful: a comfortable if not luxurious life with loving parents and
a little brother and sister in a big house on a three-hundred-acre
strawberry farm on Happy Woods Road four miles from Hammond.
(William Hodding Carter, Jr., was born February 3, 1907; his brother,
John Boatner, eighteen months later; his sister, Corinne Henderson,
soon after in 1909.) When Hodding was a child, the house on Happy
Woods Road had no electricity. The Carters used kerosene lamps and
the cook presided over a wood stove in the kitchen. They rode to
town in a horse-and-buggy or in a surrey that actually had a fringe on
top. Hodding once said his earliest memory was of making the journey from the farm to Hammond on a dirt road that "was practically
paved with homemade pacifiers for me that we called sugar tits."[1]

Hammond, population 1,200, was more cosmopolitan than most
small towns in the Deep South. The Illinois Central Railroad and
other businesses and development groups had recruited Scandinavian
farmers from the Midwest, and Hungarian and Sicilian immigrants
to settle in the area. Hammond was in Tangipahoa Parish, just north
of Cajun and Creole country, and thus had a scattering of French-
speaking residents. With this diversity came an easy tolerance for
Catholics (except Sicilians) and northern Europeans. One Jew lived

in Hammond, as Hodding remembered it, and he was so completely assimilated that he went to church with his Christian wife.[2] Blacks, of course, were condemned without thought to a segregated, second-class life. The Anglo-Saxon Tangipahoans, many of them descendants of Tennessee and Mississippi farmers who had come down to fight at New Orleans with Andrew Jackson, had a reputation for violence, which gave the parish the name "Bloody Tangipahoa."

Strawberries provided the chief source of income, and buyers came to Hammond for the strawberry auctions in early spring and then shipped the crates of berries out on the Illinois Central. Before the Civil War, a Tangipahoa man had grown the first strawberries in the area; one of his slaves carried them to Tickfaw and shipped them to New Orleans by train.[3] After the Civil War, a local grower produced the Klondike variety, which became world-famous. Hundreds of farmers in the area grew strawberries.

Hodding idolized his father, and his autobiographical writings are full of stories about Will Carter. Will taught his son to ride a horse, shoot a gun, swim, and make camp, and he refereed boxing matches in a lighted ring in the backyard after Boy Scout meetings on Friday nights. He had lived in Tangipahoa Parish most of his life, and had attended Tulane University in New Orleans. He was a founder of the First Presbyterian Church in Hammond.

Hodding made his father into a mythic figure, writing in one book that Will had saved his wife and the three children from drowning when they were swimming in the Tangipahoa River,[4] and in another that Will was the first person in town to be summoned when violence broke out or the sheriff needed a posse. One day, Hodding wrote, a drunk man started shooting up a small short-order restaurant and dared the town marshal to come and get him. The marshal asked Will Carter to go inside and persuade the drunk to give himself up. Will walked in, unarmed, and came out with the drunk.[5] Hodding remembered sitting in a barbershop and listening to two customers discussing another man; one of them, to clinch the argument, said, "He's as honest as Will Carter!"[6]

12

Will Carter, beloved by young and old alike in Hammond, was quick to use his fist. He taught his son to fight back if someone attacked him or cursed him and to take on anyone who picked on his brother. If an older boy attacked, Hodding was to look around for the nearest stick or brick. "Fight back!" was Will Carter's code.[7]

Will had enough land to rent out to Sicilian sharecroppers. When he grew older, Hodding deplored the community's attitude toward the Sicilians; he recalled that his mother was genuinely frightened of them. Very late in his life he remembered how his father, that ordinarily kind and generous man, had supervised the horsewhipping of a drunken Sicilian tenant who had said something so grossly insulting to Hodding's mother that she, in the tradition of delicate southern ladies, fainted.[8] Hodding and his brother were fascinated by the Sicilians, however; these were the most exciting people they knew. The Sicilians had cone-shaped clay ovens in their backyards where they baked crusty bread. They kept goats and made cheese from the milk. (Hodding's mother swore the cheese would kill her children if they ate it.) They made strawberry wine in crocks. Hodding and John visited the Sicilians, and not only ate the bread and cheese and drank goat's milk but encouraged the addition of a thimbleful of strawberry wine to the milk.[9]

Hodding's mother, Irma Dutart Carter, was a pretty woman, gay and full of life. Younger than her husband, she used to tease him about the many suitors she had "given up" in Natchez for him. Never in her life, people in Hammond said, did she cook a meal, because the Carters had plenty of servants, all black.[10]

Irma Carter grew up in Vidalia, Louisiana, just across the Mississippi from Natchez. Her father, John Dutart, a South Carolinian of Huguenot descent, had ridden with General Nathan Bedford Forrest in the Civil War and was captured at Vicksburg. (It was he who had been an active member of the Ku Klux Klan, wearing robes sewn by Hodding's grandmother.) Until his mother disillusioned him with the truth, Hodding believed his grandmother's tales that the family would have owned uncounted acres of rich land had it not been for the Civil War and Reconstruction. Hodding grew up convinced that General Benjamin Butler, the Yankee commandant in occupied New Orleans, had stolen spoons and ordered his troops to despoil the women of the city, that William Tecumseh Sherman was a devil incarnate who had laughed out loud at the starving women and children he left behind on his march to the sea, and that Thaddeus Stevens, the hated militant Radical Republican leader in Congress who sponsored the strongest Reconstruction legislation, had married a Negro woman and wanted to find white southern wives for his Negro cohorts.[11]

Hodding's father's family had been in Tangipahoa Parish long before Hammond was founded. Alfred Hennen, Will Carter's great-grandfather, a lawyer, arrived in Louisiana soon after the Purchase, became a Louisiana Supreme Court justice, and acquired a 1,320-acre hunting preserve in the parish with a house that the family used as a retreat during yellow fever epidemics. Hodding felt that some of their neighbors resented the Carters' air of assurance that came from belonging to a past that antedated the community.[12]

Hodding's great-grandfather Needham Jennings died at the Battle of Shiloh during the Civil War. Since Jennings had voted in the Louisiana legislature in favor of secession and had served in the Confederate army, he was officially a traitor to the United States and his property was confiscated. His widow went to Washington to seek a presidential pardon for herself so that she could regain her modest properties in New Orleans. Hodding always kept on his office wall the framed document signed by President Andrew Johnson on which the engraved phrase "the late traitor" was edited in longhand to read: "the late traitress, Anna Maria Jennings."

Hodding's grandfather Thomas Lane Carter grew up in Charles Town, in what is now West Virginia, attended the University of Virginia, and served as a militiaman at Harpers Ferry when John Brown was captured. In spite of a wound that made him angry with the North the rest of his life, he was a telegraph officer for the Confederate army during the Civil War. After the war, while he was up North, he met Anna Hennen Jennings, who was visiting from Louisiana, and they were married in New Rochelle, New York. Right after the wedding they went to Europe, where Carter sold bonds for a telegraph company. Four of their eleven children were born abroad, in England, Switzerland, Italy, and Germany. Hodding's father, the ninth child, was born in Amite in Tangipahoa Parish, after the family had settled in Louisiana.

Since Will Carter, according to one of his grandsons, "never made a penny in his life,"[13] he was lucky to have a benefactor. One of his cousins, Hennen Jennings, was a mining engineer in South Africa, where he worked for Wernher Beit & Co. (Julian Wernher and Alfred Beit), which was associated with Cecil Rhodes. Jennings moved to London, and in the 1890s, when an aunt took two of Will's sisters, Lilian and Marguerite, to London, Hennen Jennings introduced them around. Lilian became engaged to Sir Otto Beit, a brother to the extremely wealthy Sir Alfred Beit. She married him in 1897 and lived the rest of her life in England. Marguerite, who returned there for the birth of Lady Beit's first child, also remained the rest of her life.

The Beit connection was extremely important to Hodding and his immediate family. Several times, when Will Carter encountered serious financial difficulties, Sir Otto and Lady Beit bailed him out. Will was the only one of Lilian's siblings to inherit money when Sir Otto died. Hodding accepted bounty from his English relatives but resented his position as a poor relation, and he loathed the Buster Brown suits and English sailor suits that Tante Marguerite sent for him and John to wear. He hated the whole idea of patronage, and he never forgot that when he was a little boy these relatives would visit and he would hear them say things like "*pauvre petit*" and "*un jeune homme de bonne famille*," shaking their heads in pity.

Everything depends on point of view. While the Carters saw themselves as poor relations, the people in Hammond saw them as part of "the money group," as one Hammond resident phrased it.[14] The Carters—even Lady Beit—talked about the hardships of their childhood. An English descendant said that Marguerite and Lilian remembered their childhood as impoverished and talked about eating squirrel pie.[15] Hodding's family led a good life by Hammond standards.

Irma Carter taught her older son to read and write by the time he was five and tutored him at home from *The Book of Knowledge*. When Hodding was seven, his parents decided to move into town so he could go to the Hammond school. They bought a big house, with a porte cochère, that occupied almost an entire block. Hodding appeared at school a few days after the school year started in 1914 and seemed to know more than his classmates in the fourth grade, where he was placed. He often quoted from *The Book of Knowledge*, which none of the other children had heard of.

Hodding soon moved to the top of the class. He took elocution lessons from Mrs. Rosa Sowell, who urged him to become a politician when she heard him recite florid patriotic speeches written by New England clergyman Elijah Kellogg—"Regulus Before the Carthaginian Senate" ("Now bring forth your tortures! slaves! While ye tear this quivering flesh, remember how often Regulus has beaten your armies in the field and humbled your pride. Cut, as he would have carved you! Burn, deep as his curse!") and "Spartacus to the Gladiators" ("Oh, comrades! warriors! Thracians! if we must fight, let us fight for ourselves! If we must slaughter, let us slaughter our oppressors"). He was a newspaper carrier for the New Orleans *Item*, delivering the papers weekdays on a bicycle, hauling them Sundays in a soapbox cart, and earning $1.25 a week.[16] He entered a letter-writing contest sponsored by a boys' magazine, hoping to win the first prize, a bicycle. He won fifth prize, a pair of ice skates—of very little use to a Louisiana boy.[17]

Hodding remembered all his life a trip to New Orleans in 1916 to see the movie *The Birth of a Nation*, on the night the residents of the Confederate veterans' home attended. Rebel yells filled the movie house, and he heard the old men around him saying it had been just like that or worse. Will Carter was so exhilarated by the filmed exploits of the Ku Klux Klan that he threw his hat in the air and never got it back.[18]

When Hodding was ten, the entry of the United States into World War I fed the inherent militarism that was part of his southern heritage. He cut pictures, maps, and poems from magazines and newspapers and pasted them into old-fashioned plantation ledgers labeled "War Scrapbook." (Irma Carter showed them off to her circle of volunteer knitters.) Hodding and his sister worked on the scrapbooks on Sunday afternoons, when they were forbidden to go to movies and baseball games. He relished the stories of German atrocities and memorized newspaper and magazine verses that showed up "the vile Boche," including "The Poem on the Tin Plaque." Paste failed to keep this poem in the scrapbook, but Hodding always remembered the last lines:

> The moaning low and the moaning wild
> Of a ravaged French girl's bastard child.

The scrapbooks, 406 pages in all, were full of stories about the murder of nurse Edith Cavell, the sinking of the *Lusitania*, and the destruction of French villages and churches. He followed the progress of the war on maps and knew how close the Huns were to Paris. He became the neighborhood authority for the number of Belgian babies the Huns had bayoneted and the number of Frenchwomen who had endured the "unspeakable bestiality of the Prussian beast." He could pronounce and explain *camouflage*. When the children played war games, Hodding could be General Pershing or Sergeant York if he chose.

Moved by a Liberty loan drive, he wrote a poem himself and submitted it to the weekly Hammond *Vindicator*, which printed it, just as it printed everything submitted. Hodding later recalled part of the poem:

> A war is going on now which America is in,
> And is sending her boys to France to keep the world from sin.

The culmination of his wartime activity was volunteer work every day after school in the Red Cross influenza epidemic headquarters.

He shredded lint, made antiflu masks, and carried soup to the sick families of servicemen. This work ended when Hodding caught the potentially deadly flu himself and gave it to his entire family.

Hodding always liked to read. One book in particular, Kipling's *The Drums of the Fore and Aft, and Other Boys' Stories*, which he got for Christmas, moved him to tears. Family lore had it that he would be reading on the porch when his brother would run up and say somebody was after him. Hodding would stand, lay his book aside, take off his glasses, go knock the aggressor down, and return to the porch and pick up glasses and book. In fact, all his life he was protective of John, who was forever a shadowy figure beside the colorful Hodding.

The Carters were hospitable people, and Will built a tennis court next to the house in town where all their friends could play. There were family feasts on holidays, when the bounty from the farm and the sea was put on the table. Irma Carter much preferred New Orleans to Hammond and went at every chance she had, buying books of railroad tickets and taking the children to visit Aunt Telle, Will's sister Ellen Rundle, and her family, to shop, and to go to the movies.

Threading through this pleasant life, always present for children to absorb without question, was the unspoken code of strict segregation. Hodding *knew* he was better than any Negro; it was simply a fact of life. He and other white Hammond children sometimes draped themselves with sheets and chased black children through the woods with toy guns.[19]

At times, however, the racial mores were too much for young Hodding. A thirty-eight-year-old black woman named Emma Hooker lived in what the people of Hammond called "the quarters," the black neighborhood. In 1916 the town marshal, Fred Marlton, visited her on several occasions, apparently seeking sexual favors. Finally Emma Hooker shot and wounded him. When other officers came to arrest her, she tried to fire on them. They shot her in the face and reportedly found more weapons in her house, as well as inflammatory racial literature. They took her into custody and placed her in the Hammond jail. Just after dark, officers decided to move her to Amite. Outside Hammond a group of unidentified men stopped the police car, took her away from the officers, drove her to the Notalbany River, and hanged her on a tree just beside the bridge. This was where people parked their cars when they went for picnics beside the river.[20] Hodding rode with a group of boys to see the body dangling from the tree, and he wrote about the incident several times in later years. "Even now," he said, "I sometimes see that body in my sleep."[21]

Tangipahoa Parish had a history of lynching. Five blacks were hanged from trees in Ponchatoula in 1907; a little later two were hanged from the water tank in Hammond, and three others were hanged near Hammond.

But no one in town challenged the status quo. In high school Ned McCready, the Episcopal parson's son, would argue with the history teacher and declare baldly that Abraham Lincoln was an atheist and the illegitimate brother of Jefferson Davis, the president of the Confederacy, and that slavery was the foreordained and natural state of Africans. (McCready, an eccentric youngster who went to school barefooted year-round, grew up to become vice-chancellor of the University of the South at Sewanee, Tennessee, and an expert in many areas, including paleontology and ornithology.)

As an adult, Hodding wrote nostalgically about the closeness of black children to white children in the segregated rural South, especially about his relationship with a black boy named Son McKnight, the third of six children who with their mother became dependent on the Carter family. Son was Hodding's companion, servant, sparring partner, and bodyguard, and the catcher when the boys were learning to pitch curves. When Hodding had to meet the afternoon train to pick up his New Orleans *Items* to deliver, he would be wearing his Buster Brown suits from Tante Marguerite and the other boys would maul him. Son went along as protection. In turn, Hodding taught Son to read and write and helped him financially as they grew older.[22]

Religion was important in the life of Hammond. Hodding's Grandmother Carter was a strict Presbyterian who disapproved of gambling. The Carters went to Sunday school and church on Sundays, young people's meeting on Sunday nights, and prayer meeting on Wednesday nights. As the children were not allowed to go to Sunday baseball games or movies, Hammond young people used to go to the Carter house on Sunday afternoons to make fudge. Corinne played the piano while the fudge cooled; when Grandmother Carter was there, Corinne was not supposed to play anything but hymns on Sunday, but she would play other songs to tease her.[23] Still, Hodding's Presbyterian parents were not as rigid as the parents of his Methodist and Baptist friends who forbade dancing and cardplaying at any time.

In spite of the religiosity around him, Hodding was not interested in church. Once he went to a revival meeting with two friends and sat in the back by the wood stove, listening in awe as the revivalist worked himself and his audience into hysteria. All the congregation crowded to the foot of the pulpit asking for salvation—except the three boys in the back. Even after a man came to pray over them, Hodding sat there, doggedly refusing. He felt "a strange, sickening resentment, a disbelief that this performance had any basic relationship to religion."[24]

Sometimes the Carters took vacations in a big rented house on the Mississippi coast of the Gulf of Mexico. Irma and the children also went for long visits to her mother's in Vidalia, on the Mississippi River. Nearly every summer Hodding's family went to Maine for a Carter family visit. The trip took days and nights in Pullman cars and involved several changes of trains.

Hodding's grandmother Anna Hennen Jennings Carter, a widow, had visited her daughter, Cora Carter Hall Robbins, in Camden, Maine, in 1900 and loved it. Sir Otto Beit helped his mother-in-law financially, buying her Undercliff, a huge house in Camden with wide lawns that sloped down to Penobscot Bay. Old Mrs. Carter lived there with Cora and her family when she was not visiting her other children.

The Carter clan held family reunions at Camden, the biggest lasting all of July and August in 1911, when Hodding was four. When the English cousins, Lilian's four children, came over one year with their parents, Sir Otto rented the big house across the road from Undercliff for extra lodgings. In Maine, Grandmother Carter presided over family prayers every night and got up early to take the comics out of the paper every Sunday because she did not think the children should read them on Sundays. All her grandchildren in residence had to recite verses from the child's catechism and the Shorter Westminster Catechism, and she paid them to memorize Bible verses. Hodding invariably learned the most verses and earned the most money. "We knew God was everywhere," Hodding wrote later. "Grandmother said the air was 'God's breath.'"[25]

A Camden legend had it that Tommy McKay, the town druggist, taught Hodding a lesson when he was seven. Hodding came into his drugstore with his black nurse, a little girl cousin, and her black nurse for sodas. When a black man came into the store, Hodding, acting very manly, went to the door and ordered the man to leave the store. The druggist grabbed Hodding and said, "Don't ever treat a customer of mine like that." Like Hamilton Hall, McKay in later years maintained that it was he who had made a liberal out of Hodding Carter.[26]

In high school Hodding took part in statewide elocution contests. He played football his senior year—all the senior boys did—but was no star. He shone in other ways. He could quote poetry, including Shakespeare, and he wrote flattering notes to all the girls. The notes contained compliments, "comparing us to flowers," recalled one classmate. "We loved them." He kissed all the girls, apparently, but had no serious love affairs. On dates they went to the picture show, to the infrequent dances, or across Lake Pontchartrain to Mandeville for picnics and swimming and dancing. The Class of 1923 was wonderful, everyone remembered, with nobody too rich or too poor.[27]

Hodding and Dick Gates, the doctor's son, competed for the best grades. Hodding was valedictorian, Gates salutatorian. Everybody thought Hodding would be famous, and he thought so, too. "He had a lot of ego," said a classmate, "but he had a lot to be egotistical about."[28] Hodding was genuinely liked by everyone, students and teachers alike. "He was bright. He was a leader. He knew how to make people like him," said one of his classmates.

During the last six weeks of school in 1923, most of the seniors rehearsed every night for the class play. Maxine Carr, Hodding's "pal," not a girlfriend, had the female lead and Hodding played her father. One of the few high school students who had the use of a car, he drove to rehearsals in an old touring car. He would pick up Maxine, then go out to the country to get somebody else, and then stop for another student; after rehearsals he would take them all home. The car was hard to steer on the country roads, but his driving went well—until the time of the class picnic at Carpenter's Landing on the Tangipahoa River, where there was a sand bar for swimming and an old bathhouse in the woods. Hodding and Maxine and their passengers were late leaving the picnic. "We came to a place in the road where the gravel was deep and loose. The car swerved and I grabbed the wheel. That was the worst thing I could have done," Maxine Carr Shannon recalled. "The car turned over. I was hurt on my left shoulder, and I still have a scar over my left eyebrow. Hodding's arm was cut right across the artery." A passing car took the young people to the nearest house, where they called Dr. Gates. When Hodding's mother arrived, she embarrassed him with her excessive concern. "My baby! My darling!" she kept repeating.[29]

At commencement Maxine wore a patch over her eye and Hodding had his arm in a sling. The *Vindicator* ran a picture of the graduating class on the front page (taken before the valedictorian was injured) and printed Hodding's speech in full.[30] Hodding gave Maxine a commencement album with a note: "To the best little girl pal in all the world."

After graduation the entire class went to the train station to see Hodding off for Maine, where he would spend the summer and attend Bowdoin College in the fall.

Hodding's family could never have afforded to send him to Bow-

doin, but Sir Otto and Lady Beit paid for the college education—
graduate school as well as undergraduate—for each of her nineteen
American nieces and nephews. Nearly all the nieces and nephews
took advantage of the offer, and they all received the same graduation gift: a trip to Europe, which included a visit to the Beits at their
country house, Tewin Water in Hampshire.

After four years at Bowdoin, Hodding took his trip to Europe. He
was at Tewin Water for the wedding of his cousin Angela Beit to
Arthur Bull. Not much is known about the rest of his trip, except that
he bicycled through Ireland with a friend.

Back in the United States, he enrolled in the journalism school at
Columbia University, where he remained for only a year and made,
for once in his life, no great impression. In turn, the year had little
impact on him, except for three Louisiana friends he made there—
Hart Bynum and Annette Duchein of Baton Rouge and Rose Corne-
lis, daughter of a Presbyterian minister in New Orleans. None of his
work appeared in *The Columbia Journalist*, the book issued each year
to showcase the best newspaper stories that students in the school
had published. Hodding is not in the class picture taken in 1928, and
years later none of his surviving classmates had vivid memories of him
as a student. He shared an apartment with John Sheffey, just out of
Harvard Law School, and Richard Tompkins, a reporter for the New
York *Times*. He took as many English courses as journalism courses
and made fairly good grades. Later he said he had learned more from
Jim Abrahamson, who had been a year ahead of him at Bowdoin and
was now in graduate school at Columbia, than he did from his professors. Abrahamson took him to some of his lectures on economics and
encouraged Hodding to "think of other things than poetry."[31]

Having decided to try for a Rhodes scholarship, Hodding secured a
foothold at Tulane University in New Orleans with a teaching fellowship. He would work on a master's degree in English, specializing in
Emily Dickinson, and teach two English classes. He was going back
to the South for good.

3. 1928–1932

"He's Probably Dangerous"

In Hammond, idling away the summer of 1928 waiting for school to start, Hodding went one day to meet his sister, who was coming on the train from New Orleans.

"Who was that girl with the curly hair and the suntan?" he asked Corinne, who had turned back to wave at the friend with whom she had been sitting.

Corinne told him it was Betty Werlein, who was spending the summer at Amite. She was a classmate of Corinne's at Sophie Newcomb, the woman's college connected to Tulane. "She's a Pi Beta Phi, but there are lots of Kappa Kappa Gammas who are nicer," said Corinne, a Kappa.

Looking out of the train window to catch a glimpse of Corinne's brother, Betty Werlein saw a handsome young man with curly black hair and dark eyes, who obviously had what people in those days called "personality."

Not long afterward Corinne asked Hodding if he would like to go to Betty Werlein's eighteenth-birthday party. She couldn't go herself, but Betty had asked Corinne to bring men. Hodding said he had nothing else to do, and so he went, along with his friend Albert Stansel. Hodding won all the parlor games, including guessing how many beans there were in a jar, and had a fine time on the front porch talking to Betty's mother, the glamorous, capable Elizabeth Werlein.

Betty confided to Peeps Kemp, a girlfriend who stayed over that night, that she thought Hodding was the most fascinating man she had ever met. "But he's probably dangerous," she said.

Betty Werlein was an "uptown New Orleans girl": she had been carefully brought up by a good New Orleans family with money. Her father's grandfather, Philip Werlein, had come from Bavaria in 1832, a violin under his arm, to teach music in Clinton, Mississippi, and by 1853 he owned a large music store in New Orleans. During the Civil War his son Peter Philip left Louisiana State University at age eighteen, joined the St. Mary's Rifles, and went to Avery Island to defend the salt mines from invading Yankees. After the war he re-opened the business with all that was left of the Werlein stock— five pianos, which a faithful employee had hidden from the Yankees. Werlein began publishing sheet music, including the song "Dixie"; family stories do not make clear whether he pirated it or not. He later became an invalid, confined to a wheelchair, and his wife, Bettie Parham Werlein, rode downtown in her carriage every day to look after the store. (It was not considered proper in nineteenth-century New Orleans, but she did it.) Philip Werlein, Betty's father, went away to Emory University in Atlanta, but when he turned eighteen, his family called him home and had him declared of age so he could run the store.

Betty's mother was Elizabeth Thomas of Bay City, Michigan. As a young girl she had studied voice with Jean de Reszke in France and gravitated to London, where she did such daring things as ride in a balloon across the English Channel. Her daughters kept a picture of her outfitted for ballooning in a black-and-white-checked dress by Worth. Her fiancé, Charles Yorke, heir to the Earl of Hardwicke, was embarrassed because the dress was too short. "This is a sport outfit, and it has to be a little above the ankle," said Miss Thomas. After her father told her she could not be married until she had traveled in America, she set out on a grand tour of her native land. Visiting friends in New Orleans, she ran her finger down the list of dinner guests expected that night; she came to the name Philip Werlein and said, "He sounds interesting." She decided she needed some sheet music and set out for the music store. Philip Werlein was in his shirt-sleeves, helping a black man push a piano, when he saw her. He stopped, put on his seersucker jacket, and went over to meet her. He left the store and took her to the French Quarter, which Elizabeth Thomas saw not as a slum where Italians lived, but as something European and beautiful. They walked down Chartres Street to the cathedral and sat for two hours without speaking a word. Very soon they were engaged. She cabled Charles York the news. He cabled back: "Hold everything. I'm coming over." Her father then cabled York: "Too late. She's married."

The wedding was in August 1908 in Bay City. Betty was born on July 19, 1910, in a house rented from the Flower family at the corner of Felicity and Race in the Lower Garden District of New Orleans; the Werleins moved later to a house on St. Charles Avenue, which was perfect for watching Mardi Gras parades. Two younger sisters, Evelyn and Lorraine, and a brother, Philip, followed. Betty's name was never Elizabeth—as a child she said, "I was born, baptized and circumcised Betty."[1]

Betty's father was handsome, charming, and civic-minded. He played poker far into the night at the Boston Club and was also a member of the Pickwick Club; the Progressive Union; the Chess, Checkers, and Whist Club; the Polo Club; and the Purity League, whose goal was not to close down Storyville, the legal red-light district, but to ensure that white prostitutes would not be available to black men. He was chairman of the state central committee of the Democratic Party. He once stood his oldest daughter on a table and told her, "If anybody ever asks you who you are, say, 'I'm Betty Werlein. American. Episcopalian. Democrat.'"

The Werleins, all musical, entertained visiting concert artists. Betty practiced the piano every morning before being driven by car to kindergarten at the Isidore Newman Manual Training School. She would go home for lunch and nap, and then she and her sisters, dressed alike, were taken for a walk. Two afternoons a week Madame Nagle came to the house to give French lessons. On Saturdays, Betty had golf lessons.

Her father came home one day and saw her playing with little boys in the backyard, and said his daughter could no longer go to the co-educational Isidore Newman School. Later Betty found out he was upset because she was playing with not just any boys, but *Jewish* boys. She went, as Protestant girls from uptown New Orleans did, to Miss Louise McGehee's (Catholic girls went to Sacred Heart). She started in the middle of the first grade and stayed there, with a few breaks, until she graduated from high school.

After the death of her father, in 1917, Betty's life was ruled by three strong women: her mother, Mama Dees, and Mamoo. Mama Dees was Elise Wagner, a German woman hired as Mrs. Werlein's lady's maid who instead helped with the children. Mamoo was her formidable paternal grandmother, Bettie Parham Werlein, who had gone down to run the business until her son was old enough to take over—and who, in fact, still ran it.

Betty's mother was almost as formidable as the older Mrs. Werlein. During World War I, she organized the Red Cross canteen services for soldiers who came through New Orleans, and her house was head-quarters for the French officers on liaison duty. She made speeches to sell Liberty bonds and chaired a committee on airplane landing fields for the Army air corps in Louisiana; she even won a "Wings" award from the New York Aero Club for her work.

After the war it became apparent that Elizabeth Werlein had made disastrous investments in German marks. She received a pension from the Werlein Music Company, but its size was set by Mamoo, final arbiter in management decisions. The younger Mrs. Werlein sold the house on St. Charles and had a smaller one built on Nashville Avenue, on a lot her mother-in-law gave her. She was not one to stay at home, though, and devoted her time to various activities. She helped organize Le Petit Théâtre and founded the Orleans Club for women. She was instrumental in the preservation of the French Quarter, and was honored by the American Institute of Architects for her work; on the fiftieth anniversary of the establishment of the Vieux Carré district, Elizabeth Werlein Medals were distributed. She directed public relations and education for movies in the South under Will Hays, of the Motion Picture Producers and Distributors of America. Hays was the czar of the movies, and southern newspapers referred to her as the czarina. Her office was in the Saenger-Richards-Shears building, and the Saenger Company, which operated two hundred theaters in the South, paid her salary. Her job was to prevent state legislatures from imposing censorship on movies, and to this end she spoke and lobbied throughout the South. In the company's screening rooms, she viewed two to five movies a day, selecting parts that would have to be cut for particular towns.

Elizabeth Werlein became a Theosophist and a vegetarian; she saw that her children got their protein from red beans and rice, peanut butter, roasted pecans, and plenty of milk. When the children took naps and little Betty was bored, she tried the trick of swallowing a spool of thread. She put the free end of the thread in her mouth, swallowed, and kept swallowing. Nap time was just long enough to swallow a whole spoolful and then pull it out, rewinding it on the spool. The exercise, Betty was told, had something to do with yoga.

The house on Nashville Avenue was always full of company, some from New Orleans, others from out of town. The bridge authority Hal Sims came every year for horse-racing season. Once the girls advised him to bet on a horse called Rollo, because that was their dog's name. When the horse won, Sims returned with four new bicycles strapped to the roof of two taxis. Novelist Kenneth Roberts came one spring, and afterward he always said it was Elizabeth Werlein who had talked him into writing fiction.

When Betty finished the eighth grade at McGehee's, her mother gave a hot-chocolate-and-cookie party at the Quartier Club, which she had organized in the French Quarter. (Before Mrs. Werlein, men would not let their wives go to the French Quarter alone.) A class-mate named Catharine Conn played the piano at the party. Catharine left New Orleans, to become Kitty Carlisle.

After Betty graduated from high school in 1927, she went straight from the ceremonies to the train station and the New York–bound Crescent City Limited. She and three other New Orleans girls were, off for a well-chaperoned eight-week tour of Europe with the Bureau of University Travel. After two weeks in England, she finally, as in-structed by her mother, telephoned Lady Beit, her mother's friend, the former Lilian Carter, at Tewin Water. Lady Beit, to whom Mrs. Werlein had written, told Betty her daughter Angela was being mar-ried in two days; could Betty come to them after that? Betty answered that she would be in France by then. Betty, who was pudgy and still in braces at the time, later gave thanks that the meeting had not ma-terialized. Hodding Carter was there for his cousin's wedding, and Betty was sure he would not have been interested in her—ever—if he had met her that summer.[2]

Betty entered Sophie Newcomb in the fall of 1927 and was elected president of the freshman class. (She would major in French, be-come president of the senior class and the student body, and captain of the rifle team.) She met Corinne Carter during rush week her freshman year, and they were physics lab partners. ("Corinne always had better results and I always understood the principles," Betty said years later.[3] "Betty always said I passed her, and I said she passed me," was how Corinne remembered it.)[4] Corinne often talked about her brilliant brother, who was in school at Columbia, and when she needed an original ballad for a class assignment, she wired Hodding, "Send simple ballad collect," and he did. His poem did not help her; she made a C-plus and could have made a C by herself—and she had to knit Hodding a sweater as payment.[5]

In the summer of 1928, Betty's mother, as usual, rented a large antebellum house at Amite in Tangipahoa Parish, up the Illinois Cen-tral line from New Orleans. Not long after her birthday party, Betty, her two sisters, and Peeps Kemp went to nearby Smiling Acres, where people danced on a platform in the woods. Hodding was there and asked Betty to dance, but he also invited her sisters and Peeps. Betty heard no more from him for what seemed like ages, and then he asked her out to a fraternity picnic.

When Hodding registered for graduate courses at Tulane, he settled in a suite at the home of Gus Capdeville and his wife, who lived in a big house on Calhoun Street, near the campus. Cleanth Brooks, another graduate fellow, who would become one of the nation's leading literary critics, moved out of his boardinghouse to join Hodding at the Capdevilles'. The couple had recently lost a young son, and Mrs. Capdeville's doctor had recommended that she fight her depression and grief by taking in college students. The Capdevilles made no money from their boarders; it was impossible, the way the table groaned with the best of New Orleans cuisine. The house always smelled of coffee and garlic and bourbon and cigarette smoke.[6] Brooks, the son of a Methodist minister in Tennessee, was dazzled by his introduction to New Orleans society; Hodding was already somewhat familiar with it because of his relatives.

"They took us into the old Creole homes on Esplanade," Brooks remembered years later. "I remember hearing Mrs. Capdeville chatter on the telephone in French. She had been queen of Comus and that outranked the queen of Carnival. We contrived costumes for Mardi Gras and one night we put on dinner jackets and Mr. Capdeville took us to the Rex ball."

Brooks recalled that both he and Hodding were "still very boyish, interested in buying old run-down cars and that kind of thing."[7] They pooled their resources and bought an old car for forty dollars, then drove it everywhere.[8] They were also writing poetry. Brooks, who had studied under John Crowe Ransom and Donald Davidson at Vanderbilt, interested Hodding in the Fugitives and regionalism. Brooks called regionalism a "healthy provincialism" and talked of "lovers of the good soil" and "good pecan crops."[9]

Hodding was only twenty-one, very young to be teaching. He later looked back and saw 1928 as a halcyon time: No one dreamed the stock market would collapse. No one took Huey Long seriously. No one outside Germany had heard of Adolf Hitler. The United States, which was scrapping its navy, had not recognized the Soviet government. In the South, feeling against the Democratic nominee for president was running high because he was a Catholic and because he was against Prohibition. In this "halcyon time," southern mobs lynched an average of twenty Negroes a year.[10]

Charged with teaching the principles of unity, coherence, and emphasis in freshman English, Hodding found his classes packed with athletes looking for easy courses. One of his students, a prospective All-American guard, wrote on his examination book, "For gods sake prof, be lenant." Hodding, a football fan, did his best for the flunking football players. Each week he let them guess what the score of the next Tulane game would be, and passed whoever came the nearest to being right.[11] He decided that only three out of ten students were ready for freshman English; when he gave a spelling test of a hundred ordinary two- and three-syllable words, less than half of the class spelled fifty or more correctly. He was convinced that southern schools were inferior to northeastern schools.

While Hodding continued to date other girls, he saw a great deal of Betty. Sometimes she and Hodding double-dated with Cleanth and his girlfriend, Tinkum Blanchard, going to dances and afterward to the French Market for coffee and beignets. Sometimes they went to the beach at Gulfport or Bay St. Louis, where friends had houses.

Hodding and Cleanth, who had both applied for Rhodes scholarships, were supposed to go to Baton Rouge for interviews. Hodding drove Cleanth to Hammond to meet his family, and then to Baton Rouge. "I don't think I'll go in," Hodding said after they parked. "I don't think Betty will wait for me while I'm in England." It might have been the smartest thing he ever did. Betty Werlein was more important than a Rhodes.

"Tinkum will wait for me," said Cleanth with confidence, and hurried inside.

31

Hodding sat outside and wrote a poem, "River Plantation," about a tenant family he had seen living in an abandoned river mansion below Baton Rouge:

> Above the pock-marked mantel where the patch
> Of lighter brown betrays, a portrait hung.
> Beneath it lay a saber. Both were his,
> The last male Corbin, slain when he was young
> Deep in the Wilderness. The jimsons snatch
> At the white columns, marked by flood and grime.
> The windows gag, the gallery stairway is
> Scratched by complacent hens, stained with their lime.
> Mose Turner, Negro tenant, and his spawn
> Work the thin fields in fief to state and bank.
> Theirs is the broken house, the furrowed lawn,
> And theirs the privilege to scrape and thank
> When gawking tourists toss a coin and share,
> With ghosts they cannot see, the humbled stair.[12]

Cleanth won his Rhodes, but he always insisted modestly that he would not have gotten it if Hodding had interviewed. If Hodding gave up a Rhodes, Betty gave up making a debut in New Orleans society, and thus incurred her grandmother's displeasure. "I didn't think Hodding would wait outside ballrooms for me," she said.

Turning his back on academia that fall, Hodding went to work for the *Tribune*, the *Item*'s morning paper. He was dumbfounded at his paycheck, only $12.50. "There must be some mistake," he said. But there was no mistake. He was too embarrassed to tell Betty—or his father—how little he made. He practiced the most rigid economy when alone—nickel breakfasts of stale doughnuts and coffee, and ten-cent po'boy sandwiches for lunch. He made money for dates by betting on Tulane's football team, which was fortunately good that year. The *Tribune* assigned him once to go to an out-of-town Tulane–Georgia football game with one dollar in his pocket and write about what happened. Many young people used to "hobo" on the special trains the railroads ran to out-of-town games, hiding under berths when the conductor came to collect tickets. After evading the conductor, Hodding got in a dice game in the baggage car; he won twenty dollars, and thus proved a ticket to the game and food attainable goals.[13]

Hodding left the *Tribune* to work for the United Press bureau in New Orleans. He moved into a French Quarter apartment with Hart Bynum, a UP colleague from Baton Rouge whom he had met at Columbia. Annette Duchein, another Baton Rouge friend whom he had met at Columbia, who now worked for the *Times-Picayune*, lived in the same building. Other newspaper people lived there as well, and they all shared a cook, Adele, who concocted marvelous gumbos, jambalayas, and daube with rice.

Meanwhile, Betty, socially a late bloomer, in her junior year was suddenly extremely popular, dated up for every available hour for three weeks in advance. She began to schedule Hodding in whenever she could, but it was hard. Hodding's hours with United Press were from early afternoon until late at night, every day but Sunday. That left him lunchtime, Saturday mornings for tennis, and all day Sundays to see Betty. They could go to the movies free with Mrs. Werlein's Golden Key pass from the Hays Office, and meals were cheap—they could have a three-course lunch at Arnaud's for fifty cents. Hodding hated never seeing Betty at night except on Sundays, but he soon solved that. He bought a Ford, paying for it with the dollar a night that Tropical Radio paid whoever delivered its UP night news release for ships at sea to the transmission office on Lake Pontchartrain. If Mrs. Werlein would let Betty ride out with him after she had an earlier date with someone else, he would pick her up at eleven p.m. and have her back by midnight. Mrs. Werlein consented, but decreed that Hodding could not come in when he brought Betty home, since no one would be up to chaperon. He and Betty got around this with Hodding's regular emergency need for a glass of water. With the glass handy on a hall table, they would engage in "a kiss so warm it should have led to immediate cohabitation."[14]

They spent the weekends at Hammond, double-dating with

Corinne Carter and Isadore Dyer. One couple got the porch swing, and the other the living room sofa. Betty recalled that she was extremely naive. Hodding once told a joke about a girl who slapped a man's face because she mistook his asthma for passion. When Betty said she didn't understand, Hodding replied, "You're so sweet you don't know what passion is!"

"I know passion makes you huff and puff," Betty said, "but I don't know the first thing about asthma."

Betty worried about those weekends on the front porch in Hammond. Could she get pregnant from kissing? Intellectually she knew she couldn't, but she still worried occasionally. (A lecturer had come to town whose press releases claimed it was possible.) Later she was proud that she went to the altar a technical virgin three years after she met that "dangerous" man.[15]

"If you marry Hodding, it will be exciting, but there will be no money," Mrs. Werlein told her daughter.[16] She was not at all sure he was an eligible spouse for her oldest daughter; he was a *jeune homme de bonne famille*, but with no prospects.

When Lady Beit and her sister Marguerite arrived from England for a visit and learned that Hodding had serious intentions toward Betty Werlein, they asked him to bring her to call at the Pontchartrain Hotel. Hodding had always resented being taken to the Pontchartrain, where Tante Lilian held court, and he still did not like it, but he went there with Betty. The next day Tante Lilian and Tante Marguerite handed down their judgment, received respectfully because of the generosity of Lady Beit and Sir Otto. The sisters told Hodding that Betty was "charming, lovely, and intelligent, but you will certainly meet other young women as charming when you are older."[17]

Hodding hurried to report to Mrs. Werlein that his aunts had said he would certainly meet other young women as charming. "Did Lilian Carter indeed say that Hodding would meet anyone else as charming as *my* daughter?" That settled it. From that moment on, Mrs. Werlein was Hodding's ally.

They hoped to be married right after Betty graduated. One night

Hodding's boss at United Press accused Annette Duchein of the *Times-Picayune* of some deceptive practice. Hodding swung his fist, knocking his boss onto his typewriter and slamming boss, typewriter, and table to the floor.

"I quit," said Hodding, already on his way downstairs.

"You're fired!" his boss yelled after him.

Hart Bynum followed Hodding down the stairs, shouting back, "I quit, too!"

New Orleans newspapers and press associations had an agreement that one organization could not hire a staffer from another organization for six months after the staffer had left the previous job. Hodding and Bynum went to Hammond and collaborated on writing short stories, which they hoped to sell, while they waited for the six months to pass. "Carter Bynum" was very prolific, and they sent several stories off to their agent, Rowe Wright at Curtis Brown. Almost immediately, Wright sold a story, "Lose a Friend," to *American* magazine for $300. Bynum offered his half of the fee as a wedding present to Hodding. (The story, under the title "Brothers Under the Skin," appeared in the magazine in March 1932. It was about the friendship between "Irish" O'Rourke and "Frenchy" LeBlanc, two Marines stationed in Haiti.)

Hodding wired Betty, who had graduated and was working as a tennis counselor at Chunn's Cove Camp near Asheville, North Carolina, the news: "I'm standing on my left ear," he said. "Cheers. Whoops. Heart throbs and all my love."

Mrs. Werlein did not think the sale of one story meant Hodding could earn a living. She was right. Wright liked their other stories and sent them out, but none sold. Then a friend of the Werleins' returned from Mexico and said it was possible to live on $500 a year in Taxco. Mrs. Werlein and Mr. and Mrs. Carter gave their consent. The wedding was set for October 14, 1931.

A point of etiquette almost derailed the marriage. Hodding and Betty had been to a celebratory dinner at a friend's apartment in the French Quarter. As they left, Hodding ran down the stairs ahead of Betty. When they got to her house, she told him she could not marry a man who was so discourteous as to walk ahead of her. The wedding was off. ("How immature I must have been! Stupid! Stupid!" she wrote years later.)[18] Betty wept all night at her own folly; her mother heard her and told her to phone Hodding and tell him she was sorry. Betty was not used to calling men—it's hard to re-create the rigid rules of a time when nice girls did not call boys—but she called Hodding, who came right over and explained that he ran down the stairs ahead of her because he was eager to get her to himself.

The marriage plans were back on, but Hodding and Betty didn't go to Taxco. Two weeks before the wedding, Associated Press offered Hodding a job as day manager for its bureau in Jackson, Mississippi. Making $50 a week, a good salary for the time, sounded better to everyone than surviving on $500 a year in Taxco.

Hodding went on to Jackson and started work, having left a trunk in Mrs. Werlein's dining room. "It held his clothes for the wedding and a pair of red pajamas," Betty remembered years later. One of her sister's boyfriends asked him if he was going to wear those after the wedding. "No," said Hodding, "no pajamas." Everyone was pleasantly titillated.[19]

Before the wedding Betty wrote him about the presents flooding in and told him how much luggage she would have. She had put a bucket out to catch rainwater, she said, to wash her hair with so it would look nicer on the wedding day.

"You have the peachiest kind of nature," she told him, because he was "thinking of all the things I haven't had time to and listing them so that I won't have to bother to think at all, but simply check as soon as an article is provided for."[20] She had recognized a salient trait of Hodding's. Although he often appeared totally disorganized, all his life he made lists and worked down them methodically.

After the wedding, which took place in the big double drawing room of her grandmother's house in New Orleans, Betty and Hodding went to Pass Christian on the Mississippi Gulf Coast for a honeymoon in a house borrowed from a friend. The trip was interrupted when Governor Theodore Bilbo called a special session of the legislature to deal with the state's fiscal crisis. Hodding had to go to Jackson.

The honeymooners drove to Jackson by way of Hammond and settled with their wedding presents into an apartment. While Hodding covered the legislature's battles over the enactment of a sales tax, which seemed inevitable, Betty went to Episcopal ladies' meetings. There were two groups, one that made patchwork quilts and one that played bridge. She chose the bridge group and soon was playing three times a day.

During the first months of 1932, the leader of the anti–sales tax legislators accused the entire capital press corps in Jackson, including the two AP men, Hodding and Kenneth Toler, of "selling out" to the sales tax people. Hodding, furious, prepared a story featuring interviews with AP client newspaper editors that cleared the two reporters. The AP division manager in New Orleans told Hodding to hold off until he could get to Jackson before he put the story on the wire. Hodding waited impatiently for his boss's arrival, then finally went ahead and moved the story.[21] The man fired both Hodding and Toler.[22] Subsequently, on March 7, 1932, the Mississippi legislature passed a resolution that the coverage by Hodding and Toler had been "fair to both sides."[23]

Afterward Hodding liked to say that the managing director of Associated Press wrote him a letter stating that he would never make a newspaperman. Kent Cooper, the managing director, denied this story and denied, in fact, that Hodding was fired at all. "I would have had to approve it and I did not," he wrote Hodding more than a decade later, mentioning "the advice I gave to you in two or three letters in the spring of '32, to the effect that your ability would have the best possible chance of development by getting a newspaper of your own. . . . I think it ought to be said that the connection was broken by mutual agreement."[24]

Hodding decided he and Betty had better go to New Orleans, where he could look for a newspaper job. He could not bring himself to stay with his mother-in-law, so they packed up the wedding presents, stored their furniture, and drove to Hammond.

4. 1932–1936

"If We Had Known Anything, We Wouldn't Have Tried It"

Angry and humiliated, Hodding took Betty home to Hammond, where the Carters welcomed the newlyweds. Irma Carter—a mother who liked to have her children nearby—suggested that he start a daily paper in Hammond.

Hammond, which had grown to a population of 6,000, already had a prosperous, well-established weekly paper, the *Vindicator*, but perhaps the town could support a daily, too. Hodding and Betty ignored the grim national economic situation in 1932 and saw that Hammond seemed to be flourishing. The strawberry crop the year before had been good. They decided, perhaps irrationally, that they had no choice: it was their own paper or nothing. "If we had known anything, we wouldn't have tried it," Betty Carter said.[1]

They had a total of $367 in cash—the money left of a wedding present from Betty's grandmother and payment for the short story— and nothing else but energy and brains. They rented a tiny office in the arcade of the Hammond movie theater, for which the manager agreed to take advertising in lieu of rent. Hodding hired a printer named Sidney Williams, who knew of an ancient, discarded Chandler and Price job press for sale at a New Orleans junk dealer's for seventy-five dollars. It was broken in four pieces, but Sidney Williams said it could be welded back together. Designed to print circulars, it would take a tabloid-size sheet of paper. Hodding loaded it on his father's farm truck and went by the *Times-Picayune* offices, where the production chief gave him column rules, leads, slugs, advertising borders, and other supplies that Williams said he needed.[2] He spent $150 at the E. C. Palmer Company, a newsprint and printing equipment dealer, on hand-set headline type. A desk, a kitchen table, and two straight chairs from Hodding's parents furnished the office, and Hodding built tables and racks for the print shop.

If Hodding was carpenter, trader, editor, reporter, and publisher, Betty, who had sold advertising for the school paper at McGehee's, was advertising manager and society editor. On April 18, 1932, after four weeks of intense effort, the first edition of the Hammond *Daily Courier* appeared. They framed the first dollar they took in—it was for some sheets of colored cardboard from their supplies for job printing—and hung it over Hodding's desk. The next day somebody stole it. The first job printing order came from Alsia Corbera, who taught dancing and wanted programs for her yearly recital.[3] (The *Courier* picked up the information from the program and ran the names of Alsia's students and the numbers they performed.)

The welded-together press ran unwillingly, and a little lopsidedly. Its flat bed was big enough for only one page at a time. The editorial page was printed first, the first page last. Sheets of newsprint the size of two tabloid pages were used; each had to be folded by hand, then fed, one at a time, onto the bed of the press. This process was repeated for each of the four pages of the paper. It had to be a morning paper: it took at least eight hours, all night, to print 2,000 copies. Betty and Hodding found out on the first night that folding the sheets of paper was a hideous job: it was hard to make the corners of the folded sheet square perfectly with each other.

The *Courier* was delivered free to every house in town for a few weeks. The first issue trumpeted a subscription rate of fifty cents for a year, with half of the money to be donated to Hammond High School. A thousand subscribers signed up right away.

That first issue contained very little news, but many letters congratulating the new paper. The second issue carried more congratulatory messages, including one from the mayor, C. C. Carter, Hodding's uncle. A front-page story reported that strawberry shipments were in full swing, with strawberries selling for $2 to $2.25 a crate, and on the inside a story noted that the paper had its first out-of-town subscriber, Brandon Woolly, Hodding's roommate and colleague when he had worked on the *Tribune* in New Orleans. The issue also invited everyone to see the painting of the Androscoggin River in Maine that had been presented to the *Courier* to mark its birth by retired Maine clipper captain F. A. Stinson.

On the second night of operation, a tramp named Brick appeared in the shop, and sat on the floor and began to help with the folding. He used a short strip of lead column rule to crease the fold, which struck Williams, Hodding, and Betty as an act of pure genius. Hodding thought Brick was a friend of Williams's, and Williams thought Hodding had hired him. At any rate, Brick stayed for nearly a year, sleeping in the shop and helping with the folding, eating food and wearing clothes that Hodding and Betty brought him.

Since they could not afford a Linotype machine at first, they had the type set at the Ponchatoula *Enterprise*, a weekly newspaper in a town several miles south of Hammond. This was expensive, and a great strain on the *Enterprise*, which could set the type only in the late afternoon and at night. Hodding had to carry the *Courier* type back to Hammond in galley trays, and once a tray of type became hopelessly jumbled. On April 25, the *Courier*'s front-page headline read: "Look What We Got for Our Birthday," above a line drawing of a Mergenthaler Linotype. Hodding and Betty borrowed $600 for the down payment from a Hammond bank, Will Carter cosigning the note. Crisis was the dominant motif those first months. The dolly carrying the Linotype when it arrived got stuck between an Illinois Central track rail and the bordering asphalt just before the arrival of the Panama Limited. The *Courier* story noted that it was the only Linotype in Hammond and one of only three in the parish. Headline type was still set by hand; once, when he could not find a capital C, Hodding carved one out of wood.

Prices for strawberries were falling each day. If they had waited another month, Hodding said, they would not have gone into newspaper publishing at all.[4] It became clear that the strawberry crop was a disaster that year. A crate of berries would not bring what the crate itself had cost. Soup kitchens opened and banks foreclosed on land they did not want. Newspapers were folding across the South. On October 24, 1932, the *Courier* printed the largest delinquent tax list ever published in Tangipahoa Parish.

The Carters' difficulties were enormous. They tried to start the press at five p.m., but sometimes they could not begin to print until two a.m. or even later. Hodding came home from the office every morning filthy with printer's ink. Betty, the uptown New Orleans girl who had never washed so much as a pair of stockings for herself, tried to get his shirts clean in the bathtub. Irma Carter found her one day in the bathroom on her knees, in tears. From then on, Hodding's shirts went with his parents' laundry to the washwoman in Yellow Water. Hodding's parents indulged the young people in any way they could. When Betty mentioned it would be nice to have a tennis court, Will Carter pulled up the trees in a young peach orchard near the house and built one. Betty and Hodding were always too tired to play tennis when they got home.

The *Courier* survived and even began to get a little national advertising. Hodding and Betty moved into their own home, a small rented house heated only by fireplaces. They cooked on an oil stove passed on to them by the Episcopal minister and his wife, whose parishioners had given them a new gas stove. They bought an icebox, not electric, from the Hammond Ice and Coal Company and paid five dollars a month for it, which covered also a supply of ice for twenty months. They unpacked their wedding presents and drank from silver goblets and ate from silver dishes because they could not afford to buy china and glasses. They caught crawfish in a muddy creek. They tried recipes from a cookbook titled *101 Ways to Use Stale Bread*. As the Depression deepened, they learned how to barter. They swapped advertising for groceries, for drugs, for printing equipment, for farm-fresh produce, for gasoline, and for clothes, including a blue sailor dress for Betty. A stranger drove into town and opened a small cannery, planning to can local produce for farmers and keep—and sell—a tenth of the cans he filled. The *Courier* printed his labels and gave him advertising in return for pears, string beans, chili, Hungarian goulash, tomatoes, and peas. The labels came off, and often Hodding and Betty didn't know what they'd be eating for dinner until they opened a can. National advertisers offered razor blades and other items; Hodding and Betty took 50,000 blades and gave them as gifts. The Carters loved J. C. Penney and other chain stores, which paid cash for advertising. A little cash went a long way—a restaurant at Pass Manchac served all the boiled shrimp, boiled crabs, fried fish, fried oysters, fried frog legs, and sliced tomatoes you could eat for fifty cents. Precious dollars were needed for newsprint, which had to be paid for on delivery. Every day after Betty had made the rounds of merchants, she and Hodding tallied her sales under swap or cash.

The Hammond *Daily Courier* was in many ways a terrible paper. It is hard to look at microfilms of it and believe that the editor had attended the Columbia University School of Journalism or worked for daily newspapers and wire services. It was lively, sometimes passionate, but often silly.

A gambling raid was reported thus on April 28, 1932:

"GO IN AND OUT THE WINDOW"
PLAYED AFTER DICE RAID HERE

Window jumping was in fashion in downtown Hammond last night when Mayor C. C. Carter and Marshal Gordon Anderson eased unexpectedly into a crap game of large proportions.

The two raiders found approximately 50 leading and other citizens crooning to Little Joe, but in the rush were unable to get more than 13 names.

Immediately afterward the Courier office resembled Pontchartrain beach on the Fourth of July and the Courier staff got hoarse explaining that names secured in crap-game raids are of no more value to us than are the chips which some of those carried in their pockets.

The *Courier* printed some of the excuses of the participants: "Believe it or not I was waiting for a streetcar." "I didn't know it was loaded." "I thought we were going to play tiddley-winks." It also printed the names the participants gave to law enforcement officers: Patrick Henry, John Doe, Ol' Man Adam and his Chillun, Apollo Belvedere, Dun and Bradstreet, and Ada from Decatur. No real names were listed.

In his memoirs Hodding said that one of the house men came to the paper and said his boss didn't want the story printed; he was willing to make it worth Hodding's while to keep it out of the *Courier.* "My first impulse was to hit him," Hodding wrote, "but why bother?" Hodding told him the story would be in the paper the next morning and asked him, as a friend, how high his boss would have been willing to go to keep the story out of the paper. Ten dollars, said the emissary. "Remember," wrote Hodding, "those were Depression days."[5]

The paper covered all the local news it could—a flower show, a Boy Scout honor court, a case of shoplifting, swimming lessons, Daughters of the American Revolution meetings, church activities. Frank Di Maggio wrote a column in Italian for the benefit of Sicilian farmers in the area, and later a history of Sicily, which appeared in installments, in English and Italian.

Local news coverage increased when Bert Hyde, just out of high school, joined the staff part-time in July 1932. He was paid five dollars a week, which Hodding often had to borrow back in order to pay the mailing deposit at the post office. By the end of the year Hyde was making fifteen dollars a week, working full-time after dropping out from Southeastern Louisiana College in Hammond. When a man named Low, who had been writing a column, "Low Down on the High Ups," left, Bert took it over and made it a much-enjoyed or—to some of the people some of the time—a much-feared column. He rode around town with a tire emblazoned "Daily Courier" on the back of his car, and when he and his girlfriend went to the drive-in restaurant where *tout* Hammond went after the movies, many cars would pull out. The fleeing passengers did not want it reported in the newspaper that Mrs. Jones was out with Mr. Smith.[6]

Hodding wrote once that during its four-year existence the *Courier* chronicled more homicides and fewer resulting convictions in Bloody Tangipahoa than the New Orleans papers reported in a city where the population was ten times greater. Next to a front-page story headlined "Chalk Up One More Killing for Hammond," Hodding ran a front-page editorial, "A Call to Arms," in the form of an open letter to the Krupp, Du Pont, and Remington companies, touting the advantages of Tangipahoa Parish for factories that made guns and ammunition. "You cannot equal anywhere the spirit in which [our men] sally forth of nights with a playful forty-five and a sparkling pint beneath their belts. . . . The parish would demand all that you could supply."[7]

The *Courier* could not run photographs because it had no facilities for making photoengravings. It had no wire services and depended on the radio for any national news. Thus the May 13, 1932, story—headlined in the biggest type yet used for the paper—began: "A horror stricken nation learned last night, through press and radio dispatches, that the decomposed body of a baby identified as Charles Augustus Lindbergh Jr. had been found four miles from Hopewell, N.J. yesterday afternoon."

Some editorials commented on national affairs. One in particular attacked the bonus marchers, unemployed World War I veterans who went to Washington and camped out while they sought assistance from Congress. A few months later, on August 1, 1932, the paper ran a long, sympathetic interview with a bonus marcher. Hodding could always be touched by an individual's plight.

Hodding's concern for the Bill of Rights would become legendary in later years, but he showed concern for its application only once while he was in Hammond. He was never remotely sympathetic to communism, but he deplored the arrest of eight men in New Orleans for attending a communist meeting, and he quoted Voltaire: "I don't agree with what you say but will defend with my life your right to say it."[8]

His editorials seldom showed even a faint interest in racial justice, but one did praise a New Orleans black group, the Association Against Radicalism and Communism Among Negroes. One very early editorial displayed blatant racism as well as a naive approach to solving economic problems. Remember the battle royal staged every Fourth of July? Hodding asked his readers. "A dozen darkies, all blindfolded, milling around in a boxing ring and swinging wildly at each other. The winner—meaning the last man left standing—won a sack of flour." The joke came, Hodding wrote, when the referee winked at the crowd and pulled the blinders off one fighter. This man, who could see, would knock down the others and win the sack of flour. The moral, Hodding pointed out, was that in times of economic stress like the present, battles royal for a sack of flour flourished. Now "the blindfolded ones are socking each other with every weapon they possess—class hatred, religious animosity, pet prejudices, political barbs and personal peeves." The fellow without a blindfold was the common enemy, fear. They should all pull off the blindfolds and work together. "A sack of flour divided is better than no flour at all," he concluded.[9]

In an editorial on Huey Long, Hodding raised his first real cry against racism. He said, in part:

> When an unnerved politician in the South today starts shouting about "negro lovers" and waving his good old color flag in matters which can in no way pertain to these former Southern problems, then we may conclude that his back is against the wall. This is just what Huey Long is doing, and this is just where he is standing now.[10]

If racial justice was not a paramount concern at this time, money and pride were. On December 24, 1932, Hodding and Betty went to New Orleans to celebrate the holiday with Betty's family, who came home late after attending many Christmas Eve parties. After a buffet supper of gumbo, chicken sandwiches, champagne, and fruitcake, the

Werleins opened their presents. Betty's sister Evelyn had just married Donald Smith, a well-off young easterner whose Christmas gift to his wife was a pair of matched silver-fox furs. Betty and Hodding were giving each other a set of the *Encyclopædia Britannica* with a bookcase, all for a monthly payment of five dollars, but they could not show this off. Hodding went upstairs and wrote Betty a check for a thousand dollars (there was less than fifty in the account), then came back down. "I couldn't decide what you wanted most," he told her in front of everyone, "so I thought I'd just give you the money." Betty knew their bank balance as well as Hodding did, but she acted her part. Hodding thought his in-laws were suitably impressed.

Early the next morning Hodding and Betty went to the farm at Hammond for Christmas Day with the Carters. There was the traditional distribution of presents to servants, employees, and their families, and then a family dinner including Hodding's brother, his new wife, and Corinne. After a little eggnog came oyster cocktails, country ham, turkey stuffed with pecans and hot sausage, homemade rolls, tomato aspic, at least six vegetables, and fruitcake and charlotte russe.

By the end of the year, Betty and Hodding had bought a new flat-bed press that could take full sheets without hand-folding, and they felt better about the future. At first it looked as though the strawberry crop might bring prosperity to Hammond in 1933. On February 3, the *Courier* reported that the first pint of mature strawberries was on display in C. C. Carter's garage. A hard freeze a few days later was seen as a blessing by strawberry growers. Hope fell, though, as prices reached a new low that year: fifty-five cents a crate.

When President Franklin Roosevelt ordered the nation's banks closed on March 6, 1933, Hodding had five dollars in his pocket— and a payroll to meet, the rent to pay, and more newsprint to buy. He met the payroll with grocery trade-outs, writing orders to the merchants who advertised with the *Courier* and owed him money. On Friday afternoon, March 10, he and Betty drove to the gas station that advertised in the paper, filled the tank on credit, and started out for New Orleans to spend the five dollars on a good time before Hodding went out on Monday to look for a job.

After dinner at Mrs. Werlein's, they went to a gambling casino on the outskirts of New Orleans. Hodding sent Betty to watch the roulette wheel while he squeezed in at a dice table. He tossed his five-dollar bill at the croupier and "got five blue chips and a pitying look."[11] He put two chips down, and a short time later he and Betty walked out of the casino with $400 in crisp new bills. It was more money than they had when they started the *Courier*, and probably more cash than anybody else in Hammond had at the moment.

It was Betty's idea to issue their own scrip that would be good with the advertisers who owed the *Courier* money. Emblazoned with the words "Daily Courier Co-operative Scrip," a picture of Roosevelt, and the slogan "We bank on him," the documents announced that "The Daily Courier will accept on Advertising and Printing Accounts the full amount of this scrip which has been used in trade between employees of The Daily Courier and the Merchant herewith named," and were signed by Betty Carter.

Whatever the difficulties they encountered, Hodding approved of Roosevelt's economic program. "It is the second American Revolution," he editorialized on April 10, 1933. "Truly it is a privilege to live through times such as these."

When the banks reopened, the Carters were in good shape. Merchants had squared most of their accounts and the Carters still had some cash left, while the payroll was only slightly in arrears.

In spite of hard times, Carter had only pity for the editor who had never had a subscription canceled, "for it only means that he has no opinions on any subject, save sugar-coated ones."[12] The *Courier* had had four cancellations, and while Hodding regretted the loss of cash, "we have not really lost . . . readers. Because, you know, they still read what we might have to say about them. They're reading this. It's human nature." Who could resist him?

Good friends rescued him. Hodding mentioned that money was very tight to Hermann Deutsch, a friend of his at the New Orleans *Item*. "Would a thousand-dollar loan help you out?" asked Deutsch, who asked for neither note nor collateral. The timely loan enabled Hodding to buy a second Linotype.[13]

Next, he acquired a new building with no effort. In 1934 a homestead association, a type of building and loan association, offered to sell him a repossessed two-story structure in good condition for $10,000, no money down. Hodding could pay for it with $10,000 in homestead association stock, which he could buy in the open market for $30 a share instead of its book value of $100. Moreover, the association offered to lend him the $3,000 to buy the $10,000 worth of stock; it would accept the $3,000 as full payment for the building. He could repay the loan at $40 a month. Hodding, Bert Hyde, and the men from the shop moved the office furniture and equipment one weekend, pushing Linotypes and press down the street on a dolly three blocks to Thomas Street. Alsia Corbera, the dancing teacher who had given the first printing order, rented a room upstairs for her dance studio.

A year later, when Bert Hyde married Alsia Corbera—after he had sold enough advertising in Hammond and Baton Rouge to get due bills for his new wardrobe and furniture—they rented living space on the second floor, next to Alsia's dance studio. Alsia began to operate a service known as the ARN, Alsia's Radio News. The *Courier* still had no wire service, and Alsia listened to the radio all day long. When there was hot news, she would call downstairs and report it to Bert or Hodding. Sometimes Bert, Alsia, Hodding, and Betty would listen to the eight-o'clock news at night and take notes, which Hodding would amplify for the next day's *Courier*.

In the summer of 1934, Hodding and Betty felt they could take a vacation. Packed suitcases in the car, they drove over the cattle gap in the driveway to the Carters' farm and paused before getting on the blacktop road. To go to California, they had to turn right. "Oh, let's go to Maine," said Hodding, and turned left. They drove to Maine and stayed with Hodding's aunt in Camden. Summers in Maine were once again a part of Hodding's life.

Soon Betty was pregnant, but their excitement about the new baby was dimmed in January 1935, when Irma Carter died after several months of illness. After the funeral, which was held at Will Carter's

48

house, Betty and Hodding moved back to the farm to keep him company.

One night when Betty was far along in her pregnancy, Hodding went back to work after supper. Betty made plans to go to the movies with a friend. They drove downtown at about eight and parked the car in front of the Central Drug Store. As they got out, Betty noticed the street was crowded. She saw a car stopping in the middle of the street in front of the drugstore and heard someone cursing. Suddenly the air was filled with the sound of gunshots; people ran for cover, and the plate-glass window of the drugstore broke right beside Betty.

"The bullets must have passed just in front of my stomach," Betty wrote the next day. ". . . Oddly enough I wasn't scared." A man lay dead in the gutter. It was the culmination of a feud between Ike Starns and his father on one side and a dentist named Sedge Newsom, who had been having an affair with Ike Starns's wife, on the other.

The Starnses, who were not rednecks but substantial farmers and businessmen, had threatened to kill Newsom if he was not out of town by seven o'clock. Newsom stayed in his office and told the police. All three Hammond policemen—the city manager who was ex officio police chief, the night marshal, and the day officer—had gathered to protect him. Ike Starns's father was killed; Newsom stood unharmed on the steps to his office above the drugstore.

"I guess I'm a full-fledged bloody Tangipahoan now," Betty told Hodding when he appeared.[14]

Two weeks before the baby was due, Hodding drove Betty to New Orleans; she would stay with her mother until she went to the hospital there. Instead of the shorter but bumpier road through the swamps of Manchac, they took the longer, smoother road through Covington. They planned to have lunch at Béchac's. They stopped first for target practice in the sun-dappled pinewoods. Hot and thirsty, they stopped again at a roadside stand, and Hodding brought tall, frosty mugs of root beer back to the car. Looking back much later, Betty said she knew "*that* had been the happiest day of my life."[15]

A front-page story by Bert Hyde in the *Courier* of April 8, 1935, announced the birth of William Hodding Carter III in a New Orleans hospital. Hammond friends sent flowers to Betty on the afternoon train. Hodding was enormously proud. "I can't concentrate on anything. Tertius Carter has already put over sixteen winning touchdowns, run the quarter in 47 flat, made straight A's in school, and disappointed me only by being elected president of the Christian Endeavor."[16]

Very early on, Hodding and the Hammond *Daily Courier* began a war against Huey Long, the flamboyant, earthy politician whose populist policies had won him enormous power in Louisiana. Hodding saw Long's use of his power as corrupt and his policies as a threat to democracy. Still in his twenties, Hodding was without fear or pity as he kept up a barrage of attacks against Long. These were often ineffective, but the campaign gave Hodding an opportunity to practice his assault skills, to polish and sharpen his editorial weapons. He learned, too, that he could bludgeon the power structure and survive. And through this bombardment of Long he would win his first national recognition.

Huey Pierce Long had come to power in Louisiana, where, as in other southern states, "gentlemen" and planters had teamed with industry to run the state's politics since Reconstruction. Long wanted to change the game. Elected governor with an overwhelming majority in 1928, he immediately forced through the legislature progressive laws to provide free textbooks, inaugurated a bond issue to build highways (Louisiana had only three hundred miles of paved roads when Long took office), and raised taxes on utility and oil companies. He acquired a nickname, "the Kingfish," won enormous popularity, and scared the "gentlemen" to death. Their fear was justified: he began to consolidate his personal power throughout all levels of state government, and used patronage ruthlessly to reward his friends with jobs at the same time he removed not only his enemies but also their sons, fathers, and brothers-in-law. Long traveled with gangsterlike bodyguards and broke all the rules of decorum.

After only two years in the governor's office, Long ran for the U.S. Senate in 1930 and was elected. He refused, however, to leave Baton Rouge while an unfriendly lieutenant governor occupied what he regarded as his governor's chair. Not until O. K. Allen, a faithful Long henchman, was elected governor in January 1932, did Long spend any time in Washington. Then his flamboyance and his call to limit personal fortunes began to attract nationwide attention.

Although a U.S. senator, he still controlled all state appointments. He came back to Baton Rouge in the summer of 1932 to run the legislature and moved Allen out of the governor's office so he could have it himself. His social program had emptied the state treasury, although he had raised income taxes and imposed a severance tax on oil. Now, in 1932, he proposed a tax on tobacco, soft drinks, insurance premiums, electricity, corporations, and gasoline.

Hodding and his family were anti-Long from the beginning. They saw real dangers in his total control of every phase of state government and, considering themselves members of the aristocracy, had no sympathy with his populism and Share Our Wealth notions. Like almost every newspaper in the state, the *Courier* opposed Long and his regime, but Hodding fought him more emotionally than did anyone else in the news columns and on the editorial page. He attacked Long sometimes with passionate seriousness, sometimes with heavy-handed ridicule, referring to him in satirical editorials as "Senator Screwy P. Swong" with his "Share Our Swag" program.[17]

After the legislature passed Long's tax bills and adjourned, the *Courier* commented: "It's all over but the paying. Louisiana's representatives are coming home now, like dutiful boys who have obeyed Daddy, and want other folks to pat them on the back."[18]

Not long after the legislative session, Bolivar Kemp, the congressman who represented the Sixth District, which included Hammond, was up for reelection in the Democratic primary. (There were no Republicans in Louisiana at the time; the Democratic primary was the ultimate election.) Kemp, who was from Amite, was the father of Betty's old friend Peeps, and the Kemps were also friends of the

Carters. Kemp's son and Hodding had competed in high school oratorical tournaments. Hodding and Betty had spent hours with Peeps and Mrs. Kemp on the Kemps' front porch, which had a ceiling fan that made it cool on the hottest summer days. Betty had worked for Bolivar Kemp's campaign when he first ran for Congress. But Hodding and Betty opposed Kemp for reelection this time because of his failure to "disassociate himself from Long,"[19] and supported his opponent, Paul Borron. The *Courier* also supported for reelection to the U.S. Senate Edwin Broussard, whom the Long forces wanted to replace with John Overton.

A front-page editorial that summer shows how emotionally involved Hodding was in the election. An anonymous letter called him a liar for inflating his crowd estimate at a Borron-for-Congress rally. Hodding admitted his estimate might have been high. "For in looking over the gathering, we doubtless made the mistake of including among the men present this saffron colored jelly fish who isn't man enough to say what he thinks—if he thinks—without hiding behind an unsigned epithet."[20]

A front-page story on August 14 announced that Long would speak in Hammond that night in support of Kemp and Long's other candidates. Years later Betty Carter would say, "We used to try to think of ways to kill [Long]. He would come and speak in the bandstand in the park and his listeners would sit on folding chairs. I thought we should take a sharp nail with the point made even sharper, and dip it in tetanus and stick it up in one of those chairs, where he'd sit on it. He wouldn't know it, and he'd die the death he deserved, the death of a mad dog."[21] Nothing so dramatic happened, and the next day the *Courier*'s report on the speech carried the headline "Huey's Hooey Falls Flat with Crowd."

Most of the solid citizens said they opposed Long, but on election day, September 14, Betty was surprised at the respectable people and leaders of the community who wore Long badges. All of the people whom the *Courier* had opposed, including Bolivar Kemp, were victorious.

After the election, the *Courier* relaxed a little, but now and then an editorial breathed a wisp of fire. On September 22, the front page featured a one-column box headed "Run Out?" "We understand," wrote Hodding, "that a certain Hammond supporter of Huey Long has recommended that we be 'run out of town' for our anti-Long activities in the recent election. If this fathead wants to exercise anything besides his mouth, we suggest that he try it."

Then the axe fell, or as the *Courier* put it: "The Hydra-head of the Long–Allen administration has again protruded itself venomously into the affairs of Tangipahoa Parish and Southeastern College."[22] In May 1933, at a meeting from which the press was barred, the State Board of Education ordered an investigation of the Southeastern Louisiana College president, L. A. Sims, and summarily dropped Will Carter from his position on the board of trustees, which he had held for seven years, ever since he had donated the land on which to build the school.

"Considerable wisdom was shown on the part of those most concerned in the failure to make any personal criticism of Mr. Carter," his son editorialized. "We seriously doubt that even the most insane demagogue or puppet representative would have the temerity to cast any aspersion upon him . . . because we know from past observation that it wouldn't be healthy."

On June 10, the *Courier* began running daily front-page editorials attacking the Long machine. Displaying such headlines as "Crawfish Senator a Tin Horn Sport," "Cowards and Grafters," "The Whale and the Crawfish," the pieces typically called Long "a destructive demagog who owes his political existence to Long RULE and Long RUINATION." One editorial described him further: "First on one foot and then on the other, right-about facing, worming, squirming, and wool-pulling, Louisiana's senior senator is establishing an unprecedented record for dancing, twisting, and wool-pulling in his intoxicating whirl for a toe hold on the winning band wagon in the magnificent March of Progress."[23] The paper described Long as "fox-brained, magnificently clothed and shod," and had him crying, "I am the

State."[24] One editorial trumpeted: "Wilful waste and woeful want; road construction means state destruction."[25] Another claimed that Long's "'redistribution' means taking away riches from the citizen and the gathering in of wealth by the pie-eating army of political parasites."[26] These editorials and stories were angry and vituperative, but they included few facts or real revelations. It was an exception when the *Courier* used objective statistics, such as the rise in the per capita cost of state government in Louisiana from $3.50 in 1917 to $12.55 in 1932, to buttress the case against Long.[27] Or when it quoted Judge Nat Tycer of Hammond, who pointed out that Long's salary was $7,500 a year but that he paid his wife more than that to run the house and traveled to and from Washington in a private Pullman car.[28]

The Sixth District congressional seat became the prime topic of news when Bolivar Kemp died on June 19, 1933. In spite of its editorial opposition to Kemp, the *Courier* ran a long, laudatory obituary, which closed: "Mr. Kemp enjoyed a tremendous popularity throughout the Sixth District, and a pall hung over the parish yesterday when his death was reported."[29]

The law required the governor to call a special Democratic primary election to choose Kemp's successor. As always, the primary winner would be the new congressman, since there was never any Republican opposition in a general election. While O. K. Allen delayed, the *Courier* hounded him to call the election. Mrs. Kemp announced herself as a candidate to fill her husband's seat. Other candidates did as well, among them "Little J. Y." Sanders, a Baton Rouge lawyer. His father, "Ol' J. Y." Sanders, a former governor from Hammond, had been a strong foe of Long's.

To make sure his own candidate won, Long decided to bypass the primary and have Mrs. Kemp named the Democratic nominee. When he called for a general election instead of a primary, with only Mrs. Kemp's name on the ballot, voters in the Sixth District were outraged. A *Courier* front-page editorial called Long a "damnable vulture" and proclaimed that the time had come for shotgun government in the district.[30]

Judge Tycer, whose judicial district included four of the congressional district's twelve parishes, enjoined the balloting in his district. Maintaining that it was a poor judge who could not enforce his own decisions, Tycer started swearing in deputies to support his injunction. Hodding Carter was one of these deputies.[31]

In early December, as election day drew near, Hodding was a member of the crowd of three hundred who broke into the courthouse in Amite and publicly burned about 11,000 ballots to be used in the special election. "For mark our words, we have started a revolt against Longism which will not be stopped," said a front-page editorial. "The flames of the burning ballots of Tangipahoa and the Felicianas stand out starkly against the Louisiana sky. And like the fiery hill-side torch which summoned the Clansmen in 1876, a beacon has been lit to call free Louisianans to stand and fight for their homes and their state. Answer that summons, Louisianans."[32]

When Long warned that their actions would bring heavy fines and long jail terms, Hodding's crowd burned more ballots. They constructed an effigy of the senator in the *Courier* office and burned it at noon at the corner of Cherry and Thomas streets in downtown Hammond. Years later, Alsia Corbera Hyde would recall that "they burned Huey Long in effigy and claimed there was a big crowd. There wasn't. There wasn't anybody there."[33]

Sometimes Hodding's opposition to Long took on an air of opéra bouffe, especially when he was trying to get outside publicity for the anti-Long cause. Hodding and Bert Hyde took pictures of the effigy-burning and rushed them to New Orleans in time for the afternoon papers. The *Courier* obtained the engraving from the New Orleans *Item* and finally ran a picture on December 6.[34]

The events connected with the election were widely reported; Hyde was correspondent for United Press and the New Orleans *Times-Picayune*, and Hodding for Associated Press and the *Item*. Stories appeared in the *Times* of London and on the front page of the New York *Times*.

Judge Tycer swore in more deputies. Long threatened to call

out the militia. On the night before the election, Hodding heard rumors that National Guardsmen were coming from New Orleans and that state policemen were bringing fresh loads of ballots from Baton Rouge. Ol' J.Y. Sanders lent Hodding a beautifully chased sawed-off shotgun, complete with leg holster. Hodding also had his own .38 caliber pistol. Plans called for the deputies to split into groups of eight or ten men and begin patrolling their parishes at about midnight. Before Hodding's group left, Betty served coffee and sandwiches to some of his fellow deputies and several newspapermen who had come up from New Orleans for the occasion. As Hodding was leaving, Betty said, with great aplomb, "Honey, you forgot your shotgun." [35]

Some of the deputies were sent to Pass Manchac to stop the militia by raising the drawbridge there. Other deputies lay in ditches along the border between Tangipahoa Parish and East Baton Rouge Parish, waiting for the state police and their ballots. There was some shooting but no one was killed. After being fired upon, the state policemen with the ballots withdrew to the capital. Hodding spent the night "scared witless" as he patrolled polling stations in his parish. On election day voting was sparse indeed, with the turnout about five percent of what it usually was. In Slidell only eighteen votes were cast; in Franklinton, seventy; in East Feliciana Parish, fewer than fifty; in Tangipahoa, St. Helena and Livingston parishes, none.

Ignoring the election, the district's Democratic Executive Committee declared Mrs. Kemp the representative. The anti-Long forces chose Little J.Y. Sanders in a rump election. It was up to the House of Representatives in Washington to decide on the legally elected representative.

"Widow Bolivar E. Kemp has rushed to Washington in the hope that she may prevail upon members of the House of Representatives to seat her on the strength of the scant 5,000 votes cast for her by penitentiary, insane asylum, and Crawfish followers of the state of Louisiana in the attempted steal," read a front-page *Courier* editorial on January 2, 1934. After trying to decide which of the two candidates was entitled to the seat, the House rejected the claims of both, and Long, through Governor Allen, had to order a special primary. In that election, Hodding supported a victorious Little J.Y. Sanders, who the next year won a full term, unopposed.

Hodding confessed years later that he was uneasy at his own willingness to resort to violence, even in the face of the "sordid, bribed rape of Louisiana," and he conceded that the people of Louisiana had legitimate grievances that Huey Long addressed. The biggest mistake he and other opponents of Long had made, he said, was to fight everything that Long did, even the good things.

In 1934, with a series of special legislative sessions, Long rammed through bills that concentrated even more power in his own hands. Although he was a senator, he personally ran committee meetings and spoke on the floor of the Louisiana House. Laws and regulations were aimed at any of Long's enemies who might still have power. He was bound to remove them, humiliate them, and get his revenge. Opposition seemed almost futile, but angry men in the Sixth District organized Square Deal associations to fight Long's Share Our Wealth clubs, and drilled under arms while they talked of a revolt by force. In January 1935, Square Dealers in Baton Rouge tried to seize the city's airport and courthouse. State officials called out the National Guard. When Square Dealers from all over the Sixth District went to the capital to help, Hodding could not go because of his mother's serious illness. Ten Square Dealers surrendered, and the movement died.

Long's men visited Hodding and urged him to "get right"; they pressured tradesmen in Hammond not to advertise in the *Courier*. A Long henchman even left with an employee an offer of cash and fat state printing contracts if Hodding would lay off Long. The Carters felt they were under siege.

It was through his bête noire, however, that Hodding first won national attention. Westbrook Pegler quoted one of his anti-Long editorials in his syndicated column.[36] Wayne Parish, a writer for *Literary Digest*, went to Hammond in the summer of 1934 to discuss Louisiana politics with Hodding and in an article quoted him as an authority on

Huey Long; Hodding, Parish said, was "one of the most articulate of the Louisiana newspapermen fighting Long."[37]

In 1933, Bruce Bliven of *The New Republic* had written to Hodding, in care of Mrs. Werlein in New Orleans: "It has been suggested to us that you might write The New Republic an excellent article on Huey Long. We aren't exactly pining for such an article—certainly not to the point of ordering one—but on the other hand if you should happen to write one, of about 2,500 words, we'd be very glad indeed to have a look at it."[38]

The letter lay on Hodding's desk for a month, and then Betty took charge. One Sunday morning, when they were about to drive to Will Carter's for dinner, she told Hodding he had to stay at home until he at least started writing the article. "As a gesture, she locked me in, and by the time she brought me a platter of fried chicken from the farm, I had written my first political analysis for a magazine."[39]

Five months after Bliven's letter, the article, "Kingfish to Crawfish," appeared.[40] In it Hodding was very optimistic about the crumbling of Long's power. He said that "laughter and ridicule" were proving more effective against Long than "libel proceedings, impeachment . . . alleged income tax evasions," and the investigation of the election to the Senate of his designated candidate, John Overton. Also, Long's feud with Franklin Roosevelt had made him lose the power of federal patronage in the state. Hodding cited the rebellion in the Sixth District and said all this "had put him on the spot."

Bliven asked Hodding to write another short article explaining how Long had won his victories in the legislature and in a New Orleans election in which he had soundly defeated the Old Regular machine.[41] In this piece Hodding conceded that while it had seemed Long was on his way out, his grasp on the state was stronger than ever and "his national stature, instead of diminishing, is attaining Gargantuan proportions." He added that the anti-Long forces needed a leader.[42]

Hodding did another article on Long, "Louisiana Limelighter," for the *Review of Reviews* of March 1935, in which he bluntly described Long as a dictator, recited his abuses of power, and predicted the appearance of a "Brutus or Corday" to get rid of the tyrant. "There are many sane, thoughtful citizens who believe that only through a .45 can the state regain its political and economic sanity." Albert Shaw, editor of the *Review*, wrote Hodding that it was "the clearest and most complete story on the gentleman that we have ever seen."[43] Hodding received a small fee and a hundred copies of the magazine. He did a third article on Long for *The New Republic*, which ran with an article by Gerald L. K. Smith, a Long supporter. The magazine headlined both articles "How Come Huey Long?" and placed "Bogeyman—" over Hodding's and "or Superman?" over Smith's; it also printed a disclaimer of Smith's views.[44]

Hodding's articles are often cited by Long's biographers, and T. Harry Williams describes them as "rising above the general level [of the journalism of the time] although marked by a strong antipathy to Long."[45]

A publisher wrote Hodding about a possible book, suggesting that it be "powerful, picturesque, and distinctly anti-Long in character." Hodding replied that he had exhaustive material, could begin the next week, and finish it in seven weeks.[46] He seemed bored with the *Courier* and began writing special Sunday articles for the *Item* in New Orleans. He also turned out a series for the *Daily News* in Jackson, Mississippi, on Long's plans to enlarge his sphere of influence outside Louisiana.

On top of his newspaper work and his outside political writing, Hodding continued writing poetry and fiction. His poem "Mother's Day" was published on the front page of the paper on May 7, 1932, and his Christmas poem "They Who Hunger" ran on the front page on December 24 of that year. (The Carters used it years later for a Christmas card.) Earlier in 1932 his agent, Rowe Wright, sent him a check for $22.50 for the poem "Appleblossoms," which he had sold to *Pictorial Review*. He sold a short short story, "Election Bet," to *Liberty*, and still had a few other stories he was trying to sell.[47] In 1933, Wright sent back all of Hodding's manuscripts; he wrote that *American* was still looking for short stories by Hart Bynum.

Hodding's output was prodigious. He had already learned the trick of delegating responsibility on his paper—Bert Hyde was now listed as managing editor—to give himself time to write for magazines and other papers. At one point he typed up a list of works in progress: a play, a novel, two articles, and ten short stories. None of the titles duplicated those mentioned by Rowe Wright.

Hodding sent *The Ballad of Catfoot Grimes*, a long narrative poem in the manner of Stephen Vincent Benét, whom he much admired, to *Esquire*. It did not sell, but its characters—Cancy Dodd, a white law officer in a small southern town, Catfoot Grimes, a young black man whom Dodd kills—would haunt Hodding and appear in his first novel a decade later. The poem decries the methods used by Dodd and treats Catfoot with great sympathy, but Hodding's sensitivity to the feelings of blacks was far from acute, as the opening lines indicate:

> Catfoot Grimes was a blue-gum nigger;
> He backed up his money with an easy trigger
> And a seven-inch switch that could slice a hair,
> Bull of the quarters, but his dice were square
> And he kept to his color and he knew his place.
> He didn't mess around outside his race.[48]

The Atlantic Monthly bought a poem, "Southern Reconstruction 1935 and 1865," which contrasts the bravado of the soldiers of the Lost Cause and the plight of Depression-era plantation blacks.[49] *The Southern Review*, the new literary magazine edited by his New Orleans roommate Cleanth Brooks and Robert Penn Warren at Louisiana State University, bought "River Plantation," the poem Hodding had written in 1929 while he waited for Brooks to be interviewed for the Rhodes in Baton Rouge.

In November 1935, Hodding wrote to Bowdoin and asked that his transcript be sent to LSU; he was doing graduate study there three afternoons a week, "working in the sixteenth and seventeenth centuries under Cleanth Brooks and Robert Penn Warren, two Rhodes scholars of about my vintage."[50] Hodding was so well known that the LSU *Tower* pictured him in "This Month's Hall of Fame," as the "author of several published articles, a short story or two, and poems" and "editor of the [Hammond] *Daily Courier*" who had decided to pursue graduate work in English.[51]

He and Hermann Deutsch, his reporter friend at the *Item*, worked on a novel, apparently a murder mystery, called "Small Town Stuff" on his typed list. He told Deutsch he had written the first chapter "between phone calls."[52] He didn't feel he had the right "tempo or swing or something," but he thought he had come up with a good way to introduce the characters. He urged Deutsch to do what he wanted with the first chapter and then to get on with the second, where he could introduce the detective chief and work in false clues. The two also worked on a play, "an utterly libelous farce" about Huey Long, to be called "The Kingpin." An agent, Content Peckham, showed the play to the Group Theatre in New York, but nothing came of it.

On September 8, 1935, Huey Long was shot in Baton Rouge. Alsia Hyde heard the news on her radio and phoned downstairs. The *Courier* staff quickly set a story in type, as well as the two possible headlines: "Huey Long Dying" and "Huey Long Dead." When Alsia called with the news that Long had died, they put in the appropriate headline and hit the streets with an extra edition. A number of people, when they heard the news of Long's assassination, wanted to know where Hodding Carter was. Elizabeth Werlein called from New Orleans to find out. "It's all right, Mother, he's right here," Betty said. And in England, where Hodding's Aunt Telle was visiting her sister Lilian, both women worried until they heard that Hodding had not been involved.

Ten days after Long's death, Hodding announced that he was running for the state legislature, on a platform of "Home Rule and Honesty." He continued working five days a week as assistant campaign manager for Cleveland Dear, a candidate for governor.

In December, when Hodding was out of town, Earl Long, Huey's brother, spoke in Hammond and attacked candidate Hodding. In his response in the *Courier*, Hodding said that Earl Long was a "foul-mouthed and contemptible scoundrel" and that if the Longs—"political rapists"—didn't have so many bodyguards he would make his answer "a more personal and effective one."[53]

Earl Long's speech in Hammond triggered a letter from a Long supporter in nearby Punkin Center that said that if Hodding Carter ever spoke against the Long machine in that town, he would be sent back to Hammond in a pine box. With a sound truck and a bodyguard, Hodding hurried to speak at Punkin Center, where his listeners booed him and threw rotten fruit at him. Afterward a farmer told Hodding that he admired his courage, and promised that he and the other three members of his family would vote for him. On January 23, 1936, the postelection headline in the *Courier* read: "Machine Carrying Everything." Hodding was soundly defeated throughout the district (his father would win the same legislative seat in 1940); he got four votes in Punkin Center.[54] Statewide, all the Long candidates won.

The Long administration set up the State Printing Board, to approve or reject any newspaper as the official journal—the designation meant contracts for printing tax lists, official proceedings, and records of sheriff's sales—of a town, school district, or parish. The new board rejected only one official journal, the Hammond *Daily Courier*. Thus the paper would lose the contract with Tangipahoa Parish for printing the delinquent tax list of 1934, and the crucial several thousand dollars the parish would pay.

Hodding and Betty hired Eberhard Deutsch, a New Orleans lawyer, and brother of Hermann Deutsch of the *Item*, to contest the loss of printing. Since the Carters had no hope of winning a suit in the Long-controlled state court, Deutsch filed in federal court. The Carters won in U.S. District Court in New Orleans, but a battery of lawyers from the Louisiana attorney general's office won a reversal in the circuit court of appeals. The Carters took the case to the Supreme Court, which ruled that it belonged in a state court. The process cost the Carters several thousand dollars, which they could ill afford.

Faced with certain financial failure, the Carters sold the *Courier* in the spring of 1936. They also sold out. The buyers were three Long men, John D. Klorer, George French, and Tom Gillen, who promised to change the name of the paper. They called it the *Daily Progress* and made it compulsory for state workers to subscribe. Editorial policy took a 180-degree turn.

Hodding bade farewell to his readers under the headline "Ave Atque—We'll Be Seeing You!!" With the final issue of the *Courier*, he said, he ended "four years of tilting at windmills." He pointed out that he was leaving his hometown with considerably more experience and money than he had had when he came home in 1932. With the *Courier* he had proved two things: "It is possible for a young man to make a place for himself in his home town although the years intervening between his boyhood and his return are sometimes forgotten by the town elders to whom he is still the kid who used to race his pony in the meadow which is Southeastern's new campus. And a daily newspaper could and does survive in Hammond, despite four years of crop failures and political retaliations."[55]

"Little of what I wrote was good journalism," Hodding said later about these years, "but I still think most of it was good citizenship."[56] He learned a great deal in Hammond. When he next ran a newspaper, he would display fewer heroics and more real heroism.

5. 1936–1938

"We Weren't Mississippians, but We Weren't Yankees"

In the spring of 1935, Hodding had gone to Baton Rouge for a southern literary conference sponsored by the nascent *Southern Review*, edited by Robert Penn Warren. Roark Bradford and Lyle Saxon came from New Orleans, John Gould Fletcher from Arkansas. Allen Tate and Caroline Gordon brought the British writer Ford Madox Ford. One night Hodding and David Cohn, who was also attending the conference, left the heat of the hotel meeting room and went out on the fire escape to talk. Cohn had grown up in the Mississippi Delta, made money with Sears, Roebuck in New Orleans (where he was a friend of Betty's mother), and returned to Greenville, Mississippi, to write a book about the Delta that was being published that year. In the book, *God Shakes Creation*, is Cohn's famous one-liner that defines the Delta as stretching from the lobby of the Peabody Hotel in Memphis to Catfish Row in Vicksburg.

Hodding told Cohn some of the troubles his paper was having in Hammond, and Cohn suggested that Hodding go to Greenville and run a newspaper there. The town needed a lively paper, he said, and he promised to speak to his friend William Alexander Percy, lawyer, banker, cotton planter, published poet, and acknowledged cultural tsar of Greenville.

Cohn easily convinced Percy that Greenville needed a "courageous, incorruptible, intelligently edited newspaper" and that Carter was the man for the job.[1] Greenville at the time had a pallid, ineffectual paper, the *Democrat-Times*, published by Ernest "Pink" Smith. It printed the news the way people brought it in. While Hodding believed that nothing good was accomplished without controversy, Pink Smith did not think a paper should hurt anyone's feelings. Cohn warned Percy that it would be expensive to start a new paper and that anyone who invested in it might lose money. Citizens who backed a new paper should think of it as a contribution to community welfare rather than an investment.

In December 1935, Hodding and Betty went to Greenville to talk to Percy and other potential backers. They ran into torrential rain on the way, and their car skidded into a ditch. Hodding carried Betty piggyback to look for help. They arrived at Percy's house covered with mud, and three hours late for dinner.

"You've got Delta mud on you," Percy said with delight when he saw them. "We'll never get rid of you."[2]

Percy was a legendary figure in the Mississippi Delta. He was then fifty years old, small and frail. Hodding found him beautiful, with blue-gray eyes, silver hair, and "a sad sensitive mouth above a fighter's jaw."[3] To Betty, he was "charming, perfect, a cameo." He was described by a younger friend as "slight and effeminate. When he played tennis, he hit the ball like a lady. He had more courage than I did, and he taught me a lot about behaving myself."[4]

Percy had published four books of poetry and had a modest national reputation as a poet. He kept open house in Greenville and always had a visitor in his study or his garden; as Hodding wrote later, it might be a young ex-convict just released from the state penal farm or the chief of police asking his advice. The big brown stucco house was an obligatory stop for out-of-towners. Poets Carl Sandburg, Vachel Lindsay, and Stephen Vincent Bénet had all been Percy's guests. Hortense Powdermaker stayed there when she was preparing *After Freedom: A Cultural Study in the Deep South,* as did Harry Stack Sullivan when he was engaged in research on race and Jonathan

Daniels while he gathered material for *A Southerner Discovers the South*. A black man came on a Sunday and played the blues on his harmonica for several hours. David Cohn came for a weekend and stayed for a year while he wrote *God Shakes Creation*. William Faulkner played tennis on Percy's tennis court, when he was sober enough to stand up. The New York sculptor Malvina Hoffman, whom Percy commissioned to do a sculpture for his father's grave, was a houseguest, and Percy's old friend Huger Jervey, dean of the law school at Columbia University, visited frequently.

Percy helped poor youngsters go to college and set up ambitious men in business. He had not yet written *Lanterns on the Levee*, which was published in 1941; the book would be the last grand, elegiac defense of the "southern way of life," including the sharecropper system. Since 1929, Percy had tried to run his 3,343-acre Trail Lake cotton plantation with its six hundred employees and tenants by the Golden Rule. His neighbors thought he was crazy to sell his tenants everything at the plantation commissary at cost; to charge no interest on "furnish," or seed, on fertilizer, and on other necessities that farmers had to buy on credit until their crops came in; and to screen every tenant house to prevent malaria. For his time, Will Percy was a model of progressivism, the last example, Dave Cohn said, of noblesse oblige. Because of his enormous prestige in Greenville, people forgave him what they considered his "eccentric" views on race. He called some black men "Mr."—an unheard-of practice in those days. Yet he was not completely purged of racism, and later was said to have treated his black chauffeur "like a puppy."[5]

Poet Langston Hughes was appalled at the chasm between the races he found during a reading tour of the South in 1931. The fact that the "patrician" Percy respectfully introduced him to a mixed audience at the black St. Matthew's A.M.E. Church as "my fellow poet" impressed Hughes. "I met less than half a dozen gentlemanly Southerners on my winter-long tour," he said.[6]

Percy had no use for what people called poor white trash. When James K. Vardaman defeated Percy's father in his race for reelection to the U.S. Senate, Will Percy said, "The bottom rail is on top," meaning trash was in the ascendancy.

Educated at Sewanee and at Harvard Law School, Percy had done more than his share of public service. He had worked for Herbert Hoover's relief commission in Belgium before enlisting in the army; he had fought in World War I and had been awarded the French Croix de Guerre. In the early twenties he and his father led a successful fight to keep the Ku Klux Klan out of Greenville. When the Mississippi River flooded and inundated the Greenville area for months in 1927, the younger Percy was chairman of local flood relief, charged with supervising the rescue and care of 60,000 people and 30,000 head of stock.

He played the piano and grew flowers and avoided baseball and heavy drinking. He never learned to drive a car, but he traveled everywhere—the Caribbean, the South Seas, Europe, Japan. Taormina, in Sicily, was one of his favorite places. In 1930 he brought the widow of his first cousin and her three sons to live with him. In 1932, after the death of their mother, he adopted the boys and educated them. The oldest was Walker Percy, then sixteen, who would become a doctor and a novelist; LeRoy was next, and Phinizy the youngest.

Walker Percy credited Will Percy with the appreciation for literature and art that prevailed in Greenville. "Our house was upperclass Delta—Mr. Will's was upperclass world," said Shelby Foote, a friend of the Percy boys who would become world-famous as a novelist and Civil War historian.[7] Will Percy made a great impression also on Hodding, who would write about him with awe on several occasions.

It is not clear how firm a commitment anybody made that night. Hodding stayed in Hammond for several more months, but at some point Percy persuaded Greenville businessmen to put up money, sums that were not small to them, for a newspaper to be run by a stranger to the community. Percy vouched for Hodding's intellectual integrity, according to David Cohn's account, and put himself down for a substantial contribution. He was followed by Colonel Alexander Fitz Hugh, a Vicksburg man with business interests in the Delta;

William T. "Billy" Wynn, the most prominent lawyer in the Delta and owner of a 10,000-acre cotton plantation; Edmund Taylor, of the Goyer company, a big wholesale grocery that did business with the plantations; Joe Virden, a lumber dealer; Frank England, the Ford dealer; J. S. and J. Q. Strange, who ran the local Coca-Cola bottling plant; Mrs. Paul Gamble; Walter Swain, of Leland; Harry Wetherbee, who owned a hardware store; and Cohn.[8] Among them they agreed to invest $10,000, matching the money that Hodding and Betty were to receive for the Hammond *Daily Courier*. Hodding was given editorial and managerial control and the right to buy out his partners.

On July 7, 1936, Hodding wrote out a list of proposed features for a newspaper to be called the *Delta Star*. Included were a column by Hodding, "Star Dust"; a letters-to-the-editor feature, "Controversy Corner"; a poetry column, "For Better or Verse"; a promotional front-page box, "The Rising Star"; sections for recipes and Bible verses sent in by readers; another front-page feature, "Gist of the News"; columns for correspondents from each town in the area; a calendar of club and lodge meetings; a daily farm column by the county agent or farmers, with questions and answers; a river column, "Over the Levee"; a weather box with almanac quips; radio news, "It's in the Air"; "three good comics"; cartoons; a high school column; news of books, theater, fine arts, and stocks and markets; a women's page with society and club news; and interviews. The paper would have wire news from either Associated Press or United Press. There would be a daily photograph contest that would "use correspondents, readers and delivery boys," with prizes for "best pictures." There would also be news photographs.

This was an ambitious outline, calling for wire services and photo-engraving, expenses that the Hammond paper had never been able to afford. It revealed a more professional attitude toward newspaper proprietorship than Hodding had ever dreamed of for the *Courier*.

Hodding was still not fully committed, however, and on July 26 he, Betty, and little Hodding left Hammond, bound eventually for Maine but going by way of the Texas Centennial Exposition in Dallas. They stopped in Chicago, Toronto, and New York to visit friends and editors. After ten days in Camden they drove to Bennington, Vermont, where one of his professors from Bowdoin thought Hodding might get a teaching job.

Betty put her foot down and told Hodding that he certainly could not teach at Bennington. She and her friends wore shorts to play tennis, but she had never seen girls sitting in shorts at the feet of their professors. "It wasn't puritanism. I saw it as a threat," she said years later.[9]

It was to be Greenville, Mississippi, then.

The Carters knew very little about Greenville and the surrounding area, except that the Mississippi Delta was supposed to be "wild." At Sophie Newcomb, Betty had known a girl from the Delta who was full of tales of hard drinking and dancing on tables. The Delta was different from the rest of Mississippi, they would learn. It was by no means "Old South," as were Vicksburg, Natchez, and Holly Springs. When planters from the Upper South brought slaves and settled the Delta for the first time—just before the Civil War—they found the land so swampy and disease-ridden that they built houses in the hills on the fringes of the Delta. They went down by day to clear and plant the soggy, cypress-filled land, and returned each night to the comparative safety of the hills. These settlers coped with river floods and yellow fever and federal raiders who burned Greenville during the Civil War. When white Southerners regained control of the political system after Reconstruction and established white supremacy, they reduced the number of black voters to insignificance. Racial subjugation was a way of life.

In 1936 the cotton plantations still brought their cotton crop to the compress in Greenville to be shipped down the Mississippi River. The Delta was indeed wild; planters, who had moved down to the valley when the land was clear, were still making it big and going broke on a large scale. The Delta, somebody said, was a place where "credit is easy and the crashes are hard." Delta people drank hard and partied long. The Delta elite were well-traveled, well-read, and sophisticated about everything but race. Surrounded by blacks, who outnumbered them nine to one, and on whom they depended to work the vast fields of cotton, they were irrational about race. Flamboyant Hodding, with a fire in his belly to remake the world, was destined, in one way, to fit right in and, in another way, to infuriate the aristocrats of the Delta.

Betty and Hodding learned that the population of Greenville was around 15,000, while all of Washington County had 54,300 people, 40,000 of them black. Greenville in many ways was livelier and more progressive and more tolerant than other Mississippi towns and cities. It was a river town, with a towboat industry that brought a more cosmopolitan population and outlook. It had a large Syrian population and an even bigger group of Chinese. When other towns in Mississippi had country clubs that did not admit Jews, Greenville's country club had a Jewish president.

The bridge across the river at Greenville would not be built for several years, and the river ferry was very much a part of the town's life; sometimes it ran at night so young people could have dances on board. Later, the Corps of Engineers would straighten out the bend in the Mississippi and Greenville would end up beside a backwater called Lake Ferguson, while the river would flow some miles from town. But in 1936, Greenville was still tucked in beside the levee that kept the river in check. The levee at the foot of Main Street was twenty-seven feet high and three hundred feet wide at the base.

Although there was diversity, there was a rigid caste system, with blacks in the lowest stratum and the people who worked in stores and filling stations in the middle. In the upper crust were the white people who ran the town; they all knew each other and were often related. In fact, everybody knew everybody else in town. One man who grew up in Greenville remembered that as a small boy, he would go into stores, pick up candy, and say, "Charge it to Sonny Boy." Storekeepers knew who he, Sonny Boy, was, knew his father, and charged it. Everybody knew everybody else so well that there was no physical danger; people could walk the streets safely at night.

Most of the top layer of Greenville people were Presbyterians, some Episcopalian, a few Jewish. They were not necessarily rich; in fact, the Depression still held the South in its grip and nobody had much money. Old ladies whose grandfathers had made fortunes in cotton lived in genteel poverty in large houses with the high-water mark from the 1927 Mississippi River flood visible on the walls.

Poor or not, everybody in the upper stratum had black servants. A cook, who prepared breakfast, dinner, and supper, was paid as little as three dollars a week, plus the food she could carry home to her family, who lived in a shack without plumbing or electricity.

Black sharecroppers on the plantations in the county (except possibly for Will Percy's Trail Lake) lived even more wretched lives. Plantation owners thought fair financial dealings with black tenants were useless—"They'd only waste the money," planters said. Schools for black children operated only a few months a year, and there were no school buses. Black pupils used worn-out hand-me-down textbooks from white schools. Blacks were called by their first name but had to call white people "Mr.," "Mrs.," or "Miss." White people clung to the idea of the lazy, carefree black, on whom education would be wasted. Whites also believed in the tremendous sexuality of black people, who should be kept under tight control.

The Delta was a very social place, with parties going on all the time. Nobody lived in the Billups Plantation house, which was used strictly for parties. There was always a weekend house party there to mark the opening of the dove-hunting season. In the twenties, the Columbus and Greenville Railroad used to bring sleeping cars onto the plantation railroad siding to provide sleeping accommodations. There was a Christmas Eve dance in the Bolivar County Courthouse in Rosedale and the Rosedale Mule Race every Fourth of July.

Greenville, the largest town in the Delta, had its own social customs. In 1936 ladies still made calls and left cards. A visitor from out of town would provide an excuse for a round of social activity—Coca-Cola parties every morning, luncheons at noon, bridge parties in the afternoons, and dinner parties at night. There were often dances at the Elks Club and the Elysian, a dance hall. Sometimes a steamboat came down the river and everybody—white people—boarded it for a cruise that lasted from late afternoon until midnight.

The Carters arrived in Greenville in September, with a baby bed on top of their car, and noticed Greenville's distinctive smell—soft and warm, not unlike baking ham, from the cotton gins. They stayed with Will Percy while they looked for an apartment, and when they found one, young LeRoy Percy and Shelby Foote helped them move. Will Percy gave a buffet supper for the Carters and introduced them to people of all ages whom he thought it was important for Hodding to know. The Percy imprimatur helped overcome the local xenophobia and removed the "outsider" stigma right away. "We weren't Mississippians, but we weren't Yankees," Betty Carter said years later.[10]

Hodding leased a store, which had been empty since the 1927 flood, next door to Harry Wetherbee's hardware store on Walnut Street, between Main and Washington. He borrowed some garden hose from Will Percy and set to work, barefooted and in his undershirt, to clean out the silt from the overflow. What followed, Hodding said later, was "one continuous nightmare."[11] Once more he had bought secondhand typesetting and printing equipment and had trouble assembling and installing it. A Jackson man who came through Greenville remembered Hodding in ink-stained, dirty clothes installing his own Linotype and press. "The *Democrat-Times* was a neat, attractive paper," he said. "Nobody thought Hodding had a chance."[12] The first issue of the *Delta Star* was delayed while the staff learned to work together and deal with the shambles of machinery. A Florida salesman for Mergenthaler recalled "the bunch of us gathered around the first old Linotypes" while Hodding, "with the aid of splints, castor oil, and other devices," tried to get enough type out of them to produce the initial issue of the *Delta Star*. When someone remarked that he had known other papers to give up under lesser handicaps, Hodding replied, "They didn't have to keep on; this one does." That ended the conversation, and everybody went out for coffee.[13]

Meanwhile, Betty trudged the downtown streets trying to sell advertising to the owners of Tennenbaum's, Hafter's, the Smart Shop, Steinmart, Nelms and Blum, Johl and Bergman, and other stores. She was an anomaly in Greenville, where women in the upper stratum did not work. A woman who moved to Greenville from Massachusetts as a bride remembered that she and other young wives would drive around town every morning and end up on top of the levee— it was a society where women did absolutely nothing. Betty Carter got away with working because the Carters were immediately seen as "different," but acceptable, because Will Percy said they were.

Hodding rounded up a staff. He put his younger brother, John, who was floundering around in Hammond after having left Tulane, in charge of circulation and photoengraving. He hired Electra Atcher to keep the books and also to write a column. Shelby Foote, who had dropped out of the University of North Carolina at Chapel Hill, became a cub reporter and proofreader.

Hodding told Will Percy that the society editor's job was the most important one on the paper. Readers were more interested in one another's business than in Washington news and editorials. The society editor had to know everybody, had to be somebody herself. Percy thought it over, then laughed and suggested Louise Eskrigge Smith. If Hodding could show her the job was a cause, she might do it. "Louise has to have causes," Percy said.[14]

Smith, a good-looking widow in her thirties, had been born in Greenville to a Mississippi mother and an English father. She had gone to Sophie Newcomb in New Orleans and Virginia Intermont in Bristol, and finally graduated from Mississippi State College for Women in Columbus. Betty and Hodding took Smith for a drive, and they ended up on top of the levee discussing the *Delta Star*. Smith tried to figure them out, while Hodding told her what he would like to have in a society editor.

"Tin cans," she said suddenly. "Tin cans." She pointed at a can lying on the sloping concrete wall of the levee. "That's the very first thing we must get started. Everyone must punch holes in tin cans."

Betty and Hodding, bewildered, looked at each other.

"Malaria," said Louise Smith. "Mosquitoes breed in tin cans. We have to get everybody to punch holes in tin cans before they throw them out, so they won't fill with water. That's one of the first things we'll campaign for."

And the *Delta Star* energetically backed the state health department's campaign against the mosquito and malaria. Some observers attributed Mississippi's slow economic development to the fact that malaria made a large percentage of the population shiver with chills and burn with fever until the first frost in the fall.

Louise Smith became far more than society editor and instigator of campaigns. She would organize Beta Sigma Phi, the Junior Auxiliary, the Newcomers Club, and the Little Theater and spearhead innumerable civic projects. She would be mother confessor to everyone in the office and, most important, would act as interpreter and buffer for Hodding. When Hodding's news policies hurt feelings, Smith salved the wounds in her column. "Louise saw that people didn't talk about us too much," Betty Carter recounted. "If somebody said, 'I don't like Hodding,' she would say, 'Oh, but Betty's so sweet.'"[15]

On November 17, 1936, after three or four false starts, the first issue of the *Delta Star* appeared, its front page adorned with a photograph of a ferryboat pilot. Hodding had counted a lot on this picture to capture the atmosphere of Greenville, but poor, ineffectual John Carter never did anything quite right and the picture came out fuzzy and dark. Hodding tried to rise above it and wrote in the caption, "Because this camera study in silhouette seems to us to personify the Delta and the river, the *Star* has selected it as the first engraving made in our plant."

A front-page editorial compared creating a newspaper to producing a play or becoming a parent. "So as the *Delta Star* rises and makes its belated bow, we hope that the reaction of our readers will be that of a new father or a director at a first rehearsal, both of whom usually are disappointed in the immediate result but hopeful of the future." The editorial promised that the paper's columns would present, "as far as we can glean them, every significant event in the life of Greenville and the Delta. Some of this news will not be pleasant. Nevertheless, if it is news—and in that we shall be our own judge—it will be printed as fairly and impartially as we know how." As for editorials, "the editor of the Star will write with both legs on the same side of the fence."

Within a few weeks, Hodding had hired Bob Brown from Hattiesburg, who was said to be able to produce twenty-five to thirty-five stories a day. Otherwise, things went badly. It was hard to find and keep compositors and printers since the hours were long and the equipment poor. A little over a month after publication of the first issue, Will Percy wrote to Hodding that the stockholders would see to it that the paper continued for a year. "If at the end of that time, it is not self supporting, they will then feel no obligation, moral or otherwise, to go further."[16] He suggested that after Christmas the board of directors meet monthly for advice and consultation. Percy enclosed his check for $3,000 and said that Edmund Taylor, who liked the paper and thought it would serve a "useful purpose in the public life of Mississippi," would put in another three thousand. "We can decide whether this should be taken out in stock or evidenced by notes to the corporation. . . . You have had every kind of bad luck and hard knocks. It is good that they should have come at the beginning, heartbreaking, of course, but vastly educating." Hodding and Betty and John, he said, were "good editors and fine sports."

Hodding worked hard. "He banged out those editorials at press time," Shelby Foote recalled some fifty years later with wonder. "And no matter how hard he worked, he was still cheerful. He had this marvelous enthusiasm. He had a good brain. He could organize a story, organize an editorial, and bat them out."[17] Other staffers were amazed at the facility with which Hodding wrote. "Tell him you wanted an editorial on polka dots and moonbeams forty lines long," said one, "and in ten minutes you would have it. It might be superficial, but it would be readable. I never saw him rewrite anything."[18] Foote added: "He wrote all the editorials and half the news stories and tried to look after the business side, which he knew nothing about. He and Betty worked so hard they hardly knew what was going on. When Hodding did slow down, Betty kept pushing him." [19]

Years later, Betty would say that they were the upstarts who came in to buck the opposition, which was "sitting there like a stuffed straw man," although nobody knew it.[20] "We didn't get advertising, not even from the people who backed us," she said. Will Percy had nothing to advertise. Frank England and his Ford agency "had something to advertise, but he had to get results. How could he tell whether this little new paper would get results?" Merchants preferred to split their advertising budgets, so each paper received only half as much as it should. Betty, who considered herself good at selling advertising, gloomily speculated that some merchants bought space because "I was a rather cute girl."

Betty and Hodding had told the other Greenville paper they didn't want an advertising-rate war, and the *Democrat-Times* gave Betty its rate card, which contained its advertising prices. When trying to get a full-page ad from the Goyer company, Betty never undercut the *Democrat-Times*; she did not realize that the rate card was absolutely bogus. When she gave the man at Goyer, Billy McGehee, the rate from the card, he said, "I can get it cheaper."

"We'll meet the competition," said Betty.

"I'm going to give it to you at the price you told me first, and I'm going to tell your father on you," said McGehee.[21]

"Merchants bought ads from Betty sometimes because they felt sorry for her or because they admired her. She was self-assured and competent. She may have worked harder than Hodding. She kept the paper afloat," recalled Don Wetherbee.[22] This tall, lanky young man from Greenville joined the staff in 1937 as soon as he graduated from the University of North Carolina at Chapel Hill, where he had roomed with Walker Percy. He was copy editor, wire editor, and makeup editor.

Whether Betty worked harder than Hodding or not, everyone agrees that without her, Hodding—whatever his talent, charm, good looks, brains, enthusiasm, and ability to meet a challenge—could not have succeeded in Greenville.

Hodding covered the Rotary Club, Don Wetherbee the Kiwanis, and Shelby Foote the Lions and the Wise Men. Foote also ran the poetry column. "Hodding laughed his head off when I wanted to print one of Walt Whitman's poems that was obscene," he recalled.[23] Foote was also the office joker. "Shelby had the devil in him," said Wetherbee. "He read proof. It's my considered opinion that Shelby let things slip through. When Sarah Farish, the daughter of Will Percy's law partner, married LeRoy Percy, it was the social event of the Delta for generations. The headline on the engagement story said 'Bridge Elect.' The wedding story said the bridesmaids wore 'gowns of pink lice.' One day the weather 'ear' on the top of the front page read 'cloudy with shitting winds.'"

From the first the Carters were entertained; in return they entertained. It was hard to resist the handsome, energetic young editor and his pretty wife, even if they were outsiders. Not long after they got to Greenville, Hodding had to have a mastoid operation. Greenville rallied, as it always did when someone was in trouble. Hodding was touched by the outpouring of sympathy, attention, home-cooked dishes, and offers of help he and Betty received.

The spring of 1937 was rainy and gloomy with threats of another big Mississippi River flood. "It was a horrible spring," recalled Betty Carter. "You can't sell advertising after Christmas. The Depression was not over. Who wants to go out in the rain to buy a dress you can't afford? I was enervated and depressed and I kept thinking, 'All I do is work on this damned paper. And the town can't support two papers.'"[24]

In many places the water was as high as the levee; the staff could look from the office window and see Coast Guard cutters moored twenty feet above street level. But the levee held. And by the fall of the year, the *Delta Star* had hired a "real" advertising man, Rodney Deffenbaugh, from Louisville, who was assisted by Herman Cohn, David Cohn's nephew. Betty helped out in news.

Although Will Percy and the other stockholders had agreed not to interfere in any way with Hodding's editorial direction, Percy occasionally broke the rule. At least once he sent Hodding a handwritten note to this effect: "Your editorials continue good, but [Huger] Jervey says they are too aggressive to convince your opponents. Perhaps."[25] And one spring day in 1937, he appeared in the newspaper office and demanded of Hodding why he had no editorial on the lynching at Duck Hill.

"I did," said Hodding. "It's on the front page."[26]

The editorial was a stinging attack on the men who lynched two black men who were to be tried for the murder of a white store-keeper in the nearby Duck Hill community; it likened the lynchers to Andaman Islanders, except that they "did not feast on the bodies of their two black victims after they had tortured and burned them" and the Andaman Islanders did not have the "precepts of a Christian civilization as signposts on the road away from bestiality. . . . In Washington, congress debates a federal anti-lynching bill, extreme in its encroachment on state's rights. To the vindicators of that encroachment Mississippi has now contributed a mighty bludgeon. . . . Is there justice in Mississippi? Then, punish the Duck Hill mobsters."[27]

Hodding also attacked mob action in Tupelo, where one night a group of women roused Ida Sledge from her bed and escorted her out of town in her nightgown. Miss Sledge, a member of an old and distinguished Memphis family, was attempting to organize workers at a Tupelo clothing factory for the International Ladies Garment Workers Union. "Running people out of town is not only illegal, but it is downright stupid and ineffectual," Hodding wrote in the editorial column. He added that he had no use for unions, but the treatment of Miss Sledge would "redouble the efforts of the CIO in Mississippi."[28]

The *Delta Star*'s news policies electrified the community. Not long after Bob Brown arrived, he was preparing the police blotter. Pink Smith never printed the name of a white person arrested for a crime, but wrote something like, "A white man was fined twenty-five dollars for assault with a dangerous weapon." From its beginnings, the *Delta Star* printed the names of whites who were arrested, although no one noticed it because for weeks no prominent person was arrested. Then one of the town's leading citizens got drunk and drove his car off the levee. The Greenville police, who were usually impartial, booked him for drunken driving and locked him up overnight. Brown put his name in the paper. "We made enemies with that story, but we also made friends and converts," Hodding wrote years later, "and we established ourselves as a newspaper neither beholden to nor influenced by anyone in town, not even our stockholders."[29]

One campaign caused more turmoil than the tin-can effort. Hodding and Brown decided to print for the first time in a Mississippi newspaper the taboo words "syphilis" and "gonorrhea" in stories about the state health department's program of free treatment for people with venereal disease. When a woman called the newspaper to object to such usage in a family newspaper, Brown told her, in a remark to be quoted and howled over by staff members for fifty years, that before they were through at the *Delta Star*, they hoped to have syphilis on the tongue of everybody in town.[30]

A photograph caused a furor—and brought more national attention to Hodding. It was a picture of Jesse Owens, who had won four gold medals at the 1936 Summer Olympics in Berlin, thus challenging Aryan claims to superiority. Owens came to the Delta in 1937 to celebrate the fiftieth anniversary of the all-black town of Mound Bayou. No southern newspaper (and few northern ones, for that matter) ran pictures of blacks at that time, and many readers berated Hodding for the impropriety of the *Delta Star*'s action.

Hodding, undeterred, published an editorial that was a ringing defense of the paper's policy: "Jesse Owens is a remarkable athlete. And so we printed his picture. We'll print it again when we feel like doing so. We fail to see anything traitorous to the white race in acknowledging the accomplishment of a negro boy." Still paternalistic on matters of racial progress, he defended the *Delta Star*'s "giving a helping hand to a little town which is proud that for fifty years it has tried to follow the white man's ideal of good citizenship and self-government."

The editorial defended also a feature story on Nelson Street, the local equivalent of Memphis's Beale Street. Nelson Street, Hodding wrote, represented "undeniably one aspect of southern life, humorous, colorful, cheerful, barbaric."

And the editorial defended the stories it had run about blacks who had achieved something "besides misdemeanors and brutalities.

Would you have us publish only crime and police court news of negroes—and omit the white offenders to boot? Does that encourage our negroes to live decently and honorably? We have attacked the murderous blot of lynching in the South, but we have also fought the anti-lynch bill so ardently espoused by a Democratic president whose background is not the South. Do these stands violate the taboo? When the negroes of Greenville banded together in the spring flood panic and offered their services, we gave the humble gesture full credit. Should we have taken their aid for granted?

Get this straight, everyone of you. We were brought up on a Louisiana farm. To our knowledge, every member of our family, as far back as any of you in Greenville can trace that mythical attribute called ancestry, has been of the South, has fought for it, and loved its ideals and its foibles as well. But we personally have never felt so unsure of our status as a white man that we had to bully a negro, to return courtesy with rudeness, or to make him think that he was a despicable beast who could sense neither kindness nor gratitude nor trust.

Here in the Delta we make our living, in the ultimate analysis, from the negro. He tills our fields. His ready spending of his scant funds has built our business sections, and maintained our economic balances. . . . Is it more revolting to try to instill in him a pride in his worthwhile actions than to—hush, hush—make him think that his race is fit only for mockery by day and concubinage by night?

We're not apologizing. We're pitying. The object of our pity is the hypocrisy expressed by what we know is an indefensible minority of a lovable town which we have made our home.[31]

Claude Barnett, of the Associated Negro Press, and Jesse Thomas, southern field director of the National Urban League, wrote to congratulate Hodding on the editorial. Philip Hanna, editor of the Chicago *Journal of Commerce*, not only congratulated him but asked whether he would write an article for the *Journal*'s back page on the Ku Klux Klan and the appointment of former Klansman Hugo Black to the Supreme Court. Hanna offered to pay five dollars. Hodding wrote the piece.

Thus, as early as 1937, Hodding had laid out his stand on racial matters, a position perceived by Northerners—and Hodding himself—as moderate and by his neighbors as radical and alarming. Will Percy began to think he had bitten off more than he could chew, that "his" editor was more progressive than he had expected.[32] Betty Carter recalled the years before World War II as economically difficult but peaceful, without controversy, but they were not entirely so. Editorials and news stories caused rumbles even in the early days.

Don Wetherbee, perhaps the least enchanted of Hodding's former employees, remembered that "half the people in town hated him. He loved to stir people up and he alienated a lot of people. Anything that was not ultraconservative enraged the people and was not considered 'normal.' When the newspaper printed a picture of a black man, it changed the relationship. It was unsettling. No one could deny Hodding's courage. He was not afraid of anybody when it came to saying what he thought was right, not even advertisers. But I had the feeling that Hodding looked for subjects that would win acclaim."

When Rodney Deffenbaugh went home to Louisville for summer vacation, he played golf with John Gibson, a young man who was working in the *Courier-Journal*'s circulation department and wanted to move to a small paper. Deffenbaugh suggested he come to work on the *Delta Star*. Gibson went to Greenville in 1937, expecting to stay two years, and never left. He started as circulation manager and after the war would become the business manager Hodding desperately needed, the most trusted and indispensable partner—except for Betty.

By then the *Delta Star* was clashing head-on with the *Democrat-Times*. Bob Brown suggested that the line "You read it first in the Star" be run in very small type beneath each story the paper printed before the competition, and the line began to appear under even the most insignificant stories. The *Democrat-Times* was still undercutting the *Delta Star* on advertising. Gibson began an all-out circulation drive, inspiring carriers to knock on doors and offer trial subscriptions. The *Delta Star*'s circulation grew, but the *Democrat-Times* added to its figures to stay ahead.

The *Delta Star* celebrated its first year of existence with a public reception and a large special edition that pictured every member of the staff on the front page of the second section. There were six editorial employees, not counting Electra Atcher, the bookkeeper who also wrote a column. There were three people doing advertising, an assistant bookkeeper, three circulation men, ten people in the composing and press room, all looking young and handsome.

Undercapitalized and chronically short of cash, the paper survived because Will Percy and Billy Wynn and Edmund Taylor came through, one with a thousand dollars more, another with two thousand, while Betty and Hodding borrowed from banks, on Hodding's life insurance, and from their families. Once a month, as Percy had suggested, the board of directors met and heard the latest bad news from Deffenbaugh, Betty, and Hodding. The directors energetically criticized Hodding's business sense, and Hodding always replied cheerfully that the *Democrat-Times* was doing just as badly. Tired of their criticisms, he wrote a poem addressing the charges that he was a poor business manager.

> Alas, alack, alas, alack
> Ye pots who call the kettle black;
> And lack of management decry—
> Are ye then functioning in high? . . .
> Why blame me for failing to foresee the red that
>   makes us blue?

I did not cause the cotton slump
Or kick the market in the rump. . . .
"I'm slightly irked, though not because
You credit me with business flaws.
I grant I can't adjust a ledger,
Or recognize a hedge or hedger . . .
And as for budgets, mine go wrong—
But still, did F.D.R.'s last long? . . .
Oyez, oyez, from far and near
Come greetings on the Star's first year . . .
But not a single greeter said
"We praise you for your business head."
I haven't got one I admit;
I don't know what I'd do with it.
The one I have is full enough
With plans for running on the cuff,
With payroll nightmares, pension taxes,
And editorial prophylaxes;
With debtors who refuse to pay
With creditors who plague each day,
With John Q. Public's lethargy,
With visitors who bother me,
With rising costs and static trade,
With tempers often sorely frayed
And unfair rivalry from that
Amazing Greenville Democrat
(I guess I should have added Times,
But it's behind them.) Here my rhyme
Comes slowly to belated close,
Forgive me if I thumb my nose.

The poem must not have been very effective: the board decided Deffenbaugh would be a better business manager than Hodding. "Nobody seemed to realize there was no money to manage," Betty recounted.[33] At the next directors' meeting, Rodney Deffenbaugh commented, "Frankly, I'm stymied." Hodding raised more money from his aunts in England, Lady Beit and Marguerite Carter, and from his old Bowdoin roommate Joe Darlington. On a trip to New Orleans to raise money, he found he could sell for only $850 a $1,000 bond Mrs. Werlein had given him and Betty. Will Carter had signed a note for another thousand. Hodding and Betty felt desperate. "We *had* to succeed," she said.

The staff was working eighteen-hour days, and didn't always get paid on time, according to Don Wetherbee. "Hodding showed me how he kited checks with the help of a friend. To meet the payroll, he would swap checks with somebody and they would each deposit the checks and keep shuffling checks until some money came in."[34]

Gibson, the circulation manager, did not see how the *Democrat-Times* could have the circulation it claimed. In the summer of 1938 he persuaded Hodding to play detective. The *Democrat-Times* press was in the front of its building behind a large plate-glass window. Anyone could look through the window and count the papers as they came off the press. Hodding rented two rooms upstairs in an empty office building across the street and sat there with a notary public and a pair of binoculars, counting aloud as the papers came off the press. Hodding and the notary did this for four days, then drew up an affidavit that the true circulation of the *Democrat-Times* was only a little more than half of what was claimed. They sent the affidavit to Pink Smith and informed him that unless he amended his circulation statements they would inform the post office. (It is a prosecutable offense to falsify the statement of circulation figures given to the post office.)

The *Delta Star* was barely hanging on. When Don Wetherbee went away for two weeks that summer to get married, he could only hope the paper would still be in existence when he returned. Rumors spread through Greenville that Pink Smith was about to do something. Hodding and Gibson knew that he was bleeding—he had lost circulation, advertising, and prestige to the *Delta Star*. Smith talked with the *Star*'s backers. Billy Wynn took over the negotiations, and a month later arranged the purchase of the *Democrat-Times* at what Hodding thought was an excessive price. Wynn, however, insisted that as a Greenvillian, Pink Smith was entitled to the fair price he had received.[35] The *Delta Star* bought out the *Democrat-Times* for $130,000, less the accounts receivable, which went back to Pink Smith's family. They were paid $15,000 in cash, which Hodding raised from his family and friends. He signed mortgage notes at five and a half percent for the $105,000 balance. These notes were for $5,000 a year for the first three years, $8,000 a year for the next six years, with a balloon note of $40,000 to be refinanced the tenth year. It was an immense debt for Hodding and Betty to assume. Will Percy put up $20,000 in United States Steel stock as collateral to secure the annual notes, and Hodding and Betty put up a similar amount in the Werlein Music Company.[36] Preferred stock was issued jointly to Percy and the Carters "in behalf of the risk of collateral."[37] Percy signed his block over to Hodding and Betty, because, he said, the risk was theirs.

Hodding announced the new, combined paper would be called the *Delta Democrat-Times* and operations would move to the *Democrat-Times* building on Main Street. The staff put the last issue of the *Delta Star* to bed on August 7, 1938, fully a year and eight months after the first issue appeared. They all stood around the old flatbed press in its pit. "Bill Yarborough, the old printer, was down in the pit, so drunk he could hardly manage to walk," recalled James Robertshaw, a young member of the staff who would go on to practice law in Greenville. "We had some half-pints of Old Forester, and we all drank our bottles and threw them in the pit."[38]

"Being now the only paper published in Greenville, we feel more than ever a deep obligation to be just and temperate and kindly. We shall fight whenever we believe a moral issue is at stake, but we'll not fight for the love of fighting," read an editorial on September 1, 1938, the first day of publication of the new paper.

The backers breathed a sigh of relief when the competition was eliminated, but Hodding found himself burdened with an immense debt, enormous fatigue, and problems of what to do with Pink Smith's staff. Charles Kerg, a 312-pound native of Greenville, had started delivering the *Democrat-Times* when he was nine years old and had become sportswriter and reporter. A tireless worker, he had slept nights on the paper's circulation counter during the 1927 Mississippi River flood while he reported on the biggest news story in Greenville history. Kerg was one of the two *Democrat-Times* employees whom Hodding kept on; the other was Lillian McLaughlin, a highly respected former schoolteacher who had been society editor. McLaughlin soon left, but Kerg would stay on at the new paper for more than fifty years. "He could get more news stories sitting by the telephone waiting for his dozens of sources to call him than we young reporters could dig up running all over the Delta," wrote a former staffer.[39] "He was barely literate," recalled Don Wetherbee. "He used clichés that set my teeth on edge, and referred to himself as 'your correspondent.' But he had sources. He was a good reporter."[40] In his novel *Follow Me Down*, Shelby Foote included a cameo newsroom scene based on the *Delta Democrat-Times*. The description of Benny, "giving his machine old two-fingered hell about how the Cats made baseball history in Sportsman Park last night," fits Charlie Kerg, and there is Louise Smith as Gladys, "steamed up because of a printer's error in yesterday's paper" and "dressed for the garden club luncheon in one of those hats."[41]

6. 1938–1940

An "Unfortunate Liking for Excitement"

This day can be the most fateful for mankind since Gethsemane," warned an editorial in the *Delta Democrat-Times* on September 29, 1938, the day British prime minister Neville Chamberlain and French premier Édouard Daladier met with Adolf Hitler and Benito Mussolini in Munich.[1] After the infamous "peace in our time" pact was signed on September 30, Hodding had coffee with stockbroker Gervys Lusk and raged about Britain's folly.

"What about us?" asked Lusk, a World War I hero who believed democracy was doomed because the democratic countries were unprepared to face Hitler. "What about you?"

Hodding was at a loss. He was patriotic and ready to serve his country. On the other hand, he was thirty-one, married, a father, editor of his own newspaper, and without military experience. Lusk told him that when the Great War broke out, he had been in the National Guard, which at least was able to provide a few trained men.

Hodding went back to the office and talked to Betty. Then he hurried—Betty remembered that he ran—across the street to see Gallatin Paxton at his cotton brokerage. Paxton was another veteran of World War I, a colonel in the Mississippi National Guard, commanding officer of the 114th Field Artillery Regiment. Hodding asked him whether he could obtain a commission in army intelligence; Paxton said no, since he had had no military training at Bowdoin. He suggested Hodding join the National Guard. Would he get a commission? Hodding asked. No, but he could enlist as a private, then study and take exams to become an inactive second lieutenant. Hodding signed up immediately, lying about his age, since the National Guard did not accept married men as privates if they were more than thirty years old. His action, he said later, resulted from a mixture of professional curiosity and his "unfortunate liking for excitement," which he disguised as a willingness to practice what he preached.[2] "Everyone in town, including Betty and Galla Paxton, thought [he] had entered second childhood."[3]

At drill the next Monday night in Greenville's new armory, he was twelve years older than his fellow privates, young men who had joined the Guard for the dollar a week for attending drill and a two-week camp in the summertime. The uniform, dating from 1917, included broad-brimmed campaign hat, wool shirt, laced riding pants, and leather boots. Hodding was eager to fire the ancient howitzers, but Paxton made him serve as headquarters clerk and keep records. Hodding rose to the rank of corporal and, striving to become a second lieutenant, read courses on gunnery, sanitation, and military law.

He suited his words to his actions. His editorials continued to be solidly anti-appeasement. On the day a front-page story reported the banning of Jews from German schools, an editorial featured the headline "The Unspeakable Hun," which recalled Hodding's childhood scrapbooks about World War I. The editorial warned that "unless Nazism is checked the United States will eventually be forced to defend itself against the barbaric ideology of the German nation."[4] Two days later, an editorial condemned Colonel Charles Lindbergh, "once America's Lone Eagle," for accepting a German Eagle decoration and looking for a furnished apartment in Berlin in which to spend the winter.[5]

On November 22 a memorable editorial commented on a joint meeting of Christians and Jews at the Hebrew temple in Greenville and a union service for the persecuted of Europe. The editorial, written as though for a Nazi paper, read in part: "Greenville, Miss.—The Jew-lover Will Percy, the communist Episcopal Philip Davidson, and the communist Jew Rabinowitz defiled the name of the Fuehrer and the great German Reich in a hate-meeting held by Jewish swine and communists in the Jewish synagogue here."[6]

In other editorials that fall, Hodding urged the sheriff to resign. "Mr. Chaney was a good private citizen before he became sheriff, and we hope he will again be a good citizen. But he has not been a good sheriff. . . . We are not prejudiced against men who drink." It was the frequency of the sheriff's drinking, he said, that was important.[7] When the sheriff and his son threatened to come over and kill them both, Hodding and Don Wetherbee hid an iron bar under the counter in the front office. No one came.

They laughed when the mayor, among others, complained that Don Wetherbee's graphic story about a picture essay in *Life* on the birth of a baby was "in bad taste." But when the mayor objected to the newspaper's "occasional criticisms of the mayor and council" and said that "persons who attend council meetings do so as the 'guests' of the council," Hodding pulled out all the stops and referred to the mayor as "Herr Milton Smith, local fuehrer, and ex-officio commandant of the Greenville Gestapo." Furthermore, the mayor had threatened that if reporters came to council meetings to ridicule and criticize, the "law would reach out and grab them by the neck." Hodding wrote that he would "like to remind the fuehrer that he is nothing but a hired employee of the citizens of the city," and that reporters who attended council meetings did so not by sufferance or invitation.[8]

One editorial so angered a man that he called Hodding at home one Sunday morning and said he was coming over to kill him. Hodding waited, shaking, with shotgun and pistol, on his front porch, while friends phoned and passed by to offer support. A policeman warned him not to shoot until the man crossed the sidewalk. Eventually Hodding and Betty went to church, Hodding carrying the pistol. ("He left the big gun at home," Betty said.) The man never showed. "If I had called upon the police for protection that day, I might as well have closed shop," Hodding wrote later.[9] At the country club New Year's Eve ball a few nights after the missed showdown, Betty found herself dancing with the man during a Paul Jones. As they waltzed, revelers on the sidelines cocked their fingers to imitate a pistol and shouted "Bang-bang."

Often Hodding's editorials dealt with race and bigotry. One called the attempt by Florida members of the Ku Klux Klan to scare a white pastor and his congregation into canceling the appearance in their church of a visiting black choir "incredibly wicked."[10] Another attacked Jehovah's Witnesses because they tried to prevent Catholics from mailing certain pamphlets.[11] An editorial, "The Decent Houses on Clay Street," called for better housing for blacks in Greenville, and a fight against disease, crime, and hunger.[12]

When the Daughters of the American Revolution refused to permit Marian Anderson to perform in Constitution Hall in Washington, D.C., Hodding was outraged. He produced three editorials in March 1939 about the episode. "We fail to see how the DAR achieved a single worthy purpose in denying the hall to a negro woman whose voice brings pleasure to men and women of every race," he wrote. In Greenville, George Washington Carver had spoken to an audience of whites and blacks, and "Delta pleasure seekers danced to the music of a nationally known negro orchestra." In Hodding's mind it was possible "to preserve racial taboos without erecting new barriers," and he commended Eleanor Roosevelt for resigning from the DAR in protest. "Incidentally, it is possible that some black ancestor of Marian Anderson fought for [George] Washington along with the forebears of those who would not let her sing."[13]

Like all other southern editors, except for Virginius Dabney in Richmond, Hodding continued to oppose federal anti-lynching legislation. It was neither an answer, he said, nor

an honest attempt at an answer to the curse of lynching. . . . If we thought for one moment that the elimination of state laws demanding segregation would mean that a partial solution of our race problem would result, we would advocate such an elimination. . . . The white people of the South would not accept such a procedure and their refusal would react forcibly and cruelly upon the negroes. . . . We happen to believe in racial segregation which does not mean racial persecution.[14]

After the district attorney used the National Guard to raid sixteen "negro joints" in the all-black town, an editorial asked: "Why Single Out Mound Bayou?" The National Guard might find sixteen joints around Greenville, Hodding said. "It's pretty hypocritical to descend on a negro town in Bolivar county to raid whiskey and gambling places, and seize slot machines, when the Delta offers so many other targets not operated by negroes. . . . If Mound Bayou is ridden with vice dens, they got the idea from the white folks."[15]

A description of the Carters' good Thanksgiving dinner of turkey and home-cured ham opened an editorial that commented on the reality that blacks on Delta farms had to scrape nickels together to buy an inadequate chicken at Christmas and Thanksgiving. The Delta could never enjoy a real, deep-rooted Thanksgiving "until men and women who work the soil"—the richest land in the world, Hodding called it—learned that land could "give comfort and delight and health instead of perhaps one money crop in three and a fluctuating credit at the store."[16]

After the presidential election of 1940, Hodding commented, illogically, that boxer Joe Louis's support of Wendell Willkie because of his promise of an anti-lynching bill was "an appeal to racial prejudice." But so were the smear sheets that showed Eleanor Roosevelt being escorted by black officers. "Personally, we think the wife of the President of the United States is fine enough and sure enough of herself to walk with any Americans, regardless of color, without losing caste or dignity."[17]

These editorials were making some people in Greenville uneasy, but Hodding learned one lesson: It was all right to write editorials about syphilis and bigotry, but it was also important to be a booster and find things to praise about Greenville. So he praised Greenville people who together pledged $1,500 for a federal arts project,[18] and the men who thought up the idea of a river bridge at Greenville and arranged for its financing with federal bonds, to be paid off with tolls.

In late 1938 the *Delta Democrat-Times* was able to report the largest surplus in history and the lowest world prices for cotton, and it noted that representatives of the American cotton industry would meet in Memphis on November 21 to form the National Cotton Council for the promotion of cotton products and the sale of cotton. Two Greenville men, Oscar Johnston and Billy Wynn, were the chief organizers. Wynn, lawyer and planter, was one of Hodding's original backers. Johnston had been in the Roosevelt administration, in charge of all agricultural loans for the Department of Agriculture; now he was president of the British-owned Delta and Pine Land Company, which operated a 38,000-acre plantation at Scott, near Greenville. Hodding, fascinated by Johnston and the Cotton Council, helped them with publicity. In a press release about Johnston, he mentioned a message from the manager of the United Press bureau in Memphis to the *DD-T*, which had been submitting dozens of trivial stories that the bureau did not want: "The United Press is interested only in stories from your territory of more than local interest . . . murders, unusual and fatal auto accidents, airplane crashes, lynching, floods, large fires, cotton research, and Oscar Johnston."[19] Hodding tried, unsuccessfully, to sell an article on Johnston to *The Saturday Evening Post*.[20] He wrote long articles for the *DD-T* about the Cotton Council and urged planters, ginners, and factors to unite in this one organization that could lobby, promote cotton, and sponsor research.

Finally, leaving Don Wetherbee in charge of the paper, Hodding went to work full-time for the Cotton Council for four months, writing editorials and feature stories that could be used as press releases. These articles ranged widely in subject matter, discussing everything from the use of cotton membrane filler between layers of asphalt for resurfacing streets, to the fact that payrolls in the textile mills of Fall River, Massachusetts, in the summer of 1939 were running $50,000 ahead of those of the previous summer, and even to the "stylishness of long-wearing, color-fast, non-shrink" cotton fabrics.[21]

Hodding spent months touring the cotton-producing states for the Cotton Council, driving to cities across the South and talking to every daily newspaper editor about the Council and its work. The Council paid his expenses and a small fee. He went as far west as Amarillo, as far north as St. Louis and Cape Girardeau, Missouri, and as far east as Charlotte, Durham, and Raleigh. Many newspapers printed stories about his visit, with his picture, in which he wore a mustache and rimless spectacles.

Joe Darlington rode the train from New York to Raleigh to meet Hodding on April 22, and the two drove to Charlotte, Asheville, Chattanooga, and Nashville for meetings at newspaper offices. Darlington kept a diary of the trip and noted that they stopped for fried catfish, French fries, fried corn bread (surely hush puppies), and slaw right after they crossed the Tennessee River on their way from Nashville to Memphis. They spent the night in one of the new "auto camps" and had breakfast at a Toddle House. They left Memphis, descended the bluffs to the Delta, and reached Greenville, where Hodding took his old roommate to meet Will Percy. Darlington realized that for Hodding, Percy "epitomized the aristocrat of the Delta."

Hodding then took Darlington to Baton Rouge. On the way they stopped in Hammond to see Will Carter and his new wife, Lucille. Mrs. Carter, Darlington remembered, "gave us each a bowl of the most beautiful and luscious strawberries I had ever eaten. To 'wash them down,' she suggested a glass of bourbon (it was excellent) and a little ice." They ended up in New Orleans, where they met Betty and her mother. Mrs. Werlein had prepared *café brûlot*, "a pleasant Creole drink."[22]

That it might be unethical for a newspaper editor to promote the Cotton Council and write its releases never entered Hodding's mind. He thought the Council would help the Delta and the South, and in his booster role he supported it in every way he could.

In 1938, Hodding had read in *Time* magazine about the new Nieman Foundation fellowships, which gave journalists a year in residence at Harvard, paid them a stipend equal to a year's salary, allowed them to take any classes they chose, and provided seminars with luminaries in communications. He decided to apply for the year 1939–1940, and went to New Orleans for an interview with Archibald MacLeish and Arthur Wild.[23] In April 1939, he learned that he had been accepted and that his stipend for nine months would be $3,040, which included an allowance to boost his salary of $150 a month so he could live in Cambridge.[24]

He called Will Percy from New Orleans to tell him about the Nieman and met icy fury. "If you go, you'll have to take your chances on coming back," Percy told him.

Percy, who had begun to sense that Hodding was probably not a suitable editor, explained his feelings a short time later to Betty. She had written him about a New Orleans job offer (long since forgotten) that Hodding had received, and Percy replied:

> Hodding has a natural flare [sic] for writing, but I do not believe that he has a natural flare for being the editor of a small town paper because nine-tenths of the time such a paper is humdrum, is not engaged in fighting anything or anybody and is not going through a crisis. When things are humdrum he loses interest and when he loses interest his writing is dull. I have always conceived him more of a poet than a newspaper man by temperament, but I believe his natural outlet would be writing special articles, pinch-hitting in emergency, and inviting his soul.[25]

Percy acknowledged that Hodding and Betty could not live on Hodding's $150-a-month salary in Greenville, but the newspaper could not pay him more until the bulk of the Smith indebtedness was paid off. Hodding was a terrible money manager, Percy said, and liked nice things; he did not care for money in itself, and was naturally warmhearted and liberal and liked to give. Yet he had a position to maintain. No matter what salary he made, he would always live beyond it, unless Betty guarded the exchequer. "But no amount of guarding on your part can permit . . . your living on $150.00 a month," Percy told Betty.

Although the paper had just gotten on its legs, Percy said, Hodding should not feel it was his duty to refuse a job because of the money Percy and Billy Wynn had put into the paper. A more serious consideration for Percy was the money his friends and relatives had put into the paper. They would lose it if the paper failed. If Hodding left, the local people would try to make the paper a success, not only as a matter of pride, but in order to save what they had put into it. If they saved their own investment, they would salvage what Betty, Hodding, and Mrs. Werlein had put into it. *"As I recollect, Hodding owns not quite a majority of the stock* [italics added], and he would have to trust the other stockholders to make a go of the paper. He would have no more share in directing its policies except as a minority stockholder." If Don Wetherbee stayed with the paper, Percy believed, he would make it a success, "but of course, not as interesting and brilliant . . . as it was under Hodding." Percy seemed to be gently urging Hodding to take the job.

"Hodding was an opportunist in a way," said Don Wetherbee. "The Nieman fellowship didn't do the *Delta Democrat-Times* any good, but it did him good." Wetherbee admired the way Hodding grasped at opportunities. He had once persuaded Wetherbee to apply for a Rosenwald fellowship. "I had to think up a project," Wetherbee recalled. "We finally came up with a study of syphilis in the Mississippi Delta. I knew nothing about it and had no credentials. I would have been gone from the paper for a whole year."[26]

Hodding was determined to take advantage of the Nieman. He and Betty both thought he needed a break. He had worked hard on the *Courier*, and then at the papers in Greenville. He felt he needed to replenish himself, and then there was his insatiable curiosity.[27] He had a good staff now. In addition to Wetherbee, there was Bert Hyde, who had come up from Hammond. Charles Kerg did sports, and Vincent Maggio, a veteran of the old *Democrat-Times*, had come aboard as shop foreman and had brought order into the back room.

A new staff member was Wells Lewis, son of Sinclair Lewis, the Nobel Prize–winning novelist. Young Lewis, hired at the instigation of David Cohn, baby-sat for young Hodding and endeared himself to the Carters generally. He did not, however, stay long.

Betty had misgivings about a year at Harvard. Pregnant with twins in the summer of 1938, she had miscarried. She had lost a great deal of blood, and the Carters had been touched by the fact that everyone in town went to the hospital offering to give blood. Betty then developed puerperal fever and was plainly dying. Hodding's sister, Corinne, had married Perry Thomas, a gynecologist in New Orleans. Betty's brother, Philip, drove Thomas as far as Jackson, where John Carter met him and brought him back to Greenville. The three-hundred-mile trip, over gravel roads, took only four hours. Thomas asked Betty's Greenville doctor if he had considered using sulfa. The doctor replied that he had read about sulfa but didn't have any. Thomas had some with him, and he gave it to the Greenville doctor. And Betty got well. She went to New Orleans, and stayed on her mother's sleeping porch for six weeks, taking wheat germ and cod liver oil. Now, in 1939, Betty was pregnant again, and she had no wish to go to Massachusetts to have her baby.

Worried about what to do, Hodding went for his two weeks of active duty with the National Guard at Camp Shelby, Mississippi, and by late August he thought he had worked out a compromise. The Nieman committee agreed to let him start at Harvard in the spring semester of 1940, after the new baby's safe arrival, and do the fall semester another time. In fact, the committee agreed to pay his way to Cambridge for a two-week stay at the beginning of the fall semester, when he could meet the other fellows, attend some classes, and obtain a reading list.

Hodding talked to the newspaper's board of directors and persuaded them that he needed the Nieman fellowship. Alarmed by Percy's remark about having to "take . . . chances on coming back," Hodding consulted Joe Darlington about gaining corporate control of the paper. "Be sure and bring all the facts," Darlington wrote

Hodding, just before he left for his two weeks in Cambridge. "All this loose talk in your letter about not being sure how many thousands of unsubscribed dollars are kicking about I hereby assume to be sheer bravado, evasive, disarming and ex parte." Darlington instructed Hodding to bring complete information about the corporate structure, the stockholders, and the amount and class of stock each one held, and copies of agreements, provisions, and bylaws. They would change all of Hodding's (and Darlington's) preferred stock, including what Will Percy had made over to Hodding and Betty, to common, and thus give Hodding a bare majority of the common.[28]

Meanwhile, war was obviously on the way. The day Hitler invaded Poland, the staff watched the teletype in the newsroom for the latest news from Associated Press. Even Charlie Kerg went over to look at it, pleasing Hodding, who thought that at last Kerg was interested in world affairs. When Kerg returned to his desk and began typing, Hodding went and looked over his shoulder, and saw: "It looks like a good season for the Greenville High School football team. . . ." "The world's going up in flames," Hodding commented, "and Charlie writes about the Green Hornets."[29]

Hodding went to Harvard later in September as planned. While he was there, Ralph Ingersoll, who had worked at *The New Yorker* and been an editor at *Fortune*, came to talk to the Nieman fellows about his plans for a new paper without advertising, to be called *PM*.

Hodding was back in the South in time for the birth of Philip Dutartre* Carter in October, in New Orleans. He was feeling very restless, and he wrote to Archibald MacLeish asking if he would recommend him for a job on Ingersoll's paper. MacLeish replied that he would be very glad to recommend Hodding for almost any job on any paper, but that Ingersoll had not yet ironed out all his money problems. MacLeish advised Hodding to write directly to Ingersoll

---

*Hodding's mother's family had spelled the name "Dutart" for several generations. When Hodding's second son was born, however, he decided to restore the original French spelling, "Dutartre," and use it for Philip's middle name.

and "tell him the situation."[30] Hodding did so, and Ingersoll replied that he had had Hodding's name near the top of his list ever since he had spoken to him in Cambridge. "You will be pleased to know you have good friends who have talked to me about you since then."[31]

In early 1940, Hodding and Betty drove to Cambridge, with three-month-old Philip in a basket on the backseat and young Hodding, almost five, standing up behind the front seat most of the way. They stopped in Lexington, Virginia, to visit Hodding's fraternity brother George Jackson, who taught at Washington and Lee, and in Washington, D.C., to visit Betty's cousin Elizabeth, married to Robert Wittoeff-Enden, a World War I German naval hero and naval attaché at the German embassy. (They met Manfred Zapp, head of the German press agency, actually a propaganda agency, who twice offered Hodding access to his wire service for the Greenville paper free of charge.[32] After two days, Hodding was nervous enough about being with these Germans to call the FBI and explain why the Carters were staying in a Nazi stronghold.) They stopped again in Upper Montclair, New Jersey, to see Betty's sister Evelyn and her husband, Don Smith.

Finally in Cambridge, they settled at 17 Wright Street and put little Hodding in kindergarten at the Buckingham School. His father enrolled in a class on propaganda and in Paul Herman Buck's southern history course, and attended seminars with, among others, Arthur Krock, Washington correspondent for the New York *Times*; Vincent Sheean, author and journalist; Professor Hans Zinsser of the Harvard Medical School, who answered the fellows' questions about reporting scientific material; H. L. Mencken of the Baltimore *Sun*; John Chamberlain of *Fortune*; Virginius Dabney of the Richmond *Times-Dispatch*; William McCleery, who would be picture editor of *PM*; and Archibald MacLeish. Other Nieman fellows that year included Carroll Kilpatrick, from Montgomery, Alabama; the political editor of the New York *Daily News*; a labor columnist for the San Francisco *Chronicle*; and a reporter from the Nashville *Tennessean*.

Betty experienced culture shock. She enjoyed such events as the meeting of the Harvard Dames where she met the speaker, Eleanor Roosevelt, but she often felt at sea. Once a friend of a friend gave a luncheon for Betty. "The other guests were wives of the Harvard intelligentsia, all in their tweedy suits and sturdy walking shoes," Betty recalled. "When I arrived in my dear little blue-green wool dress, mink hat, and high heels, the hostess announced, 'Our southern belle!'"

They saw Jimmy Robertshaw, the young Greenville man who had worked at the *Delta Star* one summer, who was now at Harvard Law School, and caught up with old Maine friends from time to time. Will Carter visited, and expressed relief when he did not have to eat meals with blacks—he was afraid a photograph of him eating with a black man would get back to Hammond.[33]

Harold Strauss, an editor at Alfred A. Knopf, wrote to each of the Nieman fellows asking whether their period of reflection and research had given them any occasion to think about writing a book. "Concrete suggestions which you may make would receive the friendliest consideration from us," Strauss said.[34] Hodding wrote back with ideas for two books, one to be called "Watchwords of Destiny," and one analyzing the reasons behind the southern racial and political situation. Strauss replied that the first did not "fit in with our program."[35] The second idea, however, interested him. There would be obvious merchandising difficulties, but if such a book were "realistic and direct and very human and to dwell but lightly on theory and on abstract argument, it might achieve considerable success." He suggested that Hodding send a chapter or two as they were written.

Betty did her first research for Hodding for this book. When she turned in her call slips at the Harvard library, she was astonished to find that women could not sit in the main reading room; she had to wait in the Radcliffe Room. Hodding finished five chapters and sent them to Strauss, who replied that they were very interesting but he was afraid Hodding's opinion had no validity.[36]

In April 1940, Ingersoll offered Hodding a job running *PM*'s press section; if Hodding found he did not have a flair for it, the national news department would still be there.[37] Hodding and Betty decided the *DD-T* was in good shape with Don Wetherbee acting as editor, and that Hodding should go to work for *PM* for four or five months. They could use the money to pay off some of the paper's indebtedness. Hodding left Harvard early to settle Betty and the children in Maine before he joined *PM* in New York on June 1.

While the Carters looked for a house in Maine, Hodding's commission as a second lieutenant in the National Guard came through. The war situation looked so grim after the Low Countries fell to Hitler that Betty refused to stay in Maine. They went to New Orleans, and Betty and the children moved in with her mother while Hodding went back North.

"Hodding worked like hell, and then the next thing you knew, he was up in New York working for *PM*," said Don Wetherbee, who was somewhat dismayed. "He was intrigued by the thought that Ingersoll wanted him. When he started on these projects, he'd say, 'Good-bye, Don, I'm leaving it in your hands.' And I was making $120 a month." Wetherbee was sometimes forced to serve as business manager. "That basically involved going to the bank to get a loan to buy a carload of paper."[38]

At the *PM* offices in Brooklyn, a tall black man checked Hodding in at the receptionist's desk, and Hodding observed that "apparently not even *PM* was ready for a Negro reporter."[39] He felt lost for a while—he knew no one but Ingersoll, and Ingersoll had no time for his new press editor. His researcher, a pretty, sarcastic blonde, shocked Hodding with her far-left views. *PM* was to have no advertising, no stock market tables, no comics, no society page, no editorial page, no sports page, no syndicated columns. It was to have thirty-two tabloid pages printed in two colors, with sections on labor, the press, and home economics, the last called "News for Living" and the mother of all "Style" sections. Hodding's fellow staff members were constantly condemning the South, and he became disenchanted with their "dreary, humorless, consecrated insistence upon conformity to a fixed and condescending liberalism."[40] Nonetheless, the work for *PM* influenced him politically and journalistically.

In New Orleans, Betty was responsible for a new development. Carl Carmer, an author, editor, former New Orleans newspaperman, and friend of her mother's, was in the city to cancel a contract with Lyle Saxon for a book on the Lower Mississippi for Farrar & Rinehart's Rivers of America series. Betty told Carmer that Hodding would be perfect to write the book, and showed him the five chapters he had written for Knopf. Carmer was interested.

Betty and the two boys then went to spend the summer with her sister near Lake Waramaug in Connecticut. During the week Hodding and his brother-in-law Don Smith stayed at the Smiths' house in New Jersey, and on weekends commuted to Connecticut in Smith's two-seater aquaplane.

Hodding investigated racial and religious discrimination in the classified advertising of the New York newspapers, and he was surprised at the number of job listings that specified an applicant must be Anglo-Saxon and Christian. The discovery reinforced his conviction that racial prejudice was not just a southern phenomenon.[41] He went to Memphis in July to cover a convention of the American Newspaper Guild, which was rent with dissension as a number of communist members tried to gain control of the union. "The charges of communism . . . had official Memphis so alert for the worst that the chief of police forbade a Negro high school's drum-and-bugle corps to parade on Beale Street because 'these niggers are communistic enough without parading for the Guild,'" Hodding wrote in *The Nation*.[42] Always generous, Hodding offered to share his room with a man who was not on an expense account, and then found himself entertaining his roommate's communist friends. Memphis was too close to Greenville, he thought, for him to be consorting with communists. He left.

In late July, Hodding signed a contract with Farrar & Rinehart to write the book on the Lower Mississippi, receiving a $400 advance from the publisher. Ingersoll and Hodding agreed that he would rove the South and write stories about the "disregarded good" and the "overplayed bad," and talk to civic groups about the potential of *PM*.[43] He could do some of this while he did research for the book. On September 21, Hodding finally resigned from *PM*.

He had come back to Greenville not because he disliked the *PM* job, he wrote in a *DD-T* editorial in early October, but because Greenville was a better place to live in than New York, "where the contrast between success and squalor is tragically inescapable." And besides, he preferred to be his own boss.[44] Some days later he wrote that it would be better that no millionaires existed if, to maintain them, any family "should live at the sub-human level at which hundreds of thousands grovel today." It was better that a hundred drones be fed than that men should lose self-respect and go hungry for lack of government relief and jobs. "We believe this is democracy, and, if we have the right to say so, it is Christianity."[45] And more than a month later, he wrote that white Southerners took for granted the terrible conditions under which too many blacks lived. He was not prepared to offer a solution, but he knew it must lie "in further travel along the road which the New Deal belatedly began, the road toward social responsibility."[46] The reconstruction of Hodding Carter was well under way.

He and Betty left the children in Hammond with Will and Lucille Carter while they went to New Orleans to do research in the Tulane library. They lived, Betty said, in a world of Jean-Baptiste Bienville and Bernardo de Gálvez, colonial governors of Louisiana, and looked up no friends, saw no relatives.[47] There was an urgency to their work because the National Guard might soon be called to active duty. Hodding had the option of resigning from the Guard, since he was over thirty, with a wife and two children, but he chose to go—he thought it would be for a year.

Once again, Will Percy displayed his anger, this time in a two-page, single-spaced typewritten letter. Hodding seemed to have disappeared "into the vast inane," he wrote. Meanwhile the *DD-T* directors "were pretty badly jarred" by Hodding's actions. "You made yourself Editor-in-Chief and fired Lillian McLaughlin without . . . the slightest authority." (Hodding had inherited McLaughlin, the society editor of the old *Democrat-Times*.) Percy said that when Hodding reclaimed the editor's title, Don Wetherbee was left dangling. "If you go with the National Guard he is needed as editor and if he gets another job the paper is left dangling."

The directors, Percy wrote, were surprised to learn that Hodding owned a majority of the stock. They had never thought particularly about who owned the majority; they considered the venture a sort of partnership. "We were also surprised at your action in exchanging preferred stock for common stock in order to gain control. Billy [Wynn] and I checked over our stock list yesterday and it doesn't appear to us by any means clear that your group does own a majority of the stock. That group would own it if stock were issued to you and to me for putting up the necessary collateral in the deal with Mrs. Smith [Pink Smith's widow]. Billy tells me this stock was issued in your and my names jointly. I paid no attention to it one way or the other. Personally, I don't see why anybody putting up collateral should have stock unless their collateral were sacrificed."

It was not good for the paper, whoever ran it, for Hodding to "ignore the directors and make such vital changes in the paper without consultation with them." Percy had "no doubt under the circumstances that their inclination would be to resign," although he couldn't imagine that as being helpful to the *DD-T*.

Percy repeated what he had told Betty earlier, that he did not think Hodding's "very marked talent" lay in editing a small country newspaper. "As a pamphleteer, you have unusual ability and I believe very real literary ability which will undoubtedly call you to the literary field and not to the newspaper field." In the past Hodding had not always been interested in editing the paper. The *DD-T* had been founded on the supposition that Hodding would be the editor, but he left it to take the Nieman fellowship and the job at *PM*. Hodding would probably want to do that kind of thing in the future. "Even when you are really on the job," Percy stated, "you frequently lose interest in it, your editorials varying between brilliance and complete apathy."

To Percy, the question of the ownership of the stock was urgent. Hodding had refused an offer to sell the paper without consulting the directors, and the directors wanted to explore the possibility fully. "You did not wish a sale made by a purchase of the preferred stock because that would not recoup . . . your loss in the Delta Star," Percy told him. "All of us lost in the Delta Star and the rest of us consider that loss final and absolute. It seems to me you should take the same point of view."[48]

Hodding took this letter, underlined phrases in it, numbered Percy's points, and answered them one by one.

First, about Lilly Mack: "When I decided to go with the Guard when it is finally called out, the only thing I could think to do was to have Betty work on the paper." For the past two years, he said, Lillian McLaughlin had been talking to him about finding a job at a larger paper, and it was understood that she would leave as soon as a job presented itself. "I didn't think any change in personnel, especially one which was not to occur until October, November, or December [1940]—depending on when our unit is called out—required a meeting of the board. Nor do I think it unfair that if and when our unit is called, Betty should do society. The paper is our only source of income. She worked for its two most difficult years, harder than anyone else, and for less than anyone else, and she wanted to be in Greenville while I was away."

Next, Hodding did not see that his reassuming the editorship left Don Wetherbee dangling, "although we have discussed the eventual possibility of his outgrowing the paper if I remained as editor." This didn't mean that Don would be forced to look for a new job, now or later, any more than Hodding would have to. He had not dangled during the time Hodding was actively serving as editor. Don should stay with the paper, he thought, because he might have a hard time finding a job "as good as his experience warrants." Besides, in another year, when Hodding would be through with the Guard, the paper could certainly hold them more easily than it had in the past. Hodding felt that if Don got another job immediately, he would have to take advantage of the dependents clause in the Guard call and not go. "Either Don or I must be there in the next year," he said.

As to his control—not ownership, he was careful to say—of the majority of stock: "Until a year and a half ago, Will, I hadn't thought much about the majority angle except, as frequently and casually expressed to you and Billy [Wynn], I hoped some day to own control. There was no secret about this. What made it seem pressing to me was a telephone conversation with you from New Orleans, right after I had won the Nieman fellowship. I'll never forget the shock that what you said gave me—'if you go you'll have to take your chances on coming back.' Before then I had also, as you put it, considered the venture a sort of partnership and I do now. But I felt and still feel that fellowship was pretty vital. I couldn't take a chance on not being able to come back. That's when I swapped stock, as the records will show."

Then Hodding took up the issue of majority control. "It has been my understanding that it has been up to Betty and me, by virtue of the collateral, to raise any difference needed to pay Mrs. Smith." Percy's stock was "the guarantee required by Mrs. Smith rather than collateral which itself should be sold in time of shortage. Under this assumption I sold $4,500 more last fall, to Don Smith. Under the same assumption I have been busy down here making arrangements to raise whatever difference is required this time. The stock for this collateral was originally issued to you and me jointly—but you must remember telling me that the stock was mine since the risk on the collateral was Betty's and mine. We were in your study, and you signed over the block, issued jointly to both of us, to me. And the question about whether anyone should have stock before collateral was sacrificed was discussed in the reorganization. Billy [Wynn] said the stock was issued in behalf of the risk of collateral. That was not my idea, but it was adopted, and on it I got Dad and Mrs. Werlein to put their stock, following which you backed it up, and thereby made it acceptable."

Hodding said that he had taken the Nieman fellowship and the job with *PM* for the money he could make to pay off debts incurred for the paper, and that he had told Percy he would come back. Even the money for the book he was writing would go to pay off the paper's debt.

He was very interested in the *DD-T*, and concerned for its welfare: "Everything we own is in it." If Percy would talk to Rodney Deffenbaugh, John Gibson, shop foreman Ted Lovell, or even Don Wetherbee, he would find that Hodding had been useful to the paper in other ways than writing. He had been away from the paper for eight months, but he had planned to be back by October 1. "Besides, contrary to your idea, I do think I have some talent in editing a small daily, and I like it," he said.

He had refused to sell the common stock owned by him and his group because the price would not pay off the rest of the preferred stockholders. All he had was the common stock, and he wanted to keep it. "Eventually the paper will work out, I know. I cannot see why any of you would want to sell simply for the preferred [stock] you would have in a new paper. And obviously we wouldn't want to make a sale of a going concern and get nothing out of it for the years and money we put into it—in fact, being left owing the balance of the note."[49]

When Percy replied the next day, he said Hodding was "entirely correct" about the stock issued for the collateral. "I had quite forgotten that I had transferred it to you and Betty. I never made any attempt at any time to get a majority of the stock, and if by transferring this batch to you I gave you the majority, I didn't think of it and if I had thought of it, it would have made no difference." He was only sorry that he could not have told Billy Wynn the facts, which had entirely escaped his recollection.

Percy conceded that Hodding was right about his attitude toward Hodding's taking the Nieman. "After your four months' absence on the Cotton Council I did not think you had any business going off to

Harvard. You were either editor of the paper or you were not, and if you were the former I thought you ought to attend to it. After our long distance conversation I think you talked over the whole matter with the directors and they acceded to your wish. I guess it was natural of you, when I as a director disapproved of your going, to guarantee that in the future my disapproval would be of no consequence and the simple way to do that was by securing control of the stock."

Percy confessed that he was worried over the duties of the directors. Hodding was right to require that they not control the paper's editorial policies, but they should elect the management and the management should appoint or fire its employees. "When you returned from New York a few weeks ago you were not the editor or the business manager of the paper. You were merely a stockholder and a director. But you fired Lilly Mack, which was Don [Wetherbee's] prerogative, and you announced that you would be the future editor-in-chief, which was the directors' prerogative." It seemed, said Percy, that Hodding wanted to be editor in chief, that John Carter would be business manager, and Betty society editor; Don Wetherbee would be either assistant editor or assistant manager, and while Hodding was in the Guard, acting editor. "I take it that your plan further contemplates on your return . . . Don's services will be retained, though in what capacity I cannot figure out. If this is your plan, it puts three instead of two executives on the pay-roll. I am certain the paper cannot stand this. My doubt has always been whether the paper could pay salaries to an editor-in-chief and a business manager, or whether those two jobs must, in the interest of economy, be combined in one as they were under Ernest Smith."

Percy thought that since he had "a congenital dislike to being a dummy sub-director," the simplest course would be for him to resign. His only concern was to have a decent paper that would last. He had put money in the paper and he hoped to get it back, but he never hoped to make money on it. "If the paper lives and is as good as it has been under both you and Don my larger objective will have been accomplished," he said.

Percy repeated that he thought Hodding was gifted with ability and imagination as an editor, but he felt his greater talent was on the literary side. "With your abounding imagination you will never be satisfied editing a small town paper, nor do I believe you can edit it without giving practically your whole time to it." He hoped he was wrong about this, he said in closing, "because you and Betty are always a great addition to the town and to my own particular happiness."[50]

Surprisingly, Hodding and Percy remained friends. Hodding's admiration for Percy was genuine, warm, and expressed often. He devoted chapters in two of his books—*Lower Mississippi* and *Where Main Street Meets the River*—to Percy, wrote many magazine articles about him, and countless times quoted Percy's farewell speech to him when the National Guard was called to active duty not long after this correspondence:

"You can't do anything on the grand scale. But when this comes to an end, you can work again for your own people in your own town. It isn't national leaders we need as much as men of good will in each of the little towns of America. So try to keep Greenville a decent place by being a correct citizen yourself. The total of all the Greenvilles will make the kind of country we want or don't want."[51]

7. 1940–1943

"The Colonel Thinks I Am a Miracle Man"

The National Guard was called to active duty in late November 1940. Hodding, by now a second lieutenant, refused to buy the boots that Galla Paxton wanted all his officers to wear and was, according to the adjutant, the only "character in tennis shoes throughout the war."[1] He had his khaki officer's shirts, khaki slacks, and campaign hat with cord and chin strap. He passed his physical, weighing 179 pounds, stripped, a pound under the maximum. "We're glad we're going," he commented in the editorial columns of the *Delta Democrat-Times* on November 24. "We hope we can learn to be a soldier."

In December, after a farewell banquet, at which Oscar Johnston of the National Cotton Council spoke, and a special community worship service at the junior high school, led by all the white ministers in town and Rabbi Rabinowitz, the 114th Field Artillery Regiment left Greenville. Since Hodding was in charge of the regiment's advance detail on its motor march to Camp Blanding, near Starke, Florida, he arranged for refueling the 120 trucks in which the 1,200 officers and men made the eight-hundred-mile trip. The trip took several days, with overnight stops in Biloxi, Pensacola (in a huge warehouse), and Tallahassee (in the gym at Florida State College for Women). It rained every day after the troops left Biloxi.

On Christmas Day he wrote Betty from Camp Blanding that he shared a tent with three other officers. It was raining, but the tent had a wooden floor, sides that went up four and a half feet, and a Sibley stove. It was hard to work on the river book, he said. "Some of the officers are just what they are in civilian life—horses. But I do think that given time, the United States is going to have a real army. I hope that I can be a worthwhile part of it."[2]

Hodding soon reported to the readers of the *Delta Democrat-Times* that he had gone from one newspaper job to another: he was the editor of the regimental newspaper.[3] In Jacksonville on a laundry detail, he went by the *Florida Times-Union* offices and found that his would be the first newspaper in camp. He planned to drop in on the *Times-Union*'s stringer at Camp Blanding and "inveigle him into writing a promotional story in which I'll figure—all with an eye toward getting the general staff's attention and possibly a future transfer with promotion."[4]

(In Greenville that Christmas Day, Betty and her brother-in-law John helped little Hodding put together the toy train Will Percy had given him. Betty attended the Junior Auxiliary Tacky Party in a sailor suit and played "Home Sweet Home" on the harmonica.)

The day after Christmas, Hodding went to Dixie Division headquarters, found the press tent, and talked to a reporter from the Birmingham *Age-Herald*. Major General John Persons, commander of the division, was a banker from Birmingham. "I think I have a story that the general might like to see in the Birmingham papers," Hodding said. "The camp's first regimental newspaper will appear Friday." He wasn't looking for personal publicity, he added, but he was a former Nieman fellow, a veteran of *PM*, a Mississippi publisher, and a public relations expert from the National Cotton Council. The Birmingham reporter said, "Why you're just the kind of fellow the general is looking for. He's having a press conference in fifteen minutes and he said yesterday he was going to select a public relations officer today."[5] Persons liked Hodding and transferred him to the division staff as public relations officer and asked him to edit a division newspaper.

Hodding wanted to call the regimental newspaper "The Rebel Yell," but the general chose *Dixie* for the division paper. Hodding wrote Betty that the paper was very good—"just the old Carter touch."[7]

A friendly colonel from Yazoo City recommended Hodding for promotion to first lieutenant; this meant his monthly salary would be $260 instead of $183. The colonel liked Hodding and his assistant, Lieutenant O. C. McDavid, former city editor of the Jackson *Daily News*, and let them use his car for errands. It was a gray-green Ford V-8 with a big "G-2" on the windshield. Captains and majors saluted them as they passed, and a driver leaped out to open the doors for them.[6]

Hodding sent editorials for the *DD-T* and promised to send one or two a day. He and McDavid were planning to serve as correspondents for a number of newspapers, and this would bring him forty or fifty dollars more a month. He also sent notes from their Memphis bank for Will Percy to sign. He was taking a course in intelligence, which he liked better than the artillery—"a lot of signal corps work, map reading, compass, aerial observation and the like all for the purpose of collecting, evaluating and disseminating information on the enemy . . . the same technique as newspaper work, only with different tools."[8] He was positive he would be a captain in intelligence before the year was out, "which is as far as Will or Gervys Lusk got."[9]

When he interviewed the generals in the division for the newspaper, he found out that one had been an aide to Huey Long. The man asked Hodding whether he was the Carter from the Hammond paper. Hodding told him yes, but this wasn't the same kind of paper and the general would be safe in telling him his life story. "The old boy," Hodding said, "spent an hour practically apologizing" for the Long administration.[10]

From Greenville, Betty, on her own for the first time in her life, wrote Hodding that she was doing features for the society page and working at night on the notes for the book. She described a party at Helen Generelly's. "First of all, we, including Will, had a right stiff drink. . . . I was right proud of myself, pulling off several bon mots—

without your air but still with enough punch to be appreciated. I may even have impressed W.A.P. [Percy] though of all egocentrics, he is the greatest and for that reason the hardest to impress. And you know something, Hodding, I think he doesn't really know so much but waits to find out what he would like. I may be wrong but that's the impression I've been developing. He is interested in the world— but it is the world that has him at its center. And that's not unkind because I still like him and think he's an interesting center. However, he's only one of the firmaments."[11]

Hodding thought her estimate of Will Percy "penetrating." She was really "much deeper" than he was, he said. He'd known it all along, and "I suspect you have, too, and that part of the depth is exemplified by your trying to keep it from me, you adorable armful of intelligence activated by sex, or vice versa."[12]

The *Times-Union* took pictures of Major General Persons and Hodding looking over the first issue of *Dixie*, which appeared on January 11, 1941. "As a matter of cold fact, I have gotten in pretty solid at headquarters because of my soldierly, serious, intent, purposeful, proudly respectful, ambitious, deferential, intelligent determined attitude," Hodding told Betty.[13]

O. C. McDavid recalled that for a while he and Hodding shared a tent as well as work. "Hodding was the outside man and spoke to Rotary Clubs. I put out the weekly newspaper. Except on rare occasions when somebody wanted a speaker, Hodding lay on his cot with his hands behind his head thinking about his book. When we rented a cottage on the St. John's River, Hodding would pull out for home and write all night long. I rustled up people to put out the paper. I should have hated him but I didn't."[14]

Hodding, who started bayonet and hand grenade practice as well as rifle and pistol practice and continued his intelligence classes, found he did not have time to string for the Memphis *Commercial-Appeal*, New Orleans *Times-Picayune*, and Associated Press and work on the book. Regretting the lost income, he gave up the correspondent's work to concentrate on the book. He had sent six chapters to Carl Carmer, who wrote back that it would be one of the two most significant volumes of the series and that Hodding should not worry about the June 1 deadline; the book was too good to hurry.[15]

Betty left the boys with John Carter and his wife, Margaret, who were living with her, and drove to Camp Blanding with four other Guard wives for a visit. She wrote her mother that she was the belle of the ball at the regimental dance, since the other wives were mostly old and fat. They partied all weekend, but on Monday she and Hodding worked on the book for several hours.

Back in Greenville, Betty kept Hodding informed of local news. The Garden Club wanted a sculpture by Leon Koury at the foot of Washington Street, where it dead-ended into the levee by the river. Seguin Allen, who was in charge of the levee, vetoed this plan. He wanted to be able to watch for "boils," swirling upheavals on the surface of the river that would indicate danger to the levee. At home Betty found mouse tracks in the baby's bed and advertised in the paper for a cat she could rent. The boy who answered her ad wanted fifty cents a night; they compromised on a dollar for three nights. The cat caught nothing the first night, but ate three mice the next afternoon.

John Carter also wrote to his brother. "Betty sits up all night figuring her expenses. . . . The next few days we eat leftovers." He had an even harder time at the office. "Saturday was tax day. Had to put out fifteen hundred on taxes besides trying to make a payday. Learning to throw grenades and running with a knife on the end of your gun is child's play compared to trying to collect just and honest debts in Greenville." He had to "use some of Gibson's money" to pay the taxes, and the next month the interest was due the Smith family. But advertising linage was up 2,000 inches over the previous January. "We are actually making ends meet if we could only collect for it." John had had a talk with Will Percy, who said Hodding was just like a bird dog, running off after every scent. John agreed and said he hoped Hodding would come home and run the paper. His experience in the Army might be good for him, but "the experience of a poorly run or bankrupt newspaper will linger in your mind a lot longer."[16]

Betty wrote Hodding about the food stamp controversy. Washington County had been certified for food stamps, but there was a move on to remove the certification outside Greenville. Some of the planters, led by LeRoy Percy, Will Percy's adopted son, and Bill Hardies, felt that "if you feed a Negro too much he won't work." Others seemed to want to have their workers certified, because the price of food was so high. Betty dreaded the excitement in the northern press when reporters found out why Washington County wanted to be "*un*certified." It was, she said, perhaps for the best that Hodding was too far away to get involved in it. "However, were you here, I'm afraid we'd be leading the fight *against* the planters—and would also be unpopular with the haberdashers who kowtow to the planters."[17]

At Camp Blanding, Hodding was not worried about the welfare of black residents of Washington County. When he learned he could not be promoted as long as he was on the headquarters staff, he voluntarily went back to the regiment, hoping for a promotion. His regiment went on maneuvers. When Betty's letter reached him, he was delirious, nauseated, and suffering with excruciating pain from a perirectal abscess. He had endured a hundred-mile ride from maneuver bivouac to hospital, in a bouncing reconnaissance car. (Galla Paxton had refused to authorize an ambulance.) After surgery relieved his pain, he complained violently about the care he received, the flies in his room, the lack of air cushions, the ignorance of orderlies, and the callousness of doctors.[18] Later he had to have another operation for a thrombotic hemorrhoid that developed in the aftermath of the first operation. He was in the hospital nearly three weeks.

In March, while in the hospital, he first noticed the loss of all central vision in his right eye; only the peripheral vision remained. The doctors could find no cause for the loss of vision, "or rather," as one Army medical report said, "any cause of the central retinitis, which caused the loss of vision."[19]

In the hospital Hodding received a letter from Captain George Smith, a regular Army officer who had been stationed in Greenville as an artillery instructor for the National Guard, asking him if he would like to go to Washington to do public relations. If he went to Washington, Hodding realized, Betty could join him. He would have more time for the book and might even get a promotion, which would mean more money. Meanwhile, letters from Carl Carmer and another editor, Stephen Vincent Bénet, were enthusiastic about the chapters he was sending in.

Hodding wrote to Betty every day while he was at Camp Blanding, once three times in one day. The third missive that day was a love letter with an added paragraph pointing out "the sheets of yellow paper on which you jotted the chronological notes on the Spanish acquisition of Louisiana. They're the kind of notes which your lackadaisical, easily dejected husband hates to, and rarely will take."[20]

In April, Hodding's transfer to Army public relations came through. He went to Washington, where he wrote releases that almost always opened: "The War Department announced today . . ." Two releases a day, he said, was considered an enormous output.[21] He also began to send regular reports to the *Delta Democrat-Times*, which were printed under the heading "A Shavetail in Washington." Betty was excited "and a little scared" about moving to the capital. She warned Hodding that her personality had changed, not her fundamental personality, but her "social-contact" personality, since he had been away. "I find that I'm now the life of the party, that I am supposed to have a beautiful voice and a wonderful lot of backtalk. . . . Having suddenly developed self-confidence, I feel able to handle any situation."[22] In June she and the children were settled in a new three-bedroom apartment at 8471 Piney Branch Court, Silver Spring, Maryland, just outside Washington.

Hodding reported from Washington to the *DD-T* on the movement led by A. Philip Randolph, head of the Brotherhood of Sleeping Car Porters, to organize a march on Washington to demand that discriminatory hiring practices in the defense industry and segregation in the military be ended. Hodding blamed the agitation on communists.[23] (The charge was false. Randolph limited participation in the march to blacks, and that effectively eliminated communists.) Threats of the march led President Roosevelt to issue an executive order banning discrimination in hiring for defense work and establishing the Fair Employment Practices Committee. The appointment of Mark Ethridge, a lukewarm liberal editor from Louisville, to head the committee, reassured Southerners that it posed no danger to segregation. At its first hearing, held in Birmingham, Ethridge charged that black leaders who demanded all or nothing were misleading their people and "playing into the hands of white demagogues." He declared that the blacks must recognize that "there is no power in the world—not even in all the mechanized armies of the earth, Allied and Axis— which could now force the Southern white people to the abandonment of the principle of social segregation."[24]

Farrar & Rinehart had asked Hodding if he would collaborate with Colonel Ernest Dupuy of New Orleans on a book about civil defense. Hodding accepted. He and Dupuy would split royalties fifty-fifty, but Hodding was to write thirteen chapters, sixty percent of the work. Chapter topics included propaganda, priorities in conservation, potential means of invasion, women in defense, shelter construction, firefighting, air-raid warning organization, public health, saboteurs, and morale. As soon as she arrived in Washington, Betty began research on the book in the Library of Congress and through interviews with government officials.

She and Hodding discussed writing a novel set in Louisiana and found Farrar & Rinehart receptive to the idea. They also planned to write a book about Betty's mother, to be called "Mother Is a Lady." Betty wrote her mother: "We want to make it the full picture of you and your activities . . . treated with reverential irreverence. The general plan being to balance energy against New Orleans. Please let us have as much good stuff as you can for the original chapters. Eventually, we'll have to see the scrapbooks, do a lot of interviewing, etc. If you're cooperative, we'll split with you, so rush us the material for the first two chapters."[25] Later she asked Elizabeth Werlein to send diaries, scrapbooks, pictures.[26] Publisher John Farrar thought it might be a best-seller.

The state of Hodding's right eye, now virtually useless, made writing hard for him. As an outpatient at Walter Reed hospital, he had tests for tuberculosis, venereal disease, sinus trouble, and tooth infection as doctors tried to determine what had caused a scar patch on the retina. "We think it was a result of having a branch stuck in his eye [on night maneuvers] at Camp Blanding," Betty wrote her mother.[27] Hodding recalled that a palmetto frond had pierced his eye while he was on the maneuvers during which he got the perirectal abscess, and while he was hospitalized for that, doctors had neglected his eye. Hodding's medical records do not mention the palmetto frond accident, or any accident, but they do state that the condition was acquired in the line of duty. The doctors at Walter Reed felt that the condition in his right eye, now diagnosed as "choroidoretinitis, chronic, non-suppurative," might spread to the left and that he should retire from the military.

In October 1941, Hodding decided to resign and return to Greenville. Don Wetherbee had left in September, abandoning the newspaper business for medical school. Bert Hyde had taken over as acting editor. John Carter was clearly incapable of handling the business side. When the Japanese bombed Pearl Harbor on December 7, Hodding was an inpatient at Walter Reed. The attack made him decide to stay in uniform. "When we have whipped our enemies, I will come home," he wrote in the *DD-T*, "and not before, unless the army decides otherwise."[28] The atmosphere in Washington changed abruptly—no lights burned in the Capitol at night, and bayoneted guards stood outside War Department buildings. Eager to convince the Army that he was fit for service, Hodding memorized the eye charts. He returned to intelligence and was finally promoted to first lieutenant. He was startled to read the cables in the War Department map room and see what really had happened at Pearl Harbor; newspapers had headlined the lightness of United States losses.[29] Soon he was promoted to captain and transferred to another branch of intelligence to write intelligence manuals. Until he was given two assistants, he had to "work so hard that it interfered seriously with the completion of the Rivers of America book."[30]

Betty bought new clothes and, since their payments on notes at the bank were more than Hodding's salary, set out to find a job. Through Archibald MacLeish she got a position with the Office of Facts and Figures. She started work on January 15, 1942, at $3,200 a year, and was assigned to do research for Malcolm Cowley, who was writing a booklet on the Four Freedoms. Her first task was to read Pope Pius XI's encyclical *Quadragesimo anno* to see if there was anything in it relevant to the Four Freedoms.

"It's really the propaganda branch," she wrote her mother about her employer. "We write booklets, bulletins, and news releases, all sorts of things, on the war aims, on postwar America, on ways of building morale." It was wonderful, she said, that Archie MacLeish was in charge; he was resolved to make the American people hate not the Japanese people, but what the Japanese warlords were doing. After the Office of Facts and Figures became the Office of War Information, Elmer Davis was in charge. At various times, Betty worked with Philip Wylie, Reinhold Niebuhr, Samuel Lubbell, Charles Poore, McGeorge Bundy ("a pink-cheeked Yale graduate"), Arthur Schlesinger, Jr., Adrienne Koch, and Christian Herter. She carpooled with Robert P. Tristram Coffin. She was crazy about her work, and enjoyed the camaraderie of going with coworkers to lunch every day at the Neptune, where they had a table reserved.[31]

After she took Hodding to an office party, he said he thought the writers looked like a brainy crowd with very pinkish leanings; he told her she was "Alice among the Brain Trust." Betty said that in his column Westbrook Pegler picked at Malcolm Cowley, a former communist, but that "if we gave him Cowley, there'd be no one else he could point to as being a big naughty Red."[32] Cowley later resigned, to "take the heat off" the agency.

Hodding needed to go back to Greenville to talk to the directors of the *DD-T*, and Will Percy's death on January 21, 1942, gave him the chance to ask for leave. In Greenville he faced the directors, who were still upset over his having gained control of the stock. He explained again that he had wanted control to prevent Will from ever being able to tell him that he would have to take his chances on coming back; that was the only thing he and Will had ever quarreled about. The meeting went very smoothly.[33] Nevertheless, the paper cut Hodding's salary in half, and he had the distinct impression that Billy Wynn was going to try to fire some of the staff, possibly John Carter.[34]

While Hodding was in Greenville, the editor of the black newspaper asked him why the War Department never sent positive news about blacks in the military. The only news about blacks from Associated Press, he said, involved race troubles. When Hodding returned to Washington, he discussed this with several generals and was unofficially put in charge of releasing good publicity to the black press. The colonel who organized the first black division in the Army asked Hodding if he would like to be public relations officer for the division. Hodding refused.

The racial situation in the country was very much on the minds of both Carters. Betty told her mother about going dancing with another couple. "He was terribly provincial," Betty wrote. "We were talking about the Negro problem and he said, 'Well, after all, the Bible said they should be hewers of wood.'"[35] Thoughtful young southern white people in Washington discussed the race problem a great deal. The Carters were seeing a wide range of people, including Clifford and Virginia Durr from Alabama. Durr was a young lawyer who had just joined the Federal Communications Commission. Because of their activities in the Southern Conference for Human Welfare and in behalf of black voting rights, the Durrs were destined to be completely ostracized by the white community when they returned to Montgomery.

Another new friend for the Carters was Milton Starr of Nashville, a former member of the Fugitives, a group of poets who had gathered together at Vanderbilt University in the twenties. He had later made a great deal of money from a chain of black movie theaters in the South, and was, Betty told her mother, "genuinely interested in doing something for the Negroes—within the limits of what is practical and would not offend Southerners." Starr, who was working as a dollar-a-year man with the Office of War Information, in race relations, was very quiet, she said, and "[thought] straight."[36] Through Starr the Carters befriended Tom Mabry, a young writer also from Nashville, who had been dropped from local society, according to Starr, because of his liberal ideas about race.

Betty wrote her mother that the Nazis were using all sorts of propaganda to whip up conflict between the races. "Something will have to be done—but what? It should probably be a liberalization of the entire white population's attitude and an increase in white tolerance. How you're going to get it, I don't know. In the meantime the Negro press is becoming more inflammatory—in great part, unfortunately, simply presenting the truth about discrimination. We can't tell these people to fight for democracy. They don't know, from experience, what that means."[37]

In her letters to her mother, Betty returned often to the subject of the "Negro problem," which, she said, "interests me more and more. It is so insoluble except by the obvious solution [integration] which is so unacceptable."[38] On one occasion she told her mother that the FBI had reported it could find no trace of a single person belonging to an "Eleanor Club."[39] (The rumors about Eleanor Clubs—named for FDR's wife—were widespread and tenacious; Southerners claimed that their black servants were organizing such clubs, whose purpose was to overthrow the established social order.)

The civil defense book Hodding was writing with Colonel Dupuy came out, and Hodding struggled to finish the last chapters of the Mississippi River book. At one point he became depressed and said he believed he would finish the book and then die. In late February 1942 he saw a doctor at Johns Hopkins Hospital, who told him the depression was caused by injections the Walter Reed doctors were giving him to keep the condition in his right eye from spreading to his left. The Johns Hopkins doctor cut the dose in half.

Lower Mississippi was published in the fall of 1942, to good reviews. While it is a history of the Mississippi valley from Hernando de Soto to William Alexander Percy, Hodding brought to it his genuine love for his native heath and his memories of boyhood visits to his grandmother's house in Vidalia, where a rowboat was tied to a chinaberry tree in the backyard, right on the river. He also brought the sensibility of his time: the Spanish, French, and English were justified in taking the land from the Indians. A very readable book, *Lower Mississippi* includes chapters on people and places—Davy Crockett, Andrew Jackson, surveyor Andrew Ellicott, Natchez—and some surprises, such as excerpts from the diary of an antebellum cotton planter in Feliciana and an account of a trip on a Mississippi pilot boat. Typical of the reviews was one by Horace Reynolds in *The New York Times Book Review*, which said that Carter was articulately sensitive to the beauty of the region, but was no exploiter of the southern tradition. "A man of thought and conscience, he is troubled by the social problems of a section to the intensity of whose plight the phenomenon of Huey Long is an index."[40] *Lower Mississippi* more than paid back the advance, and pleased Farrar & Rinehart no end.

With this success, Hodding immediately started on a novel. Betty thought it was the finest realism she had ever read, even better than Hemingway. The novel would be timely, she told her mother, because it would demonstrate how "fascism can take hold in a small Southern town" and show "weaknesses that must be solved by democracy before we can feel that America has cleaned up its own doorstep."[41]

Meanwhile in Greenville, Rodney Deffenbaugh, the *DD-T*'s advertising manager, was leaving for another paper, and John Gibson, the circulation manager, was going to war. The stockholders, led by Billy Wynn, were in revolt. Betty and Hodding were afraid they would stop sending Hodding any money at all.[42] Finally, in February 1942, a letter arrived from Billy Wynn summarizing the situation at the paper.

The *Delta Democrat-Times* had been in operation about three and a half years, since September 1, 1938. Its circulation had grown from about 2,000 to 6,000, and its advertising rates had increased considerably. It lost money the first and second years but made a profit of

$5,000 the third year. (If the paper had paid a dividend on its pre-ferred stock of approximately $1,800 a year, it would have been in the red.) The paper could not expand its circulation much beyond the present level because the press and the other mechanical equipment could not handle it. The amount charged for depreciation had not been saved and thus there was no reserve for contingencies, to take care of breakdowns, or to buy new equipment. "The paper must either go forward or backward. It will not stand still," Wynn wrote.[43]

John Carter was not competent to manage the business side and the editorial side, Wynn continued, and Hodding could not run the editorial side from a distance. The directors had decided that the paper could not justify paying Hodding a salary. The sum, more than $5,000, that he had drawn in the past two years could have paid the dividend on the preferred stock for three years. The directors wanted to be frank with Hodding, Wynn said. "This paper was organized to back you as the editor. You have not been here for two years and only Hitler, possibly, can tell when you will return." Therefore the directors thought it would be wise to sell the paper so Hodding could protect his investment as well as theirs. If Hodding was unwilling to do that, he might prefer to purchase the balance of the stock, since he claimed "to have procured already a majority control."

Betty wrote her mother to sell $2,500 worth of Werlein Music Company stock for her so she could pay off a bank note and get rid of a $100 monthly payment. Hodding, she said, was working hard at the office in the daytime and on the book at night. He was afraid that his good eye was going bad, too, and he would not want to live if that happened. If she went back to Greenville, she wrote, and John Carter went into the army, she would have to run the paper with no Don Wetherbee, no John, no Rodney Deffenbaugh, and no Will Percy to fall back on.[44] Betty was a strong, talented woman, but she did not want to head a corporation or win power for herself. She was Mrs. Hodding Carter and regarded it as her calling to provide a support system for her husband.

Hodding did not see how he could buy out the other stockholders, and he felt under enormous pressure to do something about the paper, especially because he expected to go overseas soon to start the Middle Eastern edition of the service magazine *Yank*. At what seemed a fortuitous moment, he met Captain Donald Reynolds, who owned newspapers in Muskogee, Oklahoma, and Fort Smith, Arkansas. Reynolds said he had no interest in the editorial side of newspapers but was looking for an editorial partner so he could expand his holdings. After he heard something about Hodding's difficulties in Greenville, he offered to buy half of the *DD-T*. "It seemed like a godsend," Hodding said later.[45]

Betty, who went with Hodding to a party at the Reynoldses' thought the captain was "not very attractive looking—rather on the not-too-porcine side." She liked his wife and their "charming old house in Alexandria" and the supper they served—smoked turkey and Virginia ham. The Carters had the Reynoldses to breakfast the next morning—waffles and fried chicken—before they went to a Washington Redskins game.[46] Hodding and Reynolds agreed, verbally, that after the war they would own a whole chain of newspapers together, Reynolds running the business side, Hodding the editorial. They signed a contract stating that Reynolds would buy fifty percent of the *DD-T* stock outright, five percent from Hodding, forty-five from the Greenville group. Reynolds would hold another one percent in escrow, and thus have control, until Hodding could acquire in his own name the stock held by the group of his friends and relatives. The deadline for the acquisition was March 1, 1945. If Hodding did not personally own his group's stock by that time, the one percent in escrow would revert irrevocably to Reynolds. If Hodding did own the stock, that one percent would revert to him, and he and Reynolds would be equal partners. When Hodding acquired his fifty percent outright, a buy-sell clause would go into effect, the person to whom the offer was made having first choice of selling or buying at the stated figure. The purchaser would have ninety days to pay. When and if one partner sold to the other, the selling partner would also be paid, in addition to the selling price, any money the corporation owed him. "I ought to have read our contract more carefully," Hodding would say ruefully later.[47]

The Greenville stockholders were delighted with this arrangement, especially LeRoy Percy, who was trying to settle Will Percy's estate and wanted to retrieve the $20,000 worth of United States Steel stock Percy had put up as collateral for the Smith notes.

Hodding had a hard time finding out exactly how many shares of stock were outstanding. His brother sent him a penciled scrawl, undated, that said he thought there were 1,079 shares of common stock, only 523 of them Carter shares. If Hodding could get hold of the twenty shares that Billy Bell, an old friend from New Orleans, owned, that would give him a majority,—if, that is, Rodney Deffenbaugh remained on his side. John pointed out there was a difference of twenty-three shares between what he had found and what Hodding had told him in a telephone call. But the agreement went through.

Reynolds immediately sent his agent, A. R. Dillard, to Greenville to reorganize the paper. Reynolds and Dillard arranged for John Carter to spend a week in Fort Smith, observing the operation there. "They really have a smooth working organization," John reported to Betty in April 1943. "Money and business first, then eddy policy. This guy Dillard . . . is quite smart and very exacting. He never misses a thing. Louise [Eskrigge Smith, the society editor] has started calling him 'The Wizard of Oz.' . . . Everyone seems a little afraid of him including me. . . . We have fished together and gotten tight together but he never seems to want to stop working."

Dillard spent money on the paper, buying $1,200 worth of new type and a new feature service. He said he would plow back into the paper all profits for the next two years. He changed the bookkeeping system, introducing a new kind of ledger, "the kind that Davis Drug uses," John explained. "Can't buy a thing without a requisition and purchase order, a new form for every department." Dillard added a classified advertising department with a young woman soliciting ads over the phone and on the street. Advertising rates had gone up on January 1, 1943 ("before we ever heard of Reynolds practically"), and

Dillard raised them again. He raised circulation rates as well, "and the strange thing is," said John Carter, "we have lost very few customers." An additional thousand dollars a month came in from circulation.

But John had some reservations. "I am a little apprehensive about his intentions for me and I cannot quite figure him out in this respect. I used to have a few daily duties such as making the daily advertising schedule, working some on the circulation books and a few other little odds and ends. Well all this has been put on either Mrs. A [Electra Atcher] or the advertising department. I really have very little to do except look important, which I surely do not feel. I really believe if it were not for the fact that I am Hodding's brother and he doesn't know exactly how far he can go with me, he would let me go."[48]

John complained that some of the staff worked a lot harder for Dillard than they ever had for him. He felt betrayed by someone at the paper when Dillard called him from Fort Smith one day and he wasn't there. The advertising manager heard Dillard tell the long-distance operator to try the Elks Club or John's home. This was "at ten in the morning. I didn't go to the Elks Club the whole time he was here and I am sure he had no way of knowing that I ever went there at all unless someone in the office told him. I don't know how much longer I will be able to take it, even though I don't get fired." John warned Betty that Reynolds could "get this paper in a couple of years for practically nothing." He had seen Hodding do "some swell pieces of finance but I cannot believe he could raise the twenty-one thousand that Reynolds has put into the paper plus the sale price of the paper." Reynolds could offer almost anything for the paper and Hodding would have to sell. John said that Reynolds retained control of the paper until Hodding could show ownership or power of attorney of all outstanding stock.

There was a problem with the power of attorney for Tante Marguerite's stock, since she could not locate the certificates. Dillard would not release the money for the stock until the documents were returned or a bond made for the stock. It took Betty months to find an agency that would provide the bond. The Carters could write no more "no par" stock, John pointed out, until they got all the old stock in. If any stockholders worried, Betty should tell them the old stock was as good as the new would be.[49]

Two months after relating all this to his sister-in-law, John informed Hodding he was an ex-newspaperman. He hadn't been fired, he said, but he might as well have been. He was told he could leave or become a job printing salesman, working entirely on commission. He started to "give it a whirl," but realized the *DD-T* did not have the equipment to produce enough work for him to make a decent living. About seventy-five percent of losing out, he admitted, was his fault; the other twenty-five percent was bad luck or having a knife stuck in his back. He did not know what he would do now—defense work or the service, he supposed. "I guess I should have broken away from you a long time ago but it was so much fun as well as comforting to have you to depend on. It is really make or break now."[50]

Hodding knew John as well as anybody, he told Betty, but he would still rather be associated with him than anybody else. He did not want to see his brother adrift. When the war was over, John should be associated with him on some newspaper or other.[51]

Captain Hodding Carter went overseas in February 1943 to start the Middle Eastern edition of *Yank*. Before leaving, he wrote a letter to Betty explaining why, loving her as he did, he seemed to go "so readily and gladly."

> Some of us have a compulsion to seek out the evil that menaces us, and to try to come to close grips with it. It brought me into the army. The Washington inertia that hides men from this evil, and perhaps hides this evil from men, has kept me unhappy. Now, I am going toward it, to attempt in my small way to help end its menace, so that the world of you and my boys and the people I love will be surer and brighter.

Hodding looked forward to a "long and annoying life, in which I can tire you and all my friends with impossible tales." He and Betty would both learn from the separation; nothing could really keep them apart.[53]

Hodding flew to Cairo by way of Miami, Trinidad, Brazil, and Accra, where he had two days of swimming in the surf and riding in native dugouts; he saw the pyramids and the sphinx as he flew into Cairo. He traveled with Lieutenant Colonel Jack Stanley, a West Point graduate who had written books for boys and was in Special Services, which oversaw *Yank* and other educational and recreational enterprises for the Army. In Cairo, Stanley stayed at Shepheard's Hotel, but Hodding said he wasn't going to live in any boring hotel and got himself a houseboat on the Nile, complete with servants.[53] "Never have I seen such poverty and filth and such a contrast between the present and the past," he wrote Betty. "America is a golden dream here." He expected to go to Iran, Iraq, and Turkey on business. There was much more meat, butter, bacon, and fruit than in Washington. He was to edit the weekly *Middle East News*, which he found "high schoolish," for a month while he prepared to publish *Yank*. Then the Army hoped to turn the *News* into a four-page daily tabloid. *Yank* would be the Sunday magazine supplement. He would have Slim Aarons, a photographer, and Burgess Scott, a legendary reporter, in the field. He needed rewrite, circulation, and makeup men. He would probably have to fashion them out of company cooks, but, as he told Betty, "you and I have done that before."[54]

Hodding could not find a plant in Cairo or Tel Aviv that could print *Yank*. Finally, in the Arab city of Jaffa, Hodding and a colleague, Major Ross Shattuck, hired Arab typesetters who knew no English but could set type. They found a Cockney printer and hired him as foreman. He in turn found a German-made press that had been used to print orange wrappers in prewar days; it was owned by three brothers in fezzes, and it needed some complicated overhauling. American Army engineers said they could make the needed parts if someone designed them. Shattuck found a German-Jewish refugee, a master printer, in Tel Aviv. Because of the strained relations between Arabs and Jews in Palestine, Hodding and Shattuck dressed the printer in an American soldier's uniform and smuggled him into the Jaffa plant and out again. The first day they tried the press, everything—the printer's designs, the parts, and the press—worked. "The colonel thinks I am a miracle man, but it was just another Courier and Delta Star," Hodding told Betty.[55] After that he did not write much about his work, except to mention an editorial for *Yank* about a United Mine Workers' coal strike that ended: "Speaking for the American soldier, John L. Lewis, damn your coal black soul." The editorial was broadcast to the United States and picked up by *Time*.

Hodding ran into a British officer named Archie Chisholm, a friend of his Beit cousins with whom he had played tennis sixteen years before at Tewin Water, his aunt's country home in England. He had dinner at a French mess, which reminded him of New Orleans—red wine, lentils flavored with garlic, fluffy omelets, and caramel pudding like that served at Arnaud's. He worried about the *DD-T*, and asked Betty in every letter for news. By July he was working on his novel again, telling Betty that "it can be the white side of Native Son with Farley Bennett as the prototype."[56]

Hodding met Aziza Hassanein, a friend of Joyce Thompson, who worked on *The Stars and Stripes*. He described Hassanein to Betty as "native, divorced, attractive, Moslem," speaking no English but good French, German, and some Italian, besides Arabic. She lived in a beautiful house, like a California villa, with tremendous gardens. He was going there for dinner, but he told Betty, "Don't get jealous."[57] A little later he wrote her that he had bought her a scarab; "I couldn't find a real one until Aziza took me to the right place."[58] He mentioned Hassanein in subsequent letters that also told how brown he was, "as dark as a quadroon," and how he had lost weight.[59] Hassanein wrote to him lovingly after he left, describing how eagerly she awaited his return.[60] Through her and Joyce Thompson and her husband, who all lived in the Cairo suburb of Maadi, he met Egyptians and began to acquire new insights into race. The British attitude toward colonials and "natives" horrified him, and he saw such dis-

crimination as destructive to the people in power as well as to those
who were subjugated.

Betty, in the meantime, was on a social whirl in Washington. She
often stayed in town after work to "play." One man compared her
with Marlene Dietrich; Adlai Stevenson, executive assistant to the
secretary of the Navy, with whom she went in line of duty to a ship
launching in Baltimore, said that the two most fascinating women
in Washington were Clare Boothe Luce and Betty Carter. Betty had
several dates with writer Julian Street, Jr., went to a party at the
house of Arthur Schlesinger, Jr., and to another where she saw the
Roark Bradfords and the Lyle Saxons. She and two colleagues gave
a cocktail party in honor of Christian Herter. (It cost them twenty
dollars apiece.) She worked on the celebration of Norwegian Day and
did such a good job that she was released to be secretary of the United
Nations planning committee. "That means I'll be in the thick of it,"
she wrote to Hodding with great pleasure.[61] She wrote her mother
that Hodding had said she was living up to what Elizabeth Wertein
had wanted for her. "And I think so, too," Betty agreed.[62]

Letters about money, the newspaper stock, and the debt flitted
back and forth across the Atlantic. In August 1943, Hodding urged
Betty to "pay off the stock loan as quickly as possible and let the rest
ride. It would give us all that collateral as a damn good nest egg and
release the company stock for any use we wanted to make of it. And
it would also make the monthly payments less difficult, as they could
probably be reduced. What I want to do is have about $25,000 in cash
in sight for buying out Reynolds if he wants to buy or sell in a year and
a half; and I think I've got a way to do it. More financial miracles."[63]
Hodding had seen issues of the *DD-T* and thought it looked good,
but he had not had a financial report. He asked Betty to have A. R.
Dillard send him one.

8. 1943–1945

"Just a Newspaperman Pretending to Be an Author"

Hodding came home from the Middle East in the fall of 1943, tan and slim, more handsome than ever, wearing shorts and bearing presents for Betty and the boys. "It seemed like the riches of the East that poured out before our eyes—long flowing robes, knives, and coins," recalled young Hodding years later.[1]

Jack Stanley, assigned to establish a propaganda branch of intelligence, asked Hodding if he knew anything about propaganda. Hodding replied that he had taken a course in it at Harvard in 1940, and Stanley signed him on. For thirteen months Hodding analyzed propaganda—and worked on his novel. He sent seven chapters, about 20,000 words, of the book, then called "Carvell City Incident," to his agent, Bernice Baumgarten at Brandt & Brandt, on November 19, 1943. She forwarded it to Stanley Rinehart, who wrote Hodding to go ahead on this "so terribly grim book" about the "race stresses in the South."[2] In fact, people at Farrar & Rinehart were quite excited about the novel. "This book is pure dynamite," read an anonymous reader's report. "God help him, he is writing an honest novel with vigor and dramatic insight that will alienate him from most of his Mississippi friends. If he were writing a purely biased *PM* type of thing, I should say to hell with it. If he were writing a defense of the noble Southerner and his troubles with the bad nigger I shouldn't

130

countenance it. But here is a man who knows both sides of a very serious question, who has guts enough to come out and try to write both sides." The book might even cause bloodshed, the same reader speculated.

Rinehart offered $250 on signing and $250 on publication. Hodding told Baumgarten that was all right, but he was more interested in an advertising clause, because *Lower Mississippi* had been handled badly, even in St. Louis, Memphis, Baton Rouge, and New Orleans, the cities where it should have sold well. Farrar & Rinehart agreed to spend no less than $2,500 on advertising.

While Hodding worked on the novel, he and Jack Stanley also wrote a scenario for a movie, a radio program, and a play, "Forever Ends the Dawn." They began work on another play that Hodding described to Baumgarten as being about "a predatory officer who has returned to the Pentagon from a soft overseas berth—Middle East, though not autobiographical—where the pickings were easy, to a wife whom he believes to be more domesticated than she is." It's somewhat bedroomy, takes place in four days and nights, in Washington and New York. Tentative title: A Goose for the Gander."[3] The "drama man" at Brandt & Brandt had a very poor opinion of these efforts.

When *Strange Fruit*, Lillian Smith's novel about miscegenation, appeared in 1944, Hodding worried that it would preempt the audience for his novel. (In Greenville, Louise Smith, now Louise Crump, devoted a column to *Strange Fruit*, denouncing the kind of Southerner who would write that sort of thing, and observing in closing that she preferred a carpetbagger to a renegade anytime.)[4] Hodding worried, too, about Stanley Rinehart's decision to delay publication until the spring of 1945. "A good part of the book would be dated by that time, i.e. the returning invalided soldier, the attitudes toward Mrs. [Roosevelt] and the administration," he wrote Baumgarten. "Further this Negro crisis will have become so explosive in the South in another year, I'm afraid, that the book will have more of a historical reporting flavor than a current or anticipatory note. . . . I suspect that there will also be several more race novels in the interval."[5] Convinced, Rinehart scheduled the book for the autumn of 1944.

Hodding technically went AWOL and slipped up to New York to confer with his editor, Philip Wylie. Wylie's suggestions for changes were few, and agreeable to Hodding. Nobody liked the title "Carvell City Incident." Hodding offered several—from "Go for a Gun" to "Cauldron Bubble"—and at the last minute settled on *The Winds of Fear*. He used the new title to make some points in his foreword: "If you have not lived in Carvell City, it is too easy to denounce its masters, forgetting that they are also the slaves of the fear which impels them. If you have lived too long in Carvell City, it is too easy to accept the inevitability of its ways." He went on to say that the hate and suspicion in Carvell City were neither peculiar to the region nor innate. "Nevertheless, within our country, it is principally through the South that the winds of fear are rushing today."

While he worked on the revisions, Hodding wrote some short shorts, one of which, "Election Bet," Baumgarten sold to *Liberty*. She refused to handle a story about a returning Japanese-American veteran because it was "too controversial." He wrote Baumgarten about a novel he had in mind that "concerns the investigation of a carpenter who has applied for a job with the government. . . . The story is told in a series of reports by a veteran civil service gumshoe who has investigated the carpenter. . . . His mother was talked about pretty much when he was born, the family left. . . . Interviews show that the carpenter is radical, a pacifist, has tied up with the village strumpet, practices medicine without a license, is suspected of patronizing the Black Market . . . has organized a group of crackpot followers, is an agent of a foreign power, and altogether very dangerous. The carpenter, in case you haven't guessed, is Jesus."[6] Baumgarten's reaction to this outline is not known.

Betty continued to flourish. In 1944 she left the Office of War Information to become a personal researcher for elder statesman Bernard Baruch. To find out the things Baruch wanted to know, she did not hesitate to call government officials at the highest level. "I'd call the

Secretary of the Army and say to his secretary, 'This is Betty Carter. I'm the confidential researcher for Mr. Baruch and there are certain things he needs to know and I would like to speak to the Secretary,'" Betty remembered. "And the Secretary's secretary would say, 'How soon can you get here, Mrs. Carter?'"[7]

"We used to be impressed with them both during the war in Washington," recalled Georgina Stanley, Jack's wife. "We used to wonder which of them would be the most famous after the war."[8] When Betty was asked to open a United States Information Agency office in Australia she turned it down because of her family, but she enjoyed the challenge of her work in Washington, the sensation of growing, and the secure feeling that she was holding her own on a big stage. Yet she was still very much Mrs. Hodding Carter. Once when she was in New York researching the future of air transportation for Baruch, Hodding called from Silver Spring. The apartment was infested with fleas, he said, and if she intended ever to come home, she must come home immediately. Betty came home.

The Winds of Fear appeared in the fall of 1944, resplendent in a book jacket designed by Honka Karasz in which a strong diagonal separated the dark "Negro quarters" from the sunlit white-columned "big house." The story takes place in Carvell City, a fictional town of 4,000, loosely based on Hammond. (Hodding said later that the all-night restaurant in the book was the beanery at the Illinois Central Railroad station in Hammond.) A drunk black soldier passing through Carvell City on a bus is arrested for demanding his right to a seat. Trying to escape, he kills the town marshal, and then is killed himself. The new town marshal is Cancy Dodd, modeled on a law enforcement officer in Hammond, the worst kind of redneck bigot. Dodd fans the flames of racial hatred in Carvell City and ultimately murders in the most brutal way Catfoot Grimes, a young "blue gum nigger" who is rather well regarded in town. (Dodd and Catfoot are lifted from Hodding's narrative poem *The Ballad of Catfoot Grimes*, which he had written years earlier. It is interesting to note that in the poem

Hodding is frankly racist, accepting southern traditions of segregation and subjugation as facts of life. In the novel, his ideas on racial justice have changed, if not 180 degrees, then at least ninety.) The whites in town at last begin to move against Dodd. Among the leaders of the revolt are Kirk Mabry, editor of the town's newspaper, and Alan, his son, a wounded veteran just home from New Guinea. A reporter from *PM* adds to the tension. Details of segregated life—welding school only one day a week for blacks, the public libraries closed entirely to them—fill in the background. Themes that Hodding would sound over and over in his life were present in this book: Northerners cannot solve the South's problems, nor can blacks alone. Southern whites must clean their own house. Minor themes that he would repeat in his journalism are also present. The newspaper editor, for instance, says that "they lynch up north and a damn sight more people than we do. Only they call them race riots." There is very little artistry in the book, and no sense of Hodding's old poetic yearnings; it is journalistic in the worst sense, and didactic, but its energy and sense of urgency make it gripping. It is remarkable as a very early attempt by a white writer to come to terms with the problems of the segregated South.

The Winds of Fear became a best-seller. Farrar & Rinehart spent more than the promised $2,500 on promotion, placing advertisements in newspapers in New York, Boston, Philadelphia, Chicago, San Francisco, and Washington, D.C., and in *The New Republic*, *Harper's*, *The Atlantic Monthly*, and *The Nation*. One advertisement run in December 1944 featured quotations from reviews by Richard Wright in the New York *Herald Tribune*, Roy Wilkins in the Louisville *Courier-Journal*, Adam Clayton Powell, Jr., in the Chicago *News*, Julia Peterkin in the Birmingham *News*, and Roy Garvin in the Washington *Afro-American*. It is too bad that this was before the days of the author's tour and television—Hodding would have been an immense success with audiences.

Although Ernie Pyle's *Brave Men* beat it out for a Book-of-the-Month Club selection, the BoMC newsletter recommended *Winds of Fear* ahead of *Forever Amber* by Kathleen Winsor, *Try and Stop Me* by Bennett Cerf, and *Tragic Ground* by Erskine Caldwell. The book won the Southern Authors Award for 1944, with Josephus Daniels's *The Wilson Era* and Katherine Anne Porter's *The Leaning Tower* runner-ups.

Hodding's book received excellent reviews. The New York *Herald Tribune* called it a "persuasive, swift-moving Southern novel with banners flying in a big crusade." C. V. Terry in *The New York Times Book Review* saw it as "an attempt to anatomize the groping toward fascism . . . endemic in the small towns of the South" and found Hodding's viewpoint "balanced and almost clinical in its detachment." While *Winds of Fear* was more polemic than novel, it showed how white hatred and fear of blacks, together with boredom, poverty, and rank pride, had poisoned the South. Bucklin Moon in *Book Week* said it was "one of the clearest pictures of the mounting racial tension in the South thus far to appear."[9] The *New Yorker* reviewer summed it up very well indeed, as "intelligent . . . and without an ounce of sentimentality"; while it was not much of a novel, it was "an interesting and useful exploitation of a new phase of an old problem."[10] A review in a British newspaper termed it "unaffectedly powerful," with "complete imaginative conviction"; not many novels about discrimination in the South had been "quite so persuasive. . . . or . . . left a stronger impression of thoughtful and fair-minded good sense. Parts of the novel, one should perhaps add, are strong meat, but nowhere does one suspect Mr. Carter of sensationalism."[11] Burton Rascoe, who wrote a book column, and Samuel Hopkins Adams, a novelist and muckraking journalist, both said it was a much better book than *Strange Fruit*.

Almost the only negative review, by Ben Burns in the Chicago *Defender*, a black newspaper, struck a tone that would be repeated often in the next few years by blacks who felt Hodding did not go far enough. "Louisiana-born Hodding Carter is one of those super-liberal dixie fence-sitters on the race issue. Carter tries to walk the literary tight rope in 'The Winds of Fear' and present the view of the middle-of-the-roaders like John Temple Graves and David Cohn. The results are a sorry hodge-podge of confusion that will . . . certainly leave a bad taste for even the Deep South's so-called liberals."[12]

Hodding's agent tried to sell *Winds of Fear* to the movies. Twentieth Century–Fox declined by saying: "This is a horrifying novel. The characterizations are excellent and the story tense and dramatic, and it might be a public service to film such a story in the interests of tolerance and race equality, but I am afraid Mr. Hays would definitely say thumbs down." Baumgarten did sell foreign rights, however—in Great Britain, Holland, Italy, Norway, and Sweden.

Betty's mother read the book and said, "It's infuriating, but it's true and I couldn't put it down."[13] When Farrar & Rinehart sent out flyers announcing the book's publication and calling it "a fierce, compassionate first novel about the Negro problem," Mrs. Werlein wrote hastily to Hodding that "the word compassionate was a mistake for down here. At least nine people told me they didn't want to read a book that was *compassionate* about the Negro—the people who needed compassion were the whites who suffered from the negroes' impertinence, laziness, dishonesty, and arrogance." She was, however, delighted that the book was doing well, and she took a flyer to New Orleans bookstores, as Hodding had asked her to do.[14]

Soon after *Winds of Fear* came out, Jack Stanley sought his advice on where he and his wife might go for a vacation. Hodding sent them to Camden, Maine; his cousin Hamilton Hall, he said, would look after them. The Stanleys went for a week and on their third day bought a house. Grande dame Mary Curtis Bok Zimbalist was selling off some of the many houses she owned in Camden and Rockport, and she interviewed prospective purchasers carefully. The Stanleys met her standards. Jack Stanley phoned Hodding to tell him there was another house, called the Boat Barn, that Hodding should buy for himself. Hodding applied for emergency leave and rushed to Maine for the first time in five years. The Boat Barn was 135 years old and furnished with antiques. A big studio-barn was attached to the green-shuttered house, which sat in the midst of a green lawn and an orchard. Mrs. Zimbalist's terms were generous, and Hodding bought the house. It would drain the Carters' financial resources, but it gave Hodding a wonderful feeling of security.

Hodding applied for a post-service grant from the John Simon

Guggenheim Foundation to write a historical novel. He intended to go to Maine, if he got out of the Army in May, and finish the "flood book," a novel about politics and a threatened Mississippi River flood. "Then I don't know," he wrote Bernice Baumgarten. "Maybe Greenville, and the paper, with writing as the sideline; maybe Maine and nothing but writing and lobstering for a year or so."[15]

By November he was working on the flood novel, and he wrote to Baumgarten that the reviews of *Winds of Fear* had been enormously helpful. "As you know what little writing I've done has been done pretty much by ear and with no knowledge of techniques or anything. A number of the reviews, in pointing out good points and weaknesses, have made me curious about the whys, with the result that I think that I have a better idea about how to do a book."[16] The first reaction in the South had made him so mad that he decided to return to the paper and "spend most of my time thumbing my editorial nose." But as he realized that people and reviewers in the South actually liked the book, he no longer felt that he *had* to go back. "That's why this Maine idea seems attractive. I'd like to try it. Financially, I could chance it for several years, anyway, and if I flop as a fulltime writer I could go back to editing."

A little later, he decided to become a part-time writer for a while. "I can either sell out to my partner for about sixty thousand or buy the newspaper in at that and I think I can swing the purchase. Being full owner, I can hang around as little or as long as I please, after the war; so if things work out that way we'll spend four or five months in Maine, writing books and potting lobsters and the rest of the time in Mississippi championing civic virtue and fighting for better garden shows each year."[17]

Finally Hodding got busy and tried to nail down his control of fifty percent of the stock in the newspaper. (He had forty-nine percent, Donald Reynolds fifty, with one percent in escrow.) In spite of his many requests he had not received financial reports on the paper, and he was uneasy. He asked Holland Felts, a Greenville attorney, to rep-resent him. A. R. Dillard, Reynolds's manager, wrote Hodding that he was very glad Hodding had given Felts power of attorney: "Some one taking an active part in the interest of the *minority group* [italics added] will be most helpful."[18] Financially, the paper seemed to be doing well, Dillard said, and he was paying off the Smiths ahead of schedule. Still, Hodding did not like the fact that so many of his employees, including John Carter, shop foreman Ted Lovell, and Rodney Deffenbaugh, had left in anger or been fired. Now Electra Atcher, the bookkeeper who had started out with them on the old *Delta Star*, was gone. Reynolds himself wrote Hodding from London that he had insisted she be fired. "She was inefficient and you know that"; Hodding should not pay attention to "old wives' tales" that might be circulating.[19] Acting editor Bert Hyde was next. He had written an editorial warning that since Greenville now had air service to Memphis and New Orleans, its merchants would have to offer competitive prices and services.[20] Some merchants objected and called a meeting so Hyde could "explain how he knew so much." G. D. Guilkey, the advertising and business manager brought in by Reynolds and Dillard, who spent most of his time in Arkansas and Oklahoma, ordered Hyde to apologize. He refused. Dillard and Guilkey told him to take expense money and go to New Orleans, so he would not be available for the meeting. Again he refused. Gervys Lusk, the stockbroker, got up at the meeting and told the merchants that trying to bring pressure on a newspaper was wrong. Then Guilkey arrived and apologized for the editorial. Dillard sent a telegram, also apologizing. Hyde, in a fury, left for New Orleans, where he found a higher-paying job with the *States*.

Hodding was optimistic as he set about trying to get proxies for the stock his friends and relatives owned. Then he found out that proxies would not be sufficient. He had to own the stock outright, his lawyer said, or face the prospect that on March 1, 1945, Reynolds would say the proxies weren't worth a damn and the one percent in escrow would revert to him; Hodding's group would become "perpetual minority stockholders."[21] The proxies and their form had been

Reynolds's idea, Hodding told his brother-in-law Don Smith, and he was very suspicious now. "I hope Reynolds isn't trying to pull a fast one, as I'd hate to be disappointed in him," he wrote his father. "We're very good friends, but he's first of all a hard businessman, so I'm not taking any chances."[22]

On June 13, 1944, Hodding stayed home from work at the Pentagon—he had a dreadful case of poison ivy—and sat down and wrote many letters, one to each of "his" stockholders, to explain the situation. "It seems that I have to buy $14,000 worth of stock. I don't have the money to do it outright," he admitted to old Army buddy Bruce Manning, to Billy Bell's mother, to Dave Cohn, to his own father and his aunts in England, to Don Smith and Betty's brother, Philip, and to Joe Darlington. "I am wondering if you would sell me your stock on a time payment plan, with the privilege, of course, to buy it back if you want to as soon as I acquire the entire paper which I hope to do." He wanted to pay for the stock in four annual installments, unless *Winds of Fear* "does better than I think it will. . . . I may be a fool to hang on to the paper this way, but I know it's a good thing in the long run. We've paid off $60,000 of the $120,000 we paid for the opposition, but that hasn't helped the stockholders, including myself, in respect to dividends. But it's a good long shot, and something I can go back to after I get out. I want to go back, or to have the thing there for me to go back to, whether I click as a writer or not." He described the prospect of minority ownership as a "nightmare."

A buy-or-sell clause is tricky. When one person makes an offer, his partner may either accept the offer or buy him out at the price he has offered. If the offer is too low, the partner may promptly buy out the one who made the offer. If the offer is high, it is difficult for the second person to buy out the offering party. But if the offer is too high, it may give the seller a bonanza. Hodding wanted to delay a showdown and decided to try for all of the stock, except one certificate belonging to Betty, or someone in his immediate family, well before the deadline. "I will hold that one certificate out," he wrote to Holland Felts in Greenville, "as I do not want the buy or sell clause invoked until the last possible minute—as the longer I have, the more money I can save, raise, earn or steal."[23] Felts told Hodding that he thought his attitude was "extreme," and the situation "in the long run" would probably be all right; Hodding had, Felts admitted, "certainly entered into a most unusual contract with Reynolds."[24]

Both Mrs. Gamble, one of the original investors, and Dave Cohn had misplaced their stock certificates, and there was endless correspondence about posting bond for the missing stock. But things seemed to be working out: all of the investors rallied. Hodding offered his Aunt Marguerite in England $1,000, and a promissory note for the rest of the money, for her stock. She sold it to him for one dollar. Darlington turned over his stock immediately. Billy Bell's mother's lawyer wanted to hold the stock as collateral for the note Hodding signed, but Hodding pointed out he had to have physical possession of the stock certificates and proposed Werlein Music Company stock instead. The lawyer accepted it.

John Gibson, the young circulation manager, offered to help Hodding financially. He had saved part of his paycheck since he started working—at first two dollars out of fourteen—and now was able to offer several thousand dollars. He expected to be business manager when Hodding got the paper back, and he looked forward to the prospect. Gibson was incensed at the circumstances under which Bert Hyde had left.

"Really, it's pitiful," he wrote Hodding, "that the merchants can force the issue. . . . It's hell to swallow. The paper . . . has lost more prestige through their apologies than you built during your time. Bert's resignation is their victory. . . . I hope to see the day when you can stop such shilly-shallying. I hope to see the day when I personally can fire Guilkey. I hope to see the day when this newspaper can be run by a newspaperman for newspapermen and for the joy of living. When working is a pleasure and life is friendly. It's hell to be the only man left in the lions' den. . . . There's no need to discuss what this paper can do, and I can run it better than it is now. I know. I see it all over."[25]

When Hodding had the stock in hand, Holland Felts wrote him that it seemed too good to be true, but everything looked shipshape.[26] Indeed, it was too good to be true. When Reynolds returned from overseas in late October, Hodding discovered that it would be very hard to buy him out. A clause in their agreement stated that if the buy-or-sell clause went into effect, the buyer had to pay the seller everything the paper owed the seller. And Reynolds had made sure the paper would owe him money.

He had, for example, financed the purchase of a new press himself, instead of financing it through a bank. For months, the *Delta Democrat-Times* had rented the press from Reynolds, who now told Hodding that he would change the deal to a $9,000 loan from him to the paper and that this loan would fall due immediately when the buy-or-sell clause was invoked.

Reynolds also had had Dillard buy $5,500 worth of notes from the Smith family. These notes would not have been due until 1948 if the Smiths had kept them, but that money was now owed to Reynolds and would have to be repaid when the buy-or-sell clause went into effect. Reynolds had instructed Dillard to buy as many Smith notes as he could. This added at least $5,500, possibly more, to the cash Hodding would have to have on hand to buy Reynolds out.

In addition, when Hodding and Reynolds signed their agreement, the paper bought up the preferred stock with $34,000 that Reynolds lent the paper. The stock was canceled, and Reynolds received a second mortgage for $21,000. This had seemed a great idea at the time, because it improved the paper's financial structure by $13,000. The first installment on the mortgage was not due until 1949, but now Reynolds said that in case of a buy-or-sell move, the $21,000 mortgage would fall due immediately.

Hodding wrote to Holland Felts about this and said that he could raise the $30,000 to buy Reynolds's stock and perhaps the $35,500— or more—to pay him for the press and pay off the second mortgage and his notes from the Smiths. "But there has to be an end to it some time, and soon."[27]

Reynolds now said it would be foolish for Hodding to return to Greenville. He could get a young newspaperman just starting to put out the paper for thirty dollars a week, and Dillard could continue to come over from Fort Smith a few days a month. Reynolds also said he planned to buy a new building and possibly a radio station, further adding to the paper's indebtedness to him. "He intends to make it impossible for me to buy him out at any cost," Hodding told Felts. "I want to acquire my 50 percent of the stock immediately even though it means that he may call on me to buy or sell the next day. Under our contract, I will have three months to raise the necessary money. I think I can do it. The paper is in a very sound financial position; it is two years ahead on the Smith notes; and it must be said, moreover, that such investments by Reynolds as the second mortgage and the new press are good investments. However, I can't let the paper's indebtedness to Reynolds keep rising, through purchase of a building, a radio station, and for all I know, a department store and a concession at the next Olympics."

Hodding and Reynolds had discussed these matters, and amicably. "The odd thing is I like him personally," Hodding wrote Felts. "He isn't dishonest, but he is the sharpest, shrewdest person with whom I ever had dealings, and completely ruthless in a business sense." Reynolds even offered Hodding a "damn good job" in the chain of papers he intended to build.

In spite of the urgency in his letter to his lawyer, Hodding decided to wait until February to bring things to a head. He did not think Reynolds had any idea he would attempt to buy him out. Hodding was a good poker player, and he tried to make Reynolds believe he wasn't interested in returning to Greenville. The Maine house became a ploy to show Reynolds he had no intention of doing anything but writing books.

Hodding wrote to Joe Weinberg at his bank in Greenville about lending him the rest of the money he would need. Weinberg agreed eventually to a loan of $40,000, the most his bank could loan to one customer. (Weinberg told Felts he would like for someone else to run the business side of the paper, with Hodding serving only as editor.) "Mr. Weinberg was very complimentary of both you and Betty and said he would like to do anything he could, financially or otherwise, to have you return to Greenville to live," Felts reported to Hodding.[28]

Hodding felt he could raise the balance with what he had saved, what he could borrow from John Gibson, and what Betty could borrow on her Werlein stock. Then he learned to his horror that Donald Reynolds had bought $50,000 more of the notes due the Smiths. To regain control of his paper, Hodding would have to accumulate $113,000 in cash, if Reynolds's half-interest was considered worth $30,000. He gave up hope of getting the paper back. "We're thinking seriously of selling our paper," Hodding wrote the dean at Bowdoin, "and spending most of our time in Maine, with me writing and making Knox County safe for Democrats."[29] He was determined to put a good face on the situation.

Milton Starr, the dollar-a-year man at OWI who had become a friend of the Carters, and his wife, Zaro, asked Betty and Hodding to go with them to a party at the home of Allen Tate and Caroline Gordon. Starr had known Tate at Vanderbilt, and he warned the Carters that there would be nothing to drink but Jack Daniel's. (The Tates were famous for their wartime parties in Washington, at which, legend has it, each guest was served his or her own bottle of Jack Daniel's.) Betty and Hodding, who were as depressed as they had ever been, decided they might as well go. While they were at the Tates', Starr said, "Well, I guess you'll be going back to Greenville soon." Hodding told him he might not, and explained the situation at the paper. "Come around and see me tomorrow," Starr said. Later Hodding and Betty decided that he "couldn't talk that kind of money or that kind of business" with a good friend. The next day Starr phoned and said, "I thought you were coming to talk to me about your troubles. Come on now." Hodding went and stayed until eight o'clock that night.

Starr thought that he and a partner could lend Hodding the money he needed, but it would take time to arrange it. For now, though, he could provide sound advice on proceeding in the war with Reynolds. Since Reynolds might buy real estate, new machinery, or a radio station, Starr urged Hodding to claim his fifty-percent ownership as quickly as possible, and to demand a stockholder meeting for setting up the fifty-fifty directorate so the directors could impose limitations on the functions of management. He also advised Hodding to have his attorney ask the Smiths whether they were willing to sell any of the remaining first mortgage notes; he had a potential customer for them. Felts should ask whether the notes were available at discount and, if not, whether they were available at par. This would keep Reynolds from buying the notes at a bargain price.[30]

On December 30, 1944, Starr notified William Keady, Reynolds's Greenville lawyer, that "Major Hodding Carter has in his hands title to 49 percent of the common stock of the Delta Democrat Publishing Company," and asked that the one percent of common stock held in escrow be transferred to Carter. He went on to request that in light of the fifty-fifty ownership no additional purchases outside the normal operation of the business be made with company funds without Carter's consent.

Reynolds wrote to Hodding in January 1945 that the year's end had found him with "a little surplus capital"; he was going to look at the Greenville note possibilities.[31] Hodding was afraid Reynolds would buy up more of the Smith family notes, and he wondered whether, if Reynolds bought them during the ninety-day grace period, he would have to pay Reynolds even more. The back of Reynolds's letter to him, in fact, is scribbled with Hodding's figures.

That same month Hodding went back to Walter Reed for what he hoped was the first stop on his trip out of the Army. He had had no central vision in his right eye since 1941, and now he was having trouble with his left, which always seemed "full of shimmering pinpoints of light."[32] He was wearing dark glasses all of the time now. The diagnosis was "chorioretinitis, old, central, healed, right, cause undetermined" and "chorioretinitis, active, left." Nonetheless, he worked on the flood novel when he could, but as he told Bernice

Baumgarten, "I just can't get to writing until some of these things like fatherhood [Betty was expecting a third child], civilianhood, and freelance hood are settled one away or another."[33]

He would know soon whether he would win his "small, capitalistic war for possession in toto" of his paper. Until that was settled, he said, "I aint a fit knight for man, beast or crusades."[34] John Gibson wrote Hodding that Dillard had "an inkling that you are prepared to buy."[35]

On January 12, Felts sent the escrow agreement to Hodding and Betty. He urged them to read it three times and then let "Betty be Reynolds and you be yourself . . . and place yourselves in each position shown in the contract in order to see the effect it will have if signed in its present form. . . . I believe it is fairly drawn and I am of the opinion that it operates to protect you and your interests to the same extent that it does Reynolds."[36]

Milton Starr suggested Hodding ask for three changes in the agreement. Reynolds readily agreed to two minor alterations but objected to one that both parties declare their creditor positions. "If we set up our existing creditor positions . . . it would be impossible for us to advance any moneys to the Delta Democrat Publishing Company. . . . With my sizeable creditor position I would not want to be prevented from advancing money if necessary to protect myself."[37]

Hodding answered him from Walter Reed, where he was still a patient. Starr had instructed him to make Reynolds think he was interested in maintaining the fifty-fifty ownership and to crawl on his hands and knees if necessary, so Hodding told Reynolds that he wanted to be sure he had understood correctly: Reynolds did not want him to return to Greenville as editor but was open to an arrangement whereby Hodding could work for some of his papers in an editorial capacity. He thought Reynolds should give an active partnership a trial. "I still believe I can offer you as much as you can offer me."[38]

The idea was to make Reynolds believe that Hodding could not possibly pay the money the paper owed Reynolds. He would then believe he could offer the lowest possible price for Hodding's fifty percent. "We had to convince him that we weren't interested in coming back," Betty Carter said years later. "And he had to make the offer, and a low offer. Hodding made him think his eyes were so bad that we were going to live in Maine."[39]

"Until I get my mind made up about Maine or Mississippi I'm not going to be able to write a line," Hodding told Bernice Baumgarten.[40] "Each night I decide that I've decided, and . . . each morning it's all scrambled again." He would have about $250 a month disability pay, plus the interest on whatever he got from selling out to Reynolds. Did Baumgarten think he could make $3,000 a year as a full-time free-lancer? The paper was worth $12,000 a year, but if he could just write, he and Betty might be willing to live on half of that. Baumgarten replied that he could surely earn a minimum of $3,000 a year.

Meanwhile, doctors at Walter Reed had decided Hodding's left eye was improving, and he received his Army discharge with retirement pay of $2,500 a year because of his right eye. On March 28, 1945, the Carters' third son, Thomas Hennen, was born. The maid had quit the day before, and while Betty was in the hospital, Hodding "cooked, shopped and entertained the two yahoos unassisted." Immediately afterward he learned that he was one of the fifty-five civilians and forty-one servicemen who each received $2,500 from the Guggenheim Foundation.

Meanwhile, the bargaining bluff had worked. Reynolds offered Hodding $38.40 a share for his 539 shares, for a total of $20,697.

Hodding wrote back a week later that he would advise Reynolds in due course of his decision on the offer. Meanwhile, he wanted a special meeting of the stockholders called as soon as possible; for the duration of the fifty-fifty ownership he wanted representation on the board of directors. On March 30, Felts wrote Hodding that the sooner he came to Greenville the better. Reynolds agreed to a meeting on April 12 in Greenville.

Hodding followed Milton Starr's instructions and spent his time with Reynolds, urging him to continue the fifty-fifty arrangement. Reynolds, however, said he was a lone wolf and wanted no partners.

He told Hodding he could be editor of one of his other papers at $12,000 a year, but he would not be allowed to write controversial editorials, or even editorials about local matters.

Hodding went back to Washington to confer with Starr. "Well, it looks like we're buying the paper instead of selling it," Hodding wrote Bernice Baumgarten. "I guess I'm just a newspaperman pretending to be an author."[41] He figured also that he could do as much writing in Greenville as anywhere else, especially since the Carters planned to spend several months a year in Maine. Both the race novel and the flood novel had come from the South, so perhaps he should stay there. He prodded Baumgarten to get all the money she could for him, from any source, as he was in the process of raising $102,000 to buy the paper back and was "willing to take two bits here and two bits there."

While Betty took the three boys to the house in Maine, Hodding returned with Starr to Greenville just in time to meet the deadline. At the bank that had acted as escrow agent, Billy Keady, Reynolds's lawyer (and the bank's), announced, "Gentlemen, I want to go over this agreement to buy or sell. What do you propose to do, Hodding?" "We'll buy," said Starr. Hodding tried to be nonchalant when "I handed over a check for $104,000 and got back our newspaper."[42]

Hodding went to the *DD-T* offices and personally fired G. D. Guilkey; this was the only person he would fire in his life. His action deprived John Gibson of a pleasure he had longed for. (Gibson immediately became advertising manager as well as circulation manager.) Hodding rehired Electra Atcher and set about rebuilding the news staff.

"As you will doubtless have learned before you receive this letter," Hodding wrote Reynolds on June 15, "I have exercised my option to buy your interest in the Delta Democrat Publishing Company and to take over your creditor position. . . . I cannot see how you expected me to sell, in view of the price and the techniques involved." He then rubbed a little salt in the wound and reminded Reynolds that he had once said that given a worthwhile price he would sell anything he had. Hodding mentioned that his friend Milton Starr was interested in acquiring newspapers; he wondered whether Reynolds wanted to sell any of his papers, and at what price.

Years later, at a newspaper editors' meeting, Reynolds, then worth almost $1 billion according to *Forbes*, would point to Hodding and say, "He's the only man who ever walked away from a poker table with me and took all the chips."

As soon as he got his paper back, Hodding wrote and signed an exultant front-page editorial. He was in Greenville again after four and a half years, and

> I have come back here because I wanted to. Of all the places my family has been . . . we believe that there is nowhere as happy a conjunction of place and people as here. And I have also felt the pull of one man's spirit, the spirit of a man no longer living. William Alexander Percy was instrumental in bringing me here, and in keeping me here in more competitive days. I have repeated over and over those of his words to me which I shall longest remember. I do not think they can be repeated too often.
>
> Will Percy said: "We can't do anything on the grand scale. But you can work for your people in your own town. . . . The total of all the Greenvilles can make the kind of country we want or don't want." [43]

Hodding stayed with a friend in Greenville while he looked for a house for his family. There were none for rent, and two for sale. He called Betty and told her to come down to look at them. She left the boys with her mother, who was visiting in Maine, and somehow, with no wartime travel priority, flew to Greenville and chose a house on Arnold Street; then she hurried back to Maine.

Hodding wrote to Milton Starr that any resentment in town would vanish as soon as Betty returned. The letters he wrote in the next few weeks—and he wrote many to acknowledge the congratulations and "welcome home" messages—reflected his enormous relief and joy at returning to the paper.

And he had John Gibson, soon to be business manager with one-fourth interest in the paper. He was almost as important in Hodding's life as Betty. The man who once had written Hodding that he wanted the *DD-T* to be a "newspaper run by a newspaperman for newspapermen and for the joy of living" was also a peerless manager. If it had not been for him, Hodding's former employees agree, Hodding would never have made money—he would have thrown it away.[44] Gibson watched purchases, controlled expenditures—and backed Hodding's controversial editorial policies almost one hundred percent.

"The Small City Is the Most Potent Soporific I Know"

When Hodding repossessed the *Delta Democrat-Times* in the early summer of 1945, he flung himself into the work of the newspaper as if to make up for his four-and-a-half-year absence. He borrowed from an insurance company to repay Milton Starr and Joe Weinberg; it would take him fifteen years to pay off the insurance loan. But he had his paper back.

As soon as Hodding's name reappeared on the masthead, on June 18, 1945, the editorials, which had been as limp as Pink Smith's, came to life. Ten days later, Hodding wrote that "Germany should be erased as a nation, its people made to rebuild the rest of Europe, members of its general staff jailed for life, the Nazi party leaders and SS officers shot." But the same editorial took up the cause of German POWs working on cotton plantations in the Delta. They, it said, "should not be mistreated."

On July 3, Hodding lashed out at Senator James Eastland, who had said that the black soldiers had been "an utter and abysmal failure." Eastland, Hodding wrote, had done a disservice both to the tinderbox of race relations and to historical truth. The editorial cited Crispus Attucks, the first man killed in the Revolutionary War, who was black; the black battalion that Andrew Jackson singled out for commendation after the Battle of New Orleans; and the black soldiers who carried the day on San Juan Hill in the Spanish-American

War. And on July 22 he attacked Representative John Rankin, who, "taking his usual advantage of Congressional immunity to malign his betters," had accused three wartime leaders, including Secretary of War Henry Stimson, of being communist sympathizers. Stimson, said Hodding, was "about as communistic as Herbert Hoover."[1]

Of course, Hodding wrote also about local issues, great and small. He prepared a long editorial about Bobby Henry, a former news carrier for the *Delta Star* who was killed in Germany.[2] On June 20 he commented on topics that people in town considered among the most important—schools, prohibition, proposals for business and industrial growth, and politics. "But it's too hot for politics," he commented. On July 1 he wrote an editorial, in the form of a skit, in which two veterans discussed the lack of recreational facilities for veterans in Greenville. He chastised cotton planters for trying to set a ceiling on wages for cotton pickers. Soon after, he argued that the people promoting a new country club for Greenville should also support a new public swimming pool.[3] A few days later, Hodding returned to the subject of race: "The so-called race question is an economic one, not social. Pay the Negro good wages for his work, give him the opportunity to demonstrate his own capacity to learn, work, and earn, give him his Constitutional rights and you have solved this distorted so-called race problem. Only the demagogue tries to make political capital of social equality and racial marriage."[4] ("Social equality" was a code used by white Southerners, who could not bear even speaking the word "integration.")

Hodding queried Bernice Baumgarten about the possibility of an article on Mound Bayou, the all-black town in the Delta, where a young doctor had built a hospital, the only swimming pool for blacks in all of Mississippi, tennis courts, and a dance pavilion, and had started building a zoo. (*The Saturday Evening Post* snapped up the Mound Bayou story idea, paid Hodding $600 for it, and ran it in the issue of February 23, 1946, under the title "He's Doing Something About the Race Problem.")

"I am having a whale of a time," Hodding wrote in one letter to Baumgarten. "I am a Redneck but I come from a good family and I'm a Southerner. . . . I like these people."[5] In another letter he mentioned his attacks on Representative Rankin and "some of the other darlings of the Old South. This place is really the battle ground between Democracy and Fascism, and the horrible part is that almost all of the Fascists honestly believe they are democratic—excusing a little color blindness."[6]

Hodding got into hot water at an American Legion meeting when he stated his opposition to a resolution condemning the admission of Chinese-American children to Greenville's white public schools. A major battle over the issue went on for months, and resulted in a general investigation of the leadership of the public schools. During this period someone called the *Delta Democrat-Times* offices and said, "Did you know that our schools are run by an atheist, a Jew, and a Catholic?" It seems the superintendent, who strongly supported the admission of Chinese-American children to the schools, was the atheist, one of two school principals a Jew, and the other a Catholic. The full-scale investigation vindicated the superintendent, Dr. Forrest Murphy, who was supported strongly by the *DD-T*. Nonetheless, Murphy left to become dean of the University of Mississippi School of Education.

At the beginning of August, Hodding left the paper in the hands of a young woman editor, Edwin Vincent, and departed for Maine and the Boat Barn, to join Betty, young Hodding, Philip, and Tommy. He had the Guggenheim grant and plans to finish the flood novel. He wanted to do a million things. And all things seemed possible.

The Carters began their custom of weekly square dances for all of Camden and Rockport—summer people and permanent residents alike—at the Boat Barn. Georgina and Jack Stanley were at their house nearby, and there were plenty of picnics and cookouts, hikes, overnight camping trips, and reunions with Carter cousins and childhood friends. Hodding bought his first boat and added sailing to the day's activities. He tried to work on his book in the mornings, and he took time to write an editorial for the Camden *Herald* when the United States dropped the atomic bomb on Hiroshima; the genie was out of the bottle, Hodding said, and the world would never be the same again. The lead story of that issue of the *Herald* was a report on his talk to a local Lions Club, and on the left side of the front page was an account of a fire at the Camden Opera House, written by ten-year-old Hodding III.

Hodding wrote several editorials for his own paper on the atomic bomb, one announcing "an instantaneous revolution in human thought,"[7] another calling on the United States to renounce and outlaw the bomb.

He sent one of his most often quoted editorials, "Go for Broke," to Greenville for the *DD-T* of August 25. This editorial saluted Japanese-Americans in Company D of the 442d Infantry Regiment and the 100th Infantry Battalion of the U.S. Army. No troops had chalked up a better combat record, he wrote, than these nisei, who had been chosen to lead the final victory parade in Leghorn, Italy, marching "in commemoration of the defeat of the nation from which their fathers came." They had spearheaded the attack that opened the doorway to Strasbourg and had rescued the Thirty-sixth Division's lost battalion of Texans from encircling Germans. As soon as these soldiers took off their uniforms, people might say that "a Jap is a Jap," but it seemed to Hodding that their slogan, "Go for Broke," could be "adopted by all Americans of good will in the days ahead. We've got to shoot the works in a fight for tolerance. Those boys of Company D point the way."

Senator Theodore Bilbo, possibly the most repulsive man ever to enter American politics, a longtime controversial figure in Mississippi, announced in late August 1945 that he would run for a third term in the Senate. Immediately, Hodding wrote that Bilbo had sought "public office with sickening regularity. . . . Now approaching senility after nearly forty years of feeding at the tax payers' trough, he announces again."[8]

Hodding once termed Bilbo a disciple of "the cults of the Master Race." After a New York woman, Josephine Piccolo, had written Bilbo protesting his filibuster against the Fair Employment Practices

Committee, the senator responded with a letter that began: "My Dear Dago." Hodding commented: "It must take a great deal of courage to rampage against Italians and Catholics who in this state are such a small minority, or against Jews whose numbers here are infinitesimal, or against Negroes, who don't vote or talk back."[9]

From Maine, Hodding wrote a series for *PM* in which he tried to explain Bilbo's popularity. His "political artistry" and loyalty to the New Deal on everything but racial and prolabor matters were significant, but the most important factor was that Bilbo had the same "background, material aspirations, fears and prejudices" as most of Mississippi's electorate. Hodding pointed out that Mississippi was near the "bottom of the pile" when it came to illiteracy, venereal disease, income per capita, and public health, and unpunished crimes of violence, including lynching. "Actually," Hodding wrote, "most of the people who vote for Bilbo aren't illiterate or murderers or socially diseased or tubercular. They are terribly poor and terribly misled."[10] (Bilbo asked Hodding for copies of the series, explaining that he did not subscribe to *PM*. Hodding replied that he had only one set of clippings but that he would ask *PM* to send copies to the senator.)

Besides preparing editorials, writing for *PM*, and square dancing, Hodding worked on the flood novel; one week he wrote 13,000 words. He and Betty discussed the possibility of staying in Maine permanently.[11] Philip Carter recalled the family's talking about the possibility that his father would lose the sight in his good eye; if he went blind, he said, he would live in Maine.[12]

At the end of August, however, they packed up and drove the 1,600 miles to Greenville. Betty, who felt that all of America was heading home after the war, read *Uncle Remus* out loud to the boys. "Do they talk like that in Mississippi?" asked young Hodding, who had left Greenville when he was five.

"Not really," Betty said, "but the southern accent is more pronounced in Greenville than in Washington."

Back in Greenville, Betty settled the family in the house they had bought at 514 Arnold Street, while Hodding once more threw himself into the newspaper and the life of the town.

At the end of the first day of school, young Hodding burst through the door, shouting, "They do, Mother! They do!"

"What?"

"Talk just like Uncle Remus!"

For the first time in thirteen years, Betty did not work and ran the house without domestic help. Her coffee was terrible, and Hodding said that if it didn't improve, it would mean the end of their marriage. Betty went to Wetherbee's hardware store and asked for a granite drip pot. The people there told her they had not seen one in years. Betty went home and wept as she sorted the laundry, remembering that Adlai Stevenson had called her one of the two most fascinating women in Washington. Then someone from the hardware store called. He had found a granite drip pot in the store's attic. Her marriage was saved.

Betty finally found a maid and began to immerse herself in civic and church work. Eventually she returned to the newspaper, sometimes in advertising, sometimes in news and features, but it was her tireless efforts for the community that earned her the respect and affection of a great many Greenville people who were often furious with Hodding over his editorials.

Hodding, too, was enmeshed in Greenville civic and social life, serving on the boards of the chamber of commerce and the library and the Boy Scouts. Yet he felt lonely and isolated at times, even as he waded into the middle of a local controversy and wrote some of his finest editorials about Greenville's World War II memorial. The Lions Club planned to erect a board at the foot of Washington Street, by the levee, that would list the names of all the servicemen from the area. Lions members obtained the names of area men who had entered the armed forces through selective service. Through editorials and news stories, the DD-T urged readers to report the names of volunteers, reserve officers, Waves, Wacs, Spars, nurses, and any other men and women who entered the service by means other than the draft. "We've waited too long for the completion of the Honor Roll," said one editorial.[13] "The Honor Roll should be a hundred percent list."

When some of the more conservative whites realized that the names of black veterans would be listed, too, they erupted. Anson Sheldon, a planter, said that over his dead body would his son's name go on the board with the names of "those niggers."[14]

Hodding thundered out an editorial headlined "Our Honor Roll Is a Monument to Intolerance and Timidity":

> We fail to see any threat to White Supremacy or to segregation or to any other of the issues so useful to rabble rousers in placing the names of the Negro servicemen on the roll. In not doing so, we see only a threat to democracy itself. What the roll was intended to proclaim was simply this: here are the names of the men and women of Greenville who wore their country's uniform in time of need. . . . It is a small enough thing to do. We are ashamed of the spirit which has seemingly prevailed against it. . . .
>
> We cannot tell what is in the minds of Negroes of this community. But we can hazard a guess. We can hear them, in bafflement and humiliation, ask these things: "We are told that we must earn a better place in the sun and that the things we do for our community will be the gauge of our worth. Our people were selected for service, as the rest were selected." They wore the uniform. Must they be denied even this recognition?
>
> And then we might ask ourselves this: How in God's name can the Negroes be encouraged to be good citizens, to feel that they can get a fair break, to believe that here in the South they will some day win those things that are rightfully theirs—decent housing, better educational facilities, equal pay for equal work, a lifting of health standards and all the other milestones along an obstacle-filled road—if we deny them so small a thing as joint service recognition?[15]

Eventually the Roll of Honor went up with no names at all. The legend reads: "In memory of those who served in World War II. May the spirit of our boys who fell in battle live forever."*

Hodding continued to press the question of adequate wages for agricultural labor, in the paper and in person. Farm workers in the Delta were mostly blacks; they lived in unpainted shacks without electricity or running water and earned an average of $400 a year. Cotton pickers, who made two dollars for every hundred pounds, wanted more money. When the planters met at the courthouse to discuss the situation, Hodding stood up to urge them to raise the pay to two dollars an hour; it would be better for the merchants and the whole community, as well as the pickers. This was a radical suggestion. The planters, who of course wanted to hold costs down, were furious that he would even suggest such a munificent sum. "We gotta keep it like it is," they shouted angrily at him, and called him a communist.[16] Two of Hodding's friends went home with him that night— they were afraid for him to drive home by himself. "Not too long after that we went to a cocktail buffet at Mr. Will Francis's," remembered Betty Carter. "He was a big shot in the Goyer company that dealt with all the planters. He had been a good friend of Will Percy's. One young planter came in and saw Hodding, and turned on his foot and left the room, very conspicuously. But the effort at social ostracism did not catch on."[17] Later some of the angriest people came to agree with Hodding. "He certainly influenced me," said LeRoy Percy.[18]

Public health was another important concern to Hodding. He applauded the Washington County Health Department's proposal to X-ray everyone in the county over fourteen years old for tuberculosis, hailing such testing of 40,000 people as a "visionary and ambitious undertaking." He supported a new hospital to serve the county's "low-

*In 1988, Helen Generelly's maid told her she would not be able to work on Memorial Day because she had to demonstrate. "What on earth for?" asked Mrs. Generelly. "We're going to demonstrate at the war memorial," the maid said, "because they didn't mention women on the board."

income white citizens and its 40,000 Negroes,"[19] but he infuriated the town's doctors when he came out in favor of Blue Cross. Dave Hollowell, the president of Will Percy's bank, had sold Hodding on Blue Cross, but the Delta Medical Association passed a resolution attacking him.

People in Greenville who disagreed violently with Hodding's editorials called him a communist, a "damned Republican," a Yankee, a radical New Dealer, a moderate, a liberal, or any other insulting name they could think of. He might be called a conservative and a communist for the same editorial. On Lincoln's Birthday in 1946, he quoted that president's remarks to a group of New York workingmen in 1864: "The strongest bond of human sympathy, outside of family relations, should be the one that united all working people, of all nations, and tongues and kindreds." (Communist! cried some people in town.) "Nor should this lead to a war upon property or the owners of property. Property is the fruit of labor; property is desirable." (Conservative! cried other people in town.)

Hodding continued his boosterism, editorializing, for instance, that the Delta Fine Arts Association was "a fine thing for a community."[20] With John Gibson's enthusiastic backing, he increased local news and covered high school athletics intensively. In the fall of 1945, a ninth-grade student at Coleman, the black high school in Greenville, tried to see Hodding at the paper's offices about that sports coverage. "Black veterans were coming home," recalled Matthew Page years later, "and waking people up. I was interested in sports, but I didn't see anything in the newspaper about my school. I wondered if I could write something about Coleman's sports. My principal said he didn't think they'd run it but to ask. The first time I went, they said he was busy. The second time he caught a glimpse of me from his office and called to me to come in. I told him I wanted to write about sports from my school. He said, 'Let me think about it.' Then he sent word through the principal that I could start."[21] It was the beginning of a long friendship between Hodding and Page.

Hodding's writing was very much in demand outside Mississippi. In the same week: *Esquire* asked him to do a thousand-word piece to accompany the reproduction of a painting of the capture of pirates in the Gulf of Mexico in 1819 (he was paid $150); Roger Butterfield asked him to contribute an article on Huey Long—defaming the regime in 8,000 words, said Hodding[22]—for a Simon & Schuster book on significant events between the wars (he received a $400 advance, with the promise of royalties); and Walter Bernstein asked him to write 3,000 words for a new magazine that alumni of *Yank* were starting (he was to receive ten cents a word). All the assignments came directly to him, but he asked the editors to pay him through Brandt & Brandt.

He put aside the flood novel to do research for the historical novel, officially the book for which he had received the Guggenheim. It was to be a story of aristocrat against frontiersman in the early-nineteenth-century Florida parishes of Louisiana, which were not part of the Louisiana Purchase and over which the English, French, Spanish, and Americans (among them, Aaron Burr) plotted for control. The book would have "lots of freebooters, river pirates, doubloons, and octoroons," said Memphis newspaper columnist Paul Flowers, who called Hodding the "busiest young man in the South today, a tireless and fearless writer who contrives to keep a dozen irons in the fire, all of them hot."[23] (The Guggenheim administrator explained to Hodding later that he was not required to write the historical novel but could do another one if he chose.)

Hodding also continued his assaults on Theodore Bilbo. He suggested an addition to the English language: *bilbo* as a noun, meaning "reckless, intolerant vilifier," and as a verb, meaning "to seek to destroy the character of another; to arouse racial animosities; to make a political nuisance of oneself."[24]

There was not a chance of defeating Bilbo for reelection, Hodding told Bernice Baumgarten in a letter in early 1946, but he was swinging away nevertheless. "It is depressing, mainly because most people don't give a damn. Maybe they've got the right idea these days though—keep your mind on duck hunting and the price of cotton and to hell with the state of the nation. I don't mean that." He was looking forward to a trip to New York in April and three months in Maine in the summer. "We're beginning to feel like missionaries getting a sabbatical in the States. . . . Some day I'm going to write a story on how small towns gradually absorb the people who live in them. You become a vestryman, a Legionnaire, a Rotarian, a school board member, a Chamber of Commerce booster. It's incredible. You're boring from within, if you don't agree, and finally you say what the hell, and become content with remodeling your house, going to New Orleans for weekends, buying a boat and worrying about diminishing profits. It hasn't happened to me yet, and if I think it's going to I'll sell the paper. But the small city is the most potent soporific I know. The more settled and secure I feel the unhappier I am."[25]

The Saturday Evening Post sent Hodding an article about Bilbo to critique; he found it superficial, missing the boat entirely. If Bilbo was that hot, he asked Baumgarten, "why not try to sell someone on having an article by one who knows the score—meaning me."[26] *The New York Times Magazine* commissioned from him not only an article on Bilbo but one about the South in general.

In May 1946, Hodding went to Cambridge for a reunion of Nieman fellows, and on an impulse decided to go to Maine to see about putting in a vegetable garden at the Boat Barn. While he was out of reach—even Betty did not know where he was—Columbia University announced the Pulitzer Prizes. Hodding was "genuinely surprised"[27] when reporters boarded the Rockland–Brunswick train with the news that he had won the Pulitzer for editorial writing "on the subject of racial, religious, and economic intolerance." The Pulitzer committee cited specifically "Go for Broke," about the Japanese-American infantry unit, but it had considered also his editorial about newspaper boy Bobby Henry; his attacks on Senator Eastland for his aspersions against black military units and on Representative Rankin for calling Secretary of War Stimson a communist; his reprimand of Senator Bilbo for his "My Dear Dago" letter; and the eloquent series on the Greenville veterans' Honor Roll.

Hodding denied to the Portland *Press-Herald* that he had been horsewhipped for the editorials. "Occasionally we do lose subscriptions," he said, "but Southerners will take opinions such as mine from another Southerner, where they would resent the intrusion of a Northerner who spends two days in the South studying the Negro problem and then writes learnedly about its solution."[28] The *Delta Democrat-Times*, meanwhile, ran a story about the Pulitzer with a big banner headline.

Hodding later claimed that John Gibson had entered his editorials in the Pulitzer competition. Gibson recalled that Hodding had asked him whether he should enter and Gibson told him to go ahead, he had nothing to lose.[29] According to an article in *McCall's* twenty years later, nobody formally entered the editorials: "In 1946 a [Pulitzer] board member just happened to see reprints of a series of editorials by Hodding Carter in the *Delta Democrat-Times*. . . . Reading five of the specimens aloud to his colleagues, he swung them away from the jurors' recommendations, and the prize went to Mr. Carter."[30] Later the board member in question wrote and identified himself to Hodding—he was Arthur Krock, of the New York *Times'* Washington bureau.

The Pulitzer was an epiphany for Hodding, bringing him national publicity and validating his opinions. After the Nieman, the Guggenheim, and *Winds of Fear*, it was a coronation. *The Saturday Evening Post* ran an admiring article about him, and he received a thousand letters of congratulation. He reveled in the attention: "I am getting a big bang out of being one of Mr. Pulitzer's little boys this year."[31] John Gibson reprinted the collection of Pulitzer editorials several times— he knew how to exploit Hodding's talents. "The award provided me with the happiest and most astounded moment of my life," Hodding wrote a fellow newspaperman in Buffalo. "But my day of glory is going to be short lived. Bilbo is coming to Greenville on June 11 and has promised to tell everyone what kind of 'nigger loving communist' I am."[32]

Bilbo's primary campaign was going strong. "I believe in white superiority," he said over and over, "white domination and the integrity of my white blood. . . . We have behind us four thousand years of culture, learning, education, and wisdom . . . and the nigger, I got nothing against the nigger, I'm his best friend, but the poor devil is only a hundred and fifty years removed from the jungle and eating his own kind." He denounced attempts to register blacks to vote. "The best way to keep the nigger from voting," he said, was "you do it the night before elections. . . . I don't have to tell you any more than that. Red-blooded men know what I mean." The Fair Employment Practices Committee, he said, was "nothing but a plot to put niggers to work next to your daughters and to run your business with niggers," and the CIO Political Action Committee was a monstrosity designed to destroy the American way of life.

Bilbo vented his spleen against Drew Pearson, Walter Winchell, Eleanor Roosevelt (Southerners loathed her because of her outspoken support of integration), Henry Wallace, blacks, communists, "nigger lovers," Northerners who advocated social equality—and Hodding Carter. Not all the Reds were up North, he said; the Greenville newspaper editor was "a nigger-loving communist." Bilbo had to run against somebody stronger than his opponents and more clearly drawn than just "outsiders" or "niggers," Mississippi congressman Frank Smith wrote.[33] Hodding was ideal for this purpose, so Bilbo pitched a good part of his campaign against him. Hodding fought back, just as he had fought Huey Long in Hammond, with every weapon he could muster.

No one should underestimate Bilbo's campaigning ability. As somebody leaving a Bilbo rally in 1927 commented, "That man can make you believe him even when you know he's lying."[34] In May 1946, Bilbo spoke in Leland, some ten miles from Greenville. He told his

162

listeners to bring plenty of baskets when they came to hear him in Greenville on June 11, for he was going to take so much skin off the town's "nigger-loving communist" newspaper editor that there would be hide for everybody. "No red-blooded Southerner worthy of the name would accept a Poolitzer-blitzer prize given by a bunch of nigger-loving Yankeefied communists for editorials advocating mongrelization of the race." Bilbo maintained he was not biased. "Up there in Washington a girl reporter asked me how I stood on the Jews. I told her I stood good on the Jews. I am for every damn Jew from Jesus Christ on down." He was also "the best friend the nigger's got in the state of Mississippi. I'm trying to do something for 'em. I want to send 'em back to Africa where they belong."[35]

Bilbo spoke for two and a half hours in Leland, and while he raved, Hodding was busy moving through the crowd, going from person to person, asking whether all had heard Bilbo say he was "for every damn Jew from Jesus Christ on down" and whether they would sign an affidavit saying they had heard the remark. Several solid Delta citizens promised to sign. The next day Hodding collected affidavits from six people, including Walker Percy, "grand-nephew of the late Senator LeRoy Percy and a nephew of the late William Alexander Percy"; McClain Bowman, "prominent young planter and World War II veteran with the U.S. Army Air Forces"; and John Gibson.[36] Hodding made copies and sent one to every daily newspaper in Mississippi and the wire services.

He thought he had Bilbo in a corner on the Leland speech because of his documentation of the comment about "every damn Jew from Jesus Christ on down." While most of Bilbo's supporters "didn't much mind what a man said about Jews or niggers or Catholics or Dagoes, and he said plenty about all of them, they were God-fearing Christian folks who didn't like a man getting sassy with the Lord."[37] Bilbo, however, denied having said "every damn Jew"; he maintained he had said "every good Jew." The affidavits Hodding had collected specified that Bilbo had said "damn Jew" and not "good Jew"; Bilbo, then, sent a form letter to offended clergymen explaining that he had always loved Jesus and would never say anything sacrilegious about Him; everybody knew the editor who had spread those lies was a well-known communist who would do anything to defeat Bilbo.

In the *Delta Democrat-Times* of May 16, Hodding wrote:

Theodore Bilbo's mind is so soaked in the poisonous slime of his bigotry that he reminds us of nothing so much as a neglected cesspool.

Senator Bilbo promised at Leland Tuesday night that by the time he finishes taking the skin off the editor of this newspaper it will be moving day for someone, meaning us. . . . We'll have to tell the senator and his local janissaries that if they are taking this moving idea seriously they'd better bring along more than a road map or five railroad tickets. A whole lot more . . . Since we've been skinned in our time by one or two experts, including the late Huey Long, we won't worry overmuch about what an old man with a wormy past has to say about us.

Hodding pointed out that the Mississippi Senate had characterized Bilbo as a man lacking in "character and credibility," unfit to sit "with honest upright men in a respectable legislative body." Bilbo, he said, had accepted a bribe and then tried to explain it away by claiming he was only setting a trap. He had granted mass pardons for convicted criminals. His wife had said he associated with "indecent women" during his entire second term as governor. He had once tried to avoid a subpoena naming him as a witness in the seduction trial of Governor Lee Russell—he hid in a barn behind a heifer calf. (Hodding quoted Fred Sullens, a Jackson newspaperman: "Some people feel sorry for Governor Russell, others for the girl, and some even for Bilbo; but I, personally, feel sorry for the heifer calf.")

The editorial closed with Hodding's expression of contempt for a "jaundiced old man who makes his living with hate and slander as his tools. . . . When he dies Hell shall have gained a noisome adornment and Satan a congenial ally."

Newspapers throughout the country carried wire service stories describing how Bilbo had "turned his pyrotechnic oratory against a Pulitzer prize–winning editor" and threatened to skin him alive.

Bilbo never spoke in Greenville; he had to return to Washington. One of his flunkies, whom Hodding called "a political jackal," read the speech on June 11. Hodding, in Maine, tried to answer Bilbo's charge that he was a "negro lover." "I have tried to love and work for my fellow man—Negro, Jews, Catholics—all of those whom Bilbo has attempted to humiliate," Hodding told a Memphis *Commercial-Appeal* reporter over the telephone. "I will continue to speak and to write. . . . Neither Bilbo nor his jackals are going to stop me. . . . In another generation the shame and evil which Bilbo represents will be only an uncomfortable smudge. I am working for that generation."[38]

Hodding could not believe that Bilbo's popularity with white Mississippians was the result of his racist talk, however much the people might love the senator's filibusters against the threat of a Fair Employment Practices Commission. "I hate the little so-and-so but he's done a good job against the FEPC," seemed to sum up their opinion. White Mississippians regarded the FEPC with the fear and hatred their forebears had felt for the occupying federal bayonets of Reconstruction. Hodding pointed out that Bilbo had not single-handedly fought off the FEPC, but that in fact other southern senators had tried to keep him off the floor during the filibuster. "They knew that if Bilbo got the floor, he would substitute prejudice, hatred, and bigotry for intelligent argument. . . . He did just that."[39]

In a *New York Times Magazine* article about Bilbo, Hodding explained that white Mississippians "rural, deep-rooted and homogeneous," were afraid of "swift, drastic and forcible change from without." Part of the fear stemmed from ignorance, which stemmed from poverty, but the "traditional Southerner today is hagridden by fear. Upon this rotten meat does Bilbo feed and grow great in the eyes of resentful frightened men."[40]

Bilbo won. Against four opponents, he collected fifty-one percent of the vote, even carrying the Delta except for Washington County. A myth had been destroyed, Hodding wrote, the myth that Deltans cherished, that they were not responsible for Bilbo, that it was the hill people who elected him.[41] Later Hodding would write that voters had thumbed their noses at outsiders with a loud "To Hell with you" when they sent Bilbo back for a third Senate term.[42] "Outside interference" was to be a rallying cry for Southerners for many years; both supporters and opponents of Bilbo claimed that "if the Yankees had kept out of the election, he would have been beaten." Hodding, too, felt that the National Negro Congress resolution demanding that federal troops be sent to Mississippi just before the election helped Bilbo immeasurably. "If the organization had been 100 per cent behind Senator Bilbo, it could not have hit upon a more effective way to insure his reelection than to make such an appeal to the government for action against a state where memories of Federal bayonets are long."[43]

There was, however, a silver lining to the robe of defeat: "The frightened people should be frightened no more," Hodding wrote. "By their ballots they have saved themselves from mongrelization for another six years.

> Mississippi is no further from Moscow or New Delhi or London or Rio de Janeiro than was Huspuckema from McComb thirty years ago. What we do here is noted in remote places, in places which may yet be the dying ground for your son or ours. Democracy is an empty thing when it is posited against the reality of hate and fear. And we humans with white skins are a minority among the surging, restless people of the world. . . . We have made our full contribution to chaos.[44]

After the election Hodding hurried back to Maine, but left there again to speak on the Mutual Radio Network from Boston in response to charges Bilbo had made against him on *Meet the Press* the week before. Hodding had first refused to appear, but when John Gibson wrote urging him to, he agreed. He wrote his friend Jimmy Alsop that he had mike fright just thinking about it, but he did very well indeed, mixing down-home humor with inspirational homily.

He began by saying that he was not going to reply to Bilbo in kind. "There is an old saying where I come from: 'You can't outwallow a hog.'" It was a good thing that Bilbo had been reelected, for he could "do Mississippi less harm in Washington than . . . at home. He was twice governor of our state and left it bankrupt." And it might be good for the nation to see him in the Senate—an example of what the combined forces of bigotry, anger, and fear could produce in a democracy. Hodding explained at some length that bigotry and intolerance infected the entire nation, not just the South. People often asked him whether he did not get terribly discouraged. "No Southerner, in all of the South's history, could afford to get completely discouraged," he said. "If we had, there would be few populated places in the South today."[45]

The pastor of the First Christian Church in Greenville wrote Hodding that Bilbo's speech, "as usual, was characterized with bigotry, intolerance, ignorance, and so much duplicity," while Hodding's was "the very epitome of kindness, charity, thoughtfulness, enlightenment, and faith."[46]

After the radio speech and two articles that summer in *The New York Times Magazine*, George P. Brockway, of W. W. Norton, and Alfred A. Knopf asked Hodding to write books. *The Woman's Home Companion*, *The American Mercury*, *The Nation*, and *The New Republic* asked for articles; so did *The Negro Digest*'s Ben Burns, who had given *Winds of Fear* such an unfavorable review.

When Hodding turned in an article, "Chip on Our Shoulder Down South," to *The Saturday Evening Post*, Ben Hibbs, the editor, asked him to write exclusively for the *Post*. Hodding declined, preferring the freedom to accept assignments from other editors who might suggest interesting topics. In that *Post* article Hodding took a few swipes at what he called the hit-and-run school of reporters, writers who came to the South, visited Hodding and Betty, and quickly noted that Mississippi's per capita income was thirty-six percent of the national average. "As native guides our duties were fairly simple," he wrote. "We had only to lead the hunter to the hunting ground, to act as decoy and beater, and to prod the sluggish prey into talking or posing for pictures." He compared these reporters with the abolitionists who campaigned against the South before the Civil War. "The abolitionists had Right on their side. So do our visitors from the North today. They also have the Left on their side, which is rather important." The abolitionists had helped unify the South, and "the liberal spirit of change in the South today is in danger of being similarly dissipated." But Southerners, he said, should not maintain that what they did was of no concern to the rest of the nation; unpunished lynchings and the denial of civil rights to minority groups were affronts to just men everywhere and blots on America's image abroad.[47]

Soon after "Chip on Our Shoulder" appeared in the *Post*, Hodding was clearly defined as a controversial figure in Mississippi. Things started calmly enough, when he was invited by the YMCA to speak at Mississippi State College in Starkville. He was greeted there by a billboard attacking both the YMCA and him as advocates of "social equality and the end of segregation." He spoke anyway, then went to the University of Mississippi in Oxford, where the service fraternity Omicron Delta Kappa had invited him to speak. Preceding him in Oxford was a telegram from twenty-three alumni in Gulfport, parents of current students, protesting his discussing racial relationships in front of their children.

Hodding sharply criticized these alumni in his speech. "I don't know the gentlemen, and I doubt that any of them ever heard me talk. I would be perfectly willing to make before them the same talk I am making here, with all proceeds going to the erection of a statue to fair play in Gulfport." These twenty-three individuals should honor academic freedom and the Bill of Rights, he felt. He established his credentials as a Southerner, even though, he admitted, he had come from Louisiana to Mississippi only ten years before; but an ancestor of his had been one of the first settlers of Natchez 181 years before that. Any approach to improving race relations in the South through abolition of segregation was "unrealistic," Hodding said. "I do believe that within the framework of segregation the Southern negro is entitled to decent housing, adequate medical care, equal educational opportunities, equal pay for equal work, and equal justice in the courts." Any positive effort by Southerners to reach these aims would lessen racial tensions.[48]

When Harry Truman appointed a President's Committee on Civil Rights in late 1946, Hodding applauded. As a firm believer in the Bill of Rights, he wrote an editorial commending Truman's instructions to the committee as an "admirable combination of just intent and clear vision"; the president wanted to see the Bill of Rights "implemented in fact."[49] There was no hint that when Truman's committee delivered its report, it would enrage the South and harden its resistance to change.

While he was battling for justice, Hodding was running a sometimes splashy hometown newspaper. The *Delta Democrat-Times* was the smallest paper in the country to send a staff reporter to the World Series in 1946. David "Boo" Ferriss, a Delta boy, had helped pitch the Boston Red Sox to an American League pennant, and even though the Red Sox lost the Series to the St. Louis Cardinals, the *DD-T* staged a Delta-wide homecoming party for Ferriss.

10. 1947–1954

The "Brighter Side to Life"

Hodding and Betty worked hard in the years from 1947 through 1954. They carved out places for themselves in the community, attracted and nurtured a young and talented staff, built a new house, and prepared books and articles. Always in the background of the good life they led was the nettlesome question of race. Well aware that change must come, Hodding wrote constantly about the South's racial problems. The next chapter will examine what he wrote on race; this chapter describes other facets of his life during the same period.

"Whenever the Parties Start, All the Critics Are the First to Ask Us"

Betty and Hodding were, in more ways than one, pace setters. Hodding was a mentor to a host of younger journalists in Mississippi. Older journalists still recall that when Hodding and Betty walked into the annual Mississippi Press Association meeting, everyone perked up. In his forties, Hodding was handsome, flamboyant, larger than life; Betty was slender, beautiful, and gracious. They were both glamorous and full of vitality—living proof that you could be liberal in Mississippi and survive. "He came to symbolize to a lot of people the right to speak out," said former congressman Frank Smith.[1] Hodding and Betty knew everyone, they were hospitable, they wanted intellectual stimulation—for everybody—and they were interested in maintaining ties to a larger world. As Hodding won national recognition, people flocked to Greenville to visit him and Betty; the Carters held parties for these visitors so that Greenville people could meet them. They invited Republicans and Democrats and Dixiecrats alike to their home. "Betty ran a salon," said one friend, who recalled the night Robert P. Tristram Coffin read his poetry until one in the morning. As guests realized he wasn't going to stop, they tiptoed out.[2] When Alfred A. Knopf and his wife came to Greenville in April 1950, Hodding was in the hospital, so Betty alone entertained them, inviting Tom Karsell and Edwin Vincent from the paper; Josephine Haxton, who would become famous as the writer Ellen Douglas; Elizabeth Morris of the Office Supply Company's book department; Louise Crump, the women's editor at the *DD-T*, who was working on a novel; and Shelby Foote, by that time the author of several.

There were parties of all kinds, and the liquor always flowed. Delta people drank a lot. In 1953, Hodding gave a big surprise party for Betty on her birthday, which was the twenty-fifth anniversary of the night they had first met in Amite. He invited 250 people, hired a band, and ordered the food and drinks himself.

The Carters belonged to several more or less organized social groups. They were members, with LeRoy and Sarah Percy, McClain and Susan Bowman, and Roger and Helen Generelly, of a poker club called the Pistol Dawn Club.[3] "Hodding didn't know what hand won at poker, but he'd play," recalled a friend.[4] Hodding was one of ten Terrapins, whose slogan was: "Stick your neck out and say what you think." The men met once a month at a member's home and each spoke for five minutes; once a year they had a party that included their wives. A very informal group, the Dead Heads, included the Generellys, the Percys, the Pottses, the Bowmans, and Virgil Rule. Anyone planning a party had to invite the Dead Heads first.[5]

In 1949, Hodding exulted in this popularity. "There's a big round of fall parties going on," he wrote to Hodding III, who was in his first year at Exeter. "It's funny that whenever the parties start, all the folks who are critics of us, as far as the paper goes, are among the first to ask us to the parties, which makes Greenville a nice place."[6]

In spite of what most people in town regarded as his dangerous, insane stands on many issues, Hodding—and Betty—were accepted, even popular, in Greenville. As the town's most famous citizen, Hodding was chosen to make the first direct-dial long-distance call from Greenville on April 15, 1950. He could have called anywhere in the United States but chose to call his father in Hammond. Greenvillians laughed tolerantly at Hodding's habit of constantly losing his car keys. While his brother dressed in the height of fashion, Hodding wore disgraceful clothes, which he bought at Jake Stein's Steinmart. It was a common saying in town that Hodding was the only man who owned three yachts but only two suits.

With his gift for storytelling, Hodding could make a connection with the men in town. Charming, ebullient, masculine, and outgoing, he befriended men of all classes. The Jewish community was firmly behind him, and he had the support of the Percy family. He was a member of the Rotary Club, which included the top businessmen in town. Every morning when he was in town, he met Jake Stein, Roy Hanf, Ferd Moyse, and Bob Harding for coffee at Al's #2, where, of course, they sat on the white side. Black patrons sat on the other side of a long cabinet that ran down the middle of the café. The staff picked out the same dishes for white and black from the cabinet, but from different sides. Likewise with the silverware: drawers opened on each side of the cabinet, and both sides used the same forks, knives and spoons.[7]

Hunting was a rewarding pastime for a nonconformist who wanted in a way to conform. And Hodding had enormous zest in the field, although his friends thought him a terrible hunter. "He was not a skillful hunter, but he was all right," recalled John Gibson. "He was a community man—he'd do anything with anybody. He liked people."[8]

Many Mississippians perceived liberals, or moderates, as "communists" or, worse, "sissies," and Hodding knew that hunting was manly. He liked to tell about one of his hunting companions, a game warden who was always frank. "One afternoon while we squatted in a corn and bean field waiting for the doves to come in," Hodding wrote, "he told me that a number of his friends did not have much use for me or my ideas. He added that he did not agree with me always either. 'But there's one sure thing,' he said, his eyes searching the gray sky. 'There can't be too much wrong with a fellow who likes to hunt.'"[9] Hodding used his hunting experiences to write articles for *Outdoor Life* and similar magazines.

In April 1950, after a cruise on the Tennessee River for an article for *Holiday* magazine, Hodding went home and bought a Greenville-built forty-foot twin-screw cabin cruiser for the *Delta Democrat-Times*. The boat could sleep eight and had butane gas for heating and cooking. She carried one dinghy topside and on hunting trips towed an eighteen-foot army landing boat, both of them with outboard motors. Hodding used the boat, christened *Mistuh Charley*, to entertain groups of all ages and constituencies, and often to take him, his sons, and his friends on hunting trips up the Mississippi, where they camped out on the river islands. His friends might belittle his hunting capabilities and his poker game, but they all admired his skill with boats.

Every year around Christmas, Greenville businessmen threw a spontaneous party at Galla Paxton's cotton brokerage. And every year the Little Red Soapbox, with its misspelled legend "For Making Speeches Without Provacation," was awarded to the person who, according to the consensus, had earned it that year. Hodding was one of the first recipients.

His acceptance in Greenville social circles did not rule out disagreements, and his critics made their views known. He regularly received furious, insulting letters. If a letter was signed, Hodding answered it, often angrily. Serious signed letters from responsible people in the community caused him concern, as did one in 1950 from a Greenville lawyer who complained that he was tired of "a monopoly by a newspaper whose policy is so nearly completely at variance from the views of a great majority of us."[10] Some of the reactions to his editorial policy cost the paper revenue. "His stand always made it difficult for the business side," said John Gibson.[11] Hodding referred to himself as a "tormentor of advertisers." For a time Hodding ran a campaign in the newspaper attacking the sheriff for letting bootleggers run wide-open juke joints. In revenge, the sheriff made the county give the delinquent-tax list to the Leland newspaper, which was much smaller, to print. Hodding reacted grandly: as a public service, he printed the list in the *Delta Democrat-Times* without payment.[12] He was brave enough to be often on opposite sides of the fence politically from old friends such as Edmund Taylor and Billy Wynn, who had provided financial support in his earliest days in Greenville.

Sometimes there was physical violence. People in Greenville still remember that Conwell Sykes, president of the Commercial National Bank, disagreed with nearly every editorial Hodding wrote. They were bound to tangle. The confrontation came when the men of the Episcopal church met at a hunting lodge out of town to discuss church finances. At the bar, a fixture at any Delta gathering, Sykes and Hodding had heated words over something Hodding had written, and Hodding knocked Sykes down. The Episcopal minister, appalled, said that this was scandalous behavior; Hodding and Sykes must be seen shaking hands on the post office steps the next morning. Grimly they complied. (Sykes's daughter Marion would later work for the *Delta Democrat-Times*.)

While he was never physically afraid, Hodding was assailed by fear that his whole enterprise could go under at any time. His anxiety became acute, his son Philip remembered, as the racial situation worsened. Exacerbating his fear was the ever-present worry over his eyesight.

It was up to Betty to keep him going and keep depression away. A friend said that Hodding had no doubts about himself because Betty supported him so wholeheartedly. In fact, she sometimes acted as a brake as well as a supporter. Hodding had a romantic image of himself and played the part of the archetypal Southerner—chivalrous, confrontational, hard-drinking, violent, protective of his honor, someone who did everything on impulse. Betty warned him not to make people mad when he didn't mean to. He had to make people mad over valid issues, she told him, but he should be careful not to make them mad unintentionally.

And it was up to Betty to act as good guy to Hodding's bad guy. At various times she served as president of five PTAs; the Women's Auxiliary of St. James' Episcopal Church; Atrus, a women's civic group; and the Junior Auxiliary. She was active in a garden club, a study club, and the hospital auxiliary, and in fund-raising drives. She helped establish a nursery school for what were then called "underprivileged" children. She was on the city's park and recreation board and was a Cub Scout den mother. In 1948 she was named Greenville's Woman of the Year for her contributions to the community as homemaker, in civic service, and in church activities. She was always involved with the newspaper, where it is impossible to exaggerate how influential she was. She had strong administrative and organizational ability and, some say, a better analytical mind than did her husband.

Hodding always told people he never would have accomplished anything without Betty, and most who knew him and worked with him agree. Betty pushed him, supported him, nurtured him, and gave invaluable aid and comfort and advice.

His family meant a great deal to Hodding. When Hodding III went off to prep school in 1949, Big Hodding, as he was called by now, was exceptionally proud. He turned down speaking engagements when young Hodding was at home so he could be with his son every possible minute. He wrote him long, detailed letters about what was happening at the paper, in town, and in the family. (The two Hoddings could fight, however: Big Hodding's temper was quick and hot, and his son felt the lash of his father's tongue.) When, in 1951, young Hodding decided he should leave Exeter and finish high school in Greenville, his father was delighted.

"We Were Like a Family"

In the postwar years the *Delta Democrat-Times*, like Greenville, grew and prospered, and Hodding built a staff on which he could depend. Their loyalty, enterprise, and reliability enabled him not only to spend the summers in Maine, but to go out of town for meetings, lecture tours, and free-lance work. These travels were essential if Hodding was to live in Greenville; he had to get away.

John Gibson, part-owner as well as business manager at the paper, was like a rock. The newsroom staff felt that as financial manager he waged war on them. "He wouldn't let us buy paper clips," Betty Carter recalled. "He said enough came into the building and we could save them. I still pick up a paper clip when I see one on the floor. One month he wouldn't give us any more copy pencils and said he had given us enough the month before to last. We were using *stubs*." When the employees heard a rumor that Gibson had bought duck decoys with the Christmas bonus money, their fury knew no bounds.[13] Gibson was stingy with raises and strict about vacation time, but staffers who felt they had been treated unfairly could go to Hodding. "Papa fix," Hodding would say, and then have a talk with "Johnny." The staff called Hodding "Hodding" and Gibson "Mr. Gibson," mystifying the many foreign reporters who came to visit the *DD-T* and leading to such awkward phrasings as, "Hodding, Mr. Gibson says . . ." When *DD-T* employees had a reunion after the paper had been sold, they passed out bumper stickers that read: "Will Rogers never met John Gibson." Betty was horrified.

Gibson and Hodding were fast friends; they often hunted and vacationed together. Gibson, although he maintained Hodding could never read a balance sheet, nevertheless respected his editorial ability and knew how to promote his liberalism. As for Hodding's absences, Gibson enjoyed them.

In 1949, Gibson hired Ione Lundy to work as secretary, first for him and Hodding both. The only person who could read Hodding's handwriting, Lundy was soon working solely for the editor. She retyped his messy typescripts for *Southern Legacy* and *Where Main Street Meets the River*. Hodding then began relying on his Dictaphone and her transcriptions. When he was traveling, he would call in and dictate to Lundy his column that appeared in eight southern papers; she would type it up and then mail it to the papers. When Hodding saw an advertisement for the first IBM Selectric typewriter, he told her, "Ione, I'm going to get you one of these." And he bought it, despite Gibson's disapproval.

Hodding could attract superior reporters. David Brown, one of his most loyal, faithful employees, joined the paper soon after World War II. He had gained a new perspective and revised his inbred feelings on race when he was in the service. While working toward a master's degree in journalism at Louisiana State University, he reviewed Hodding's *Winds of Fear* for the school paper. When Hodding came to LSU to speak, Brown asked him for a job. "I used to say the last place I'd ever work would be Mississippi, but working for you would outweigh that," Brown told him. "Greenville is different," Hodding said. "Do you have a car?"

Brown did not have a car, but Hodding told him to come ahead. He could do the night police beat—the station was right across the street from the newspaper office. Brown arrived after the Carters had left for Maine, and spent the summer at their house on Arnold Street with Tom and Doris Karsell, where the Carters' cook prepared their meals. Karsell, the managing editor, was fairly new himself. Louise Crump, the society editor, mothered the young members of the staff—Brown, Karsell, and Edwin Vincent, the young Greenville woman who was city editor. Crump introduced Dave Brown to Sue Harte, whom he married. After the wedding, they spent the summer of 1949 in the Carters' house; then they moved into an apartment in Crump's house. The Karsells lived in a little house in back.

Once Brown acquired a car, Hodding reassigned him to the courthouse. Brown protested that he and the chief of police had become friends. "That can be a problem," Hodding said. "I don't want my reporters too close to their regular sources." The lesson stayed with

Brown, and he has always told his journalism students about the conversation.[14]

When Hodding was out of town, Betty, as well as John Gibson, kept an eye on things; but when Hodding hired editors, he gave them guidelines with plenty of leeway. "They knew the objectives," said Gibson. "Be local. Be aggressive. Don't kowtow, but don't set out to make enemies." According to Betty Carter, "They knew where we stood and what the policies were. They did better than they would have done if Hodding had been standing over them."

By 1949, when Louise Crump was in full sway, the *DD-T*'s extensive social coverage filled several pages. Crump was a monument at the paper and in the town at large. Her civic work was legendary. She had Greenville adopt a Methodist orphanage in Jackson for three days one Christmas—people took in two or three children for the holidays. She helped found the Delta Debutante Club, Beta Sigma Phi, the Junior Auxiliary, the Newcomers Club, the Twin Cities Theatrical Guild (the twin cities were Greenville and Leland), and the recreation center for the cadets at Greenville's air base. She worked with health department personnel on a campaign to clean up public rest rooms, and persuaded the *DD-T* to run pictures of unsightly outdoor toilets in the slums on the front page.

Louise began writing her immensely popular column, "Delta Scene," in 1946, and when her husband, Brodie, began one of his own, "Mostly Old Stuff," later that same year, their columns appeared on alternate days. Brodie, who played the senator in Elia Kazan's *Baby Doll*, which was filmed near Greenville, apparently had total recall. His column might include reminiscences of icy roads or talk of hollyhock seeds, essays on Mother's Day and the virtues of Golden Bantam corn versus Paymaster or Tennessee Red Cob. Louise went in for club news and social notes—sighs of relief that a garden club convention was over, and stories about birthday parties, square dances, and the activities of prominent people in town, including some who hated Hodding. The unspoken theme of Louise's column was: If you do this, it will help you socially.[15] It worked.

178

Both columns had tremendous readership and influence. Louise once wrote one paragraph about a crippled boy that brought in six wheelchairs. A column of Brodie's yielded a truckload of furniture and clothes for a tenant farmer's family who had lost everything in a fire.

For a while Louise was also food editor—even though the staff used to say she would scorch water if she tried to boil it. Hodding liked it when she tired of "impersonal recipes" and invented a family for whom she ran menus, recipes, and shopping lists in dialogue under the standing head "Life with the Jones."[16]

One day after Shelby Foote's novel *Love in a Dry Season* was published, Crump came up to him. "She said, 'Shelley'—she always called me Shelley—'there's a brighter side to life.' That helped me decide to leave Greenville."[17] Crump later published two novels of her own.

Charles Kerg, the only holdover from the old *Democrat-Times*, stayed on and became a fixture. Henry Marsh, who taught journalism after he left the newspaper business, coauthored a textbook featuring stories by Pulitzer Prize–winning reporters, and in it he included work by both Kerg and Louise Crump.

"Louise Crump was making thirty-five dollars a week when I went there," Dave Brown recalled. "Tom Karsell made a hundred. When I arrived, Gibson asked me if I was eligible for the GI Bill. I was, and he put me on as a trainee, so the government paid most of my salary. That Christmas, Betty gave me a sterling silver bottle opener. When I was checking out at Kroger's, a pressman cashed a check for twice what I made—but I opened bottles with a silver opener."

Nobody on the staff seems to have minded the low wages and long hours, or resented the fact that the Carters had much more money than they did. "Hodding would give anything away," according to Dave Brown. "Once I said I hadn't had a steak in six months. He went to the freezer and took out two steaks and gave them to me. Later, when I had children, the kids wanted to take piano lessons and I couldn't buy a piano. Hodding said, 'I'll buy them a piano.'

He didn't, but he wanted the people he cared for to have what they wanted." This story is perhaps more valuable as evidence of Brown's devotion than as evidence of Hodding's generosity to his employees.

Far more than money, the staff valued Hodding's management style. He said he ran his paper "as a sort of free-wheeling democracy that sometimes borders on anarchy," and admitted the system did "produce prima donnas but it has also produced a good newspaper and a good atmosphere in which to work."[18]

"You had your job, and he never interfered," said Vince Maggio, the composing room chief. Maggio worked on Sundays without extra pay and often stayed late, but when he was out nine months with appendicitis complicated by an abscessed stitch and out another eight months for a thyroid operation, his paychecks arrived regularly. Hodding, generally prolabor, backed the shop's requests for raises six years in a row. In 1953, however, he told the composing room men that they were the highest-paid skilled workmen in Greenville, and resisted. The shop backed down.

Hodding and Betty encouraged closeness, and achieved it. Staff member after staff member, talking of the glory days, said, "We were like a family." And they were. Maggio and his wife inherited Philip's baby buggy for their own baby. Louise Crump was Philip's godmother. Doris Karsell, Tom's wife, kept Philip after school while Betty worked.

It was a family of writers, too, encouraged in outside work by Hodding. He helped Louise Crump with both her novels and encouraged his reporters and editors to free-lance. Dave Brown, for instance, was a stringer for United Press, the Memphis *Press-Scimitar*, cotton trade journals, and later for *Time* and *Life*.

Although Hodding spent a great deal of time making speeches and writing magazine articles and books, he was still a newsman. When a tornado hit Vicksburg and ripped out a chunk of the downtown area, Hodding wanted to see it. He invited staffers to go with him. Karsell and Brown went, but a new man, George Stroud, turned down the invitation. "Hodding worried all the way to Vicksburg," recalled

Brown. "He said, 'I don't understand how any newsman could stay away.'" After they saw some of the damage in Vicksburg, Hodding wanted to visit the newsroom at the local paper to see how the staff was managing. They were without electricity, and pots of lead were frozen in the Linotypes. Hodding was moved at the enterprise of the dedicated journalists, who somehow got hold of a generator and put the paper out.

In Greenville, there were staff parties at Christmastime—Vince Maggio cleaned off the tables in the composing room to serve as buffets—and election nights turned into big parties in the newsroom, with plenty of food and liquor. Mississippi resisted voting machines, so the *Delta Democrat-Times* had correspondents calling in results. The staff put a big bulletin board in the window and everybody in town came by to check on it; most of them then joined the party inside.

Harry Marsh, who had attended Baylor University, in Waco, Texas, came to the *DD-T* after the Korean War. He took over the "critter" page, snapping pictures and writing the obligatory stories about the biggest tomato or the man who caught the most bass. He loved the family feeling of the staff. "On Saturday nights after the paper was out, we'd go to the Browns' and watch television and talk and eat," Marsh recalled. Sue Brown made a salad and somebody picked up tamales from Doe's Eat Place, another peculiar Greenville institution, a restaurant that had opened on Nelson Street in the black neighborhood. Doe Signa, the Italian proprietor, started making tamales that became popular, and white people started going to buy them—entering by the back door. Doe's was later the best restaurant in Greenville for whites.

"Give Mrs. O'Leary's Cow Three Columns— Give Panama Three Inches"

Editorials in the *Delta Democrat-Times*—and sometimes the news stories—were partisan, personal, fervent, and emotional. Hodding was never reflective, analytical, or detached. The front page, with its heavy black gothic type, often looked cluttered with the many local stories, but it was always readable. The women's section and the editorial pages, with their lighter headline type, looked better. Ben Wasson began his critic's page in 1946, with comments on books, drama, music, and art. It ran the only book reviews in Mississippi.

By 1954 the paper had won the Mississippi Press Association's general excellence award for dailies five years in a row. It was full of local news of all kinds, some of it controversial. Hodding never let family or social ties influence the paper's policy. The practice of always putting in the paper the names of people arrested for drunk driving rankled for years. One woman came by the *DD-T* offices begging that her husband's name be omitted; she was afraid he would lose his job. Dave Brown told her that the policy was firm, that even the name of the owner's brother had been printed in the paper when he was ticketed.

Hodding, Betty, and John Gibson all knew the value of local news. And benefiting local advertisers helped keep circulation up. When Hodding was on an Asian trip in the fall of 1952, Betty proudly wrote to him that the front page that day had boasted twenty local stories.[19] "Local stories were the basis of our success," Gibson said. "Give Mrs. O'Leary's cow three columns—nobody else is going to use the story. Give Panama three inches—and that's all."

Local news could be about anything—Howard Dyer's hiccups (he had twenty a minute for eight days), or the Sea Scouts' meeting the four Frenchmen who visited Greenville while following the river trail of Father Marquette and Louis Joliet. When a really big local story came along, the *DD-T* shone. In November 1948, Dave Brown was driving through Leland and saw cars from the sheriff's office in front of the house that belonged to a prominent family, the Dickenses. Like the good reporter he was, Brown stopped, got out of his car, and found the sheriff, Hugh Foote (an uncle of Shelby's), cleaning up the bathroom. Mrs. John Dickens said she had caught a small, very black Negro hacking her mother to death in the bathroom with her rose shears. Mrs. Dickens's mother was the widow of J. W. Thompson, who had been chairman of the Levee Board and an important man in the Delta.

Nobody believed Ruth Dickens, except, apparently, the sheriff, who helped her clean up the bathroom. After she was arrested and held in the little jail in the Greenville Courthouse, people in town got in their cars and drove 'round and 'round the courthouse hoping for a glimpse of her. At her trial the next June, Mrs. Dickens was found guilty of first-degree murder. The *DD-T* duly reported after the conviction that Mrs. Dickens's cell was eight feet by ten, with a ceiling covered with corrugated iron; she had an electric fan and a rocking chair in her cell, and her nephew brought her sandwiches. The paper conscientiously followed up on the trial news with an editorial pointing out that the recent attention focused on the courthouse showed the need for refurbishing the courtroom and jury quarters.

Editorially, the paper boosted Greenville and Washington County, promoting industrial development and the establishment of a community theater. The paper fought prohibition laws that allowed Delta sheriffs to get rich from fees paid by bootleggers. The news columns faithfully reported on the activities of garden clubs and 4-H Clubs, and on the annual mule races at Rosedale; Delta Council Day in April; the Lake Village Water Carnival, held each Fourth of July; the Greenville Hornets in the fall; the town's Christmas parade; and the Christmastime Delta Debutante Ball. The paper underwrote the cost of a film series from the Museum of Modern Art in New York. In 1947, the *DD-T* served as the central collection agency to help Greenville's Jewish community raise its quota for the United Jewish Appeal; Protestants and Catholics together contributed $10,000. A few years later, Jews and Protestants contributed $20,000 to help Catholics in the community build a new school, with strong support from the paper. In 1948 it gave lavish coverage to the Friendship Barge, which it sponsored along with the Greenville Ministerial Association and the churches of Washington County. The barge was loaded in Greenville with clothing, food, and usable farm equipment for shipment to destitute areas of Europe and Asia under the supervision of Church World Service.

Hodding made a conscious effort to balance each controversial editorial with what he called a "sweetness and light" editorial. "Then," he explained, "they can't say they don't agree with anything that SOB says." The editorial of January 9, 1952, for example, decried the assassination of Florida black leader Henry Tyson Moore, while the next day Hodding used the editorial space to commend the Greenville police for rounding up stray dogs.

Sometimes the staff manufactured news. In 1948 everybody in town was disgusted with the service of the Illinois Central Railroad. The IC's predecessor, the Yazoo and Mississippi Valley line, had operated three trains a day between Memphis and New Orleans, stopping at Greenville, Vicksburg, Natchez, and Baton Rouge. When the IC took over, it cut passenger service and concentrated on its original Memphis–New Orleans line, which ran sixty miles inland from the river towns. One passenger train, nicknamed "Old Reluctant," poked along from Memphis to Vicksburg, taking six hours to travel the 150 or so miles to Greenville. Adding insult, it backed into Greenville on a spur line from Leland, which lay about ten miles to the east.

The Greenville Chamber of Commerce protested the Illinois Central's treatment of Greenville, Mississippi's fastest-growing city. Handling the story on the chamber's action, Tom Karsell commented that he could outrun Old Reluctant himself. Edwin Vincent, the city editor, didn't think Tom could outrun a balky mule.

"Let's race mules against Old Reluctant!" was Tom's idea. And so the newspaper sponsored the First Annual Mule–Train Race. Plans were made to put up relays of plantation mules against the passenger train from Cleveland, Mississippi, to Greenville, forty miles away. The *DD-T* ran deadpan stories about the upcoming race (wire services picked them up) that quoted mayors of the towns along the route and reported reactions of civic clubs, mule fanciers, and chambers of commerce.

Plans became more elaborate. One mule rider would hand over a cotton-picker's sack of what was alleged to be mail to the next rider in the relay. In each town where the rider would change mules, the mayor would hand a key to the city to the mule and a bunch of carrots and hay to the rider. "Miss Mule," a beautiful Delta girl, along with a band, the American Legion, and the mayor, would greet the victor in Greenville. The paper promised that the mules would win.

The Illinois Central, not pleased by all this, sent a representative to town. The *DD-T* said not to worry, it was all in fun. Time-Life and Paramount's newsreel division were to cover the race.

The *DD-T* ran stories of the upcoming race under big headlines. On May 21, 1948, the day before the event, there were six stories about it on the first page alone. Of course, the race sponsors cheated. John Fletcher, a Cleveland funeral director, rode the first mule out from Cleveland and then pulled off to a side road, where a cattle truck and a Greenville police car waited. The truck took the panting mule home, and the police car rushed Fletcher to the outskirts of the next town, Boyle, where he mounted a fresh mule and raced into town to turn the mule over to a new rider. This continued all the way to Greenville.

Old Reluctant arrived in Greenville on time the day of the race, and almost won. When the last mule came into Greenville, it balked at the band. Old Reluctant would have beaten it if desperate Greenville residents had not pulled and pushed the mule to the finish line.

Hodding himself wrote the main story on the race the next day under the headline "Old Reluctant Runs Last; Iron Horse No Match for Mules." The Delta mule, he said, "came into his (or its) own again Saturday in a train–mule race that a lot of folks believe was fixed. . . ."

Hodding acknowledged the criticism that the newspaper should report the news and not make it with prejudiced stunts, but he disagreed. "I can't run for public office and remain an editor, but the staff and I participate in many civic activities."

Hodding once began a speech by saying, "Some newspaper people think the editor should stay clear of what might be called local entanglements. . . . He should stand to one side, holding a mirror before the community, reporting what he sees in it." He, however, had chosen to pursue precisely the opposite course.[20] Hodding served on many local boards and believed in principle that an "editor or reporter should be free to participate in any activities that have community-building as their objective and which aren't obviously partisan in nature or remunerative to the individual or directly to the news-paper." It was his "firm conviction that the more an editor and his staff identifies . . . with the community, the better job you can do for that community."[21] He invested in the first rice farm in Washington County in order to help promote the crop, and promoted the Land Improvement Association, the county fair, civic baseball and softball leagues, a local professional baseball association, an industry-locating service, and an airline.[22]

He served on chamber of commerce committees, but this did not prevent his lambasting the chamber of commerce when he thought fit, "which was quite often." In 1949, more than a year after the mule–train race, the Greenville Chamber of Commerce board of directors, reversing its stand, passed a resolution praising the Illinois Central and saying the *DD-T*'s criticism of the railroad had done incalculable harm to Greenville. So Hodding passed his own resolution that the chamber of commerce board of directors be made honorary members of the Brotherhood of Railroad Firemen; and "be it resolved that their first duties as firemen shall be to build a fire under themselves."[23]

Hodding worked extremely hard on the chamber's campaign to bring industry to Greenville, where jobs were needed; he saw that the mechanization of cotton farming was throwing tenant farmers out of work.[24] The *DD-T* put everything it had into support for a bond issue to finance industrial acquisition. When it passed by a lopsided vote in January 1951, Hodding exulted. It was "a great triumph for the town and the paper and splendid proof of what people could do when they worked together," he wrote Hodding III, "which is what those cyni-cal little brats that you referred to from Long Island wouldn't realize because they live principally in a vacuum and sealed from neighbors and from any sense of community or personal cooperation. Don't let them get under your skin. The New York and Westchester group was just the same when I was in college and they actually have a very small say-so in this country or in the affairs of the world."[25]

Hodding did not allow sports promoters or any other profit-making group to pay reporters' expenses, nor were reporters permitted to earn money by working for political campaigns on the side. On the other hand, he defended two of his government junkets, one a Navy aircraft carrier trip and the other an annual inspection trip of the Mississippi River, because, he said, they were important to the area.

As the mechanization of agriculture continued to displace black tenant farmers, Hodding saw a basic need for decent educational facilities for the tenants' children, and he began demanding equal schools. Whites, who would have to pay the taxes to build new black schools, disagreed with him and fiercely resented his editorials. Planters accused him of meddling.

Hodding's editorials attacked Senator Joseph McCarthy from 1950 on, and warmly supported Dwight Eisenhower for president in 1952. Every day during the campaign, the top of the editorial page announced: "Eisenhower says" and then offered a quotation from the candidate.

Hodding supported Frank Smith, as much a liberal as Mississippi could produce, for Congress against Oscar Wolfe in the early fifties. He liked Smith, who had been on the staff of the *Morning Star* in Greenwood, and disliked Wolfe, who approved of the use of the lash on prisoners at the state prison farm at Parchman. In his speeches Wolfe attacked Hodding as much as he attacked Smith. Smith won.

Hodding's fight against "Black Annie," as the prisoners called the lash at Parchman, went on for years. In July 1953, Tom Karsell dug up the fact that a prison trusty-guard had fired into a group of prisoners, wounding several. Marvin Wiggins, director at Parchman, did not report the incident and said it was only a routine matter when Karsell asked him about it. Wiggins barred Hodding and the entire *DD-T* staff from Parchman, saying they were too "disreputable" even to walk through his gates.

In an editorial, Hodding suggested that a group of editors judge the reputation of the *DD-T* and a group of qualified penologists judge Parchman. "Whoever gets the low score should take ten from 'Black Annie' with the winner wielding the strap. We feel ourselves getting sorry for Marvin's backside already. But on second thought, since we don't believe in the lash like Marvin does, we suggest as a substitute if he loses, he be required to read a book on present-day penal methods."

"I Never Knew I Could Get So Delighted with Anything This Close to Home"

When Betty and Hodding decided to build a new house in Greenville in 1949, they chose a piece of land on the highway west of town between Greenville and the Mississippi River bridge. The owner, Anne Stokes, had always refused to sell, but she admired Hodding and agreed to part with 10.87 acres. At closing, after the exchange of money and title, Mrs. Stokes opened a book and read a poem about how everybody should own a bit of land where a spider could spin a web to catch moonbeams on the dew. Then she presented the book to the Carters.

Betty wanted to be on hand to supervise the construction, so during the summer of 1950 they did not go to Maine but instead rented out the Boat Barn and offered their sailboat, the *Channel Cat*, for charter. The family moved into a quickly built tenant house on the new property in Greenville so they could be close to the construction site. (John Gibson bought their house on Arnold Street.) Betty and Hodding became consumed with the building project, scheduling innumerable consultations with their Baton Rouge architect. They found a well digger, and a bulldozer dug out the cypress slough in front of the house to make an artificial lake fed by a deep well. Hodding had two little black boys kill the water moccasins in the lake with willow switches; they were paid ten cents a snake, and made more than five dollars. Hodding ordered bream and bass to stock the lake with, and put a skiff and a Navy rubber raft in it.

After buying a small tractor, he was able to cut the grass, plow up land for a fall garden, and haul gravel for a roadbed. He worked so hard clearing out underbrush that he lost his glasses, sprained his wrist, and got a case of poison ivy that put him in the hospital.[26] He bought beef cattle, a pig, a burro, saddle horses, and ducks. "I never knew I could get so delighted with anything this close to home and to nature," he wrote his oldest son. "We have about 70 laying hens now, 25 of them arriving tomorrow and presenting us with 18 eggs immediately."[27] (He became so excited about his poultry that he and John Gibson seriously considered going into the broiler business.)

Work on the new house went more slowly—and cost more—than expected, so in 1951 they sold the house in Maine. They moved into the new house, which they named Feliciana, in the late summer of 1951 and held a giant housewarming on Labor Day weekend. Their architect and other Baton Rouge friends chartered an air-conditioned bus, complete with bar and bartender, and rode up in woozy comfort for the party.

It was an impressive house, with a large central hall and a curving stairway, for which Doris Karsell painted a mural. When they decided to add a wing with a family room, Hodding embarked on another lecture tour to pay for it. Eventually the property included a swimming pool and a tennis court.

"Privately Printed and Fabulously Priced"

Shelby Foote, who had worked as a cub reporter on the *Delta Star*, came back to Greenville after the war, lived with his mother, and wrote fiction. He had had two short stories published in *The Saturday Evening Post* and decided to publish one of his longer stories, "The Merchant of Bristol," by himself. He and Bill Yarborough, who worked in the *DD-T*'s print shop, produced a slim blue-covered pamphlet.

During the production process, Ben Wasson of the *DD-T*'s critic's page heard about it and asked them to set "Levee Press" as the publisher's imprint. Wasson had grown up in Mississippi, roomed with

William Faulkner at Ole Miss during the brief time Faulkner spent in college, worked with Broadway producer Leland Hayward for a while, and then as Faulkner's literary agent. Hodding, Wasson, and Kenneth Haxton, who had started and now ran the book department in Nelms and Blum, his family's department store in Greenville, had been talking for some time about starting a small publishing venture that would print limited editions of southern writers. Since they were going to call their company the Levee Press, Wasson thought Shelby Foote might use the same imprint. He agreed, and Yarborough ran off 260 copies. Foote stapled them together.

The twenty-page booklet that Yarborough and Foote published was not as handsome as the volumes the Levee Press later produced. Autographed copies sold at Nelms and Blum for $1.50 each, and some people complained about the price, pointing out that a good shirt cost less.[28]

For the first *real* Levee Press book, Wasson suggested Eudora Welty.[29] When the others, who knew Welty, agreed, Wasson wrote to her to ask whether she had an unpublished manuscript. Her novella *Music from Spain* became the first official Levee Press book. She received a twenty-five-percent royalty on the $3.50 price. Haxton felt some of the pages should be headed with a Spanish musical score, and they chose a work by Isaac Albéniz. Haxton drew the cubist guitar for the cover. Charles Poore, writing in *The New York Times Book Review* in 1949, called the volume a "handsome example of bookmaking."[30]

After Wasson contacted Faulkner to ask whether he had a manuscript, Wasson and Hodding drove to Oxford for an evening with the Faulkners. They returned to Greenville with what Faulkner suggested they call "A Dangling Clause from a Work in Progress." Instead they titled it *Notes on a Horse Thief*, and set it to begin with a lowercase letter and end without punctuation. (It eventually became part of the novel *A Fable*.)

Faulkner's willingness to autograph all nine hundred copies of his book led to a most hectic day for Hodding. In early 1951 the Carters' house was under construction and Hodding was heavily involved in a chamber of commerce campaign to attract an industry, any industry, to Greenville. Greenville had caught the interest of the Alexander Smith company, a carpet manufacturer, and a delegation from the company was supposed to visit Greenville on January 23. The chamber had scheduled for Hodding to meet the Alexander Smith grandees at the town airport and take them for a river cruise on board the *Mistuh Charley*, the *DD-T*'s cabin cruiser, which people in town had taken to calling the "Welcome Wagon."

Early on the morning of January 23, Estelle Faulkner telephoned from Oxford to say that her husband had decided not to open the crates of books the Levee Press had sent him for autographing but to bring them back to Greenville and sign them there. He was at that moment on his way to Greenville, with the crates, in his station wagon.

A half-hour later Hodding found in the mail at the office a letter from the Mississippi Game and Fish Commission notifying him that his order for five hundred bass and five hundred bream fingerlings would arrive on the morning of January 23 and must be picked up, not in Greenville, but in Indianola, twenty-eight miles away, at eleven a.m. The letter instructed him to bring suitable receptacles, such as oil drums, to hold the fish, and to stir the water on the return trip to keep it aerated. Almost immediately Hodding received a telephone message that his 150 day-old chicks had arrived and should be put in his brooder house as soon as possible. He was now due in four places at the same time—at the airport to meet the Alexander Smith group, at Indianola, at the hatchery, and at the office with William Faulkner.

Once Faulkner had arrived at the *DD-T*, and the crates had been unloaded from his car, Ben Wasson brought him to Hodding's office. There Wasson handed him the books one by one, and Faulkner signed them standing up. Hodding sent out to Al's #2 for beer, and Faulkner sipped as he signed. Hodding, meanwhile, fled home to check on the chicks, which had been delivered, and found the electrical outlet in the brooder house did not work. He and Betty brought all the extension cords from the tenant house and plugged the heater into the outlet in the henhouse. Then he raced off to Indianola with the gardener to pick up the fish. On the way home, Phillips stayed in the back of the truck with the oil drums and kept the water stirred up with an egg beater.

Betty and Hodding made it to the hotel, not the airport, to help welcome the Alexander Smith people. Faulkner refused invitations to both the boat ride for the carpet makers and the chamber of commerce banquet afterward, but he agreed to go to the Carters' for a drink between the two events. After he finished signing books the next morning, Faulkner boarded the *Mistuh Charley* with Hodding, Ben Wasson, and John Gibson; they cruised around and talked about duck hunting. When they returned to the *DD-T* at twelve-fifteen, Hodding's secretary asked, "Did you forget you were supposed to talk to the Kiwanis Club at noon?" Hodding rushed over and described how the new Mississippi "was diversifying its agriculture and restoring its soil and bringing in industries and producing more writers to the acre than any state in the Union." He knew all about it, he said.[31]

Notes on a Horse Thief was published at the same time that Faulkner received the Nobel Prize, and the nine hundred copies sold out quickly. Irving Howe, reviewing this "privately printed and fabulously priced story" in *The Nation*, said it was "a bad piece of writing."[32]

Hodding was ready to publish next a book of poems by James Gould Fletcher of Arkansas, but Fletcher's New York publisher decided he wanted them after all. Wasson approached Flannery O'Connor, Carson McCullers, and Robert Penn Warren, but none had a suitable manuscript. Carl Van Vechten sent some unpublished works by Gertrude Stein, which the three Greenville publishers found so mystifying that they returned them, regretfully, to Van Vechten. Unknown writers submitted hundreds of manuscripts, but none of them seemed good enough.

Meanwhile, Anne Stokes, to whom Hodding felt obligated because she had sold him the land, nagged at him to publish a book of William Alexander Percy's poems. It did not seem to bother Mrs. Stokes that they already appeared in collections that were still in print. She had worked with Percy on some of his poems, she said, and there were variant forms of some of the published poems that should be printed, too. During a long and complicated correspondence with Alfred Knopf, whose company held the copyright, Hodding actually tried to encourage Knopf to refuse permission, to save the Levee Press the trouble of publishing the poems. Knopf declined to get Hodding off the hook and granted permission to publish Percy's poems. *Of Silence and the Stars* came out with Mrs. Stokes's editing and a foreword by Hodding.

He thought of publishing some "lost literature" of the South, such as "Prentiss' Defense of His Friends," a stirring antebellum courtroom plea that a Natchez lawyer, Sargent S. Prentiss, made in defense of three roistering Mississippi planters who had become involved in a bloody brawl while attending a wedding in Kentucky. Prentiss's oration, which saved their lives in a hostile court, had been popular reading around the turn of the century. Nothing came of Hodding's plan.

After trying and failing to get a manuscript from Tennessee Williams, the Levee Press ceased to exist. Hodding, Wasson, and Haxton had full-time jobs and none of them had the time to push it.

"It's Not Hard to Sit in New York and Say What's Wrong with the South"

In the spring of 1947, Hodding sent off the first section of his novel *Flood Crest*. Both his agent and his editor, John Selby at Rinehart & Company (as the firm was now named), said they loved it.

A few months later, while in Maine, he could write: "Tuesday evening, twenty minutes before train time, I finished Floodcrest and with it tucked under my arm, left for New York where I turned it over, with all its final revisions, to Rinehart & Company. Now for the first time in seven years I have no deadline hanging over my head."[33]

The situation did not last long. Hodding went back to Mississippi for an election in July, which he described as "not as bad as the

Bilbo battle last summer," although he was again "being announced
[*sic*] as a red and racial agitator." William Raney of Rinehart came
to Greenville with Hodding's manuscript to polish it up, work on
"an additional small love at the end," and "make a few other minor
changes," as Hodding put it.[34]

Flood Crest appeared in December 1947. Its author, a friend said,
loved the Delta mystique and thought no one was a real man unless
he had lived through the flood of 1927. In the book Hodding wrote
about an almost-flood. Cleve Pikestaff, a character based on Senator
Bilbo, although calculating and cynical in his Red-baiting ("A Red was
any nigger who wanted to vote and any white man who thought he
ought to," he says), is neither as colorful nor as repulsive as the real-
life Bilbo. Pikestaff says nothing to equal Bilbo's "My Dear Dago"
or "every damn Jew from Jesus Christ on down." The book does
not throb with the sincere outrage at racial injustice that fueled *The
Winds of Fear*. It is a badly written story about cardboard people.

Reviewers paid deference to Hodding's status as a strong, articulate southern liberal. In *The New York Times Book Review*, Knox
Burger wrote that Hodding had been "on the right side of more causes
than almost any other man in his region" and bore "the distinction of
having been called some of the choicest and most uncomplimentary
names" by Bilbo and Huey Long. Burger praised *Flood Crest*, citing
Hodding's "intelligent, constructive writing on important Southern
themes," his courage, and his "good reporter's eye for accurate and
revealing detail." He quoted one paragraph from the novel that seems
to sum up Hodding's personal dilemma:

> It's not hard to sit . . . in New York and say what's wrong with
> the South. It is hard to do it as an ordinary Southerner. You've
> got two strikes on you to start. Your fellow white Southerners
> hate you for it. You're scalawag, a nigger-lover in their eyes.
> Your Northern reformers deride you for not going far enough.
> And you're suspected by Negroes everywhere because you're
> Southern and White.[35]

Confirming Hodding's statements about northern reformers, *The Daily Worker* gave the book a bad review and described Carter as one of those liberals "who want to save their souls and their skins at the same time. In a timid fashion they want to correct some of the things in the South that affront their sensitive souls, but they are afraid of the anger of the Southern ruling class. If you don't bother us, these 'liberals' say, we'll take care of the Communists for you."[36] *The New Yorker* called it as "mechanical and false as a pinball machine,"[37] and other critics were of the same mind. The reviewer for the Jackson *Daily News* said it very well: "It is one thing to present an idea on politics or a social problem on an editorial page; another to have two or three paragons of liberalism state the author's opinion in rather unnatural prose in several paragraphs per quotation."[38]

Hodding later said he wished he had held on to the manuscript until his emotions were more "stable." He feared that the work would permanently damage his reputation as a writer. Late in 1947 he wrote Bernice Baumgarten at Brandt & Brandt about the historical novel he would write next. "I know it will be my best because I have been working, researching and mulling over it for two years and am not going to be rushed into finishing it too soon." Dissatisfied with Rinehart's distribution of *Flood Crest*, he wanted Baumgarten's opinion on whether he should change publishers. Meanwhile, he said, he was "in the middle of the little book that I told you I was doing to do for the Louisiana State University Press, a non-fictional and personalized study of the South."[39] This would be a "handbook for southerners, about twenty-five thousand words. . . . It is important to me that this book be printed in the south . . . for the reason that it will make people down here realize that my ideas are not so alien that other southerners do not share them even to the extent of publishing them." Admittedly, he did not expect to make money from the book. "This actually comes under the heading of being a southern publisher rather than being a writer."[40]

In early August, when Hodding was in Maine, where he was having another sloop built, John Selby asked him about writing a nonfiction

"Southern book" for Rinehart. Hodding told him about the "very short, connected essay sort of thing on this subject" he was doing for the LSU Press, "as part of the campaign to prove that I'm not in the pay of the Yankee publishers." He wanted to write an apology for southern traditions and attitudes, while maintaining his insistence on that region righting its many wrongs. He did not think the book would preclude his doing a longer book about the South. But the long-delayed Guggenheim-sponsored novel had to come first—after the LSU book.[41] Selby did not think the LSU Press book would stand in the way of a big "Southern book." It might be very useful, he said, in establishing Hodding as a current William Allen White, the distinguished editor and author from Emporia, Kansas. "The fellow is a fireball, and we . . . want to keep him happy and at work," Selby wrote in a memo to Bernice Baumgarten.[42]

Hodding did not finish the little book about the South, which became *Southern Legacy*, until the summer of 1949, and it did not appear until early 1950. Betty liked the jacket copy: "This necessity of saying uncomfortable things about his fellow Southerners has placed Hodding Carter rather in the position of a ship captain who must repel boarders and quell a mutiny at the same time."

In the book, which would appear on the New York *Herald Tribune*'s best-seller list, Hodding asserted that the southern qualities of violence and frontier self-reliance make the real man an avenger of slights. (*The Virginia Quarterly Review* bought this chapter discussing what he called the "broadsword virtues.") Because of Reconstruction, he maintained, the South had a historical basis for suspicion and fear. Hodding trotted out all the familiar puppets, including his little old grandmother (who sent him from her table because he criticized the Ku Klux Klan) and a black childhood playmate. (*The Saturday Evening Post*, bought the chapter on Son McKnight, his friend and protégé.) He deplored the way "the white South continues to emphasize the inferior status of the Negro and make separation synonymous with subordination."

Maintaining separation did not make it necessary, he said, for the white South to deny blacks their self-respect.

Hodding was realistic enough to dismiss assertions that "in the South the white man and the Negro understand each other, that their life together would be idyllic if they were let alone, and they have a great affection for each other." Except for a relatively small number of individual relationships, he wrote,

> the white man demonstrates little affection or respect for the Negro. It is impossible that the Negro loves a people who once held him in slavery, whose concessions to his citizenship have been grudging and slow, and who have made his predicated inferiority the primary unifying factor in their political, social, and economic behavior.

He suggested that the South answer outside critics: "We have not gone far enough or fast enough, but we have already gone far. Your prodding has been in a measure responsible but not in principal measure, or so we believe."

Paul Flowers, writing for the Memphis *Commercial-Appeal*, saw the point of *Southern Legacy*. "The overwhelming theme is that the South must take action to solve its own racial and economic problems . . . [and must] take a more realistic view of race relations, health, education, and economic expansion."[43]

Charlotte Capers, reviewing the book in a Jackson paper, said that three works were necessary to understanding Mississippi, and all of them came out of Greenville: *Lanterns on the Levee* by William Alexander Percy, *God Shakes Creation* by David Cohn, and now Hodding Carter's *Southern Legacy*.[44]

Another reviewer said that Hodding's book confirmed the fact that he "diagnosed [and] prescribed for the Southern scene more accurately, eloquently, and fearlessly than anybody writing, talking, or fighting the current civil war." The same reviewer, however, challenged Carter's conviction that Bilbo was reelected in 1946 because of "the damnyankee press," and claimed that Carter overemphasized the connection between the "present defensive attitude of Southerners" on the one hand and the "ravages of the Civil War" and its aftermath on the other.[45]

Lillian Smith wrote the only negative review, which appeared in the New York *Times*. She pointed out that church groups and university women had recently taken stands against specific forms of the "Jim Crow ritual." She was therefore surprised that "Mr. Carter, a forward-looking Mississippi editor and Pulitzer Prize winner," had in 1950 written a book "based on the assumption that segregation cannot be questioned in Dixie. Not only can it be questioned, it has been questioned by all of the South's serious thinkers. It is questioned and it is crumbling." Perhaps they were taking Hodding's book too seriously, she said, since it was not at all an analysis of the South but a string of breezy anecdotes about the author himself. The changing South she said, desperately needed for its newspaper editors to change with it.[46]

Hodding was furious with the *Times* for assigning the book to Smith. She had attacked him in her own book *Killers of the Dream*, which Hodding had refused to review because he could not be impartial.

Erskine Caldwell, who was editing a Folkways of America series for Duell, Sloan and Pearce, had asked Hodding in 1947 to do a book on the Gulf Coast Piney Woods country. Hodding told Bernice Baumgarten he would be happy to do the book, "as we already have enough stuff in our files to write it."[47] Later he told her it would do him good in Mississippi to turn out Mississippiana. "The only way you can get by with conking people there is to alternate with a little patting."[48] Hodding and Betty spent a month in the summer of 1950 on the Gulf Coast working on the research for the book, which Hodding finished with the help of a collaborator, Anthony Ragusin. *Gulf Coast Country* appeared the following summer, to good reviews.

Meanwhile, the "historical novel" hung over Hodding's head. He had, in fact, talked with John Selby about two different historical novels, but the lecture trips he had been making to earn money for the new house had delayed both. Still, he hoped to deliver a novel to Selby soon, and in June he went off to New Orleans and Baton Rouge to wind up research on a novel about the Louisiana Lottery.

As it turned out, he completed neither this book nor the other, about the early days of the Spanish colonies in Alabama and Mississippi. Life was too busy for him to take time to reflect and write fiction, and he continued to turn out nonfiction. When Rinehart agreed to substitute a book of memoirs, which became *Where Main Street Meets the River*, for a novel, Hodding started writing it immediately. By the time he left for Asia in the fall of 1952, a chunk of the manuscript was in the publisher's hands. Even before the rest arrived, Rinehart began having the partial manuscript set into type, and Selby demanded the remainder from Hodding. In between speech-making and sightseeing, Hodding sent chapters about Camp Blanding, Cairo in wartime, and the editor's role in the community (plus his foreword to the Percy book published by the Levee Press). As a title Hodding suggested "To Light a Small Candle," with the words, "It is better to light one small candle than to curse the darkness," printed inside. "Don't you think that's good?" Hodding wrote Betty from India, where he finished the last chapters. "It seems to fit us."[49] Selby plumped instead for *Where Main Street Meets the River*.

The book appeared in the spring of 1953, to rave reviews. It is Hodding's most charming book, warm, appealing, and full of the stories about his life and career that he could tell so well. Everybody loved it.

In 1952, he produced *John Law Wasn't So Wrong: The Story of Louisiana's Horn of Plenty*, which was published by Esso Standard Oil as a promotion and distributed to libraries, schools, educators, and others throughout Louisiana. Hodding's text about the Scottish financier John Law, and the Louisiana land bubble was illustrated with photographs and gouaches.

From 1947 to 1954, Hodding wrote dozens of articles for magazines, including *The Saturday Evening Post, Reader's Digest, Look, Collier's, Holiday, The New York Times Magazine, This Week*, and *Ford Times*, and book reviews for the *Times* and the *Herald Tribune* in New York. At one point in 1949 he was working on articles for

Collier's, Look, The Saturday Evening Post, and *Holiday* all at the same time.

In the fall of 1947, *Holiday* asked him for an article on the Mississippi River and how it dominated the life of the people along its banks. Hodding worked on this intermittently for quite a while, and the editors praised the final draft. The article appeared in March 1949, with *Holiday's* splendid layouts and color spreads. It covered Memphis, New Orleans, Natchez, showboats, tugboats, river rats, and legends of the river, and took up almost the entire issue. Hodding immediately proposed to *Holiday* a piece on the "Great lakes of the South," the area that the Tennessee Valley Authority had created out of the Tennessee River from Knoxville to Paducah, Kentucky. The magazine was interested, instead, on a definitive article on the whole state of Tennessee. Hodding wrote it, after an eight-day, 650-mile cruise on the Tennessee River, all the way from source to mouth. The article ran in November 1950.

When editors at *This Week* asked him to do one of the magazine's "Words to Live By" pieces, he chose "You Need Enemies" for a title and wrote once more about William Alexander Percy. He referred to Percy as "one of the saintliest men I ever knew," and noted that he was "hated by his fellow citizens with a hate surpassing Cain and Abel."[50] Despite his being libeled often, Percy was "untouched and undisturbed, and in the long run . . . held in honor, respect and affection." Percy, in short, found it "quite difficult to pontificate to order."[51] Hodding returned to Percy as a subject for "The Most Unforgettable Character I've Ever Met," an article that appeared in the September 1952 *Reader's Digest.*

Hodding used every experience, no matter how trivial. The speech he gave at an Episcopal Church meeting in Atlanta in May 1949 became an article that Baumgarten placed with *Ladies' Home Journal.* Philip Carter's first duck hunt provided material for an article for *Outdoor Life* in November 1952, and Hodding wrote other pieces for the magazine as time went on. Washington County's black agricultural agent, whom Hodding admired, was the subject of "Charlie Burton's

Field Day," which appeared in *Country Gentleman*, also in November 1952. And he wrote an article about Edward McCready, his old schoolmate in Hammond, now vice-chancellor of the University of the South in Sewanee, Tennessee, in *The Saturday Evening Post* of March 28, 1953.

Among Hodding's booster pieces were "My Favorite Town— Greenville, Mississippi," for *Ford Times* and an article on Biloxi for the same magazine; one about the growth of the cattle industry in Mississippi for *Nation's Business*; another, "The South Is on Its Way," discussing the regional pride in industrial and agricultural development, for *The Lamp*; and the fluffier "When a Woman Makes Up Her Mind," for *Ladies' Home Journal*. And he contributed a long piece about statehood for Hawaii—he was very much in favor of it—to *The Saturday Evening Post*.

Aside from the books, articles, and newspaper columns, Hodding managed to write—and publish—still other work in the late forties and early fifties. His article on cotton was included in the 1953 *Book of Knowledge*, and he continued to write short stories. "The Awful Encounter," about a Virginia dog "who helped his master find that Yankees have a heart," ran in *This Week*, and "Bad Check" appeared in *Ellery Queen's Mystery Magazine*. He also worked briefly with Floyd Huddleston of Leland, on the book of a musical, *The Magic Circle*, for which Huddleston was writing the lyrics.

"They Can't Call Me a Communist"

Hodding joined boards supporting the United Nations, the United Jewish Appeal, the Southern Regional Council, the National Citizens Commission for the Public Schools, and the advisory board of the Columbia School of Journalism. He enjoyed attending meetings of the Pulitzer Prize advisory board. George Peabody College for Teachers in Nashville elected him a trustee, the William Allen White Foundation tapped him for its board, and Tulane named him to its board of visitors.

Awards and honors were showered on him. In 1947 he received an honorary bachelor's degree from Harvard, which cited him as "a forward looking interpreter of the South." The same year his alma mater presented him with an honorary doctorate. At Bowdoin's commencement ceremonies Hodding noted that the last Mississippian to receive an honorary degree from the college was Jefferson Davis, who was then United States secretary of War. In October 1949, the University of Nebraska gave an award to the *Delta Democrat-Times*, citing its editorial policy as a "model for other newspapers throughout the nation" and its "conception of the newspaper as a laboratory for testing suggested solutions of agricultural and sociological problems." Hodding received a $1,500 Freedom Foundation Award for "outstanding contributions to the American Way of Life in 1951," for an editorial on India. He was honored by the University of Kansas Journalism School and named a fellow of Sigma Delta Chi, the journalism fraternity, in 1954.

He was genuinely thrilled when, in 1952, Secretary of the Army Frank Pace appointed him a civilian aide. "They can't call me a communist with this on my desk, can they?" he asked Betty when he showed her the plaque the Defense Department sent him.

II. 1947–1954

"I Have Lost Whatever Color Consciousness I Brought Along with Me"

From 1947 until 1954, when the Supreme Court outlawed segregation in the nation's public schools, Hodding Carter wrote prodigiously on race. He said it was his chief interest as an editor, and Harry Ashmore, editor of the *Arkansas Gazette*, commented that no one ever got so much mileage out of one subject. Hodding wrote about racial problems not just in the *Delta Democrat-Times*, but often in national magazines with wide circulation—*Look*, *The Saturday Evening Post*, and *Collier's*. As time passed, he refined his views and sharpened the language he used in editorials and articles.

Early in 1947, S. R. King, a lawyer in Durant, Mississippi, wrote in a local newspaper that Hodding had won his Pulitzer for "his agitations against the South and the race questions," and that the "South-hating Northern papers" were obtaining "anti-Mississippi propaganda" from him.[1]

Hodding, who was to hear this kind of abuse for the next twenty years, replied in an editorial in the form of an open letter to King. Before he expressed his opinion on the race question, he certified his southern credentials. "I suspect that my family has lived in the South as long as your own, and has rendered the South as much service." He reaffirmed his belief in segregation, saying that he had "never advocated or believed in any movement for 'social equality,'

203

the ending of segregation or the mass enfranchising of the Negroes of Mississippi," and adding that such movements were both unrealistic and dangerous to the cause of improved racial relations in the South.

He had, meanwhile, always stood for:

1. Raising educational, health and living standards of the Southern Negro to improve "the economic well-being of the South."

2. Attainment of equal justice for Negroes in Southern courts.

3. A greater recognition that the Christian concept of man's responsibility for his fellow man has a very practical meaning to the western Democracies in a Communist-threatened world.

4. Condemnation of the bigots of all sections of our country who would deny to minority groups even their right of self-respect and self-advancement.[2]

It was the first of many four-point plans. In the next several years, these would grow more specific and more liberal. Although, for instance, he said in his reply to King that he was against "mass enfranchisement" of blacks, he was already conceding privately that it would be impossible to keep them from voting in Mississippi forever; it was up to the white man of the South to "put his house in order." Later in 1947 he said he was in favor of blacks' voting, although he qualified his opinion: "whenever the education standard of the Negro approaches [that] of the white people." Even if "every voting-age Negro in Mississippi were to go to the polls, there is no state in the union where there are more negroes than whites. I do not, therefore, see that the negro vote could abolish segregation and the ban on intermarriage."[3] Three years later Hodding felt the time had come for blacks to vote. "However, we do not believe it would be safe for all of them to come to the ballot box for the first time in the same year."[4]

Among Hodding's early controversial editorials was one headlined "About Negro Education." After applauding a recent legislative move to provide black Mississippians with educational opportunities comparable to those offered blacks in other states, he reminded readers:

204

No one loses on education and especially is it valuable when afforded a group burdened with generations of superstition and ignorance. . . . It is absurdity to denounce a race for its ignorance, at the same time denying the denounced race adequate information with which to overcome its lack of knowledge.

We have yet to try solving our racial issue with education. . . . It is time we gave a test to the best answer to intellectual poverty yet devised.

Enlightenment is nearly as contagious as fear and ignorance, particularly when it is propagated with purpose. Knowledge is catching and transcends racial barriers. . . .

Education is the reconstruction to give us a future.[5]

After the President's Committee on Civil Rights released its report "To Secure These Rights," which called for the elimination of segregation from American life, Harry Truman in 1948 issued an executive order to end segregation in the armed forces. When he called for the establishment of a Fair Employment Practices Commission, the outlawing of the poll tax and lynching, the elimination of segregation in interstate transportation, a law to enforce fairness in elections, and the establishment of a permanent civil rights commission, even Northerners regarded it largely as a symbolic gesture; hardly anyone thought Congress would ever approve such a program. The South was outraged at these threats to its "way of life,"—the euphemism for segregation and oppression of blacks.

Hodding, although he had applauded Truman when he appointed the Committee on Civil Rights, did not like the report. He suspected the president's motives, and wondered whether he had "discovered his interest in civil rights when he was a member of the Pendergast society for the advancement of civil rights in Missouri."* He opposed Truman's proposals, as did Ralph McGill of the Atlanta *Constitution*, who called the program "too radical for the white South," and almost

---

*Harry Truman had entered politics under the sponsorship of the Thomas Pendergast machine in Kansas City.

every other southern newspaper editor. Hodding reiterated his belief that laws would provide no solution to the race problem. When the states failed, he said, the federal government should act to protect the constitutional rights of citizens. It was possible to legislate against the visible manifestations of prejudice, but impossible to change the hearts of people through laws. He called the poll tax "archaic" and wished the seven southern states that still had it would abolish it, but he was "unalterably opposed" to federal action.

As for anti-lynching laws, Hodding said lynching was the only crime that was on the decrease in the South and the only crime for which it was impossible to obtain a conviction. Public sentiment, he believed, would eventually make an anti-lynching law unnecessary.[6]

The South regarded the Fair Employment Practices Committee as the work of the devil.* In an editorial, Hodding quoted the New York *Times* in calling it "an attempt to enforce tolerance with a policeman's billy."[7] It was useless, Hodding wrote, to argue with most Southerners that the FEPC was not aimed at the heart of the South's racial mores. They did not believe for a minute that it was directed at job discrimination everywhere, but were convinced that the South alone would be the target area. Hodding did not think the government should intervene whenever a worker protested being fired or not hired because of race or religion,[8] yet he did not agree with South Carolina governor Strom Thurmond, who said that Truman's program would mean "forcible social intermingling of the races in the South."

The greatest danger from the program, Hodding said in an interview, was that "an angry, frustrated, and fearful South might forget that the South's ten million Negroes" had nothing to do with it. "As in Reconstruction, they may again be the victims of a resentment that

---

*FEPC were inflammatory initials in the South. The chairman of the committee from 1943 through 1946, Malcolm "Mike" Ross, whom the Carters had known in Washington, once called the Carters from Memphis; he wanted to come to Greenville to visit. Betty Carter remembered: "I said, 'If you come, I'm going to deny I know you. If you came to see us, it would destroy our position in the community.' Mike was a red flag. If he came, we might as well pack up and leave."

should be directed not against them but [against] those outside the South who harry us."[9]

The Mississippi legislature, opposed absolutely to Truman's civil rights agenda, called for a convention of the "true white Jeffersonian Democrats." States' rights supporters from across the South met in Jackson on May 10, 1948, and Strom Thurmond gave the keynote address.

Scornful of splinter parties, Hodding never took the States' Rights Democrats very seriously. He termed them "a minority segment within a minority regional group" and maintained that among the party's delegates were "a disproportionate number of mountebanks, political mediocrities, has-beens and professional axe-grinders."[10] He mocked the Dixiecrats, as the States' Righters were also known, in a front-page story headlined "South May Secede Because of Weather / Ice Sheet Seen as Secret Red Weapon." Local highways, it seemed, were iced over, and ice in the Mississippi was interfering with shipping. "As mid-South weather rapidly approached the ridiculous stage, the *Democrat-Times* learned . . . on good authority that the governors of seven Southern states and the Republic of Texas were planning to secede from the union on the icy grounds that the unnatural climatic conditions were obviously Northern interference and a violation of state's rights."[11]

"However wrong segregation is as a theory," Hodding wrote in an article for a northern publication, "it is also an actuality which the white majority in the South intends to maintain." Jim Crowism in public carriers would vanish and black college students would occasionally be admitted to southern universities, and southern draftees would find themselves in mixed platoons and battalions. White Southerners could accept that, but a "standing army would be necessary to end general segregation in the South. . . . The very intensity and one-sidedness of the anti-Southern bias . . . is welding the South into resentful unity."[12]

If federal intervention were the proper means of hastening orderly transformation, Hodding asked, why did the two major parties not unite behind other legislation that could more quickly help the "least privileged section of the country"? Federal aid to education would help blacks and whites in the South toward useful citizenship far more than would federal abolition of the poll tax in seven states, and adoption of a soil conservation program would create more economic security in the South than would the passage of fair employment legislation. A national housing program with slum segregation as its target would, in the long run, guarantee human dignity for second-class citizens better than would proscription of Jim Crow.[13] Hodding would propose this plan for federal action many times in the next few years.

He was much tougher on the South when he spoke to a southern audience. At the fall convocation at Tulane in 1948, Hodding warned his audience that states' rights and states' responsibilities must go together. The South had to admit that the records in "a thousand southern courts" proved that there was one kind of justice for the white man and another for the black man. The public schools in the South were "vivid evidence" that separate did not mean equal. Southern blacks could not always vote, and their job opportunities were few. White Southerners could not say in blind passion, "Leave us alone." The issue was urgent. Sitting in judgment were a billion and a half nonwhite people around the world who heard communist propaganda and news accounts of Georgia lynchings.

Earlier that year Hodding had spoken at commencement exercises at Alcorn A&M, Mississippi's largest black college. There he told the graduates neither to be content with the "manifold inequalities" they experienced nor to listen to the "false counsel of civil disobedience or the heady promises of communism." Perhaps more deeply affected by the experience than the Alcorn students, Hodding said later that if democracy had any meaning, "it must be extended fully to such as these," and there could be "no good reason for fearing or . . . subjugating any American who dreams our common sturdy dream of a fair chance and a place in the sun."[14]

In August 1948, Ray Sprigle, a white reporter for the Pittsburgh *Post-Gazette*, decided to disguise himself as a black man to find out what life was really like in the segregated South. After trying several skin dyes, he settled for acquiring a deep suntan and left Pittsburgh. He spent four weeks touring the strictly segregated South, and wrote a series of twenty-one articles for his paper about the degradation and discrimination in a Jim Crow world. Twelve of his articles, syndicated by the New York *Herald Tribune*, ran in fifteen northern newspapers; editors reported they received more letters about the series than about anything they had ever run before.

Sprigle traveled with a representative of the NAACP who coached him on behavior, telling him, among other things, never to jostle a white person. While no harm or even threats came his way, he wrote horrifying stories about what black people told him of life in the South. No black woman was allowed to try on clothes in a white department store. No white person ever called a black person "Mr." or "Mrs." Black doctors and dentists who treated blacks and whites alike became "niggers" outside their offices. Sprigle interviewed the widow of a prosperous black farmer who had been killed by whites, not because he had done anything, but because another black man had killed a white man and escaped; the whites, frustrated, killed the first black man they saw. Then there was the story of Macy Yost Snipes, a black World War II veteran, who registered to vote in Rupert, Georgia, and was lynched as soon as he voted.

Sprigle described the shacks of sharecroppers, bare, windowless, with holes in the roof, and told of black sharecropper after black sharecropper cheated each year by The Man, the landlord, who never gave an accounting of costs and sales. The sharecropper had no recourse, because no black man ever won a suit in the courts against a white man. Sprigle visited black schools, decrepit shanties with leaky roofs and homemade desks, and compared them with the new brick schools for white children in the same town. Taken for a black man, he was not allowed to swim on Georgia's Atlantic beaches or visit state parks; nor would he have been permitted to use a white library—and the black library that he could use was apt to be a small, dusty storefront. Segregated railroad cars and rest rooms were filthy. At some bus stations Sprigle had to eat in the kitchen, where food was prepared for white customers; at others, where there were no facilities for blacks at all, he stood outside and watched whites eating inside. And whenever he rode in an automobile, Sprigle cautioned the driver to be careful: he had heard stories of seriously injured blacks being refused admission to white hospitals in little towns, and then dying en route to the nearest black hospital in a larger town. "Separate but equal," wrote Sprigle, was a catchword white supremacists used to "justify all phases of segregation with its inevitable train of discrimination, oppression, brutality, and petty chicanery."

Sprigle reported, however, that the blacks he talked to did not hate whites, and they wanted mainly two things: the right to vote and better schools for their children. "Not one Negro did I meet who wanted to associate with white folks. . . . It was discrimination rather than segregation that they hated." From field hands to educators, they wanted as little contact with the white world as possible.[15]

Sprigle said that when he crossed the Ohio River to Cincinnati, thus leaving the South, he felt like Eliza in *Uncle Tom's Cabin*, crossing the ice to escape a life of slavery.

The Providence *Journal* asked Hodding to reply to Sprigle's pieces, and the New York *Herald Tribune* syndicated the resulting six articles under the title "Jim Crow's Other Side." Ten of the fifteen northern papers that had carried Sprigle's series ran Hodding's, as did many southern papers, none of which had run Sprigle's.

Hodding wrote that he had several handicaps. First, he was what was called a "Southern liberal." (In another context, Hodding had said that the South was the "only place in the western world where a man could become a liberal simply by urging that people obey the law."[16]) Being a southern liberal made almost anything he said suspect, not just among Southerners but among "most of the professional, semiprofessional and even amateur liberals of the North who demand unqualified agreement with their goal of complete, abrupt, and Federally enforced ending of the Southern pattern of segregation." Second, he had never disguised himself as a black to discover the widely known discrimination that "increasing numbers of sensitive, compassionate and fair-minded Southern whites are combatting openly and successfully, Mr. Sprigle to the contrary." Third, while he had to agree that certain of Sprigle's "discoveries" were tragically accurate, he did not believe that under the circumstances and within the time limits of his adventure Sprigle could have gotten "in proper perspective the whole story of the Negro's life in the South." Although Sprigle had spent longer than most investigators in the South, anybody who toured the region with a representative of the NAACP wasn't going to find anything good there, Hodding maintained. "Mr. Sprigle could have written his entire series without leaving [NAACP secretary] Walter White's office. . . . If I were going to make a study of Pittsburgh I wouldn't select . . . a representative of the National Association of Manufacturers or an organizer for the CIO as a guide."

And as for Cincinnati, which Ray Sprigle had been as happy as Eliza to reach, that city was where the Carters once could not find a room for their black nursemaid to sleep in. The motel they had chosen would not allow her to stay with them; motels in the South, on the contrary, allowed black servants to stay with their employers.

Hodding objected to Sprigle's "loaded" adjectives and pointed out that he had described an old black sharecropper's hands as "knotted and gnarled" with labor; so were a Maine fisherman's hands, said Hodding. He was further annoyed at Sprigle's judging southern-style fried chicken an "abomination."

Still, "his trip was a good stunt and offers many future possibilities," Hodding wrote. "He might disguise himself as a Mexican in the Southwest, or a Filipino or Japanese on the west coast, or a Jew in a good many American cities, or a militant, proselytizing Protestant in Boston, or a Negro in Chicago's South Side, or a truly poor white in Georgia. He'd discover the really basic and menacing fact that prejudice isn't directed solely to black skins or limited to the South."

Hodding did not deny that blacks were subject to "calculated mistreatments." He admitted that the Negro occupied a "sub-marginal place" in the South and in the rest of the nation, and that he "has a long way to go before he gains political, economic and legal equality."

But he insisted that "within the framework of segregation, the Negro is gaining ground in the South"; Sprigle's picture, in the end, was one-sided and distorted.

In the fifth article of the series, Hodding dealt directly with segregation. "The argument is that as long as mass segregation continues in the South, the Negro is still being discriminated against no matter whether all his economic, political and judicial goals are achieved. Segregation, they say, is the arch discrimination." People who wanted the federal government to force the white South to end segregation in its residential areas, its churches, its public schools and universities, and its public conveyances, in its theaters and restaurants, and in employment, and who demanded an end to laws against interracial marriage were not truly interested in better hospitals and schools for blacks. "It would be better in the long run for the living conditions of the segregated Southern Negro to get worse instead of better. The worse living conditions got, Northerners argued, the more chance there will be of Federal anti-segregation action." These critics were as extreme on one side as the Ku Klux Klan was on the other.

There was one point Hodding said he could not emphasize too strongly: "The white South is as united as 30,000,000 people can be in its insistence upon segregation. Federal action cannot change them." Blacks, Hodding said, knew that the things they wanted most—the vote and educational opportunities—would be more readily attainable if the South were not aroused against federal intervention in the field of segregation.

The vote was more important to blacks than anything else, in Hodding's view. They were already beginning to cast their ballots in increasing numbers throughout the South, and even in Mississippi more than 5,000 blacks had voted in the two previous elections. (In a state that was almost fifty percent black, that was hardly a heavy black vote.) But suffrage alone would not save blacks; basic progress could come only through education.

"And while you're working on discrimination," Hodding told his readers, "lift your sights a little. What about the discriminations against an entire region that are inherent in the Federal taxes on oleo-margarine, for instance, and the freight rate and tariff structures."[17]

John Gibson reprinted Hodding's series of articles in a booklet, while Hodding struggled to answer the flood of mail, most of it favorable, from readers. (On one occasion he mentioned 3,000 letters; on another, 4,000.) He estimated that eighty percent of the letters from Northerners were approving, and an even higher percentage of those from Southerners. Many of the letters from Southerners were long and thoughtful, indicating that the writers were deeply concerned about segregation.

Hodding later spoofed Sprigle's series in *Look*, in a mock tribute to an imaginary reporter, "the late Sherlock Meriwether . . . a Crusading Journalist who was known admiringly to the staff as Ol' Fearless."[18] Fearless and his boss decided there was nothing left to crusade about at home, now that Truman's civil rights program had scared everybody to start reforming, so they decided to crusade up North. To disguise himself as a New Yorker for his own series, Ol' Fearless lived in a cellar for three weeks until he acquired a pale yellow "skyscraper-shadow" complexion, and lived on barbiturates, martinis, black coffee, and tongue on rye, "except for a cornpone, salt-meat and turnip green jag one unfortunate weekend." He divorced his wife, married again, and divorced his second wife. He subscribed to three left-wing periodicals and the *Congressional Record* and memorized the campaign speeches of Henry Wallace. He cultivated a habit of shaking his head disparagingly at any mention of the South.

Hodding said he had high hopes for Fearless's series, which he planned to call "In the Land of Grim Snow." A typical report described the menace of New York:

I feel that I am being followed. Murder stalks these streets, brutal, unprovoked murder. Up in Harlem, the bodies of mugging victims are piled high. . . . Along the waterfront, the fishes feed on the ghastly remains of longshoremen and social workers. Gangsters torture and kill.

Then Hodding took over, and turned serious. For a hundred years the South had been "investigated, harpooned, lampooned, pestered and exposed . . . presented as a region of utter hopelessness, depravity and brutality. A lot of things are wrong with us but not as wrong as the endless 'exposés' make out." The South, after all, had never had a bund or a Christian Front, and there was genuine cause for alarm at the existence of bloc voting by ethnic groups and at the "intensity of racial and religious hatred" in the North.

James Wechsler, editor of the New York *Post*, took offense at Hodding's article.

> The lines dividing satire, sarcasm and solemnity are blurred in Carter's manifesto and we do not wish to misconstrue his deeper meaning. If he is saying that things are bad all over and that Southern prejudice has Northern parallels, we are disposed to agree. In fact we agree so strongly that we favor the immediate creation of a national Fair Employment Practices Committee that would protect Northern and Southern citizens alike against the nightmare of discrimination. . . .
>
> [But Carter] is really suggesting that we avert our eyes from the Southland because evil things also occur up North, just as the apologists for Soviet tyranny tell us we dare not attack their slave system until we have ended oppression in Dixie. The inevitable impact of Carter's sermon, written by a liberal with a capital L, is to fortify the complacency and indifference of the South. Nothing he said could not have been written with equal ardor by a Southern conservative.[19]

Hodding, believing that a strong two-party system would be good for the South, supported Thomas Dewey, the Republican candidate for president in 1948. The Democratic Party had grown "stale in office," and Truman was "an ill-advised little man, lacking the background, training and leadership qualities that our country must increasingly require for president," Hodding told Associated Press.

Newspapers across the country reported his endorsement of Dewey. While Republican leaders applauded his stand, W. Austin Seay, Washington, D.C., director of the States' Righters and a former president of the Mississippi Press Association, commented that "Hodding likes to be different." NAACP secretary Clarence Mitchell did not think Republican stock would be boosted by Hodding's declaration: "It's more . . . a case of opposition to Truman than endorsement of Republicanism."[20]

At the 1948 Democratic National Convention, delegates adopted four civil rights planks: abolition of the poll tax, a federal anti-lynching law, nondiscrimination in the armed forces, and establishment of a Fair Employment Practices Commission. Senator Paul Douglas, who was considered liberal, said that the Democrats were not proposing to abolish segregation in the South, and argued that their platform did not threaten segregation. Nobody in the South believed him. The entire Mississippi delegation walked out. States' Righters met in Birmingham and nominated Strom Thurmond for president and Mississippi governor Fielding Wright for vice-president.

On election day in 1948, Mississippi voted eighty-seven percent for the Thurmond–Wright ticket; Louisiana, Alabama, and South Carolina also went for the Dixiecrats. Truman upset Dewey elsewhere across the country, proving that the Democratic Party no longer had to rely on the Solid South.

Shortly after the election, Hodding and Harry Ashmore of the *Arkansas Gazette* went to New York to debate Ray Sprigle and the NAACP's Walter White on *Town Meeting of the Air*. The makeup man, faced with blond, blue-eyed White and black-haired, dark-skinned Carter, was not sure which one was the black. In the end, he darkened White's skin and tried to make Hodding look less swarthy.

Hodding opened his comments by quoting from an article by George Schuyler in the Pittsburgh *Courier*. (His fellow blacks regarded Schuyler, an extreme conservative, as a traitor to his race.) Schuyler had just returned from a tour of fourteen southern states. He hadn't disguised himself as a black, Hodding pointed out to Sprigle, because he *was* black. Schuyler had written that most of what was being said about the South was untrue. It was not a place of terror and persecution, nor had it been in many decades. Nowhere was there studied insult or discourtesy within the social framework, and blacks everywhere told him that persecution and police brutality were rarely encountered. It had to be admitted that blacks were better off in the South than any other minority with "comparable background" was elsewhere. There was less opposition than ever to black suffrage and, Schuyler thought, such opposition would gradually disappear. The level of tolerance in the South was little short of amazing.

Hodding said that he, like many Southerners, was acutely aware of and actively opposed to the discrimination practiced in the South, but he was disturbed by the venom and ignorance of outsiders who offered cures for southern ills. Unlike many Southerners, however, he did not object to outside pressure. "This is one country. New Yorkers and Pennsylvanians have every right to be interested in Mississippi's shortcomings. On the other hand, Mississippians have a right . . . to imitate the North's utter perfection in race relations, crime reduction and the ending of segregation, in slum clearance, equality of job opportunity and enlightened politics."

Walter White maintained that there could never be any equality within the framework of segregation. "Denial of equal educational and economic opportunity, disfranchisement, the ghetto and humiliation are the inevitable consequences of segregation." Furthermore, he pointed out, segregation and its evils lowered the prestige of the United States among the two-thirds of the people of the earth who were not white. He cited the overwhelming approval of the President's Committee on Civil Rights, headed by the industrialist Charles Wilson, as just one of many proofs that decent Americans wanted segregation abolished immediately.

To people forty and more years later, Carter's ideas may seem almost quaint and too "Old South" to be taken seriously. It is hard to remember that even "liberals" in those days were genuinely fearful of excessive intrusion by the federal government into the business

216

of the states. It was due partly to a memory of Reconstruction and partly to a trickle-down of Jeffersonian ideas. Almost *nobody* in the South publicly favored integration; one of the few who did was Lillian Smith, whose 1949 book *Killers of the Dream* condemned "the terrible curse of segregation." Smith, in fact, attacked such southern liberals as Hodding and Ralph McGill, "who spend their time fighting the 'foul drainage' from the sore of segregation itself."[21] Virtually all southern liberals believed in a gradual approach. They insisted constantly that neither the abolitionist crusade before the Civil War nor Reconstruction afterward had helped race relations in the South.

When the Washington County Better Citizenship Committee, a group of black ministers, teachers, and businessmen, asked to meet with white leaders in Greenville in April 1949, Hodding was surprised at their message. Disturbed by the frivolous way the white population accepted violent crimes by blacks against blacks, they wanted more severe punishment for black lawbreakers. They also wanted protection against crime from members of their own race.

Hodding admitted that he felt guilty that the *DD-T* would report the murder of one black by another with a few paragraphs, while a stabbing or assault was dismissed in a couple of sentences. The paper reported trials of blacks only briefly.[22] During the cotton-picking season, it was common for planters to bail black tenants or employees out of jail temporarily, so they could work in the fields, ignoring the seriousness of the offenses the workers had committed. All his life Hodding had heard tales of black killings "as if they involved no suffering or death."[23] As a child he had come to believe that loose morals and violence were characteristic of blacks.

After the meeting with the black leaders, he wrote an editorial calling for equal treatment for lawbreakers of both races. "A double standard of justice during a period of unrest—when there is a national reawakening of our democratic heritage offset by the challenging ideology of communism—is no longer practical and is no longer tolerable if it ever was," he said.[24] He was not optimistic that changes would occur. There were, for now, four different sets of justice in the South: one for crimes by blacks against blacks, another for crimes by blacks against whites, a third for crimes by whites against blacks, and a fourth for crimes by whites against whites. "Because the South discriminates against the Negro in the law's application, it finds it all but impossible to discriminate between abstract right and wrong."[25]

Hodding's attitude toward handling more routine news of blacks evolved slowly, too. He explained his paper's policy to a Texas newspaperman in 1948: Black crime news was played down and black success stories played up. The DD-T did not run social items, since there was a "relatively good Negro paper in town." The DD-T used pictures, both local and national, of blacks, but did not run routine shots of, for instance, high school graduates and returned veterans. The paper capitalized the N in "Negro," even though this was not "customary in our section." The paper followed the white southern journalistic practice of employing contorted circumlocutions to avoid "Mr.," "Mrs.," or "Miss" with the name of a black person, but it broke the "unwritten rule every now and then." In his region, Hodding said, blacks were "considerably more interested in fighting for their political and economic rights and in our refusing to overplay the unpleasant side of the news than in our giving them a larger share of the news columns."[26]

More than a year later he told a newspaperwoman that the DD-T left out the word "Negro" in headlines identifying criminals. Although the paper did not have a section devoted to black news, it was featuring more and more stories of general interest about blacks. "We have not yet begun using courtesy titles . . . and as long as we integrate the [black] news with the other news, I am afraid it will have to be postponed for quite a while."[27]

Very soon, though, the well-dressed, attractive wife of a black doctor, H. J. St. Hille, who had settled in Greenville after getting a degree at the Sorbonne, came to see Hodding and asked him to begin identifying black women as "Mrs." She chaired the black division of the Red Cross and had been referred to in the paper as "the St.

Hille woman." According to his own account, Hodding asked himself what there was to be afraid of. Was it "that somebody will write or telephone . . . us to cancel their subscription . . . to a damned nigger-loving paper? Afraid of economic reprisal or social retaliation? Afraid that our usefulness in larger matters will be impaired by our violation of the taboo against permitting a Negro self-respect?"[28] So the *DD-T* used "Mrs." when referring to the doctor's wife in a story about the Red Cross campaign. That night Hodding received several phone calls, not from critics, but from friends wondering whether he had gone too far. Hodding's insouciance was assumed; many former staffers and other residents of Greenville remembered forty years later the resentment with which a great number of people in town reacted to the change, which they considered quite radical. "They weren't ready for 'Mrs.' for blacks," recalled one woman.[29] After this incident there was for the first time talk in town of starting an opposition paper. Still, Hodding's enlightened policy must have been good for business—a third of the *DD-T*'s 12,000 subscribers in 1950 were black.

Hodding had begun sounding a theme in 1947 that he would repeat often over the years: The North had no right to attack the South for its prejudice when the northern house itself was not in order.[30] He was always delighted to point out specific examples of racism in the North. When hoodlums threw eggs at Henry Wallace in North Carolina during the 1948 presidential campaign, Wallace had said he saw "the evil face of Fascism" in his southern audience. Hodding noted race riots in Wallace's bailiwick, Peekskill, New York, when Paul Robeson tried to stage a songfest. Hodding called attention, too, to the fact that the National Guard had had to quell race rioting in Cicero, a suburb of Chicago, after a black family moved into a white neighborhood. "It appears that when anti-racial action takes place anywhere north of the Mason-Dixon line it is the work of hoodlums. When it occurs in the South it is the outbreak of an inbred cruelty that was conceived in slavery, brought to term in reconstruction and reared in resentment."[31]

Hodding often insisted that the South was improving. While blacks were still being discriminated against, the nature and the severity of the discrimination was "far less than even twenty years ago," he wrote in 1948. "And while the progress is undoubtedly due in part to national pressures, I believe that its major impetus has come from the Southern conscience."[32] He praised the biracial Southern Regional Council, the only base southern liberals had. The Council, founded in 1942, acted on the premise that the South could be prosperous and healthy, freed of poverty, prejudice, and fear. In the name of democracy, Christianity, and common decency, Hodding said, the Council advocated equal opportunity for blacks in the schoolroom, on the job, and at the polls.[33]

Hodding was especially proud of Greenville's achievements, and he wrote about them not only in the *Delta Democrat-Times* but also in articles for other papers, both regional and national. He told a dozen times how Greenville had voted in favor of a bond issue for a trade school addition to the black high school, and another bond issue to build a new black junior and senior high school. (The latter was approved overwhelmingly, 463 to 67.) When Clarksdale voted to approve a bond issue for a black swimming pool and a new black high school, Hodding praised the town in an editorial and wrote to a friend, "It's the sort of thing that makes us glad we are newspapermen."[34]

He liked to tell, too, how Washington County doctors had worked ceaselessly for six months to plan a 175-bed black hospital, and at the same time a young bank president had undertaken to bring Blue Cross to Mississippi and make it available to low-income groups, including plantation blacks. In addition, the county was paying a third of the cost of a new hospital that would serve blacks and whites. A GI trade school for blacks trained nearly 1,000 veterans in carpentry, masonry, electrical work, and the operation of mechanized farming equipment. The *DD-T* had reported that two hundred more blacks in the county became independent farm owners; one, a farming contest winner, had net yearly earnings of more than $10,000. Black citizens themselves, aided by white contributions, had built a civic center and a branch library. "Time after time in our city court, I saw a tough, honest judge take a Negro's word against a white man's when he thought the Negro was telling the truth and the white man lying," Hodding wrote. "Greenville had nothing even faintly resembling a racial clash, even though we were electing a senator to replace the late Theodore Bilbo, and the woods were full of demagogues seeking to arouse white men against the peril of the Negro who voted or wanted to vote." Greenville and Washington County had given a majority to John Stennis, the decent man who won Bilbo's old seat. And only twenty-four people turned out when segregationist John Rankin spoke there.[35]

When a man from Pennsylvania wrote Hodding that he had subscribed to the *Delta Democrat-Times* for a year and had not seen one editorial denouncing intolerance, Hodding replied that during the previous year the paper had campaigned for employing blacks on the Greenville police force; published a series of articles on the woeful state of black school facilities in the county, another on slums, principally black, in town; vigorously endorsed construction of two swimming pools, equal in size and cost, one for blacks and one for whites, and seen the proposal passed with the help of about four hundred Negro votes; chronicled the county's approval of plans for a low-cost hospital with identical white and black wings, and for a new black grammar school in town, and authorization for another; editorialized against the States' Righters' fantastic proposal to strip the federal government of virtually all its powers and end its economic programs; written against racial discrepancy in teachers' pay and against the beating by a deputy of a black prisoner who had killed a white man; applauded the inclusion of a black on a jury panel for the first time since Reconstruction, the congressional legislation for slum clearance and aid to education, and the increase in black farm ownership in Mississippi.

"But," he added, "since I didn't get around to an editorial denouncing intolerance, I herewith denounce it."[36]

Hodding found black migration to the North a hopeful sign—the "Southern problem" would soon become a national one.[37] The 1950 census showed that the Delta had lost population. "The unoccupied, rotting tenant cabins, the mechanized farm equipment sales, the decline in business in the tiny crossroads stores" were to Hodding evidence that the migration had begun.[38] He was prescient. By the time the migration was over, as Nicholas Lemann has explained eloquently, the whole country would have acquired the South's tragic sense. Race relations would stand out everywhere as the one thing plainly wrong with the United States.[39]

Hodding pointed out that the departure of blacks was impelled not only by despair at their subhuman status but by the changing agricultural economy, which made blacks no longer essential to the South. "A tragic pilgrimage is under way, and some Southerners find grim pleasure in the stories of unfamiliar tensions in Indianapolis and Los Angeles and Seattle. What of these unskilled, hopeless migrants, whose barren, suspect existences cannot be explained away by an accusing finger pointed at the South? Will their civil rights be affirmed by poll tax repeal? Will their grisly Northern ghetto become more habitable because segregation is banned? Will their untutored hands and minds be salvaged by a fair employment act? Or did the party band wagons forget about these matters when the civil rights program became the battle hymn of the Republicans and Democrats alike?"[40]

In spite of his defensiveness, Hodding was moving toward a slightly more progressive stance. In a 1949 magazine article he announced that "a strong flame, brighter and infinitely more cleansing than the fiery cross of the Klan, is burning throughout the South today. . . . The flame of purposeful liberalism is lighting up dark and tragic corners of a harried region." Southern liberals, even though they were attacked by the right and left, had limited objectives, but they were determined to make democracy work through effort "on the battle line itself and not from a distant ivory tower."

These liberals included educators, editors, churchmen, representatives of organized labor, writers, political leaders, business and professional men, farmers—and he named several. Liberalism was not new to the South, and Hodding could cite Thomas Jefferson and Andrew Jackson. Even Theodore Bilbo had sought agrarian reform, he said; Huey Long had met the road, hospital, and school needs of his state; John Rankin had bulldozed legislation for the Tennessee Valley Authority through the House of Representatives.

> But they . . . capitalized upon, or ignored, the South's ancient portentous problem in human relationships: the contradictory, enforced status of inferiority of the Negro in a professed democracy. This problem still haunts the South. . . . Man's antipathy for the dissimilar, for reason of race, religion, culture, and even nationality, is not Southern in origin. It has dogged every civilization, every century of recorded history, and is present today in every part of the world.

Defiant reactionaries at home branded the liberal a communist, a nigger-lover, a Yankee tool, Hodding said, and he was at the same time a target for the militant, all-or-nothing crusaders who fought their war at a distance. If he advocated or praised local equal hospital facilities, or pushed for equal pay and facilities in the separate school systems, or for the inclusion of blacks on trial juries, northern liberals who believed in the immediate ending of segregation "at the point of a bayonet" would denounce him for endorsing the status quo, while people who yearned for the good old days would whiplash him for endangering it. Speaking out was not as easy as it seemed.[41]

Hodding's four-point program in this article was more specific than it had been two years before. His four concrete objectives were the same ones Gunnar Myrdal had attributed to Southern blacks: equality in the courts, equal school facilities, job opportunities, and the right to vote.

Walter White criticized Hodding's article, pointing out that most of the actions equalizing education in the South had come about because of courageous southern white judges, not at the urging of white liberals. Lynchings had almost stopped because of Congress's attempts to pass a federal anti-lynching law, not because southern liberals were converting anybody.[42]

In 1949, in Houston, a town in Chickasaw County, Mississippi, three young white men were accused of beating a forty-five-year-old black farmer, Malcolm Wright, to death with a jack handle because he had "hogged the road" with his wagon. They had blown their car horn, they said, and he had refused to pull over. Wright's wife and children saw the murder. An editorial in the *DD-T* noted that the white citizens of Houston had raised several thousand dollars to help prosecute the murderers. "We hope this story receives wide publicity throughout the nation. It is the moving spirit of the New South."[43]

Because public sentiment was strong against the accused, the trial of the man who actually used the jack handle was moved to another venue. All three men were acquitted, in spite of the fund for the prosecution, after they testified that Wright had cursed them and threatened them with a harrow. Hodding was furious when the Tuskegee Institute classified the crime as one of the three lynchings in 1949. Tuskegee did not consider it a lynching when four black men, under the influence of drugs or alcohol, attacked a middle-aged man and killed him; Hodding saw no difference in the two crimes, except that one was committed by blacks and one by whites.[44] He also wondered why murders committed during race riots, were not counted as lynchings; of the thirty-four dead in the 1943 Detroit riots, twenty-five were black.

In an editorial Hodding deplored the actions of the Birmingham Ku Klux Klan, which had been flogging men who did not support their wives. "Masked men breed trouble—only men who are ashamed of their deeds need to hide their identity." Another editorial said the Klan added fuel to the flame of intolerance and helped bring communism a step closer.[45] In September 1949, Hodding remarked on the death of Dr. Samuel Green, grand dragon of the Klan. The fact that Green was a physician had perhaps brought some respectability to the Klan, but the same was not true for "the other wizards, lizards, or gizzards."[46] The next year he noted that when Lycurgus Spinks was in Greenville he did not cause a stir, although he was former emperor of the Klan.[47] Only sixty delegates showed up for a Klan rally in Jackson, Hodding wrote, and the boss of the Mississippi delegation fell off his horse.[48]

In early 1950 the *Delta Democrat-Times* ran one of its most scathing editorials on race, titled "Aw Well, Who Cares?"

Saturday night a colored boy named Odell Moore was sitting around a plantation store talking to some other folks and playing the slot machines off and on. So were the other colored folks.

Thought he was pretty smart, this boy. Had some jingling money in his pocket; and he'd been having money for several days. Ain't right for a boy like that to be having money three, four days in a row. Something must be wrong, him having cash.

Odell probably didn't notice the white man who was talking to the store keeper and eyeing him. He probably didn't know that the white man could put two and two together.

That white man was plenty smart. He knew that if Odell had jingling money he undoubtedly stole it somewhere and, come to think of it, one of his slot machines was missing. That's it, Odell did it. After all, the boy had some money, didn't he? Ain't that proof enough?

Well, Sir, he really showed that boy a thing or two. Took him out to the Bogue, he did. He rope whipped the boy while the others held him. Told the boy that he was going to hang him off the bridge.

He didn't really hang him. After he rope whipped the boy, he made him get into the Bogue. 'Course, the water was ice cold. You should have seen that boy light out for the bank. Talk about a frozen nigger! He was it.

He hardly hurt the boy at all. Just beat him up a little. Gave him something to remember, though. It'll be a long time before that boy flashes coins around in front of the white folks after there's been a slot machine stolen.

Hear tell they called in a deputy sheriff. Wonder what'll come of it. Can't think much'll happen. After all, the sheriff has been saying that there aren't any slot machines in the county.

Why, if the slot machines were to be taken out of the county, lots of folks would have a tough time making a living in these little stores. They get to keep part of the money, you know. It pays off pretty good.

Anyway, who cares? Oh sure, the "decent" folks get all upset about slot machines once in a while but they don't do anything about it. They just talk about how terrible things are out in the county and ain't it too bad that no one does anything about it.

So, nothing's going to be done about it and the man'll get off without any trouble. Who would arrest him? That's one thing about living in Washington County; you sure can do what you want to. We won't have any trouble here as long as the law enforcement people keep out of our way. A dunking in the Bogue'll do more good than all the conferences in the world.

Punish that man for what he did? Don't be silly. Anyway, who cares?[49]

In 1950, in a front-page editorial headlined "To Get the Record Straight," Hodding said he had written fifty articles in national magazines that were "a defense, interpretation, or prideful boasting about the South." His book *Southern Legacy*, published, he emphasized, by the Louisiana State University Press, had won approval from everyone in the United States, "except from the *Daily Worker*, the Northern Negro press, and Lillian Smith." People accused him of being "anti-Southern," of advocating civil rights, social equality, and the FEPC, but "whoever says that is a liar." A group had offered to buy the *Delta Democrat-Times*; it was not for sale, and, Hodding insisted, "we've done as much for Greenville and the South's good name as anybody." The newspaper would not be "sold or silenced."[50]

He continued to maintain that any attempt to abolish segregation was "both unrealistic and dangerous to the cause of improved racial relations in the South." White people would resist it. "What would happen next," he asked in an editorial, "if a state and its people simply refused to accept a court ruling that segregation of any kind was illegal?"[51] The outrage that broke out over his editorials calling for fair trials or even Blue Cross for Negroes was enough to convince him that the breakdown of segregation would indeed lead to another Civil War.

Carter warned his readers repeatedly that if Mississippi did not make the "separate but equal" facilities truly equal, the Supreme Court would surely outlaw segregation. "How one group, given all the advantages of modern information, dares indict another (never properly provided for in education) for its unenlightened outlook is the basis of intolerance. . . . It is absurdity to denounce a race for its ignorance, at the same time denying the denounced race adequate information with which to overcome its lack of knowledge."[51]

After Supreme Court decisions in June 1950 that required Oklahoma and Texas to admit blacks to their law schools and medical schools, Hodding urged careful planning to carry out the decision.[53] He recognized, of course, that the ruling should have been expected. The Court had not ruled on the constitutionality of separate school systems and thus the southern states had a breathing spell during which to live up to their own constitutions. "But the decisions do make it crystal clear that equal facilities must be truly that and not the mockery that has persisted so long." And to make them equal in Mississippi, he estimated, would take $75 million.[54]

A few months later, he wrote that "anyone believing that our system of segregated education will continue unless equal educational facilities are made available for Negroes is guilty of wishful thinking." Mississippi must not delay providing separate but equal facilities. "We must act at once."[55]

Hodding kept it up. No good could come of Governor Hugh White's "wait-and-see policy on school equalization," he wrote. The issue was a moral one. "Are we planning equal facilities for Negroes because we acknowledge a moral obligation or because we anticipate legal compulsion?"[56] In June 1953 the governor finally called the legislature into special session, and it appropriated $50 million for an equalization program. The governor said he hoped blacks would be content with the promise of improved schools.[57]

Although Hodding never condemned segregation in general, he took stands on individual cases. In June 1952, eight faculty members of the University of the South School of Theology, the Episcopal seminary at Sewanee, resigned because the trustees refused to say that black ministerial students would be admitted. The Bishop Payne Divinity School (a black Episcopal seminary in Alexandria, Virginia) had closed its doors in 1950 for lack of students. Four of the twelve white Episcopal seminaries in the country were open to black students; Sewanee was not. No black had ever applied there. Edward McCready, Hodding's childhood friend from Hammond and vice-chancellor of the University of the South, of which Sewanee Episcopal Seminary was a part, said the university had no regulations discriminating against blacks, but the State of Tennessee did, and lawyers had advised the trustees that it would be a criminal offense to enroll blacks. Publicly, Hodding called the eight faculty members heroes for letting it be known "they think Jesus Christ is more important than Jim Crow."[58] Privately, he said the seminary should say that it was open to qualified divinity students of any race.[59] When the seminary abolished segregation the next year, Hodding applauded the action; it was "in keeping with the teaching of Christ."[60]

"Carter took his Christian humanitarianism seriously and he believed thinking Southerners took it seriously, too," wrote former *DD-T* staffer Harry Marsh.[61] According to another journalist, Hodding "made a career of shoving the Golden Rule down the throats of his recalcitrant adversaries."[62]

In the summer of 1950, members of the Civil Rights Congress, which Hodding identified in the paper as "a Communist-line group," came to Mississippi to protest the death sentence imposed on Willie McGee, a black convicted of rape in Laurel. The CRC maintained that McGee had been "knowingly convicted by the state of Mississippi on perjured evidence."[63] While Hodding disagreed with the CRC, he was outraged when in 1951 white Mississippians whipped one of its members in a Jackson hotel. "Only a group of nitwits would have done such a thing," he wrote.[64]

Hodding later supported the NAACP's call for clemency for McGee; no white man had ever died for a similar crime in Mississippi.[65] The U.S. Supreme Court eventually ruled that there was no new evidence to justify a new trial, which would have been McGee's fourth.

Hodding's editorials became stronger during 1952. About the recent bombings of Jewish synagogues and black apartment houses in Miami and the assassination of a Florida black leader, he wrote: "Our own Anglo-Saxon ancestors died for the right to political expression. It is incredible that three centuries later Negroes like Henry Tyson Moore are still dying for that same right."[66]

Hodding liked to goad people in the South as well the North. "Down here I give our people the dickens on their social attitudes. Up North I defend them," he told an interviewer in 1951.[67] To the New England Weekly Press Association he described the South as "a land of churchgoers who pay little attention to the Christian concepts of the brotherhood of man."[68] He then suggested "voluntary resettlement" of blacks throughout the nation as a step toward solving the integration problem. If the black population were spread more evenly throughout the country, he said, "we could talk integration on more sober terms."

In the fall of 1952, Hodding left Mississippi for a tour of Southeast Asia under State Department sponsorship. He wrote in the paper that he intended "to answer Communist lies and distortions about the South and our Nation" and show that "dignity and self-respect and a common equality are the right of every man" and that "their attainment is the prayer of most Americans."[69] He would find that most of the questions he met on the other side of the world concerned the racial situation in the United States.

While he was gone, Betty had to make one serious editorial judgment. The newspaper covered a speech by Zelma Price, a white woman, who addressed a group of three hundred black supporters of Democratic presidential candidate Adlai Stevenson. "We . . . pointed out this was the first time the Democratic party had wooed Negro voters in a presidential election, and covered the story straight," Betty wrote Hodding. Supporters of Stevenson's Republican opponent, Dwight Eisenhower, had taken a picture of the event and wanted the *DD-T* to run it. "They wanted . . . to play on the anti-Negro sentiments of the voters. The reason they gave for wanting it run was that it was news for a white woman Democrat to be addressing Negroes." She told the Eisenhower people she thought the news story brought that fact out and that was enough. And she admitted to Hodding, "I hope I was right."[70]

Another significant incident occurred in Hodding's absence. The Junior Auxiliary was planning a Cotton Pickers Ball, and Ruth Walcott invited Betty to be in the "court" and dress as a "high yaller." Betty accepted, then changed her mind. "I'm going to . . . tell her I can't do it," she wrote Hodding. "I think it's very bad for race relations."[71] While she was writing the letter to Hodding, Louise Crump came into the office and voiced the same doubts Betty had about the ball. They talked to several members of the Junior Auxiliary and urged the group to "reorganize it on a Southern folklore basis or leave it as cotton pickers, but not have the court browned up. Cotton pickers are Mexican, poor white, and Negro."

The Asian trip was important to Hodding in more ways than one. As he wrote to Betty on November 9 from Bombay: "This is for your information only, but I have lost whatever color consciousness I brought along with me. The day I arrived in Bombay I was asked to lunch by the cultural attaché. He happens to be a light Negro, about octoroon I guess. His wife was just as light, both Californians, self-possessed and not race-inhibited. The other luncheon guests included Ed Clarke, a Westchester County, Princeton blue blood who is a state department officer on tour of the Asiatic posts; a young girl from the consulate named Celind Lee, half Chilean; an Indian editor; a very black, middle-aged Negro named Dr. Leo Marsh who is out here on tour for the YMCA and Ford Foundation—he's on the Montclair city council or something—and myself. It didn't seem odd at all. The Negroes think of themselves as Americans first and as Negroes very secondarily."[72]

Once he was back home, Hodding waited for the Supreme Court's decision on the school segregation cases. If the court did outlaw segregation, he wrote in *The New York Times Magazine*, the walls of Jericho would not come tumbling down "to the tread of Negro children marching off to hitherto all-white schools."[73] No matter what the Court did, he predicted, the next fall and for many years to come the great majority of black children would continue to attend their own, separate schools. The situation was confusing. In Greenville, as elsewhere, "segregation follows no hard and fast rules, nor is it as severe and as all-embracing today as the practice was in my Louisiana boyhood."

In that *New York Times Magazine* article, Hodding described the anomalies and contradictions in the life of a fictitious black bricklayer in segregated Greenville. The bricklayer had the right to vote, but he still had to pay a poll tax of two dollars to exercise that right. He could buy clothes in the best men's store in town, but he rode a segregated bus to his home. A few white families lived on his street. If the bricklayer went to the movies, it was to a segregated theater. He could attend an American Legion carnival with a tent show, but not a concert by a visiting artist at the white high school.

Hodding maintained that most white Southerners thought the changes were coming too fast; some blacks thought they were coming too slowly; and some people of both races were somewhere in between.

Walter White of the NAACP pointed out that Hodding had neglected to note in his article "that most of the progress has been the result of organized efforts on the part of groups which refused to accept the status quo. It is often said that Southern Negroes do not want a change, but it is significant that all lawsuits to alter the old pattern have been brought by Southern Negro plaintiffs."[74]

When it was a question of equal justice, however, Hodding was never mealy-mouthed. On April 27, 1953, a justice of the peace in Bolivar County dismissed the case of justifiable homicide against John Thomas, a storekeeper in Benoit and also a justice of the peace. In front of witnesses, Thomas had shot a black man in the back after a squabble over a thirty-seven-dollar bill for groceries. The *DD-T* reported in a front-page story the next day that the town marshal of Benoit, W. O. Lester, had said to the newspaper's photographer after the hearing exonerated Thomas, "Go tell that to your Mr. Carter."

And the day after that, in a front-page editorial, Hodding referred to the hearing conducted by Justice of the Peace E. V. Reams and County Attorney Frank Wynn as "the damndest job of bloodstained whitewashing that ever sickened us." It was, he said, "a wicked farce." Not a single eyewitness was called, although several were available. The killer himself was the only witness present.

In a quarter century of reporting and reading about unequal justice in the South, this is the first time to our knowledge that no one was summoned as an eyewitness on a publicly committed slaying except the man who used the gun. It is also the first time in our memory that a so-called officer of the law jibed at a newspaper when a killer came clear. . . .

We know and all our readers know that if the victim had been a white man, or if the killer had been a Negro, this whitewash would not have been tolerated. . . .

Until we in Mississippi can look upon the law and crime without relation to the color or faith or nationality of the principals, we have no right to lift our heads and ask for equal treatment in the concert of states or the community of nations. . . .

And to the Bolivar County officers who couldn't find any witnesses, we offer this suggestion. . . . The dead man had a hundred dollars or so in two-bit a week insurance. Enough at least for his widow to take care of the grocery account. If you can find her this go-round, make her pay her just debts. Thirty-seven bucks is thirty-seven bucks.[75]

The editorial caused a sensation in Greenville. Almost forty years later one man remembered taping it to his refrigerator door, where it stayed for years. Another man remembered reading it out loud to his elderly mother three times. Not all the reaction was admiring. Hodding left that same day for New York, and "the phone calls absolutely went crazy," Betty Carter remembered years later. "They started at dusk and built up until around ten o'clock at night and then they cut off. It was just revolting what they said to you."[76]

As 1953 drew to a close, Hodding said that he could not see how the Supreme Court could hand down any other decision than one outlawing segregation. "As a practical matter, however, I really think it will cause very few conflicts among people in the states of the Deep South . . . and I am hoping that a period of grace would be given during which adjustments could be made. My own feeling is that if we equalize our schools, very few Negroes will take advantage of a . . . decision and try to enter the completely white schools."[77]

12. 1954–1955

"A Curse Lies on Our State"

On May 18, 1954, the *Delta Democrat-Times* carried the banner headline "School Segregation Is Held Illegal." "It's about time," Hodding had remarked to his staff as the news of the Supreme Court's decision in *Brown vs. Board of Education of Topeka* clattered out over the Associated Press wire in the paper's newsroom.[1]

That same day at E. D. Bass Junior High School in Greenville, Philip Carter observed that his classmate Stanley Davidow was in a fury over the decision. (Stanley Davidow, Stanley Sherman, and Philip were always on the same side in schoolyard fights—liberals and Jews against the rest.) "Stanley Davidow started a petition that began, 'We the undersigned, will never go to school with Negroes.' The next day he stood up in class and took back the petition. He said his father had said, 'You're trying to do to Negroes the same thing the Nazis did to the Jews.'"[2]

The decision had been expected, said a *DD-T* editorial, which also advised, "Let's keep our shirts on." There was no point now "in listening to the professional politicians and hotheads." The South had asked for the decision "through its shocking, calculated and cynical disobedience to its own state constitutions which specify that separate school systems must be equal. For seventy-five years we sent Negro kids to school in hovels and pig pens," and now the South was challenged to "replace trickery and subterfuge in our educational structure with an honest realization that every American child has the right to an equal education. How that equal education will be given will largely be a local matter."

A front-page story that same day—under the headline "Southern Segregationists to Fight to Bitter End Against Court's Decision"— made it plain that few voices in the South were as calm as some of those in Greenville. The Jackson *Daily News* headlined its lead editorial "Bloodstains on the White Marble Steps," referring to the U.S. Supreme Court building, and Representative John Bell Williams of Mississippi labeled the day of the decision "Black Monday." But the *DD-T* also quoted E. A. Greene, the mayor of all-black Mound Bayou, who said that his town had "no school segregation worries" and that "the people would welcome white folks" to its schools.

A few days later the paper repeated the "keep calm" theme and praised responsible citizens who were using good sense and "refusing to be stampeded into making damn fool remarks."[3] In a signed editorial on August 22, Hodding reiterated that the Court could not have made a different decision "in the light of democratic and Christian principles and against the world background today," but he admitted that many of his fellow Southerners differed with him.

His was almost a lone voice. While Presbyterians, Methodists, and Baptists in denomination-wide conventions voted their approval of the Court's ruling, individual congregations across the South passed resolutions denouncing it. Southern bar associations and local school boards adopted resolutions opposing the decision, and southern legislators vowed undying resistance to its implementation.

"Georgia, South Carolina, Louisiana, Alabama, and Florida . . . are ranging themselves in the anti-integration columns, but nowhere have race tensions reached the same peak as in Mississippi," wrote Bem Price in a series for Associated Press on southern reaction to the decision. "Both sides have made clear publicly that this is a no-quarter battle. Each has ruled out compromise."[4]

One of the strongest opposition movements began in the Delta close to Greenville. John Herbers of the United Press bureau in Jackson wrote in his Sunday column (front-paged in the *DD-T*) that communities in the Delta were organizing secret vigilante groups to oppose desegregation.[5] In an editorial the next day, Hodding noted the "talk behind closed doors" and "veiled remarks at open meetings" about groups organizing to make sure schools remained segregated. It was time for these groups to come out in the open, Hodding felt. There was no secret about the NAACP, and there should be no secret about these groups.[6]

That same week, when David Brown was covering the Rotary Club meeting in Leland, the club president said the speaker for the day was controversial; the Rotarians didn't want anything about the meeting in the newspaper. Brown said later that although he could have left, he instead ostentatiously turned over his notepad and stayed. The speaker talked about the newly organized Citizens' Council, com-posed of prominent, law-abiding white people who thought things were moving too fast and who wanted to find some legal means to stop them.

After the meeting Brown went up to the speaker and said he had agreed not to cover the speech but would like to find out more about the Citizens' Council. The speaker told Brown to go to Bill Caraway, the mayor of Leland, who consented to talk for the record.

Brown's first story on the Citizens' Council—the first story in the country that called the group by name—appeared in the *Delta Democrat-Times* on September 9, 1954. "We are trying a peaceful and intelligent approach to a very difficult problem," Mayor Caraway told Brown. The Citizens' Council wanted to provide "responsible, sincere and effective leadership in maintaining segregation."

Caraway then referred Brown to Tut Patterson in Indianola. Robert B. Patterson was a redheaded thirty-two-year-old planter, a former paratrooper and former Mississippi State football star, who had written a letter to *Time* shortly after the Supreme Court decision, in which he used such phrases as "red-blooded Southern Americans," "unconstitutional judge-made law," and "our Caucasian heritage of sixty centuries." The flood of mail Patterson received after the publication of his letter led him to meet with five friends—a lawyer and former sheriff and a banker among them—in Indianola in July to organize the first White Citizens' Council.[7] In less than six weeks, seventeen Mississippi counties had such councils.

Brown called Patterson, who said, "Come on over to my house— but I don't like your boss." When Brown arrived, Patterson took him back to the kitchen and introduced him to the cook. "This is Martha. Don't you like it here, Martha?" And she replied, according to Brown, "Yas suh, Boss."

"Patterson said he had friends who were 'niggers,' and I nodded. I listened to him, and I went back and wrote the most objective report I could," Brown said. The *DD-T* ran it on October 24.

Patterson wrote Brown to praise his story, but at a Citizens' Council meeting later, Brown heard him blasting Hodding Carter and his paper. Afterward Brown remonstrated: "Mr. Patterson, I'm surprised at what you said about the paper. I have a letter from you that says you appreciated the story I did."

"I wasn't talking about you," Patterson said. "I was talking about your boss."[8] Hodding Carter was the enemy.

Brown was a stringer for *Time*, which ran a story based on his file. His coverage of Citizens' Councils showed that by the late fall of 1954, they claimed a membership of 25,000 in twenty-four of Mississippi's eighty-two counties. Council membership played a leading role in December of that year in the passage of two state constitutional amendments, one intended to prevent black voter registration by requiring more difficult qualifications for voting and the other empowering the state legislature to abolish the state's public school system "as a last resort"—which meant if integration ever appeared unavoidable in Mississippi. Hodding editorialized that "truly we didn't expect that even the most callous of our politicians would be so cynical or so humorless as to place themselves and the rest of us in the role of constitutional saviors."[9]

The Citizens' Councils issued a handbill that listed in one column names of people who opposed the school amendment and in another those of people who supported it. The latter included almost every political leader in Mississippi, the former included Hodding Carter, Oliver Emmerich, editor of the McComb *Enterprise-Journal*; a few legislators; and members of the CIO, the AFL, and the NAACP. Hodding knew that most white Mississippians considered the NAACP "ahead of the Communist Party . . . as the fountainhead of all evil and woe," [10] and he reacted with fury in an editorial:

> We've never run with the pack, and we've never run from it. We've been battling the N.A.A.C.P.'s own angry racism for a long time. We'll battle Patterson's identical brand of hatred for dissimilar people just as hard. . . . And we brand as a contemptible liar anyone in or out of the Council, Clan, or Kooko Koncation who says or intimates that . . . [anyone] who opposes this amendment is an enemy of the state or nation or democracy. We happen not to believe it necessary to authorize the abolition of the public school system in order to keep school children in separate public schools in Mississippi. That's all there is to it. . . .
>
> The amendment will almost certainly carry. As for us . . . we say it's spinach and to hell with it. [11]

Mississippians voted two to one in favor of both the amendments that the Citizens' Councils wanted. In fact, the Councils won every battle they entered, and by the beginning of 1955 they were organizing in other southern states. The Councils were able to silence all vocal black opposition to segregation in Mississippi. When fifty-three blacks in Yazoo City signed a petition asking for an immediate end to segregation, the local Council outlined brutal economic retaliation: employers of the signers were to fire them, and landlords to evict them; retailers were to refuse credit to black customers who had signed, and wholesalers to cut off credit and supplies to black retailers who signed. When Clinton Battles, a black doctor in Indianola, registered to vote, urged other blacks to vote, and publicly supported the Supreme Court's decision, Council members warned his patients to find another doctor or lose their jobs. Most of Dr. Battles's patients deserted him.

The Councils targeted Greenville, although one leader doubted whether a Council could ever be organized there "because of those rich Jews and that damn newspaper."[12] A circular from the Councils in the fall of 1954 threatened a boycott of Greenville because the directors of a local baseball team, a member of the Cotton States League, had leased the ballpark to a Memphis promoter for an exhibition game between a black all-star club and a white team made up of players from various southern leagues. The teams had played without incident in Louisiana, Texas, and other parts of Mississippi. Hodding was out of town at the time, and the *DD-T* printed advance stories without comment. After the first story appeared, Citizens' Council members notified the mayor and the chief of police that if the game were not canceled they would stage a sit-down strike on the diamond. The Council also used planes to drop leaflets threatening to boycott stores in Greenville if the town's "experiments in race mixing" were not stopped. The directors of the baseball team, the chief of police, and the mayor all stood firm, but the promoter canceled the game. Hodding wrote an editorial condemning the Citizens' Council and the cancellation of the game. The Council dropped another leaflet, virulently anti-Semitic, and a third, a personal attack on Hodding in bad verse, titled "The Fence Rider."

> There was a young man named Fodding Harter
> Who with his scrawlings replenishes his larder
> He is world renowned by liberals and pinks
> But with his homefolks, my he stinks
>
> The Yankees think he speaks for the South
> But we all know he just runs his mouth
> He thinks he's a statesman and takes many trips
> You can rest assured he's well paid for his quips

He begs to differ with the true Southern leaders
He knows that controversy will get more readers
We often wonder if the man is sincere
In trying to destroy what we all hold dear.

He wants our race mixing a little at a time
He knows we won't stand it quick, worth a dime
Interracial baseball will harm? nevermore!
Remember the salesman with his foot in the door!

He's a great believer in quick compromise
Don't fall for that line, folks, be wise
If you give them an inch they will take a mile
Come on, Hotshot, get in step for a while.

There's always a doubt why he left his state
If we could only get him to repatriate.
Come on, "old boy," quit riding the fence,
Are we white or black, fifty years hence?

This is anonymous and we are ashamed
Man to man we'd much rather be named
We are Southern Patriots and our number is legion
Your language is foreign to this, our region.

All is fair in love and war
Just tell us plainly what you stand for.
No wonder white people won't tell you their plans
For you to pick apart and betray? My lands!

Convicts and race mixers, you're their defender,
Service to the South you do not render.
You may write your books and ride your yacht
But express Southern sentiment you do not!

Any resemblance to persons living or dead
Is purely coincidence, so it's said

If this is a joke, will you share it
If the shoe fits, you may wear it.[13]

The "rancid doggerel" triggered a vehement editorial. "If we couldn't write better verse than that we wouldn't have signed it either." He noted that it was National Newspaper Week and he had been planning to indulge in professional bragging, just as his fellow editors around the country were doing. The *Delta Democrat-Times* was a nationally acclaimed paper, but Hodding would not mention the national honors it had won. In the annual statewide competition, however, southern judges had named it "the best in Mississippi for six out of the last seven years, including the year just past." He pointed out the community work he had done, and said that five of his eight books either defended or praised the South. Certainly, he continued,

> any newspaper worthy of the freedom guaranteed it in the first amendment to our Constitution should welcome criticism and from time to time expect antagonism from its readers. If we were one-sidedly approved by our fellow townsmen at all times, we would know that we were not living up to our obligations under that amendment. But we do expect their disapproval to be forthright and our critics to make themselves known. They know where we work and where we live. We should have the same knowledge of them.[14]

In a survey of southern newspapers for its January 17, 1955, issue, *Time* found that only one-fourth of southern dailies flatly opposed the Supreme Court's *Brown* decision. Most editors, however, were saying as little as possible about desegregation, since anything they said would anger someone. Nashville papers reported that the Catholic schools in town would desegregate, but they failed to follow up with stories on how integration worked. *Time* commented that "even liberal Editor Hodding Carter . . . who opposes segregation on 'moral grounds,' feels that the Supreme Court decision has hurt the gradual progress of desegregation in the South by forcing both segregationists and desegregationists to 'extremes.'" The magazine reported that although few newspapers had campaigned strongly against state constitutional amendments to empower state governments to make public schools private, Hodding's paper had fought the Mississippi amendment with everything it had.

The few southern liberals did try to support one another. As Harry Ashmore, the Little Rock editor, said, "We are few, but there are those who hate us." Liberal southern editors, including Hodding, Ashmore, Ralph McGill in Atlanta, Bill Baggs in Miami, and Mark Ethridge in Louisville, maintained a loose but sustaining network and exchanged news of their latest defeat or victory. Hodding, like the others, tried to hold a middle-of-the-road position, telling Northerners that putting pressure on the South would only rouse Southerners to fury and grant more power to the segregationists. Southern moderates regarded those who favored an immediate end to segregation as extremists on one side and die-hard segregationists as extremists on the other.

The majority of white Southerners regarded the few moderates as renegades and traitors. By one definition, a moderate was a person who did not say, "By God, if this keeps up, if they don't realize their place, what we were going to do to them"; a person who would use the word "nigra" instead of "nigger," and try to "find the middle ground."[15] This falls far short of capturing the courage of the moderates. In the poisonous atmosphere of Mississippi especially, a moderate lived a life of peril. Politicians referred to Hodding scornfully as "a self-confessed moderate," effectively placing him on what Mississippians regarded as the radical left. Northern liberals, ignoring how much Hodding battled against the tide in Mississippi, were often contemptuous of him. C. L. Golightly, a black professor of history at the University of Wisconsin, called Hodding, Ashmore, Ethridge, Jonathan Daniels, Virginius Dabney, and other southern moderates as "obsolete." "What are the moderates?" asked Carl Rowan. "Are they moderately *for* or *against* compliance with the Supreme Court's

242

decision?"[16] A black lawyer called Hodding "the most over-rated Southerner of our times," and pointed out that "a Southerner can be against both the Ku Klux Klan and the WCC [White Citizens' Councils] and remain . . . opposed to conformity to the Supreme Court's interpretation of the U.S. Constitution."[17]

Only a lunatic fringe believed that opposition to the Supreme Court decision was anything more than a delaying action, Hodding said in a speech at the Southern Police Institute in Louisville. Reaction to that simple, sensible statement showed how wide the lunatic fringe was. The Jackson *Daily News* proclaimed that the South's battle plan meant defiance to the last ditch: "Any attempt to ram that decision down the throats of the people of Mississippi will inevitably result in bloodshed."[18]

In his reply to two men who had attacked him in letters to several newspapers after the Police Institute speech, Hodding displayed his remarkable talent for invective. "Since you are printers I am assuming you can read," he said in a three-page, single-spaced letter. "If so, you should know that I have never advocated nor welcomed an end to separate public schools systems in the South. I said that anyone who believed that school segregation would last forever was either a blind optimist or on the lunatic fringe. If you have any doubts as to which category I would place you in, please do not hesitate to inquire."[19]

When Hodding decided to write a magazine article on the Citizens' Councils, Dave Brown turned over all his research to him. Hodding promised to split with Brown any money he made. *Look* bought the article for $2,500, and Brown was delighted, realizing he could not have sold an article himself for half of that amount. He went out and bought a new jacket and a pair of pants, his first in a long time.[20]

In the article, Hodding said that although so far the Councils had eschewed violence, he could imagine hoodlums taking over "if today's leaders give way to boredom or anger or despair." The Councils could become "instruments of interracial violence."[21] Advance copies of the issue of *Look* containing Hodding's article "A Wave of Terror Threatens the South" reached Mississippi in early March and stirred people in the state to hysterical rage.

Tut Patterson blasted Hodding for comparing the Councils with the Klan. "Citizens familiar with Carter's writings know his intolerance toward the determination of white people to stay white," he told the Jackson *Daily News*.[22] The mayors of Indianola and Cleveland took issue with the article and defended the Citizens' Councils; Mayor Martie Bishop of Cleveland said their membership represented a cross-section of "our white male population."[23]

"Our native Mississippi has received another black eye," wrote Tom Ethridge, a columnist for the Jackson paper. "Mr. Carter sees Ku Klux Klan under the bed here at home. . . . Clairvoyant Carter seems to glimpse an impending reign of terror where more experienced prognosticators see future progress and prosperity undreamed of before. . . . It is an old tune, yet one that never fails to tickle the ears of Eastern critics hostile to Southern ways. . . . Mr. Carter's article should delight the Communists, who seize every available propaganda weapon in exaggerating alleged racial tensions in the United States. Certainly his article will not help those seeking to attract new industry here." Hodding reminded Ethridge of a "self-important little rooster who heard thunder for the first time. Dashing wildly across the barnyard, the hysterical little rooster shrilly proclaimed that the world was coming to an end." Ethridge went on: "While Mr. Carter profits financially and publicity-wise from such writings, it is mighty hard on the rest of the home folks who dislike sleeping in a wet bed." Ethridge wondered why Hodding could not be more like Harnett Kane, who was a "credit to Louisiana and his beloved Southland."[24]

Other Southerners reacted just as angrily. A South Carolina columnist reported a local conversation about Hodding: "An assertion was made that Mr. Carter is a brainwashed Southerner. It was as vehemently denied. His defender stoutly insisted that a brain must exist before it can be washed. . . . All present were willing for Look to have him. For none wanted any part of him."[25]

On April Fool's Day, during a debate about the article in the Mississippi House of Representatives, members called Hodding everything from a scalawag and a lying newspaperman to a Judas who had sold out the South for fifty thousand pieces of Yankee silver. As far as the white people of Mississippi were concerned, Hodding Carter should have no rights, one House member said. Representative Eck Windham said Hodding wrote "filthy articles aimed at the Eastern market"; the *Look* piece was "a willful lie a nigger-loving editor made about the people of Mississippi." By a vote of eighty-nine to nineteen, the House adopted a resolution charging that Hodding's article "drew inferences and conclusions on the flimsiest and most speculative kind of evidence." (In spite of the lopsided vote, there were eloquent, passionate speeches, not actually in defense of the article, but at least in opposition to censure. Representative Joel Bass, who had opposed the amendment to abolish the public school system, said he had felt the sting of the Councils' pressure himself; for him, the evils of censoring were worse than the article itself.)[26]

Hodding, with four friends, a cook, and a guide, had taken the *Mistuh Charley*, the newspaper's cabin cruiser, on a turkey-hunting trip on the Arkansas shore. Betty packed up the wire service report about the House resolution, and Joe Call, a cotton-duster pilot, flew along the riverbank until he spotted the boat, then dropped the bundle on the nearby shore. While Hodding and his friends continued playing cards on board, John Gibson went to retrieve the bundle. "You'd better read this," he said when he returned. Later Hodding described feeling as though he had been kicked in the stomach by eighty-nine angry jackasses. His companions thought the resolution was funny, but Hodding did not, even when they assured him that "a Mississippi legislative majority was mentally and morally incapable of insulting anybody."[27]

Hodding went below deck and typed his reply, in the form of an editorial. His friends persuaded him to tone it down a bit, and the next morning he phoned in the milder version. Headlined "Liar by Legislation," it ran on the front page of the *DD-T* on April 3:

By a vote of 89 to 19 the Mississippi House of Representatives has resolved the editor of this newspaper into a liar because of an article I wrote about the Citizens' Councils for Look magazine. If this charge were true it would make me well qualified to serve with that body. It is not true. So to even things up I herewith resolve by a vote of 1 to 0 that there are 89 liars in the State Legislature, beginning with Speaker Sillers and working way on down to Rep. Eck Windham of Prentiss, a political loon whose name is fittingly made up of the words "wind" and "ham."

I am hopeful that this fever like the Ku Kluxism that rose from the same kind of infection will run its course before too long a time. Meanwhile those 89 character mobbers can go to hell collectively or singly and wait there until I back down. They needn't plan on returning.

The editorial had a curious effect on the legislature, recalled newsman John Herbers. "It was so potent they just shut up."[28]

The conflict with the legislature brought Hodding some praise from an unexpected source. In Montgomery, Alabama, Virginia Durr and her husband, lawyer Clifford Durr, were ostracized for their liberal views and their work for the Southern Conference Educational Fund. She had often criticized Hodding for being too moderate, but this time she congratulated him on his good fight with the legislature and the Citizens' Councils. "I always thought you were going to be able to get by as you seemed to be such a gentleman and have money and were friends of the Percys, etc.," she wrote him, "but it looks as though to the Mississippians no fine distinctions are drawn. . . . I hope you can stick it, we are sticking it here in Alabama and find it rough going, but awfully interesting." Hodding replied that it was an ill wind that blew no one any good, and he was glad that the Mississippi legislature had raised him in her estimation.[29]

In a later article for Look, "The South and I," Hodding lamented that he had always been a middle-of-the-roader but other Southerners had been conditioned by political demagogues over the years to think that anyone opposed to extremism was "in league with the Supreme Court, the NAACP, the Communist party, the mass-circulation magazines and everybody north of the Mason-Dixon line to destroy the Southern way of life." For those Northerners who also misinterpreted his situation and believed he led a martyr's isolated life, he clarified:

We live normal small-town lives in Greenville. That means we're busy with all kinds of matters besides racial problems. According to my calendar for the general period between the [March 22] *Look* article and the legislature's resolution, I was chairman, so help me, of the Rotary Club Ladies Night; planned a spring boating week end with the skipper of the Sea Scouts . . . and gave a wiener roast for the Cub Scouts, including my youngest, whose den father I am; met three times with my fellow directors of the Chamber of Commerce; awarded the annual *Democrat-Times* plaques to the outstanding man and woman citizen; served as ringmaster for our neighborhood teenagers' Cypress Saddle Club show; met with our monthly discussion group, a dozen business and professional men, in my home; began work on a talk for the convention of the Mississippi Bankers Association; helped my wife entertain for two engaged daughters of friends and for . . . our older sons home from college and school for Easter holidays; planned a board meeting of the Mississippi Historical Society, of which I'm president; and worked with my wife on the 150-year history of the Episcopal Diocese of Louisiana. This accounting is only partial, but it doesn't leave much time for scalawagging.[30]

Missing from this list were activities for the board of the Delta Council and the vestry of St. James' Episcopal Church. Hodding was voted off the board of the prestigious Delta Council, an economic development group to which the Delta's most important planters and businessmen belonged, because of his opposition to the Citizens' Councils. At the church, someone brought the question to a vote in the vestry: If a black person came to the church, should he or she be seated? Hodding and another vestryman, Jack Potts, said firmly that they would not turn anyone away. "It wouldn't be what the Lord would want us to do," Potts said. At the next yearly parrish election, Hodding and Potts were soundly defeated.[31] The rejection was a blow to Hodding.

When the same issue came up at Greenville's Presbyterian church, one man said he thought blacks should be admitted. His mother was outraged. "Mother, what do you think Jesus Christ would do if He were standing at the front door of the First Presbyterian Church?" he asked her. "I know exactly what he would do," she said, "and he would be wrong."

The community pressure took its toll on Hodding. About this time he went with Matt Virden, a Greenville businessman, to Xavier House at Pass Christian for a retreat conducted by Father Edward Sheridan, a Jesuit priest. Father Sheridan, celebrated for his work with alcoholics, had helped Virden lick a serious drinking problem, and Virden had taken other Greenville men, including a prominent lawyer and a well-known banker, to Xavier House for help. Virden, who must have recognized signs that Hodding's family did not notice, did not tell Father Sheridan that Hodding had a problem with alcohol, nor did Hodding mention his drinking to the priest.

"He made the retreat," recalled Father Sheridan. "He kept the silence. He went to the meetings. He talked to me. He and I took a liking to each other and asked each other a great many questions about each other's work. I asked him what was important in running a newspaper. He said, 'Get the name and middle initial!'" At some point Hodding talked to Father Sheridan about converting to Catholicism.[32]

Two years later, Potts and Hodding were both back on the St. James' vestry, Potts as clerk and Hodding as senior warden. There was no more talk of converting to Catholicism.

Hodding had mentioned a speech to a convention of the Mississippi Bankers Association in the June *Look* article, and he reported on it to his two older sons, who were away at school: He and Betty had had a "wonderful time" at the bankers' convention. "Despite advance predictions of disorder and the like, there was a record breaking crowd at the banquet—more than a thousand—and only two or three walked out, obviously with kidney trouble and not from animosity. Wade Hollowell made a fighting introduction and I was both surprised and delighted that they gave me an encore handclap, which meant that I had to rise and take a bow. And we had a wonderful time socially, meeting lots of people and apparently proving to them we don't grow horns."[33]

But there was an undercurrent at the convention. Alden Sawyer, a Bowdoin classmate of Hodding's and a banker, later attended a national bank convention where he met the president of the Mississippi Bankers Association; he asked the man whether he knew his college roommate Hodding Carter. The Mississippi banker replied, "Yes, and if I ever catch up with the son of a bitch who asked him to speak at our convention, I'll cut his throat."[34]

Hodding's hate mail called him everything from "renegade" to "liberal" (obviously a term of opprobrium) to "negrophile white-trash bum" to "Benedict Arnold in sheep's clothing." It put him "in the same class with a cotton-mouth, probably even lower," and described him as trying to "pacify the pro-communist negro loving judas' of the publishing world." Much of this mail was unsigned. When it did have a name attached, Hodding answered it. Almost worse than the mail was the slander. Politicians routinely referred to him as a "nigger-loving, Yankeefied communist" who advocated the "mongrelization of the race"; the *Delta Democrat-Times* was "owned by a millionaire Northern Negro" who used Hodding as his mouthpiece. His office was the "secret headquarters of the NAACP," and his editorials showed that he was a radical, a liberal, or—worst of all—a moderate.

Threats and malevolent telephone calls continued, at home and at the office. Hodding normally answered the phone in a courtly way. A visitor remembered hearing him say, "I am very fine, sir, and you?" But he could yell when the call turned out to be a threat. Lawyer Phillips, who worked at Feliciana as butler, gardener, and general factotum, learned to mimic Hodding answering threatening phone calls: "You can kiss my ass, you country son of a bitch."

Feliciana had a long, winding driveway bordered with thick bushes and trees. Hodding once got a call from a longtime resident who had had a few drinks and called up to announce that he was coming out to shoot him. Hodding got his shotgun, took it down, and waited in the bushes. Nobody came.[35] In fact, nobody ever shot at the house, but people would drive up the long driveway and honk their horns. The Carters installed an alarm bell that would ring from the big house to the little house, so whoever was staying there could get help; they kept guns in every room of the house and in the glove compartments of the cars. Hodding took the threats seriously, but he was not a coward. The people who threatened him made him mad, and he would "show them."

The dangers were not imaginary. Teenager John Keating, who stayed with Betty and Tommy when Hodding was out of town, worked for the same fertilizer company in Greenwood that employed Byron De La Beckwith. When Delay Beckwith—so Mississippians called him—found out that Keating knew the Carters, he asked him questions about the layout of Feliciana. Was there a way to get in behind the house? What kind of alarm system did the Carters have? Beckwith, who reportedly told other people he was going to kill Hodding, would later be tried twice for the murder of Medgar Evers.

"It's true that Hodding became the object of virulent hatred. He aroused venomous ire," said Roy Campbell, who was president of the Greenville school board in the fifties. "But that didn't mean he couldn't go to parties. They went everywhere. They invited the whole spectrum to their house. He still had coffee nearly every morning with a bunch of guys—John Gannon, Ferd Moyse, Roy Hanf, Jake Stein, Jack Baskin, and Bob Harding. Most of that group bellyached about the paper, but they liked Hodding."[36]

Hodding's enemies charged that Feliciana was a haven for subversives from Europe, Africa, Asia, and New York City. And visitors did come from India, from South Africa, from all over the world. Once Harry Marsh was startled to see a stuffy British general helping Betty plant a tree. A young South American, who liked to take a three-hour siesta but worked on the paper in the mornings and early afternoon, stayed with the Carters at the same time they hosted a six-foot, five-inch Afrikaner editor, Fritz Potgieter, and the dwarf son of the Canadian humorist Stephen Leacock. A visiting Korean writer went to the kitchen to ask Phalange Word, the cook, how much the stove and refrigerator cost and how much money she made.

The Carters still gave parties. Perhaps the most grateful guests were the few beleaguered liberal journalists in Mississippi, who came to Feliciana to drink and let off steam. The testimony of these few is enough to glorify Hodding forever. "Things were popping all over the state," recalled John Herbers, who later joined the New York *Times*. "The UP bureau in Jackson grew from one man to five. The atmosphere in Mississippi was atrocious, abysmal. It was the most rural state, the state with the most blacks, the poorest. It had no political figure to stand up. The whole state was so racist that I was totally surrounded by people who didn't believe what I believed. They were backed up by tradition, religion, and the law. I'd get up every morning and ask myself, 'Is there something wrong with me?' I'd think I was crazy, and I'd see people like Hodding and know the real world was out there. A few journalists kind of banded together—we were totally outnumbered. If you tried to suggest that segregation was wrong, you got shouted down. Hodding gave me a reason to think what I was doing was worthwhile. He made me want to continue in journalism. If it hadn't been for him I would have left. He gave us hope."[37]

John Emmerich, son of Oliver Emmerich who would leave McComb to work on newspapers in Baltimore and Houston and return to Mississippi to own a dozen newspapers, always looked up to Hodding as an idol. Hodding had a big house in the country, a pond, a swimming pool, a tennis court, and horses, and Emmerich wondered whether his admiration of Hodding might explain why he, too, would have a big house in the country, a pond, a swimming pool, a tennis court, and horses.[38]

It was not just newspaper people who drew strength from Hodding. According to Kenneth Haxton, who helped start the Levee Press,

Hodding may have been considered left-wing, but "he wasn't that far out in his views. It was just the times. He created a climate where you could say what you thought."[39]

As time went on after the Supreme Court's decision, Hodding was more morose and pessimistic than he ever had been. The angry letters he received, the pummeling he took from neighbors affected him.

"During the fifties I dreaded coming home from vacations at prep school," recalled Philip Carter. "I could feel the social strain. Was it adolescence? I never had any sense of being ostracized myself. When Conwell Sykes and my father did not speak, Mr. Sykes still spoke to me at church and shook hands—and gave me the Deke grip."[40] The opposition, Philip said, radicalized Hodding. "It infuriated him to have people he knew and cared about denounce him for what seemed a defensible attitude. He knew their capacity for violence. He was *one of them.*"

The Carters had heard rumors of someone's planning to start a more conservative rival paper since 1950. In 1954, as the Citizens' Councils seriously considered taking on such an enterprise, Hodding and Betty had decided to start a "shadow" competitor. Hal DeCell, the *DD-T*'s stringer in Rolling Fork, was friendly with Hodding and came by to see him every week when he was in Greenville to sell advertising. When DeCell, who owned a weekly in Rolling Fork, mentioned that he wanted to launch another paper elsewhere, Hodding said, "Why don't you start one here. See if the market wants an independent voice."[41] The *Mississippi Pilot* began publication on July 7, 1954. Although the *DD-T* printed it, the *Pilot* was independent editorially and no one knew that Hodding was involved in any way. DeCell soon determined that he should concentrate on Rolling Fork, and the *Pilot* ceased publication in October 1954.[42]

"We saw how much it would cost for a competitor to start a paper," Betty Carter said.[43]

"Competition was always in the Carters' mind," said John Gibson.

"They started a paper in Hammond and they started a paper here, and they thought somebody would do it to them. I never thought anybody would."[44]

The rage of the Citizens' Councils against Hodding became more focused as its members set out to damage him. They urged Greenville people to stop subscribing to the *Delta Democrat-Times* and advertisers to boycott the newspaper.

Hodding met these attempts head-on. In a signed front-page editorial on April 21, 1955, he called the Councils' action "gangsterism" and said that now he had

> evidence that men identifying themselves with the Councils are trying to put the squeeze not only on the Delta Democrat-Times, but upon a number of our advertisers and other Greenville citizens. . . .
>
> We're not talking about one or two incidents. This is a planned campaign, deliberately entered upon by men whose behavior in this regard makes them blood brothers of the Capone mob. Merchants, professional men, and distributors have been approached.
>
> These protection sellers make no bones about it. In some cases they tell their targets that unless they organize or join the Councils they'll get no more business from Council members. Sometimes they say to a merchant that unless he quits advertising in this newspaper he'll lose the trade of the shadowy brethren. Sometimes they warn subscribers to quit taking the paper.
>
> We have a hunch that relatively few of our fellow citizens are going to knuckle under. If we're wrong, it's not only our head that's going to be chopped off. What will also be lost is freedom of conscience and of speech and of action. These are the only privileges that basically set us apart from Soviet Russia. No matter how worthy the purpose, these tactics have no place in America. . . .

And if some of our weaker neighbors are going to buy protection, we hope that they pay off to highbinders who have the
guts to behave like highbinders instead of posing as honorable
defenders of the South.

Citizens' Council members called a public meeting at the Greenville community center where they encouraged merchants to stop
advertising in the newspaper. Howard Dyer, a lawyer and former
state senator, and a friend of Hodding's, stood up and made a speech
supporting him. The meeting disbanded. Advertisers resisted further
Council efforts. "They came in and asked me to stop advertising in the
Democrat-Times," said Steinmart's Jake Stein, "and I said I couldn't
stay in business if I didn't advertise."[45]

Likewise, circulation did not fall. It held steady at around 12,500,
but there was a feeling that it would have grown in the Delta outside Greenville if it were not for the Council efforts at boycott. (After
the Little Rock Citizens' Council called for people to cancel their
subscriptions to the *Arkansas Gazette*, daily circulation dropped 10.6
percent.[46]) John Gibson, looking back thirty-five years later, said,
"Hodding and Betty were overconcerned about the boycott. It didn't
amount to anything. These things run their course. We tried to
counteract it by constructive things. It's hard to argue with a newspaper."[47]

Hodding was "always afraid he'd lose the paper," said his son Philip.
"If circulation in Indianola dropped from 300 to 250, he perceived it
as dropping to zero."

On May 2, 1955, the Mississippi Board of Public Contracts announced that it was rejecting the state's contract with the Delta
Democrat Publishing Company to print the laws of the 1954 and 1955
sessions of the legislature, even though Hodding's company had been
low bidder for the contract. The public contracts board rejected the
contract on the grounds that the company would have had the binding
done out of state. John Gibson said Attorney General J. P. Coleman
had told him that the binding could be done anywhere, as long as the

printing was done by Mississippi labor within the state. Hodding was sure he had lost the contract because of the Citizens' Councils.[48]

Carter continued to attack the Councils in the paper and in his speeches. When he spoke to the Memphis Public Affairs Forum on May 2, he called the organizations "dangerous and unholy." His speech was interrupted by the sudden arrival of a fire engine, a police squad car, a Navy shore patrol vehicle, and two "Negro ambulances," summoned after what the police later determined were crank calls.[49]

"So far they have been able to hurt us very little," Hodding wrote a friend about the economic terrorism. "And I don't think they are going to do any better, but a whole lot of small folks can get hurt."[50] He told another friend, "I believe we are slowing these boys down a little. They tried to boycott us and threaten us and none of it has worked so far. From what my spies tell me, they are beginning to give up a little as far as Greenville is concerned, but I am not betting on that."[51]

Hodding never yielded or even flinched. When he was in Maine during the summer of 1955, Harry Marsh, who had joined the *DD-T* the year before, covered a meeting called in Greenville to organize a Citizens' Council. Representative John Bell Williams, a U.S. congressman from Jackson, was the speaker. Marsh wrote a story about the meeting and an editorial that took issue with Williams, then called the Carters to read the editorial to them. At one point Hodding interrupted: "After 'John Bell Williams,' put in 'a political punk.'" "Oh, Hodding, you don't want to say that, do you?" Betty said. "Leave it in," said Hodding. Marsh thought it helped the editorial considerably.[52]

Ferd Moyse, a Greenville businessman, wrote Hodding that there was "too much discussion going on concerning 'the subject' . . . too many meetings, too much discussion on the streets, too many forecasts of doom. . . . There are too many people just waiting for your return to see how far you can be pushed into committing yourself."[53] When the Carters came back to Greenville after the summer, Hodding found the situation had deteriorated. White Mississippians were uneasy, to put it mildly. That fall they read that 134,000 black students were enrolled in hitherto all-white schools in other southern states. Pamphlets from the Citizens' Councils dwelt on the threat of intermarriage. Segregationists looked around at military bases in Mississippi, where integration was already the rule on training fields and in barracks, clubs, and swimming pools, and swore this would never happen off the bases. Segregationists railed against the NAACP, which was now winning every court battle it fought. Everybody Hodding saw—white and black—would say, "There's going to be worse trouble. It's going to get worse before it gets better." One friend of Hodding's even put his wife and daughter on curfew because he feared racial violence. An angry farmer came to Hodding's office and told him that he and some friends had planned to give him a "going-over," but decided not to: they did not want to give the NAACP any more fuel. People whose families had lived in the Delta for generations talked wistfully of being able to move away. When a Citizens' Council was finally organized in Greenville, Hodding was astonished at the names of the town's worthies who were among its leaders. Hodding, who weighed 235 pounds in April 1955, said he was too fat to run away from controversy.[54]

Hodding's editorials calling for punishment for the Till murderers especially angered some Greenville residents. Emmett Till, a black fourteen-year-old from Chicago who was visiting his uncle in Sumner, Mississippi, was alleged to have whistled at the wife of a white storekeeper. That night he was kidnapped from his uncle's home by two white men, beaten, and shot through the head. His body was found three days later in the Tallahatchie River, with the fan from a cotton gin around his neck. Two white men, Roy Bryant and J. W. Milam, were identified by Emmett's uncle as the men who broke into his house and kidnapped the boy. In fact, Bryant and Milam admitted taking him away but denied having killed him.

On September 6, 1955, Hodding editorialized that it was becoming evident that two groups were seeking an acquittal for Bryant and Milam. One group, he said, was the NAACP, "which is seeking another excuse to apply the torch of world-wide scorn to Mississippi," and the other group included the friends of the two men, including Sheriff H. C. Strider.

Hodding felt that the "macabre exhibitionism, the wild statements, and the hysterical overtones" at the Chicago funeral for Emmett Till were "too well-staged not to have been planned to inflame hatred and to set off a reverse reaction in Mississippi," where there had been a reaction of "honest indignation." These demonstrations could make prospective jurors very angry with the "blanket indictments of a white society," and Mississippi "would go down in further ignominy as a snakepit where justice cannot prevail for each race alike." This would suit the NAACP just fine, he said.

And the sheriff was working hand in hand with the NAACP, Hodding charged. Strider held that the body found was not that of Emmett Till, although it was identified by relatives and accepted by the boy's mother. The sheriff claimed that the body, after being shot, beaten, and soaked in the river did not resemble a picture of Emmett. Fortunately, said the editorial, other officials of Tallahatchie County were acting more sensibly.

Outside Mississippi, Hodding wrote, the murder was being called a lynching. "Well, it wasn't. But it may well become a lynching post-facto if the courts in Mississippi are unable to accomplish justice in this matter. And if this happens, we will deserve the criticism we get."

When four young Memphis blacks raped a white woman that fall, they justified themselves by referring to the Till case. Hodding thought the NAACP, which blamed all Mississippi for the slaying of the boy, should take the blame for inciting the rapists. "The atmosphere of hatred created by the NAACP against white people could very well have precipitated this crime in Memphis," he wrote.[55]

The *Delta Democrat-Times* sent a reporter to cover the trial of Bryant and Milam, which polarized Mississippi. Segregationists outdid themselves to appear as bad as they could to Northerners, sniggering over such jokes as: "Isn't it just like a nigger to try to swim across the Tallahatchie with a gin fan around his neck?" An international press corps covered the trial, and its members delighted in reporting on the sheriff, who each morning greeted the white and ignored the black journalists. Warned by more clever county leaders that he should not be so pointed, he changed his tactics. He first greeted the white reporters, then turned to the black reporters and said, "Morning, niggers."

When the jury acquitted Bryant and Milam, some in the press corps wept. The tension from the murder and the trial was the worst Hodding had ever seen. "Matters are going to get more violent down this way before things take a turn for the better. I've never felt quite as discouraged about racial relations and attitudes."[56]

Later, after a grand jury in Leflore County refused to indict Bryant and Milam for kidnapping, to which they had confessed, Hodding wrote one of his strongest editorials. The grand jury, he said, had

> told the world that white men in Mississippi may remove Negroes from their homes against their will to punish them or worse, without fear of punishment for themselves. . . .
>
> That [Bryant and Milam] admitted taking the boy from his uncle's home to punish him for insulting the wife of one of them meant nothing to the grand jury. Unfortunately, it is going to mean a great a deal to Mississippi and none of it will be good.
>
> If this miscarriage of justice were an isolated incident we could be less ashamed of the present and less fearful for the future. But it is not unique.
>
> The records of our courts reveal a shocking number of related incidents. In one Mississippi county a Negro who raped a white woman has this year been executed, a fate he deserved, but the same day a white man was given a minimum jail sentence of two years for the heinous rape of a Negro child.
>
> In another Mississippi county a grand jury was unable to indict the white slayers of a Negro political worker who was shot to death on the courthouse lawn, with a large number of people nearby, because no witnesses would testify.

This can be sickeningly blatant, but there is no need to repeat what so many know when so few seem to care.

A curse lies on our state. Where are our leaders of yesterday . . . giants who would lead us away from the jungle of anarchy in which we have been lost?

Most of what is happening in Mississippi has nothing to do with segregation, although violence has multiplied in the wake of the United States Supreme Court decision on segregation in the schools. This is naked racially-inspired terror. We are paying and will continue to pay a price for it, both in the sight of God and our fellow man.

It is not happenstance that our population dwindles while in our sister states it rises; that our income lags behind that of our other Southern states and far behind the rest of the nation, and that 65 out of every 100 college graduates in Mississippi leave the state for far more reasons than just greener pastures.

All of these things are related to what happened in Leflore County Wednesday. It will be a long time before Mississippi recovers from the injury the Leflore County grand jury has done to our state and to humanity.[57]

Hodding could write a brave editorial like this and almost simultaneously blame the North for the South's problems, as he did in an article for *The Saturday Evening Post*.[58] In Memphis six black men beat a white man, kidnapped his companion, and raped her repeatedly. Why didn't the northern press play this up like the Till case? he asked. Why did the North blame a whole state for the Till murder? There was no doubt that Mississippians were convinced that they lived in a "misunderstood and abused state."

He listed newsworthy events that had been reported in the *DD-T* but had not received publicity up North: A young white woman had risked her life to rescue a black child from the same river in which Emmett Till's body was found. Greenville residents—whites and blacks together—had raised—more than $2,000 to send the black high school band, the only band invited from the state of Mississippi, to participate in a Negro Elks convention parade in New York. The school board had authorized construction of the third black school to be built in Greenville since World War II. A second black staff physician had been appointed to the state mental hospital. A new black assistant county agent had reported for duty in Washington County, and the *DD-T* had printed his picture and a feature story about him. The paper had also published a three-column picture and feature story about a black sharecropper who was grossing $200 a day with a mechanical cotton picker he had bought used for $3,000.

Hodding saw it as a hopeful sign that business-minded individuals were beginning to realize that the sizzling racial climate would not help Mississippi promote new industry. "Meanwhile," he concluded, "ours is a besieged state, but one not inclined to surrender. No one should expect that a decision of a Supreme Court can soon or conclusively change a whole people's thinking. That must be understood."

Now, why couldn't his enemies at home understand that when he wrote for the Yankee dollar, he wrote things like this, things he hoped would *explain* the South's position to the North and place the blame for the South's plight on the North?

The Boston *Herald*, editorializing on Hodding's article, referred to him as "the Alan Paton of the American South" and asked, "Except for the separate schools, do not these things give a different impression of Mississippi [from what] we have had up here? But what are we doing to encourage this Mississippi? Do we encourage it by sitting in terrible judgement on Mississippi's crimes?"[59]

The pressures mounted, and Hodding showed it. He wrote to a friend who was going abroad as a Fulbright lecturer that he envied him. "Right now I'd rather be at the North Pole than in Mississippi."[60] And yet life rocked on. As Hodding told Harry Ashmore, "Southerners will generally treat you politely until they make up their minds to kill you."[61]

The NAACP had filed suits for the integration of the public schools in Yazoo City, Jackson, Natchez, Clarksdale, and Vicksburg. Mem-

260

bership rolls in Citizens' Councils grew, and by December 1955 all petitions for integration had been withdrawn. The number of eligible black voters in the state had fallen from 22,000 in 1952 to less than 12,000. Blacks were still powerless, and the NAACP had virtually written off Mississippi as hopeless. At a convention of Citizens' Councils in Jackson on December 1, Senator James Eastland announced that desegregation was dead.

But that was the same day Rosa Parks was asked to give up her seat on a bus in Montgomery, and a citywide boycott of the buses by blacks soon followed. Hodding at first said the boycott was a lesson in "how not to go about seeking what has popularly come to be known as 'EQUALITY.'"[62] Nevertheless Eastland was wrong. Desegregation was coming, even to Mississippi.

13. 1955–1959

"Nothing Could Make Things Worse Down Here"

Hazel Brannon Smith, an editor in nearby Holmes County, led a life much harder than Hodding's. She had come to Mississippi straight out of the University of Alabama and bought the Lexington *Advertiser* with borrowed money, and she operated it as fearlessly as Hodding did his paper. In July 1954, the *Advertiser* had reported that the county sheriff, Richard Byrd, while trying to clear the crowd from a country store near Tchula, told a twenty-seven-year-old black man to "get goin'" and then shot him in the leg. Hazel Smith's story made it plain that she considered the shooting unnecessary. The sheriff denied the man had even been shot and sued Smith for libel. She was found guilty in circuit court, and liable for $10,000 in damages. In November 1955, the Mississippi Supreme Court unanimously reversed the verdict and rebuked the jury and the sheriff.

More trouble grew out of the suit. In September 1955, the Citizens' Councils of Holmes County called a kangaroo court to "try" David Minter, a white physician who had treated the gunshot victim and testified for Hazel Smith in the libel trial, contradicting the sheriff. Dr. Minter had come to Mississippi to begin medical practice at a cooperative plantation, Providence Community, in a remote section of Holmes County, which was seventy-three percent black. A. E. Cox, a native Texan, ran the plantation. Whites in Holmes

County, already suspicious of the cooperative plantation, did not like it that the two men ministered to blacks. Over the previous summer, rumors about the families of both men and mixed swimming in the plantation's small pool had been rife; Minter and Cox were accused of advocating racial integration. A newly elected member of the state legislature who was head of the Tchula Citizens' Council presided at the "trial"; the county attorney, head of the Lexington Citizens' Council, directed the interrogation. Both Minter and Cox insisted, amid heckling and audible threats, that they had not violated southern racial taboos. The men and their families were "advised" to leave the state. They did, eventually.

Hodding vigorously defended Minter and Cox in an editorial that began, "This is just a reminder that Mississippi, including Holmes County, is still in the United States."[1]

Although Hazel Smith was as brave as Hodding, her paper was not as good as his; she never covered local news as intensely as he. After the racial controversy heated up, she was always on the edge of bankruptcy. Hodding and Betty tried to tell her that in order to fight the overpowering racism in Holmes County, she first had to make her paper profitable and build a base of community support. Hodding did everything he could to help Smith: cosigned her notes at a Greenville bank, talked about her in speeches he made in the North, wrote articles about her, nominated her for awards, and finally implemented a campaign to raise money from northern liberals. These donors contributed to the Tri-County Fund, administered by Hodding, which paid for advertising space in the *Advertiser* that was used by national charity and civic organizations such as the Red Cross. Smith remained virtually friendless in Holmes County.

Hodding, on the other hand, always held on to his Greenville friends, who helped him bear the apparently endless lash of hostility and vituperation. Business prospered. The newspaper began operating an office supply and gift shop, and in 1957 he and John Gibson started radio station WDDT, which turned out to be a profitable investment. By 1960 the newspaper's circulation was almost 15,000, and they had added the Associated Press wire to the United Press wire in the newsroom, partly to keep any competing paper that might come to Greenville from having AP service.

Hodding sought to escape the pressure often, with vacations in Maine and working trips to other parts of the country. He traveled to Huntsville, Alabama, for a story about rocket scientists for *Collier's*. For diversion, he went to Louisville for the Kentucky Derby, to Baton Rouge for boozy weekends of football and parties with old friends, to Princeton to see young Hodding and to speak on Faulkner. He visited countless cities, towns, and college campuses to give speeches and receive awards.

Hodding returned to the Democratic Party before the 1956 presidential campaign, describing himself as a "mugwump"—the term for a Republican who had refused to support the party's presidential candidate in 1884, James G. Blaine. Hodding endorsed Adlai Stevenson for president, "the only candidate who had a kind word for the South."

Time was bringing changes to Hodding's family. His children were growing up: Hodding III, who had enrolled at Princeton in 1953, worked in the summers of 1954 and 1955 for the New Orleans *Item*; Philip and Tommy had gone off to Episcopal High School in Alexandria, Virginia, in 1954; In July 1955, Margaret Carter, John's wife, suffered a cerebral hemorrhage and went into a coma; John, with his daughter, Joan, moved into the little house on his brother's property so Betty could keep an eye on Joan. On August 3, 1955, Hodding's seventy-four-year-old father died of a heart attack in Hammond. Hodding was glad, at least, that his father had seen—and loved— the piece Hodding had written about him that appeared in *Reader's Digest* two weeks before he died.

Hodding and Betty and their two younger sons managed to spend part of the summers of 1954 and 1955 in Maine, renting a house from one of Hodding's cousins. They worked on books and magazine articles every morning and sailed every afternoon. Philip sailed a smaller boat, and Tommy had his own turnabout, the *Hushpuppy II*.

Betty put together feasts of boiled corn and lobster and arranged big parties. Maine was essential to repair Hodding's battered spirits.

The racial question, of course, never went away. Whites in the South were talking about the doctrine of interposition, the idea that a state could "interpose" its will against the federal government, and there was also talk of "nullification," which would involve nullifying federal laws in Mississippi. At first Hodding thought interposition was "interesting," since it might buy a little time for the South.[2] As 1955 drew to a close, he saw no hope for the idea. "We are getting ready to secede," he said.[3] He brooded about the violence in Mississippi that would hurt not only the state's "resort business but its industrial efforts," yet he felt that "the dawn may be soon breaking. If I didn't think so I would leave too."[4]

Early in 1956 the *Delta Democrat-Times* ran a front-page story on the Reverend Alvin Kershaw, a white Episcopal priest who had been invited to speak at the University of Mississippi. University officials had withdrawn the invitation after they found out that Kershaw had given the money he had won on a television show to the NAACP. Dr. Morton King, chairman of the sociology department at Ole Miss, resigned in protest at the university's decision, and the *DD-T* ran an editorial on his resignation, deploring "the shotgun blasts that shallow people are taking at the integration threat."[5]

That same week students rioted and an angry mob threw eggs and rocks at Autherine Lucy, the first black student admitted to the University of Alabama. To keep the peace, the university suspended her. Hodding wrote an editorial calling outrageous the NAACP's claim that university president O. C. Carmichael had allowed the rioting as a "cunning stratagem."[6] Lucy did not really want to attend the university, Hodding said, or she would have met officials halfway.*

Autherine Lucy's case was a reason for secret joy among Mississippi

---

*Hodding was dead wrong. Lucy went on to graduate from all-black Miles College in Birmingham, but earned her master's degree from Alabama in 1992.

moderates. For years—when their schools or public health programs or highway systems ranked second from the bottom—Southerners from Alabama, Georgia, Arkansas, and Louisiana used to sigh and say, "Thank God for Mississippi! At least we're not the *very lowest*." Now, for once, as Hodding said, Mississippians could say, "Thank God for Alabama!"[7]

This glee could not shield him for long from the real state of affairs in Mississippi. When Kenneth Douty of the American Civil Liberties Union wrote Hodding in February to ask whether there was any chance that a respected lawyer of real stature, say a former president of the Mississippi Bar Association, would take the case of Emmett Till's mother if she sued in civil court as "any mother might sue for damages for the loss of the life of her son," Hodding replied that he doubted that she could "find a lawyer of any stature in Mississippi" to take the case.[8]

Hodding was "extremely pessimistic" about the tension and "danger of sporadic civil strife in the Deep South." He and Betty both feared that the Citizens' Councils could force the South into another Civil War. "Their mentality," Betty wrote, "has created [a climate] where any kind of interracial violence could flare up overnight."[9] Hodding was so gloomy that when Bob Brown, a former *DD-T* staffer who was now editor of a paper in Columbus, Georgia, wrote him suggesting a stunt—a campaign for the return of Alabama and Mississippi to "the original and rightful owner, namely the by the Grace of God Free, Sovereign and Independent State of Georgia"—Hodding replied that he didn't think they should start the silly season right then. "Folks over here wouldn't think it was funny at all and it would just give them more stuff to jaw about. And they've got enough already."[10]

On Easter Sunday, 1956, Hodding sailed with Exton Guckes and three other friends on Guckes's forty-two-foot schooner, the *Malabar II*, from Philadelphia, bound for La Coruña, Spain. They hoped to make the whole voyage under sail, but they carried a sixty-horsepower auxiliary engine just in case. They soon ran into bad weather—high winds, rain—and waves as high as sixty feet. Everything in the cabin seemed to be drenched, and salt water fouled the engine. Hodding and his companions went without sleep for twelve days, and they had neither hot food nor dry clothes. They limped into port in the Azores for repairs, then continued on to Spain. It was the worst thirty-six days Hodding could remember, he said. He flew home and announced, "I've had enough of the High Seas in a sailboat for a long time."[11]

After his return, someone asked Harry Marsh at the *DD-T* whether Hodding might talk to the Lions Club about his trip. He was now such a celebrity that the Lions hesitated to ask him directly. When Marsh told the Carters about the invitation, Betty told Hodding, "Don't talk to them. They're enemies."

"That's why I should do it," Hodding said. And he spoke to the Lions.[12]

That same year, Hodding had to pay $11,000 in back income taxes. He had reached the stage where "Uncle Sam checks my returns every year," he lamented.[13] Various members of the Carter family have said that the Internal Revenue Service harassed Hodding unnecessarily because of his liberal views, Hodding did not help journalist William Peters, who was writing an article about the federal government's helping to maintain segregation in the South by having the IRS harass moderates there. Hodding did not want Peters to list him as a victim of IRS harassment because it would be too easy for people at the IRS to point out that they gave the president of the Greenville Citizens' Council as much trouble as they had given him. "But I do believe that your thesis is generally correct," Hodding wrote Peters. "They have been throwing the book at us on very minor points for two years."[14] Ultimately, however, anybody as careless as Hodding about money and accounts could expect the IRS to audit him.

In the summer of 1956, Hodding and Betty did not go to Maine. They stayed in Greenville, where they had a swimming pool built at Feliciana. Hodding continued to work on his history of Reconstruction over the summer.

A constant, gnawing worry was his vision. His "good" eye began bothering him in 1956, and in October he went to see a specialist in Detroit. The doctor, Jack Guyton, assured him it was not glaucoma, but told him that he would need an operation for cataracts eventually.

On New Year's Day, 1957, most of the newspaper staff was watching television at Dave and Sue Brown's. A black doctor called to say he was treating three black men who had been brutally beaten in the Hinds County jail. The men had thrown a lot of clothes in the backseat of a car, and the police, who thought they had stolen them, put them in jail and kept them six days without charging them. One of the men was a civilian airplane mechanic at the Greenville air base.

After speaking with the doctor, Harry Marsh called the Hinds County sheriff, who said the police hadn't beaten the men—they "just rubbed voodoo oil" on them. "I saw the wounds on their buttocks," Marsh remembered, "and they weren't from voodoo."

Later both Hodding and Marsh had to testify about the incident at a grand jury hearing in Jackson. On the way home they compared notes about their testimony. The prosecutor had asked each man why he had written (or run) a story about the alleged beating. Marsh said that he thought everything that happened was news; he was dedicated to working on that assumption. Hodding, however, told the prosecutor he had run the story "so you won't beat up so damned many Negroes in your jail." [15]

In a piece written for United Press about the outlook for 1957, Hodding said integration was a long way off. "Meaningful implementation of the decision in the Deep South appears at least as distant today as it did in May 1954," and years of anti-integration legal campaigns and extralegal resistance on state and community levels lay ahead. Hodding still believed that the South's push toward school equalization might be more effective than legal, or illegal, delaying tactics to keep white and black schoolchildren separated. [16]

In early 1957, young Hodding came home from Princeton to work on research for his senior thesis on the White Citizens' Councils. (Dave Brown had sent him carbons of his entire file.) "He says the double-take when he gives his name at the various headquarters and to individual leaders is worth watching," Big Hodding wrote Mark Ethridge.[17] When the thesis was finished, Hodding wrote his agents about his son's "rather remarkable" work of thirty-five or forty thousand words; "the only definitive thing written on the group," it might merit publication as a book. People at Princeton's Woodrow Wilson School of Public and International Affairs had liked it and given young Hodding a "1+" on it, the only 1+ in the school that year, and only the fourth in the school's history.[18]

Young Hodding graduated summa cum laude from Princeton in June (likewise, the only summa in the Woodrow Wilson School, as his proud father pointed out in letters to friends). Three days later, in New Orleans, he married Peggy Wolfe of Pass Christian. The bride and groom left shortly after the wedding for Quantico, Virginia, where he was due to report for active duty with the Marines.

Hodding and Betty went to Maine that summer, but Hodding flew back to Greenville to speak at a chamber of commerce convention. The city's chamber of commerce manager wrote to thank him afterward, saying that Hodding's speech "planted seeds statewide that you are not an ogre but a simple human who likewise suffers from hangovers"; moreover, he said, Hodding demonstrated that he was not "an adamant integrationist."[19]

In Maine he and Betty worked on books. He had finished a children's biography of Robert E. Lee for Random House's Landmark series, and had started work with Betty on a history of the Episcopal Church in Louisiana; later he would turn it over to Betty entirely. Although the diocese asked him to keep his name on the book, it was Betty who took an old microfilm reader home from the newspaper offices and put it in her dressing room, where she could plow through decades of church records. When *So Great a Good* was published in November 1955, it made Betty mildly famous and won her speaking engagements before Episcopal groups.

His book on Reconstruction for Doubleday's Mainstream of America series, a major project, took far more time than the few months Hodding had expected. He had thought he could limit it to the period from 1868 through 1876, but the Doubleday people wanted him to widen his focus and bring it up to 1932, the date they said Reconstruction really ended. At first, Lewis Gannett, the series editor and an NAACP board member, had serious doubts about working with Hodding on the subject; but eventually he came to believe that Hodding was the man to write the book.[20] In November 1955, Hodding was confidently predicting that he would finish the book by the following March. Betty did most of the research—all from secondary sources—and Josephine Haxton did "a mountain of research" after Hodding began having trouble with his vision.[21] He had hoped to finish the book that summer, but by the time he went home to Greenville, he was able to leave only about a dozen chapters with the publisher. He would not complete the book until the following spring.

The Carters were still in Maine when the Little Rock crisis erupted. Thirteen black students had registered at Central High School there, and everyone expected integration to go smoothly, until Arkansas governor Orval Faubus called out the National Guard. Little Rock exploded. The *Delta Democrat-Times* reported each day's events, and on September 25, after President Eisenhower ordered federal troops to Little Rock, the paper ran a front-page banner headline: "Troops with Bayonets Guard Negroes." From Maine, Hodding had telephoned an editorial backing Eisenhower in this clash between federal and state forces:

On May 2, 1792, George Washington signed a law which is still on the statute books and is, in essence, the one under which President Eisenhower acted Tuesday.

In his statement made before he invoked the law, President Eisenhower said in part, "The Federal law and orders of the United States District Court implementing that law cannot be flouted with impunity by any individual or any mob of extremists."

We go along with the first president of the United States and the present president of the United States.

The *Delta Democrat-Times* was one of very few southern newspapers to support Eisenhower's dispatch of troops to Little Rock. Papers that had long championed Eisenhower—the Montgomery *Advertiser*, the Dallas *Morning News*, the Nashville *Banner*, and the Birmingham *Post-Herald*—turned on him in fury. The *News and Courier* in Charleston, South Carolina, ran six anti-Ike editorials in one day. The Jackson *Daily News* editorial contained only one word, "Nuts!"[22] The *Arkansas Gazette* in Little Rock was courageous and backed integration, leading Hodding to predict: "Harry Ashmore will win a Pulitzer, and the publisher will lose the paper." Hodding was partly right. Both Ashmore and the *Gazette* won Pulitzers in 1958; the paper eventually lost millions, but weathered the crisis; its owners lost it years later through inept management.

Mississippi was the only southern state in which no integration test cases had been instituted. It was also the state with the lowest percentage of black voter registration. "Now its white citizens are asking whether the Federal government will use troops to see to it that . . . Negroes vote in polling places where once they never dared show themselves, and to assure the enrollment of Negro students in schools to which they have not yet ventured to apply," Hodding wrote in a special syndicated article for the New York *Herald Tribune*. Mississippians were "stunned by what has happened in Little Rock" and, as he had said before, things were going to get worse before they got better.[23] The South's reaction to events in Little Rock, Hodding told the American Jewish Congress in Chicago, had "raised racial, sectional, and political animosities to their highest pitch since Reconstruction." The use of federal troops had again solidified the opposition of southern moderates as well as extremists to mass integration of southern schools. Delaying tactics, he said, would postpone integration for many years.[24]

"Nothing could make things worse down here," Hodding wrote in the fall of 1957.[25] "I have never thought the outlook to be as grim as it is today."[26] He told Bernice Baumgarten in New York: "Things are really steaming down this way. You would have to be here to believe that folks could get so wrought up."[27] For the past few years, not a week had gone by that he did not receive angry letters, most of them unsigned and threatening. "There has hardly been a month in which either my wife or myself have not been assailed and warned by anonymous telephone calls. And periodically, there have been concerted, group attempts to punish us for what the Communists would call deviationism, through boycotts and the like."[28]

Yet Hodding continued to be a booster for Greenville and its "enviable atmosphere." Local businessmen appreciated one front-page editorial that fall, "No Recession Here," which was backed up with statistics: Twice as many people were using the airline that served Greenville as had used it in 1953; bank deposits were the highest they had ever been; mail receipts were up. It pleased Hodding especially to have a local "brotherhood" story during the Little Rock crisis: W. T. Gibbs, a Greenville Presbyterian, was in a hospital in Jackson and needed blood. His preacher alerted his friends, and scores of people in town helped out. The local Coca-Cola Bottling Company, managed by O. S. McCoy, provided portable refrigeration facilities, and I. B. Isenberg's Greenville Coal and Ice Company provided the ice. Greenville was lucky, Hodding editorialized, to have this "kind of uninhibited cooperation between Catholics, Jews, and Protestants."[29]

Hodding's article "The Shrinking South," which appeared in the March 4, 1958, issue of *Look*—about the "melancholy facts that dying farms, too few jobs and low paying industries" had prompted more than a million people, white and black, to leave the South between 1950 and 1956—aroused more anger and resulted in what Hodding called "hysterical ranting" in many small southern newspapers.[30] John Temple Graves, the conservative Birmingham columnist, said Harry Ashmore had written an epitaph for Dixie (indeed, this was the title of Ashmore's new book) and now Hodding Carter was adding "the quaintly primitive touch. He shrinks the heads."[31] The editor of the West Point, Mississippi, *Daily Times* said, "Of course Hodding doesn't believe this [that people were moving out in droves] . . . but he is guilty of pigeonholing truth in order to write what will sell, and what the North WANTS to believe." A Kentucky paper called Hodding "one of the leading collaborationists and quislings who glean Northern dollars by belaboring the South." An Arkansas editor said that "the North doesn't like the continuing influx of Negroes. . . . That puts Carter and his kind to profiteering on gullible editors."[32] *Manufacturers Record* ranted, too, maintaining that Hodding, "a professional Southerner," seemed to have "joined up with Erskine (Tobacco Road) Caldwell to dig up in odd places the 'true picture' of the South."[33]

Hodding defended his *Look* article. "I said nothing that every Chamber of Commerce office in the South has not been saying for years. Why do you think the state governments have authorized the communities to issue full faith and credit bonds to get industry? Why . . . have so many Southern states lost Congressmen when national population trends are all up?" *Manufacturers Record*'s statistics, he said, concerned payrolls in a number of progressive southern cities.[34]

Hodding's ringing defense of freedom of speech in a *DD-T* editorial caused a great deal of controversy. He lambasted Ellis Wright, the undertaker president of the Jackson Citizens' Council, for his "monstrous attack on Millsaps College in Jackson because that distinguished Methodist institution dared permit a pro-integration speaker to address a number of its students." Wright's attack was not unexpected, said Hodding, but it was intolerable.

The school had a right to admit as speaker Dr. Ernst Borinski, a white sociology professor at all-black Tougaloo College, Hodding said, and Millsaps students had a right to meet with their Tougaloo contemporaries to

discuss our nation's most perplexing problem. *This newspaper does not advocate the integration of the public schools* [italics added]; but that is beside the point. All citizens who believe in

273

freedom of speech, whether segregationists or integrationists, should be ready to defend the real issue here. Every American has the privilege under the Bill of Rights to speak or write, without undue reprisal, whatever is on his mind . . . subject of course to legal redress if his words are considered slanderous or libelous.

And every American also has the right to listen to any speaker, whatever his tenor, without being subjected to the smear and threats which Wright and his breed employ in place of reasonableness and fairmindedness which they so obviously lack.

The editorial set a fire under leading segregationists in Mississippi. They thought they had Hodding this time. Tom Ethridge, a conservative columnist for the Jackson *Clarion-Ledger*, seized on one sentence in the editorial, "This newspaper does not advocate the integration of the public schools," and ran with it:

> This is a factual statement but its clever wording carries a wrong impression. True enough Mr. Carter's Greenville newspaper does not advocate integration. Such a stand is not too healthy for circulation and advertising in this state.
>
> On the other hand, Mr. Carter himself has been identified as an integrationist by admiring newspapers beyond the Mason and Dixon Line.

Ethridge then quoted from an interview Hodding had given to the *Oregonian* in Portland, where he had spoken the week before:

> An advocate of integration, Carter believes it can be done properly, only by easy stages. He favors gradual absorption of the Negro students as they reach an educational level where they can mix with white pupils. This can be done now on a university level, Carter said.

Ethridge also quoted an *Oregonian* editorial:

> Hodding Carter, the Mississippi editor . . . is representative of

the most responsible thought in the South. . . . It is his conviction, expressed in several Portland appearances, that racial integration in the public schools is right morally, ethically, and legally.

Ethridge pounced on a report from the St. Louis *Post-Dispatch*, about a speech Hodding had made the month before at a Brotherhood Week assembly at Washington University: "More intensive legal action based on the Constitution and the Supreme Court integration decision will not achieve anything more than token integration. Our best weapon is going to be the attainment of spiritual awareness of what is right and what is wrong."

Ethridge commented:

Mr. Carter's use of the phrase, "our best weapon," clearly places him on the side of the integrationists. . . . Here in Mississippi he assures one and all that his newspaper does not advocate integration. In Oregon and elsewhere he is hailed as one who thinks "integration is right morally, ethically, and legally." Mr. Carter is working both sides of the street.[35]

The Jackson Citizens' Council circulated copies of Ethridge's column, together with excerpts from the *Oregonian* and *Post-Dispatch*.

Hodding responded immediately, with a signed editorial in which he said no one had ever accused him of "talking out of both sides of my mouth." He was willing to repeat his Portland speech, with the much shorter Washington University talk thrown in, to any audience. Both had been broadcast and recorded, after all, and he had said nothing in either that he had not already said in his editorials. "The day after the Supreme Court's decision I wrote . . . that the Court was morally obligated to hold compulsory segregation invalid. I also said then and have continually repeated that I am opposed to putting into practice public school integration in the Deep South."

Hodding said that he had written many times that his fears about integration of public schools did not extend to the college level;

even Governor Faubus of Arkansas agreed with him on that. And he pointed out that the NAACP in Portland had asked for equal time to answer him, so surely "that organization will be surprised to learn that I am an 'Integrationist.'" In the end,

> the real issue facing Mississippians today . . . is whether such treasured rights as freedom of speech, and of the press, academic freedom, religious freedom and even freedom of thought are to be permitted in a state apparently dominated by hired agitators as merciless and as lacking in compunction as a rabid dog. They specialize in isolated, vastly outnumbered victims—a minister, a doctor, a small town merchant, a college president, a woman editor of a weekly newspaper, a college student. Heroic men, these.
>
> They may eventually have their way. It is unlikely that if they do industry will come to Mississippi in quantity enough to give jobs to the multiplying thousands who are being displaced through agricultural evolution. Thus, the supreme irony can be that misled Mississippians who look upon the Ethridges . . . as their protectors will have to go outside Mississippi and the Deep South in order to find employment, and thus will find themselves compelled to send their children to the now integrated public schools of 37 of the 48 states.[36]

The Jackson *Daily News* ran a copy of Hodding's editorial as a letter to the editor, and put it on the news pages. The paper explained that it had arrived too late for the editorial page but the paper wanted to give it prompt circulation.[37]

Four days later, Hodding attacked a bill before the state legislature that would have allowed cities and counties to contribute public money to the Citizens' Councils. "A $250,000 war chest can shut up a lot of people, elect candidates galore, and show the nation just where Mississippi stands in relation to democracy," he wrote on March 21. (The bill eventually died, at the adjournment of the legislature.)

The Mississippi legislature had already involved the state government in the battle to preserve segregation when it created the Sovereignty Commission, which began a public relations campaign to sell the segregationists' viewpoint to the North. Hal DeCell, editor of the Rolling Fork weekly newspaper, was in charge of the Commission's public relations, and he brought a group of New England newspaper editors to Mississippi to see for themselves the modern school buildings that were being rushed to completion for black students. Undercover, however, the Sovereignty Commission conducted clandestine investigations of blacks, Jews, and "moderate" teachers, preachers, and students who had expressed the mildest support of civil rights.

People in Mississippi were afraid to open their mouths, Hodding said. It was a pity, since there had always been room for dissenters. Even at the time of Secession, three men who voted against it were made generals in the state's army.

Doubleday & Company bought young Hodding's senior thesis about the White Citizens' Councils for book publication, paying $500 on signing and another $500 when he turned in a revised manuscript. Managing editor Jay Milner was leaving the *Delta Democrat-Times*, and Hodding asked his oldest son if he planned to come back to Greenville when his tour of duty with the Marines was over. If he did not return, Hodding would have to hire somebody else; if he did plan to come back, then the paper could "limp along" until he arrived. When young Hodding said he would be returning, Hodding asked him whether he was sure he wanted to come back to Mississippi. "It's not exactly coming back to Mississippi," young Hodding said. "I'm coming back to Greenville."[38]

Milner was one of many employees who admired Hodding inordinately. He even named his daughter Carter in Hodding's honor. He wrote a novel, *Incident at Ashburn*, in which one of the characters is a beleaguered small-town newspaperman who is hated by his community for his liberal stands. The editor goes across the river to consult Hodding Carter, who is lucky enough to have a circle of supportive friends in Greenville.

When Hodding at last finished the book on Reconstruction, he signed a two-book contract with Doubleday. One work would be non-fiction, and the other a novel about Civil War deserters—from both sides—set in Texas's Big Thicket. Judge Edmund Talbot of Hammond had given him the idea, and Hodding was enthusiastic about it; he offered to split the proceeds fifty-fifty with Talbot. He had meanwhile done another juvenile biography for Random House, about the Marquis de Lafayette, and was planning one about British commandos during World War II. He was also planning another book for Doubleday, to be called "Here Today, Gone Tomorrow," with Bern Keating's photographs of southern farm implements and furnishings that were on their way to oblivion.

The Angry Scar: The Story of Reconstruction appeared in early 1959. It was not so much that the events of Reconstruction linked it with the situation in the South in the 1950s, Hodding wrote; it was, more precisely, the use that four generations of southern politicians had made of Reconstruction that joined the two tragic periods. "I have become convinced that it has been almost as unfortunate for our nation that the North has remembered so little of Reconstruction as that the South has remembered so much," he said in the preface.

Historians have described *The Angry Scar* as being in "the Dunning tradition." William Archibald Dunning's history, written earlier in the century, saw Reconstruction as a total outrage against the South, and his view had prevailed ever since. James Silver, a professor of history at the University of Mississippi, reviewed Hodding's book in the *DD-T* and called it "probably the best survey of Reconstruction available." *Saturday Review* said that Hodding led readers "through Reconstruction's maze of counter influences and its puzzling personalities with authority and understanding."[39] T. Harry Williams in the New York *Herald Tribune* praised Hodding's use of the "best secondary sources," and found the book highly readable, intelligent, stimulating, and unusually accurate for a volume of its scope.

In his preface, Hodding had written that while working on the book he had had serious eye trouble and was forced to dictate and to rely on assistants who read sourcebooks aloud to him. "Where does that leave a reviewer convinced that 'The Angry Scar' is a confusing, badly organized and intermittently tedious work—in the position of kicking a man while he is down?" asked Orville Prescott in the New York *Times*.[40] However, Prescott, who had admired *Where Main Street Meets the River* as one of the best books yet written about the South, termed "expert and interesting" Hodding's focus on some episodes, such as the impeachment proceedings against Andrew Johnson. C. Vann Woodward's tepid review in the *Times Book Review* pointed out minor factual errors and predicted that revisionist histories of Reconstruction then in progress would show that the "angry scar" was from a largely self-inflicted psychic wound and the heritage a product of invention.[41] *The New Yorker* dismissed the book as a popular history of Reconstruction compiled from secondary sources, with a maddening organization and pretentious style, but found the material fascinating.[42]

Southern reviewers were kind, and the Birmingham *News* ran *The Angry Scar* in serial form. It was named a Notable Book of 1959 by the American Library Association.

In 1958, Philip, who had dropped out of Yale in his freshman year, worked three weeks as a deckhand on a Mississippi River towboat, six weeks as a deckhand on a freighter-passenger out of New Orleans, had gone back to school at Tulane. At home for Christmas, he had accidentally shot himself in the foot while deer hunting on an island in the Mississippi River with Hodding and young Hodding. The high-powered rifle was loaded with soft-nosed bullets, which did enormous injury to his foot. Hodding and his oldest son did not find Philip for an hour after the accident. They made a litter on which to carry him and when it broke, young Hodding carried his brother piggyback for half a mile. At first doctors thought Philip's foot would have to be amputated, but after considerable surgery it was saved.

The accident delayed until March the Carters' departure on a long-planned trip to South Africa under the auspices of the United States–South Africa Leadership Exchange Program of the African–American

Institute, funded by the Rockefeller Foundation. Hodding, Betty, Philip, and Tommy went to New York by way of Camp Lejeune, and then on to Johannesburg. Hodding had arranged to buy a secondhand car once they landed, and they drove to Cape Town, where they rented a house.

Hodding later described the trip to South Africa as a turning point in his life, equal to his service in the Middle East during World War II. He met with groups of Afrikaners, white descendants of Dutch settlers; with white descendants of British settlers; with black Africans; and with Indians, Malays, and multiracial "coloreds." He fell in love with Afrikaners and identified with them. He found them less reserved than the people of British ancestry, and moreover, they reminded him of white Southerners. "The Boers of 1900 were the outnumbered Confederates of the 1860s," he said.

When he returned home he wrote an article for *The Saturday Evening Post*, "We Never Felt More at Home," that praised the Afrikaners and took their side. The South African government was naturally delighted. For the rest of his life, Hodding would compare Afrikaners with the settlers of Israel. "If they try to drive these brave people into the sea," he claimed, "I'll take my stand with them." The man who never stopped calling public attention to the outrages of segregationists at home seemed to accept apartheid. "He drew a line in his mind separating the American state of affairs from the South African state of affairs," said his son Philip. When Philip argued with him about South Africa, Hodding would say, "They're an embattled minority. We're the majority in America."

While they were in South Africa, Philip, who attended classes at the University of Cape Town, became a friend of Hans Beukes, a colored student. Beukes won a scholarship to Oxford, only to have his passport taken away.

At a farewell dinner given for the Carters, Hodding thanked his Afrikaner hosts for their hospitality, and then brought up the matter of Hans Beukes. He lashed out at the Afrikaners, telling them that was not the way civilized people behaved. Philip remembered this as "one of my father's finest hours." And it was typical of Hodding: when there was an individual case involved, he could always see clearly and was never afraid to speak out.

After leaving South Africa, Philip and Tommy spent four weeks traveling through the Belgian Congo by car and river steamer, while Betty and Hodding visited Ethiopia, Egypt, Greece, Italy, and France. The boys met their parents in Paris, and they all flew home together in August. They had been gone almost six months.

Meanwhile, young Hodding and Peggy, who now had two daughters, had returned to Greenville in June. Young Hodding was reporting and writing editorials, and waiting for the publication of *The South Fights Back*, his book about the Citizens' Councils.

The travelers got home on the night before the second Democratic gubernatorial primary and joined the usual throng at an election-night party at the *DD-T* office. Anonymous callers telephoned the usual threats, and staffers took turns at the door, on the lookout for people with guns. Police in the station across the street also watched from their doorway. Sue Brown remembered that was the first time she ever saw Hodding drink too much. "At parties, everybody got looped, but this time Philip and young Hodding had to persuade him to go home." Hodding had been drinking heavily, including a first-thing-in-the-morning drink, for some time, but with the wily skill of the alcoholic, he could mask his dependence from his family. Betty, like most people closest to alcoholics, simply did not acknowledge the seriousness of her husband's drinking problem. "I did not know what was going on," she said.

An argument could be made for strong drink that particular time: Ross Barnett won the Democratic primary—in those days the election that counted, since few Republicans ran for state office—to become the next governor of Mississippi. Barnett was a grotesquely evil politician of whom the kindest thing Robert Sherrill in *Gothic Politics in the Deep South* could find to say of him was that he was "bone dumb."

In the fall of 1959, Tommy entered Culver Military Academy in

Indiana, and Hodding began going to New Orleans twice a month
to lecture at Tulane, the first semester in journalism, the second in
history. It was a relief, he said, to get away from Greenville.

An unexpected attack on Hodding came in November, when J. B.
Matthews, a thoroughly disreputable onetime investigator for Senator Joseph McCarthy's committee and a "professional anti-Communist
witness," testified to the General Legislative Investigating Committee of the Mississippi House of Representatives of the legislature
that Hodding and other Mississippians were among fifty members of
"an interlocking directorate" of the Southern Regional Council, the
Southern Conference Educational Fund, and the former Southern
Conference for Human Welfare, all of which he said were "Communist tainted."

Hodding immediately called Matthews a "damn liar"; the only
one of the organizations he belonged to was the Southern Regional
Council. "I belong to it openly and believe it a worthwhile interracial organization in these unhappy times." And in a boxed "Personal
Statement" on the front page of the *DD-T*, Hodding expressed his
doubt that any fellow Greenville and Washington County citizens
who knew him "could believe that I am or ever have been connected
with any Communist, Communist-front or subversive organizations.
To the contrary, I have fought such groups all my adult life."[43]

Indeed, no one in his right mind would think Hodding was a Communist, and friends and admirers, critics and political enemies alike
rose up and said so. LeRoy Percy and Galla Paxton, the lieutenant
general and former commander in the Mississippi–Alabama National
Guard, led a group of distinguished Washington County citizens who
signed a statement of support in the form of an open letter to Mississippi. "Galla Paxton always thought we were crazy, but he was the
first one to sign," said young Hodding; "going off to war early saved
Dad's ass."[44] Greenville city attorney Albert Lake, who always disagreed with Hodding's politics, signed, as did Arch Toler, president
of the Greenville Bank and Trust, and barge line owner Jesse Brent.
The entire Washington County legislative delegation put their names
to the document, agreeing that:

We the undersigned citizens of Greenville and Washington County, Miss., wish to express our belief in the good citizenship, honesty, and patriotism of our fellow citizen, Hodding Carter, who has been accused in a legislative hearing of having Communist connections.

We have not always agreed with him, but we recognize his right to differ as well as our own.

We recognize also such rights are imperiled in our state today. We strongly condemn the smear techniques by which a man's good name can be dragged in the mud.[45]

The New York *Herald Tribune* rose in Hodding's defense on December 23. "The dimensions of a newspaper editor's service to humanity can be judged by the volume and velocity of attacks against him. Thus judged, Hodding Carter . . . measures up to the finest traditions of American journalism."

Praise for Hodding in a northern newspaper always enraged many Southerners, and the Charleston *News and Courier* replied accordingly to the *Herald Tribune* editorial. Hodding was not the voice of the South, it said. "Mr. Carter never lets his public forget that he edits a paper in Mississippi," but people should keep in mind that he was "a former staff member of *PM*, [a] New York newspaper of deepest pink hue," a "part-time resident of Maine," and "a Southern editor nowadays only by reason of geography."[46]

After the Mississippi House passed a resolution commending the General Legislative Investigating Committee for its work, Hodding spoke before the Anti-Defamation League of B'nai B'rith in Jackson. In Africa, he recounted, he had seen a "pack of baboons yelling, grinning and making faces at a pride of lions" in the same way that Citizens' Council spokesmen called on people to ostracize Mississippians who accepted appointment to a state advisory committee to the federal Civil Rights Commission. These "paid mouthpieces" of the Council, he said, listed "enemies" of the Council's in its newspaper; these enemies included the Air Force, the Treasury Department, the Interstate Commerce Commission, the United Nations, and the B'nai

B'rith Anti-Defamation League. It was "just a little boys' game to defy the government of the United States," Hodding said. The Birmingham *News*, among others, attacked Hodding for this speech.[47]

Hodding explained later that although he thought he had enough provocation to do so, he wasn't calling all members of Citizens' Councils baboons. He was concerned that the Citizens' Councils had called for the ostracism of Rear Admiral Robert Briscoe and Mrs. Wallace Schutt, two solid Mississippi citizens who had agreed to serve on the Civil Rights Commission advisory committee. "I think I let them off light," he said of Council members.[48] He knew he was guilty of "occasional intemperate remarks," but anybody would be who, because he did not agree with the majority, was subjected with his family "to the kind of anonymous abuse, threat and slander that has come our way."[49] Hodding was no more hopeful than before. "I am not too pessimistic about the outlook in our own country where the Negro is only one man in ten. But when I consider that the white man is only one in seven in the world, I am disturbed, because some of our ancestral chickens are coming home to roost." While he was opposed to "mongrelization," he did know that "Herr Hitler's East Prussians, perhaps the staunchest defenders of Aryan supremacy, are themselves a composite of Germanic and Mongoloid bloods" and that "the rest of the empires of the world for as far back as we know were an amalgamation of many peoples. . . . My own fearful belief is that before any further great 'mongrelization,' we will all be reduced to the common complexion of a very well burnt black cinder."[50]

14. 1960–1963

"Burning an Effigy Represents Real Progress"

The civil rights movement lurched into high gear in 1960. Activist black students, among others, sat in at lunch counters, demonstrated, and went to jail. What young blacks resented especially, Hodding felt, were the outward symbols of second-class citizenship and the failure of too many white juries to indict and convict white murderers, lynchers, and bombers. He doubted that organizations such as the new Student Nonviolent Coordinating Committee, founded by college students in Raleigh, would help the movement; the mounting antipathy was mutual. The Southern Regional Council could only wring its hands and say that some people felt each new black demand represented a setback in race relations.[1]

As he planned articles for *The Saturday Evening Post* and *Look*, Hodding expressed his worry about what he saw as increasing fanaticism among some blacks, in the form of "organizations like the [Black] Muslims—including one in New Orleans which has dedicated itself to the 'pink-haired black Jesus' and whose members refer to white people only as 'things.' . . . As much as the white South hates the NAACP, the time may come when both moderate and extreme Southerners will wish the NAACP were back in the saddle since it has confined itself to court action."[2]

In Mississippi the atmosphere was more poisonous than ever under

285

Governor Ross Barnett. It was a "rough time" for Hodding, but "not nearly as hard to take now that Hod is with me." It was a great feeling to have a son turn out to be all he had hoped, and more.[3] Young Hodding was "just as good an editorial writer . . . and a little more temperate."[4] His editorials may have lacked the passion, heat, and energy of his father's work, but they passed muster with some of Hodding's old enemies. Conwell Sykes, who had not spoken to Hodding for years, wrote to praise an editorial young Hodding had written. And his book on the Citizens' Councils, *The South Strikes Back*, elicited a favorable letter from Judge Tom Brady, the author of *Black Monday* and a stalwart segregationist.

Sue Brown once told Hodding that his second son, Philip, "has a hard time living up to young Hodding." Hodding replied, "*I* have a hard time living up to him."

On May 1, 1960, Hodding named his oldest son managing editor and put him in complete charge of news and editorial operations and policy. Two days later, at a meeting of the Mississippi Press Association, Hodding gave him credit for the awards won by the *Delta Democrat-Times*—first place for general excellence, first place in community service, second place in editorial writing, and several others.

Younger staff members enjoyed working for Hodding III, whom they found bright, enthusiastic, and fun; but Dave Brown, who had been at the paper for fifteen years, began to feel uneasy. On Saturdays, he and Harry Marsh took turns, one working in the morning and the other in the afternoon. One Saturday, Brown worked until noon, then went home for lunch—he knew Marsh would come in soon, and the news wire did not open until one o'clock. Young Hodding called Brown at home and said, as Brown recounted later, "Get your ass back down here." Brown explained that Marsh would be in, that the wire wasn't open, and that everything was under control. Nonetheless he went back to the office, to find that Marsh had appeared by then. Young Hodding apologized, but Brown still felt uneasy; nobody had ever talked to him that way, on the *Delta Democrat-Times*, and he didn't like it. He began to look around for another job. He did not leave until April 1962, when he became editor of the paper in Pascagoula that was owned by liberal Ira Harkey.

One night Hodding came home and told Betty he had paid off the last of the *DD-T*'s notes. "I think I'll buy myself some bath powder," Betty said, realizing she had never bought anything to pamper herself while they repaid the debt. That year on her birthday, when she tried to cut her cake, the knife would go no farther than the icing. The impediment turned out to be a jeweler's box containing a diamond wristwatch from Hodding and their three sons. Each had contributed a week's income to its purchase.

When Hodding's paean to the glories of life in Greenville, "I'll Never Leave My Town," appeared in the June 4 *Saturday Evening Post*, the chamber of commerce, of course, had reprints made. The article drew more than 2,000 letters, Hodding said.[5]

On the dark side, Hodding's eyes had been causing him more trouble, and he had been in Detroit in May for more tests. His good eye had deteriorated so much that it was hard for him to drive. His doctor in Detroit, however, was delaying cataract surgery until the last possible moment.

In August, Hodding and Betty were in Maine. They idly looked at houses for sale, and found one they liked on the first day. Brownshingled, with dormer windows, and surrounded by overgrown island roses, it was located in Tenants Harbor, about twenty miles from Camden, on a cliff above the ocean. They had to stand outside looking at it—the real estate agent had no key.

"Do you want it?" Hodding asked.

"But we haven't been inside," said Betty.

"Do you want it?" Hodding repeated. "It won't be on the market long."

"I do, I do," said Betty.

Hodding phoned the owner, a New York City admiralty lawyer. He had heard of Hodding and said he'd be delighted to sell his house to him. It was a Saturday afternoon, and Hodding wanted to guarantee that his check for the down payment would clear. He found Wade Hollowell, his banker, at the Greenville Country Club, where he and his wife were giving the wedding luncheon for their only child. "The sky's the limit," Hollowell told the real estate agent of Hodding's credit.

When they went inside the house the next morning, Hodding and Betty found hooked rugs, Chinese export porcelain, handmade maple chests, blueberry rakes, primitive paintings of Maine schooners—a treasure trove that came with the house. The house had three bedrooms with three baths upstairs, and more bedrooms downstairs. Built-in bunks lined the walls of the room above the three-car garage. As if to prove the house's desirability, a man drove up while they were there, intending to buy it himself that day. Instead of the week or two the Carters had planned, they stayed in Maine until late September.

Back in Greenville, Hodding and Betty seldom went to the *DD-T* offices. They worked on magazine articles, as well as on a book about the Spanish Trail and the novel about Civil War deserters. Hodding hoped to deliver the two manuscripts around the first of the year, but he was slowed by having to dictate. That was fine, perhaps, for nonfiction, but dictating a novel was not easy.

Hodding and the editors at McGraw-Hill had selected *Doomed Road of Empire* for the title of the book about the Spanish Trail, or Camino Real, which ran from Natchitoches, Louisiana, through San Antonio, to Saltillo in Mexico. Betty, who had done research all over Texas and written most of a preliminary draft, thought the title would kill any chance of commercial success. "What red-blooded Anglo-Texan would ever consider his highway of empire doomed?" she wondered.[6]

In 1960, Hodding supported Lyndon Johnson in the Democratic presidential primaries, and John Kennedy in the November election. He was afraid that Mississippi would go for the "independent elector dodge or for Mr. Nixon, the artful dodger."[7] Democrats and one Republican—Clark Reed—attended the election-night party at Feliciana. Young Hodding was absent: he was in Washington, D.C., working for the Kennedy campaign.

At Christmas that year, Hodding's sister visited from New Orleans with her husband and children. It was the first time that Hodding, Corinne, and John had been together for Christmas—indeed, at all—for years, and they enjoyed seeing one another. Sissy Thomas, Corinne's daughter, came out at the Delta Debutante Cotillion, and Hodding said he did not know a man or boy from ten to eighty who had not expressed an overwhelming desire to throw her over his shoulder and leap madly about the tundra.[8]

Another family matter was less happy. Hodding's Aunt Lilian had died in England and left bequests to each of her grandnephews and grandnieces. When Philip had failed to respond to letters from Angela Bull, Lady Beit's daughter, about the inheritance, Angela wrote to Hodding. He, with all his old insecurities about his English relatives still in place, erupted at his son. He sent Angela a blank check to pay any extra costs incurred by Philip's dereliction, and urged her to give Philip's share of the money to some worthy cause. He apologized in a second letter and expressed his gratitude for the education "Uncle Otto" had provided; the Carters were lucky to have received the help they did, even if

> I happen not to have liked it. I can remember as a child not too young to understand the French phrases, "Pauvre petit" and "Jeune homme de bonne famille" above my grateful, if preco-cious self. I have never forgotten it.[9]

Only young Hodding, it seemed, was pleasing his parents at the time. Tommy was playing polo at Culver in Indiana, but making ter-rible grades. After he failed the entrance exams for St. Albans School in Washington, D.C., his appalled parents decided he was learning nothing at Culver except horsemanship. Philip had reentered Yale, then left again, and was working for the *Herald Tribune* in New York. Still, Hodding wrote a friend, "we have no favorites among our sons, but the best way we can describe our feelings toward them is that Hodding is our pride, Tommy our delight, and Philip our heart."[10]

Hodding was receiving honors right and left. The Phi Beta Kappa chapter at Southwestern College in Memphis, now Rhodes College, elected him an honorary member, and he won the twelfth annual National Award for Journalistic Merit from the William Allen White Foundation at the University of Kansas. In his acceptance speech, Hodding called on newspaper editors to step down from their traditional position of Olympian detachment and take community affairs into their hands. Such action, he maintained, enriched the community as well as the newspaper.[11]

Young Hodding, too, won recognition. He was the only Mississippi journalist in several years to receive a Sigma Delta Chi award. The Jackson *Clarion-Ledger*, which had at times viciously attacked his father, said, "young Carter comes by his talent naturally. His prominent father and his talented mother have surrounded him with precept and example from his earliest days. We may not always agree with his editorials, but he is literate, articulate, gifted."[12]

By the beginning of August 1961, the Carters were back in Tenants Harbor. They began what would be their pattern for years: an extended stay in Maine, taking along Ione Lundy, Hodding's secretary, and her two sons. She later recalled: "Hodding said JoJo, my youngest, was five, the same age he was when he first went to Maine, and he saw that my boys got sailing lessons and everything his children had had."[13]

The grown-ups tried to work in the mornings—Hodding had a workroom in the garage, Betty and Ione had desks in their bedrooms—and play in the afternoons. By two-thirty they were out on Muscongus Bay or threading the needle toward Penobscot Bay, in a new thirty-two-foot sailboat, the *Channel Cat II*.

At home in Mississippi, Hodding found he was still controversial. Mrs. James Polk Morris, Jr., of the Louisiana Genealogical and Historical Society wrote to withdraw an invitation for him to speak at the Society's meeting on the LSU campus in Baton Rouge. "Very unofficially and vaguely," the message had reached her that it would be better if she made other arrangements for the program. It was best to avoid any controversy, she wrote Hodding. He replied that he was delighted to be out of it, as it conflicted with a board of trustees meeting he had to attend.[14]

McComb, Mississippi, became a hot spot in 1961. Robert Moses began a voter registration drive, and Marion Barry, later mayor of Washington, organized a workshop on nonviolent action there. Herbert Lee, a black man, was murdered when he showed an interest in Moses' work. Reporters trying to cover the attempted integration of McComb's bus station in December 1961 were beaten up. And someone hit editor Oliver Emmerich when he left the *Enterprise-Journal* office, and knocked him into a plate-glass window. Hodding was greatly distressed—he and Emmerich had been friends since Emmerich had dropped by the Hammond *Courier* when it was only a few days old to wish the young publisher well.

When Hodding spoke at Brown University in Providence, Rhode Island, shortly after this incident, someone in the audience asked him, "What do you think ought to be done when someone like Oliver Emmerich is slugged?"

"If the local police protection isn't enough, they should call out the National Guard," Hodding replied, "and if the Guard can't do it, they should call out the marshals, and if the marshals can't do it, send in the Marines."[15]

His answer was distorted by Associated Press, and the Jackson *Daily News* picked up the AP story and printed it with the title "Hodding Carter Urges Force Be Used to Integrate State."[16] A headline like that could topple Hodding from his narrow foothold in the middle of the road. It would enrage the citizens of the Delta so much that his life in Greenville would become untenable.

While still in Providence, Hodding received a threatening phone call from an unidentified man who said, "You're going to get what the others did." Apparently he was referring to reporters who were attacked at the McComb bus terminal. Hodding called Betty to see if all was well at home, and she reported only one angry, anonymous call there.

On the day Hodding was due back from Providence, Betty was at a friend's house doing garden club work. Before she left to meet him at the airport, she called home and found that the chief of police was there. Chief William Burnley had heard that people in Glen Allan, thirty-five miles south of Greenville, were organizing a convoy to come and burn Hodding in effigy in front of the *DD-T* office. When Betty got to the airport, she met the sheriff, who told her with a wink that he was there "to meet a friend." The friend was Hodding, whom he wanted to see safely home. The Glen Allan folks did not come to Greenville, after all, but burned Hodding in effigy in their own town.[17] They also burned hundreds of copies of the *Delta Democrat-Times*.

In an almost lighthearted editorial, Hodding recalled that some twenty-five years before, he and his friends had burned Huey Long in effigy on the main street of Hammond. It occurred to him that since Mississippians used to burn real people, burning an effigy represented real progress. Even if the effigy was of him.

In the same column Hodding reiterated his position on the beatings in McComb and mentioned the Brown speech, in which he had "protested the apparent open season . . . on newspapermen in Mississippi." He had been "pretty upset about the beating of a half-dozen newspapermen—admittedly Yankees from Time and Life, but still humans—and a Mississippi publisher who is a life-time friend." And he was none too happy that "Mississippi's largest and worst newspaper combined used a completely dishonest headline over the Associated Press story from Providence."[18]

The editorial appeared in the *DD-T* on December 10, the same day Hodding and Betty hosted a well-attended reception at Feliciana to celebrate their twenty-five years of newspaper publishing in Greenville.

On December 13, the *Daily News* fired back with an editorial that called Hodding's speech at Brown "another of his famous addresses criticizing his own state and poking ridicule at the people of Mississippi." Since the Jackson paper had no "special, roving correspondent to follow this distinguished speech-maker on his adjective-strewn circuit throughout the nation," it had to depend on wire services to keep readers "informed of his deep, intellectual, earth-shaking, policy-making statements." The *Daily News* claimed it was in no position to doubt that Hodding had said what the AP reported he had said in Providence; moreover, it pointed out most newspapers had used headlines in the same vein as the one it had used. "Is everybody out of step but the Delta Democrat-Times?" the Jackson editors wondered.[19]

Hodding received a flood of hate mail from all over the country after the Providence story. "You've been hitting us below the belt every time you could—especially in front of northern audiences, since 1954," one letter said. "You certainly are serving as a splendid communist agent. You really couldn't do better for their cause if you were paid for it. Upon second thought, maybe you are being paid for it." Another writer told him: "I have just read your article about sending troops to Mississippi. I've read your trash before. . . . I can't see why the good people of Greenville will allow a negro loving hypocrite who talks about his state like you to remain in their midst." Ninety-five citizens of Indianola signed a broadside that reprinted the Jackson *Daily News* story, and made it clear that they repudiated the statements of Hodding Carter.

Hodding spent a great deal of time and effort to try to make his position clear at home. Sevellon Brown, editor of the Providence *Journal* and *Evening Bulletin*, helped him with a "To Whom It May Concern" statement that read in part:

> Mr. Carter made three addresses to the student bodies of Brown and its affiliated women's college, Pembroke, and he participated in three informal discussions with selected groups of students. His topic for the first of three group discussions on the evening of December 5 was "The Role of the Journalist in the South." . . . Mr. Carter emphatically did not say, imply or even hint that he favored intervention by federal marshals or troops to enforce integration in the South; he was not at this point even discussing integration at all. Furthermore, in all of his speeches and discus-

sions, Mr. Carter made perfectly plain his own belief that all-out integration never could be and never should be forced upon the South from without.

It also seems to have escaped attention in Mississippi that the main theme of all Mr. Carter's talks while he was in Providence was a proud defense of the South, its values and its institutions . . . and distortion or misrepresentation of some of his remarks can only damage the work he did in the South's behalf.[20]

The wire services ran Brown's statement, and Hodding mailed copies to several thousand people. He was determined not to be labeled an integrationist. When copies of his book *First Person Rural* arrived at Feliciana in 1963, Betty and Hodding were horrified to discover that the jacket described Hodding as "the foremost integrationist of the South." Flushed red to the roots of his hair—Betty had seen this phenomenon very few times before—Hodding called the publishers and told them if the jacket was not immediately withdrawn and replaced, he would sue. Doubleday delayed publication until a new jacket was ready.

He wrote "Desegregation Does Not Mean Integration" for *The New York Times Magazine* to explain again why "numerically meaningful integration" was not in the cards for the Deep South for a long time to come. Mississippi, as a federal judge had said off the record, would be "saved for last" for school integration, and then "token desegregation would be accepted eventually in the larger communities."[21]

Shock waves from reports of the Brown speech continued to worry Hodding for some time. The Citizens' Council tried to organize a boycott of his Greenville radio station and talked again about starting another paper in town. "The extremists make the most noise," Hodding thought.[22] After all, "when a pot begins to boil hard, the scum is the first that rises to the top."[23] But there were also positive consequences, and the best, according to Hodding, was an invitation to speak at the University of New Hampshire "for an astonishing $1,000 and expenses" for one talk. "I ought to get burned again,"

Hodding said.[24] He also liked a telegram he got from Memphis friends who said they still liked him, whether he was "rare, medium or well done."[25]

The Greenville Junior Auxiliary pleased Hodding enormously when it honored him for his civic service and asked him to be the King of Hearts at its annual ball in 1961. No other king had ever worn a costume for the ball, but Hodding ordered one from New Orleans and went as Henry VIII, a part which, his friends assured him, he played to perfection. The royal court assembled at Feliciana before going to a local armory for the ball. Photographs show him as he wanted to be, Betty Carter wrote in her unpublished memoirs—handsome, carefree, spontaneous, gay, with a silver goblet in his hand.

That year, when Mrs. Lawrence Lipscomb Paxton of Leland, the sponsor of the Delta Debutante Club, visited her daughter in England, she was surprised by the number of people who spoke so highly of "the South's fighting editor," Hodding Carter, who lived so close by and yet whom she knew only casually. When she returned home, Mrs. Paxton asked Hodding to be master of ceremonies at the debutante ball during the 1961 Christmas season. Hodding accepted gladly. His niece Joan would be making her debut that year, and he felt the invitation was a seal of approval from the people of the Delta, just as the invitation to be King of Hearts was an accolade from the people of Greenville.

Soon after the contretemps of the Brown speech, two mothers of debutantes who lived outside Greenville demanded that Mrs. Paxton rescind her invitation to Hodding. Mrs. Paxton refused; the invitation had been extended and accepted in good faith and no lady could think of withdrawing it under those circumstances. "If Mr. Carter is master of ceremonies, we will throw tomatoes when he stands at the microphone," one of them said. "If you do, you will splatter my new gown, because I'll be standing right beside him," said Mrs. Paxton.

The two irate women called Feliciana and asked to see Hodding.

Betty and Hodding waited for them, wondering why they wanted a formal meeting.

"We want you to resign as master of ceremonies, Mr. Carter," they told him. "Our fathers worked to build the Delta, and you are working to destroy it. We stand for the South, Mr. Carter. We beg of you to resign."

Hodding's face froze. Betty thought he was saying to himself that he was a Southerner as much as they were. "Did Mrs. Paxton ask you to ask me to withdraw?" he inquired.

"No."

"Then unless she asks me to withdraw, I will serve."

The two women left, but within a day or two, Albert Lake, a lawyer and a former emcee himself, and Frank Hall, a good friend of the Carters', arrived at Feliciana. They sat with Hodding on the long sofa by the fireplace in the living room and explained how Hodding's serving would adversely affect the institution. Parents would withdraw their daughters from the ball; the organization would flounder.

Betty watched Hodding's face turn white. She was tense herself. If he gave in, she thought, the right to be different would be lost in the Delta. Anyone who didn't follow the shibboleths of the extreme conservatives would be barred from participation in the life of the community, at first just socially, but then what?

"Did Mrs. Paxton ask you to come?" Hodding asked.

"No."

Hodding drew a deep breath and said, "I will not withdraw."

Albert Lake sank back on the sofa. Frank Hall threw his arms around Hodding's neck.

One debutante withdrew, and one planter, father of another, announced that his daughter would not be introduced by Hodding Carter. The ball took place without incident, with Lester Lanin's orchestra playing. "We formed a Praetorian guard 'round Hodding," recalled one of his friends. When it came time to introduce the debutantes, Hodding did his job until the daughter of the disapproving planter was next in line. Scarcely anyone noticed when Hodding quietly handed the microphone to her father so he could read the information about his daughter and her family. Mrs. Paxton's dress was not stained. Chief of Police Burnley sent several plainclothesmen dressed in dinner jackets. When asked the next day what they thought of the debutante ball, one of them said it was just like any other dance, except that the women used more expensive perfume. Young Hodding, Philip, and Tommy went to the ball to back up their father, and their cousin Joan and Uncle John. There was some talk of staying for the breakfast after the ball, but Betty said they had shown the flag and made their point. They all went home to Feliciana, where the security man hired to protect the house reported no incident.[26]

In early 1961, Hodding, who had been going to Tulane twice a month to lecture, had told Bill Hogan, a friend in the history department there, that he would like to do more at the university. Delighted, President Herbert Longenecker and dean Robert Lumiansky named him writer in residence—which he remained from 1962 to 1970—and advisor to the student newspaper, the *Hullabaloo,* to begin in September.

Betty thought it would be ideal if they moved to New Orleans. Young Hodding and Peggy and their growing family could move out of the little house and into the big house at Feliciana. Betty and Hodding would find a place in New Orleans, and when they were in Greenville for holidays, they could stay in the guest room downstairs, next to Hodding's study. It was a good move for young Hodding, too. "There was no way on God's earth we could be at the paper at the same time," he said later.[27] But when he took over his father's chair in the dining room, he realized how courageous Hodding had been. He sat with his back to a plate-glass window, outside of which were cypress trees growing in a slough and a low brick wall. From the other side of that wall, a sniper could easily take aim on the back of a man's head.

When Hodding reported to Tulane in September 1961, he found his students brighter than the ones he had taught in 1928. He met with the *Hullabaloo* staffers, and he and Betty had them all over for dinner every few weeks. They took smaller groups to their new retreat on the Wolf River near Pass Christian, next door to Betty's sister Lorraine, and an hour and a half by car from New Orleans. The Carters' sixty acres featured six hundred feet of frontage on both sides of the river, tall pine trees, a log house and a guest house, a pier, and a swimming pool.

That same September, Philip married Marcia McGhee, daughter of Undersecretary of State for Political Affairs George McGhee and his wife, Cecilia, in Middleburg, Virginia. Marcia insisted that Philip finish college, so he enrolled at Tulane, and the newlyweds moved into an apartment in the French Quarter.

One night while Hodding and Betty were having dinner at Marcia and Philip's, they heard a noise that sounded like a gunshot. "Hit the floor!" said Hodding. "Get your gun!" Marcia sat stiffly at the table while Betty and Hodding lay on the floor and Philip crawled out on the balcony with his gun. If a car backfiring in New Orleans could cause such a reflex, Marcia thought, what a life her in-laws must have led.

In September 1962, the Fifth Circuit Court of Appeals ordered the University of Mississippi to allow James Meredith to enter. Governor Ross Barnett swore he would not obey. Young Hodding editorialized:

> For the rest of the nation what is going on now in our state in relation to desegregation of the University of Mississippi is a matter of incredulous wonder. . . . We should make no mistake about where tomorrow's expected confrontation between federal and state power will take us.

On September 25, the *DD-T* stated: "Sedition—ugly word. The nation cannot allow the governor to be successful." Over the next few days the paper reported that Barnett had rushed to the university, and that "only Meredith's absence keeps Ole Miss from exploding."

An editorial on September 29 announced that "now is the time for the silent majority to speak out."

On October 1, Meredith was in classes as riots spread. Two people had died, and the campus was in shambles. General Edwin Walker of the U.S. Army arrived on the campus and made things worse. A third of the 166 federal marshals who had been sent in by Attorney General Robert Kennedy were wounded, and forty National Guard soldiers had been hit by missiles or bullets.

Hodding and Betty decided to drive from New Orleans to Greenville to protect Feliciana. Philip and Tommy Carter and their uncle Philip Werlein, Betty's brother, wanted to go as well. They all waved good-bye to a forlorn Marcia, who stood outside on her apartment balcony. It was ten at night before they left New Orleans, and because of detours for road construction on the way it was morning before they reached Greenville. During that nightlong drive they listened to phone-in shows on the radio, broadcasting calls from Ole Miss: "Federal troops are in the dormitories with *bayonets!*" "They're in the *girls'* dormitories with bayonets!"

Once in Greenville, they approached Feliciana from Cypress Road instead of the highway, and saw a car in a ditch near the house. Philip wrote down the license number to report to the police; Chief of Police Burnley later told Betty it belonged to a "bad man." Feliciana was still standing, apparently unharmed. Young Hodding, who also had been up all night, had nothing to report but more phone calls. They went to bed early that night and slept soundly. The next morning Hodding, walking around the lake, saw the charred remains of a cross. "Thank goodness we didn't see who did it," Betty said.[28]

Doomed Road of Empire was finished, but Hodding had contracts for four other books: a biography of Andrew Johnson for World, books on South Africa and East Texas for Doubleday, and a history of Freemasonry for McGraw-Hill. None of these would be written. Hodding asked Carol Brandt of Brandt & Brandt to get him out of his old contract with Doubleday for a novel; he could not dictate it. To replace the novel, he said he would write another book like *Where Main Street Meets the River*.[29] Doubleday agreed to substitute a collection of essays. In February 1963, he signed another contract with Doubleday for a book tentatively titled "After Meredith, What?"

Hodding was tired and bitterly unhappy, worried about his vision, annoyed by everything around him. He and Betty had either too many social engagements or too few. Betty drove either too fast or too slow. He blamed his bad temper on his blindness, and Betty accepted his diagnosis. He seriously considered selling the paper, but young Hodding talked him out of it.

Hodding's lively, tenacious mind was slipping. A letter he wrote to John Starr of McGraw-Hill about the proposed book on Freemasonry reveals the feeble grasp he had of the subject.

> I would start out with an introductory chapter, fixing the Masons in time and place, as far as this book is concerned—in other words, begin with the earliest political activity in which the Masons were known to have been engaged, probably in Spain. I would then proceed to pretty well cover Europe, with the chapters regarding Masonic political activity in England, France (of the Revolution and later), Italy, the Mediterranean (Sardinia especially), southeast Asia, the United States—our Revolution, the West Florida Republic, the Mexican War for Independence and our own war for Texas independence would fit in here. The final chapter, of course, would deal with the Masons today, making it a probable point that the political activity is not as widespread and the repression in un-Democratic countries severe. The Masons maintain a fantastic library in the midwest. The name of the city escapes me now but I can get it from anyone of a number of Masons whom I know, and it will be all there.[30]

He forgot appointments and missed an important board meeting at George Peabody College for Teachers in Nashville. His behavior in public began to be "inappropriate," as social workers say. At Bowdoin, for a board of overseers meeting, he wanted to see his old friend Alden Sawyer, who was a member of the board of trustees, which was conferring in another room. "He came blundering in the trustees' room, not knocking, looking for me. He didn't know where he was," Sawyer recalled. "I got up and got him out. One time he was coming up for an overseers' meeting, and because of a mini-hurricane, all flights were canceled. He called from Boston and said that he had come that far by train and was going to hire a taxi to bring him up to the south Portland exit of the turnpike. He'd be there at one a.m. I went and waited on him until three—and I had to be at a meeting in Brunswick at eight a.m. He never thought."[31]

Medgar Evers, NAACP field secretary, was shot in the back as he got out of the car at his home in Jackson on June 12, 1963. On June 24, Byron De La Beckwith, the Greenwood man who had been so interested in the layout of the Carters' house, was arrested. The Jackson *Clarion-Ledger*'s headline, "Californian Is Charged with Murder of Evers,"[32] shows how defensive Mississippians had become. Beckwith had indeed been born in California, but he had lived in Greenwood since he was four years old. The Carters shivered when they heard of his arrest.

After Evers's death, demonstrations grew more defiant. Greenville had its first sit-in, the first racial conflict in its history. Hodding wrote about the local situation for *The New York Times Magazine*. The attitudes of people on both sides of the racial struggle were hardening, he said, and there was a widespread "fantastic belief in an eventual and inevitable showdown." Hate and fear were the two emotions that possessed Mississippians.[33]

Hodding felt more intense anxiety about losing the paper, his eyesight, everything. Betty was worried about him, but realized she needed help as well. She was eating six Hershey bars at a time and several times went to a psychiatrist to whom she could talk freely.

Betty and Hodding went to Tommy's graduation from Culver in June, then went to Greenville, where they stayed until they went to

Ford Hospital in Detroit for Hodding's cataract operation in July. The operation went smoothly, but recovery was hard. Old classmates from Bowdoin and friends who lived in the area, including Theodosia and Hubert Davis, thronged his hospital room, making him a celebrity at the hospital. The second night, with everything going well, he apparently received an overdose of painkiller—morphine, he thought—fell out of bed, suffered a slight hemorrhage in his bandaged eye, and went roaming around the corridor. In his mind Betty had been kidnapped, and he yelled for his pistol.

He complained that his head felt as big as a pumpkin. He could not gauge the width of doorways or the depth of steps. From Detroit, they went to Maine for the rest of the summer. He wrote friends that Maine had never been more beautiful, and described the daisies, black-eyed Susans, clover, and grasses outside his window. Ione Lundy and her sons did not come that summer, so he dictated letters on a Soundscriber and mailed the tubes to her to transcribe.

With none of his children or grandchildren there, Hodding, lonely, invited everyone to whom he dictated letters to come for a visit. As he could not read typescript or newsprint, Betty read to him. Betty read the proofs for *Doomed Road of Empire*, and when she finished, Hodding asked her what she wanted as a reward. When she answered, "A watch," he was indignant. Hadn't he and the boys already given her a diamond watch for her birthday? She said she felt uncomfortable wearing it to the grocery store. He bought her a gold Rolex that she wore for twenty years.

Hodding wrote the dedication for *Doomed Road*: "To my wife, without whom this book could not have been written." He stopped and said, "Hell, yes! It couldn't have been written without you! You wrote it!" He added "with Betty Carter" after his own name on the title page. His recognition came too late for her name to appear on the cover. Actually, Betty wrote all of the book except the chapter on the Alamo. "That was the only chapter that had any life to it," she would always say, referring to her own style as "pedantic."

Hodding told his editor at Doubleday that he had about six chapters of the "race book" written. He did not think it should be called "After Meredith, What?"—things were moving too fast to use Meredith as a focal point. Instead, he was using "Moderate Is a Dirty Word!" as a working title.

Hodding, a scrupulously honest man all his life, had begun to prevaricate. He told one correspondent he had lost the sight in his bad eye "fighting for my country in far places," and claimed that he had "twice helped avert a lynching."[34]

He sent his poems, most of them written in his youth, to Doubleday. The publishers hesitated to issue them, at an estimated loss of two to three thousand dollars, but they eventually agreed. Hodding told his agent he "would rather have a book of verse published than anything else."[35]

He rejoiced when he could read a newspaper for the first time. An unexpected hemorrhage in his eye, however, disturbed him—and the doctors.

In the fall of 1963, *First Person Rural*, a book of twenty-six personal essays that had appeared previously in magazines, was published, and following it closely was *Doomed Road of Empire*. Reviews of *First Person Rural* were generally favorable, most of them emphasizing Hodding's own bravery in the battle for racial justice.

Doomed Road of Empire, the sixth volume in McGraw-Hill's American Trails series, did worse. One critic echoed Betty's question, "For whom was this road doomed?" History in the book was too simplified, the reviewer said.[36]

Also that fall, General Edwin Walker sued Hodding for $2 million. Hodding, in a speech at the University of New Hampshire, had called the general a seditious psychopath. Walker also sued the Associated Press and a number of newspapers. Eventually the suits were disposed of on appeal, with Walker losing under the Sullivan ruling, which says that public figures cannot collect damage for libel unless they can prove malice. The suit against Hodding was the only one dismissed by the plaintiff, with prejudice, at the plaintiff's cost.[37]

In September, Tommy Carter had enrolled at Tulane, where, Hodding pointed out, forty-one of his forebears and relatives had gone to school. Hodding admired President Longenecker for having quietly integrated the campus that year. "Now you see Negro students—there can't be more than 30 or so but the number will grow— talking and eating with white students. How in the hell Mississippi could act one way and Louisiana in such a completely opposite way, I don't know—except as a native Louisianan, I am tempted to say in line with the old joke, 'We just got a better class of white folks down here.'"[38]

In October, Hodding received the biggest honor of his life, the Bowdoin Prize, awarded every five years to the Bowdoin alumnus or faculty member deemed to have made the "most distinctive contribution in any field of human endeavor." Judges were the presidents of Yale and Harvard and the chief justice of the Maine Supreme Court. Hodding was notified in April that he would receive the prize that fall. "I am still up in the clouds and I am afraid I can't write too coherently; he wrote to the president of Bowdoin. "My cup ran over when I was elected to the Board of Overseers. Now I have ordered a gross of cups. Please accept my heartfelt appreciation. I shall try to live up to the Bowdoin Prize."[39] As the time for the prize-giving came closer, he promised "Immediately following the anointing I plan to walk on water from Casco Bay to Soames Sound."[40]

The ceremony was festive. Thirty members of the Bowdoin class of 1927 were on hand, as well as many eastern friends. It was the most heartwarming experience of his life, Hodding said in letter after letter.

He and Betty had worked on his speech that summer in Maine and although he had trouble reading it, it was one of the best he ever made. He talked of four memorable journeys he had taken during his lifetime: The first was from Hammond to Brunswick, where the prejudices he found among other students at Bowdoin made him "begin to worry" about his own. By the time he received his diploma, he said, he had begun a process of unlearning, a process useful to those "whose minds have been clouded and whose hearts have been hardened by old and accustomed prejudices." His second journey took him to the Middle East and North Africa, where, for the first time, he "discovered the plight of hopeless dark-skinned people so impoverished and exploited and abused as to appear to be festering sub-humans." On his third journey, to Southeast Asia, he observed "desolation of the masses was more brutish still," and understood "the world-wide intrusion of Communism with its belly and vengeance appeal." And on the fourth journey, to South Africa, he "first fully realized the implications of being a small minority of the world's people—as we whites are—and that the whispers of the non-whites are rising to the angry shouting of many hundreds of millions."

It is sad that Hodding did not die immediately after this speech. Heartbreak, blindness, and wrack and ruin were to follow.

15. 1964–1972

"Hodding Was Like King Lear"

In the spring of 1964, Tommy and another freshman at Tulane made up their minds to quit school and join the military after one last spree; they ran away to the Bahamas. After a furious Hodding tracked them down in Nassau, Tommy came home and agreed to stay in school to take midterm examinations. He spent a tense Easter at the Wolf River place with his parents.

The next weekend, Hodding and Betty went to Wolf River alone. While he was unloading the car, Hodding staggered back, clutching his eyes. "I'm blind, Betty," he said. "I'm blind." It was as if, he said, a shade had come down over his good eye, the left eye. Within hours, he and Betty were on their way to Detroit for an operation for his detached retina. Tommy was to stay in their apartment on Camp Street.

Hodding's hospital room was small, so Betty slept in a hotel. Around midnight on April 27, the phone rang. Nineteen-year-old Tommy had been at the Camp Street apartment with his girlfriend, Alice Monroe, when he decided to play Russian roulette. He put one bullet in the chamber of Hodding's gun, twirled it, placed the gun barrel to his head, and fired. He was dead.

Betty waited until early the next morning to tell Hodding; he later remembered that she said, "I could just spank him."[1] Hodding wept, but Betty was dry-eyed as she comforted him. They left the hospital, Betty leading Hodding, whose eyes were bandaged. At the Detroit airport they met young Hodding and Philip, who had flown up to escort their parents home, and the four of them put their arms around each other and huddled together. A friend sent a private plane to fly them from Memphis to Greenville. More friends waited at Feliciana. In Bern Keating's memorable phrase, Hodding was like King Lear, led into the living room with his eyes bandaged and tears rolling down his cheeks. The doctor wanted to give Betty a shot. "No," she said, "Hodding needs me." When Father Edward Sheridan called to offer his condolences, Hodding wept again and said, "He was our baby."

"Betty never lost control," said Josephine Haxton. "But Hodding was the most tragic figure at the funeral I've ever seen. He was incapacitated."[2] His constant tears had the worst possible effect on the eye that had just been operated on.

On the morning of the funeral, as the family left Feliciana, they found that someone had dumped a load of garbage at the driveway entrance. It had happened before, but this morning, it seemed especially cruel. "Their tribute to the grief of a mother and father was an appropriate symbol of the filth-crazed haters who today are riding again in Mississippi. . . . It was a symbol which all the complacent, comfortable citizens of this state who would passively or positively acquiesce in the resurgence of organized bigotry should mark with care," editorialized the *Delta Democrat-Times*.[3]

After the bandages came off, Hodding could see. Then in late May his retina detached again. His doctor in Detroit was on vacation, so he went with Betty to Johns Hopkins in Baltimore for another operation. The doctor there was not encouraging. Hodding would never have direct vision in his left eye because of the wrinkling of the retina. And there was only a twenty-five-percent chance that he would have any vision at all. What would happen if the operation did not work? Betty asked the doctor. "Cold, utter darkness," he said.

Hodding emerged from the operation with peripheral vision, much like what he had in his right eye. He would never again be able to read. Once he was discharged from the hospital, he and Betty went to the Virginia home of Philip's in-laws, George and Cecilia McGhee, for ten days so Hodding could recuperate. The McGhees were away, but Philip, who worked for *Newsweek* in Washington, and Marcia, and their new daughter, Cecilia, were there.

At times Hodding drank excessively; at other times he was not lucid even if he was not drinking. He felt "like he was going to the bottom of the creek and being dragged along the bottom by the current. It was just pushing you along, and you were scraped and dragged and unable to get above it. He had that feeling from then on."[4]

He begged Betty to commit suicide with him. She told him he could decide for himself but she could not do it. He continued to urge her and she continued to refuse.

He was momentarily cheered when Doubleday published *The Ballad of Catfoot Grimes and Other Verses*, a book of Hodding's poems, in the summer of 1964. He had written most of them years before, but he had completely rewritten the title poem, to eliminate the racist phrases he had used forty years before. It received positive reviews. *Saturday Review* said it was "more illuminating than many ponderous sociological studies,"[5] but the Birmingham *News* grumbled that "Carter's verses picture the area at its worst." The first edition of the book sold out. *McCall's* bought one of the poems, dedicated to Will Percy, before publication of the book and ran it.

That summer Hodding's mood improved, and he dictated letters saying that he was better than he had expected to be. Although he could never read again, he said, he believed that without further complications he could live normally. "Even now I get around freely, recognize many objects and at rather close range I can recognize anyone," he told Carol Brandt. He planned to finish the books for which he was committed, he told her, and perhaps even write others.[6]

U.S. News & World Report interviewed several southern editors that summer on what they thought the effects of the pending civil rights legislation of 1964 would be. Each man's reply illustrated his own position on civil rights. Virginius Dabney of the Richmond *Times-Dispatch* said the bill went so far it would increase tension. John Popham of the Chattanooga *Times* saw no great impact from the law, since it was "no panacea for race problems." Leroy Simms, editor of the Huntsville *Times*, predicted that the use of force would arouse new resentments. Caleb King of the *Florida Times-Union* said the "civil rights thing has been overdone." Hodding said, "The new act won't improve relations between the races, but it's going to improve the status of the Negro. If I were a Negro, I wouldn't care whether it improved race relations or not, if I got what I thought were my rights."[7]

Hodding and Betty, still in Greenville in July, saw Project Mississippi in action. Youthful black leaders of the NAACP, the Student Nonviolent Coordinating Committee (SNCC), the Congress of Racial Equality (CORE), and the Southern Christian Leadership Conference (SCLC) had banded together to form the Council of Federated Organizations (COFO), with Aaron Henry of Clarksdale the president. A thousand volunteers, white and black, had flocked to Mississippi and Alabama to work on voter registration during what came to be known as "the long, hot summer." They were backed up by 140 paid workers from SNCC and CORE and a hundred clergymen and volunteer lawyers. The State of Mississippi prepared for the invasion, increasing the number of highway patrol personnel from 275 to 475.

On April 24, crosses were burned in sixty-four of the state's eighty-two counties. In one month, June, six black churches were burned. Between January and August 1964, thirty blacks were murdered by whites. The murders of three COFO workers, Andrew Goodman, James Chaney, and Michael Schwerner in Philadelphia, Mississippi, were the most widely publicized in the state. (In 1967 the white murderers of these three men—one black and two white—would be tried and convicted of conspiracy to murder—a first for Mississippi.)

Hodding detested the young reformers from out of town. While conceding that some of them were idealists, he said they were "beatniks who thought the way to be a brother to the Negro was not to bathe; boys in beards, and dirty little girls in tight slacks with their hair down to their waists walking hand in hand with Negro boys down streets where this couldn't possibly do anything but antagonize the local white people and stir up violently angry reactions. [Some of them] . . . were really dangerous, people who have been for years identified with the Communist cause."[8] He huffed and puffed when "the COFO boys and girls had a mixed dance in the Negro VFW Hall." It did not seem to him to be the "best way to register Negroes."[9] Time was passing the old moderate by.

Hodding did defend ministers and other volunteers who lived in the homes of blacks. It would be "impossible for them to live anywhere else," he said. "The very people who denounce them most vigorously for living among Negroes would be the first to turn them away from their own doors and seek to have them barred from public facilities." He could see that their real contribution was in showing southern blacks that there were whites who believed in the "rights and brotherhood to man to the extent of suffering indignities and even death on their behalf."[10]

During the summer of 1964, Hodding pointed out, Greenville was the "only major city in Mississippi that did not have a home bombing, a church burning, a beating, or a single harassment arrest. Not one of the demonstrators was injured in Greenville. In fact, Greenville surprised the COFO workers, who, when they formed a picket line, were always protected by the police."[11] Later COFO sent volunteers from other towns to Greenville for rest and recreation.

Nicholas von Hoffman, in town that summer for a Chicago paper, wrote that Greenville was different and that its people took pride in being different. For this, von Hoffman credited the legacy of William Alexander Percy and the influence of Hodding Carter.[12]

The Civil Rights Commission, holding hearings throughout Mississippi at which witnesses presented an unending stream of evidence of intolerance and brutality, was baffled by the favorable testimony about Greenville and Police Chief William Burnley from black people, mostly NAACP leaders. There was no place like Greenville, they said; ninety to ninety-five percent of the blacks there who tried to register to vote succeeded.[13] Hodding said the televised hearings of the Commission in Jackson "must have made some impact on viewers. Perhaps little by little people will come to realize the horror of the situation as it has been in this state. At last there seems to be a desire on the part of the power structure to at least change the image of the state."[14]

William Burnley, who later became mayor of Greenville, remembered that "in 1964 we had to walk a tedious line of control. One little pimply-faced guy called me a pig every day of the world. I received a letter from his mother complimenting me. She said her son had told her not to worry, that Greenville had a professional police department." Burnley credited the *DD-T* for helping the community move with the times. "A lot of the press, like the Jackson newspapers, were stoking the fires. They wanted it to break loose. But the Carters were very effective in helping maintain peace and harmony."

When members of the Delta Ministry, an ecumenical civil rights group sponsored by the National Council of Churches, came to town at the end of Freedom Summer, they conceded that conditions were better in Greenville than they were anywhere else. "Much of the credit for the difference in Greenville is given to the *Delta Democrat-Times*, founded by Hodding Carter, Jr., with the help of plantation owners," Bruce Hilton wrote in his book about the Delta Ministry.[15] While Greenville was the most liberal town in Mississippi, it was still far from paradise. The Ministry, which had a black secretary for its four staffers, was evicted from its office in the white part of town and moved to the black neighborhood. (The *DD-T* editorialized, under the headline "This Isn't Greenville," that "our community has a precious heritage of dissent, of going our own way no matter what others in the state might do." Now there was "evidence that Greenville is giving ground to those who would straitjacket us into a city of conformists.") The Ministry workers found that the hospitals and the white doctors' offices were strictly segregated. There were separate white and black public libraries, and the black library was small and crowded. Public schools were still segregated. Streets in the black part of town were paved—a rarity in Mississippi—but housing was poor. A drugstore had taken out the stools at its lunch counter and set up booths and tables in a room behind a sign reading "Employees Only"; the proprietor invited white people to eat in the "employees' lounge." The Paramount Theater used two doors—one for whites and one for blacks, which led only to the balcony. Maids still made a mere thirteen dollars a week. There were just two black clerks in the whole downtown shopping district, and neither was permitted to handle cash or touch the cash register. The northern-owned carpet mill employed blacks only in the most menial positions.

The Delta Ministry arranged for picketers to march to the carpet mill each day until the company agreed to negotiate and, eventually, to hire more blacks. The Ministry also organized a boycott of Steinmart and picket lines for other downtown stores.

"Why me?" Jake Stein asked in bewilderment. "I've always been friendly."[16] The owner of Steinmart was, the Delta Ministry workers conceded, a warmhearted man who had helped poor Negro families for years. White people in Greenville were furious with the Delta Ministry for "picking on" Jake Stein, who catered to Negro customers. Stein admitted to the Ministry staffers that their demand that he train a Negro clerk to be a cashier was quite moderate, but that he was afraid of a counter-boycott from the segregationists. "Jake Stein has been outspoken in seeking civil rights for Negroes," Hodding said. "He was the first merchant, I believe, to employ Negro personnel. . . . But these men of God in the Delta Ministry decided that Jake must go. He survived but through no fault of the Delta Ministry."[17]

The Ministry tried a more general boycott in Greenville the next year. Merchants held meetings and tried to think of a way to break the boycott. Sol Goodman was incensed that black demonstrators sang in front of his store, and he asked other business people to work with him to get an ordinance passed against singing on the street. "And then we could tell the city to quit playing those awful Christmas carols and the Catholic church to quit ringing its bells," said

Kenneth Haxton of Nelms and Blum. After Charles Evers, brother of Medgar Evers, came to town to speak in support of the boycott, the merchants wanted to use a tape of his speech to sue him for inciting a riot. Haxton pointed out that nobody had taped Evers's speech. Haxton was amused one cloudy day when blacks picketed Mangel's. "It started raining and they all went inside and bought umbrellas at Mangel's, and then went back outside and continued to march." Another time Haxton saw a merchant named Nathan Adams standing in the picket line at the post office. "What are you doing, Nathan?" Haxton asked. "Waiting to buy stamps," said Adams.[18] After boycott and picketing had gone on for a month, merchants began hiring and promoting blacks and it was over.

Hodding, growing ill and old for his fifty-seven years, reverted to something worse than his childhood prejudices. The Delta Ministry, he said, was a front for Stokely Carmichael, "whom I consider one of the most evil influences among the American Negroes today."[19] Carmichael, later chairman of the Student Nonviolent Coordinating Committee, was, Hodding said, "a little black Power Sambo. To be truthful, I am getting pretty damned well fed up with what I once called jigs and I am about to call them again."[20] Betty said she knew that Hodding was deranged the night a car full of black people pulled up beside them at an intersection and Hodding said to them, "Get out of the way, jigaboos." He had never in his life, she said, said anything like that in her hearing.

Hodding dictated an article for *Pageant* that praised Dr. James Silver, the history professor at the University of Mississippi who had befriended James Meredith when nobody else would speak to him. Silver spoke out before the Southern Historical Association in Asheville, North Carolina, where he said that a "totalitarian society of Mississippi imposes on all its people acceptance of an obedience to an official orthodoxy almost identical with pro-slavery philosophy. . . . Mississippi is the way it is, not because of its views on the Negro . . . but because of its closed society, its refusal to allow freedom of inquiry or to tolerate 'error of opinion.'" Silver was subjected to the same kinds of verbal abuse and threats that Hodding had endured for years.[21] In the end Silver regretfully left Mississippi.

On their way to Maine that summer, Betty and Hodding stopped in Baltimore so the doctor could check Hodding's eyes. John Emmerich, news editor at the Baltimore *Sun*, and his wife, Celia, took Hodding out to dinner in one of Baltimore's Italian restaurants. Emmerich told Hodding about the Heffner family in McComb, where John's father owned the *Enterprise-Journal*. Albert Heffner—everybody called him Red—was a prosperous insurance agent in McComb, who had recently won a community service award. He and his wife, Malva, had two daughters, one of whom was the reigning Miss Mississippi. The Heffners asked some civil rights workers, one of them a minister representing the National Council of Churches, who were in McComb for the summer of 1964, to their house for dinner. Anonymous telephone threats began at once, and cars circled their house constantly. The lease on Red Heffner's office was canceled, and his business vanished. Life in McComb became untenable for the Heffners, so they fled—first to Jackson, then to Washington, D.C. Oliver Emmerich had done what he could, but as Hodding had said, McComb was in the most "morally and spiritually bankrupt area of Mississippi"—he wouldn't be caught dead in Pike County himself. Galvanized by the Heffners' story, Hodding determined to write a book about them; he went immediately to a pay phone in the restaurant and called Red Heffner.

Hodding stopped work on "Here Today, Gone Tomorrow," the book about vanishing southern customs, tools, and techniques, and the novel about his childhood to work on the Heffner book in Maine. Using Red Heffner's diary of the daily events of the crisis, he wrote a short and angry book that became *So the Heffners Left McComb*. He planned to split any money from the book fifty-fifty with the Heffners.[22]

Back in New Orleans, he and Betty settled in a small apartment at the Andrew Jackson—they could not live in the Camp Street apartment again.

So the Heffners Left McComb appeared in the fall of 1965, to good reviews. Gene Roberts, in *The New York Times Book Review*, pointed to other dissenters who had had to go into exile—Harry Ashmore from Little Rock, Charles Morgan from Birmingham, and James Silver from Oxford. The dissent-to-exile pattern was so familiar that it explained why there was not more dissent. In spite of the reviews, *So the Heffners Left McComb* did not sell well and did not earn back its $2,000 advance. Hodding blamed Doubleday for delaying publication,[23] but the book itself—only 142 pages long, hastily written and poorly edited—was not without fault.

Young Hodding, who had been named a Nieman fellow in the spring, was off at Harvard that fall. While his son was away, Hodding contributed more editorials to the *DD-T*. In a much-quoted one, he said, "As far as I can determine, there are only two basic differences between a Ku Klux Klansman and a jackass. One is that a jackass doesn't take himself seriously. The other is that a jackass doesn't know how to murder from ambush and wouldn't try to do it if he did know how. . . . In a way, the Klansmen have done our State a favor by demonstrating what kind of vicious damn fools apparently control what is, possibly next to the Communists, the most un-American aggregation in our nation."[24]

Young Hodding, Peggy, and their children came home for Christmas in 1965 and brought with them a Nieman fellow from South Africa, his wife, and two little boys. Philip and Marcia and their daughter were there, too, as were a Japanese houseguest, and briefly, an Iranian guest, Peggy's mother and younger brother, and for Christmas Day, John Carter and his wife.

Hodding, Betty, and their older son discussed the state of the newspaper. They decided the current editor was not running it as a local paper; he was playing the Vietnam war as the main story of the day, instead of emphasizing local news. He would have to return to reporting or be fired. And one of the Carters would have to tell him of the family's decision. Young Hodding was going back to Harvard. Big Hodding had to be in New Orleans because of his commitment to Tulane; he could stay with his sister there. So it was up to

Betty to remain in Greenville, tell the editor, and return to the paper full-time.

She assumed the task; as far as the ultimatum to the editor, no one in the family had ever been called on to make so drastic a change in an employee's status. Predictably, the editor resigned. Betty immediately picked Foster Davis, a Bowdoin graduate on the staff, to replace him.

By this time, segregationists in Mississippi knew they were beaten. The Civil Rights Bill of 1964 had been signed into law and the federal government was enforcing the public accommodations law. Mass registration of blacks followed the 1965 passage of the Voter Registration Act. The politics of Mississippi changed, and white Mississippians gave in and said, "We've had it." Bumper stickers that said "Welcome to Mississippi, the Occupied State" appeared.

Ever since 1960, when young Hodding became managing editor, the *Delta Democrat-Times* masthead had carried his father's name as editor and publisher. In June 1966, when young Hodding came back from Harvard, Hodding formally named him editor and associate publisher. Big Hodding said he felt quite sad and sentimental the day the notice ran in the paper, but young Hodding reassured him, "You can still fire me." [25]

Betty and Hodding went to Maine that summer, and Hugh and Theodosia Davis came for a visit. "Theodosia Davis is the only other person I have ever really loved," Hodding wrote to his older son. "Mother is pretending to be greatly jealous that we are taking them on the cruise but she really isn't." [26] He and Betty had the Maine house enlarged, and in the fall they sold the Wolf River property and bought a little house on Prytania Street in the New Orleans Garden District.

Hodding continued to write books and articles. As he deteriorated mentally and emotionally, the quality of his writing was bound to decline. He had to dictate what he wrote, and someone, usually Betty, had to read research material aloud to him. Sometimes there was a flash of his old fire and brilliance. It was remarkable that he continued to write at all, and even more remarkable that he continued to talk about writing with such enthusiasm.

On September 14, 1965, Hodding proudly wrote to his cousin Muriel, Lady Beit's daughter, in England that at the moment three Carters were working on biographies—he on Andrew Johnson, Philip on Lyndon Johnson from birth until he came to Washington to work for the New Deal, and young Hodding on Theodore Bilbo, a project first offered to Hodding, who recommended his son.[27] None of these books was written.

In his letter, Hodding included a note of sympathy: Muriel's nephew Theodore Bull had married a black Nigerian woman. "Thank God that your mother and her brothers and sisters are not alive. It is a ghastly, nightmarish thing," he said.

In 1965, Hodding wrote two articles for *The New York Times Magazine*. One was about the South's double standard for the punishment of murderers—leniency for whites, severity for blacks—and the other deplored the way the Confederate flag had been degraded into a symbol of resistance to civil rights. In 1966, in another *Times Magazine* article,[28] he lamented that the Student Nonviolent Coordinating Committee and other groups—he termed them "black nationalist"—demanded that *Uncle Remus* no longer be read to children. Nobody would know who Joel Chandler Harris was, he complained, and in his boyhood the book was thought to be an "enduring classic, equal to Aesop and Montaigne." This defense of *Uncle Remus* was not so bad—Harris had collected the old animal stories from former slaves and written them down in the dialect the tale-tellers used—but Hodding also defended *Little Black Sambo* and went on to talk about his black "Mammy" and how much he loved her.

Grosset & Dunlap had bought publication rights to the Rivers of America series from Rinehart and planned to bring *Lower Mississippi* back into print. Betty hired a young man to read the book aloud to Hodding so he could note passages that needed updating.

In December 1967, Hodding, behaving irrationally, caused a storm over the *Hullabaloo* at Tulane. He had long ago lost interest in advising the paper's staff, and the students considered him at best a "grand old man" and at worst an irrelevance. A group of students from Louisiana State University in New Orleans had distributed pamphlets on the Tulane campus that described an antiwar demonstration at LSU in New Orleans, at which, according to the pamphlet, the chief of the campus police had "jerked off in his pants." *Hullabaloo* editor Jeff Howie, a twenty-five-year-old law student, wrote an editorial criticizing the campus police for confiscating the pamphlets because they contained what Howie termed "childish obscenity." Howie called Hodding in Greenville, where he and Betty were entertaining the members of his journalism seminar, on a Thursday night to read him the news story, by another student, and his own editorial.

Howie read the editorial, then the story. Hodding said the story was "horrible, tasteless." Howie agreed, he told Hodding, but he had to run it to back up the editorial. Hodding apparently did not understand that Howie intended to publish the story, with its excerpt from the pamphlet, in the *Hullabaloo*. When he found out Sunday that the *Hullabaloo* had indeed run it, he was furious. He resigned as faculty advisor and called the New Orleans *Times-Picayune* to denounce the "dishonest and obscene" practices of the *Hullabaloo*. The Tulane publications board met and reprimanded Howie, who resigned. "If they don't understand what I'm trying to do, I might as well." [29] Hodding said he would return as advisor to the *Hullabaloo* if Howie's resignation stayed in force.

Hodding defended his stand, even when Red Heffner wrote him to protest mildly on the students' behalf. "If you . . . think that front page news stories in a university newspaper or any other, tossing about four letter words and libelous comments are synonymous with liberalism, review your thinking," Hodding wrote back angrily. "And if either of you believe that I shouldn't have blown up over the reprinting of description of a campus official in the same front page story as 'jerking off in his pants'—love to you both." [30]

More than the obscenity—though like most men of his age he had a puritanical streak—Hodding detested the antiwar demonstrators. "Something evil is stalking the land," he wrote in a letter. "And as a disabled veteran of World War II who is old-fashioned enough to love his country, I have only admiration for the boys, so many of whom come from underprivileged families who are fighting our fight."[31] "I wish they would put me in charge of the draft board," he said later in a speech in New Orleans. "I'd know what to do with those rioters and rebels."[32]

It is a commentary on Hodding's true nature—or perhaps Betty's—that when Jeff Howie was married, his bride, who was in Tulane's a cappella chorus, which the Carters had chaperoned on trips to Mexico, invited the Carters to the wedding. They sent a wedding present, and it was a nice present, Jeff Howie said years later.

In October 1967, after editor Sanford Cobb came to Greenville on a scouting expedition, Hodding signed a contract with Rand McNally to do a picture book on the Mississippi from Itasca, Minnesota, to the Gulf. It would become *Man and the River*. In April 1968, he returned to Doubleday the advance for a novel, and that summer he worked on *Man and the River* and "Beanie," a novel based on his own childhood, which was never published. He dictated fragments, some of them inaccurate, for an autobiography.

In the summer of 1969, doctors agreed that Hodding had had several strokes, and ordered him to remove all pressure from his life. "It is all very well to tell a man to have no pressures," Betty wrote to Carl Brandt of Brandt & Brandt. "But in actual fact if he has none he is ever more restless and discouraged." Betty felt that some of the vignettes he had written for *Man and the River* were as beautiful as anything he had ever written, but she told Brandt he was handicapped by his poor eyesight as well as "his very short concentration and sudden weariness."[33]

Hodding also continued to lecture, using cue cards with one word printed in big letters on each card to remind him of what he wanted to say. It took "pure grit," Betty said, but he gave the first Carlos McClatchy Memorial Lecture at Stanford University in 1965. He spoke that spring at Clemson, Spring Hill, the National Cathedral, and Virginia Theological Seminary, where he was the first layman to receive an honorary degree. In his acceptance speech, Hodding spoke of his Grandmother Carter, who had devoutly hoped that one of her nine children or twenty-five grandchildren would become a minister; he had at least come this close.

One of Hodding's last commitments was to deliver the Lamar Memorial Lectures at Mercer University in Macon, Georgia, in late 1968. Betty went with him and remembered it as pure hell. Hodding was unable to speak, and Betty read his speeches for him while he stayed in their room. The speeches were published by the University of Georgia Press in 1969 as *Their Words Were Bullets: The Southern Press in War, Reconstruction, and Peace.*

When Hodding was hospitalized in New Orleans in 1967, Blue Cross refused to compensate him since he had been treated for alcoholism. With the vivid example of his cousin Hamilton Hall and his wife in Camden, both of whom had been institutionalized for alcoholism, before him, he quit drinking for a while. The only trouble, he said, was that "when you quit drinking whiskey you wake up each morning with the sad knowledge that you won't feel any better all day."[34]

Abstinence did not last, and Hodding acquired new habits that were downright repulsive. He began to fawn over women—among them Rene Carpenter, aspiring columnist and wife of astronaut Scott Carpenter, and Eppie Lederer (Ann Landers)—in a way he never had before. He was becoming notorious for pawing and "tweaking butts," as someone said; even Ione Lundy, who sometimes took him to the Catholic church, had to endure his fumbling hands.

He could still try new things, though. When he took on a journalism course at Tulane in the fall of 1967, he turned to David Brown, who had left the Pascagoula paper and was teaching journalism at Morehead State University in Kentucky. "I don't know how to give such a course," Hodding wrote. "Will you send me an outline of what you tell your young hopefuls? If you have an outline for the year or semester which I could use as a guide, it would be a great advantage to me."[35] Brown sent him everything he had in the way of lesson plans and syllabi, and Hodding taught the course.

In 1968, Hodding learned that he would receive the tenth annual First Federal Foundation Award for his "outstanding achievements and distinguished service to Mississippi." Being chosen for the "Missy Award," a peculiarly Mississipian honor, thrilled Hodding. He asked the vice-president of First Federal Savings and Loan in Jackson if he could "turn in the names of more than 150 people if we pay personally for the dinners of the overflow? We have a great many friends in Louisiana and Mississippi whom we would like to have with us on this happy occasion."[36] At the award dinner in March, Hodding said, "I am a Mississippian. I love the state of Mississippi. But I am also an American and I love America." It was obvious that he was drunk.

Hodding appeared on William F. Buckley Jr.'s *Firing Line* program in April 1968 on behalf of Robert Kennedy. He had always liked Bobby Kennedy, whom he regarded as "tough" and "a fighter," and he worked for him in the California primary campaign. In Los Angeles on the night of the primary, he ate supper with the whole Kennedy family, John Glenn, Roosevelt Grier, and Rafer Johnson. Hodding left Los Angeles before the vote was counted and heard about Kennedy's assassination when he was in Denver. In an oral history interview in November 1968, Hodding said:

> I hit a guy in the mouth, bruised three knuckles coming back through Texas. And a bunch of god-damned Texans got on the plane—four of them, and one of them said, "Well, we got that son of a bitch, didn't we?" And I knew who he was talking about. I turned around to give him a chance and I said, "Who are you talking about?" He said, "You know damned well who I'm talking about," and I said, "You're just a son-of-a-bitch," and I hit him in the mouth. . . . Don't make me a two-gun man in this thing because I'm strictly a newspaper observer, and that fact that I hit these guys is nothing.[37]

"Three nights ago I had supper with a man and his family and close friends for whom I had an almost idolatrous affection," Hodding wrote in a signed editorial in the *DD-T*. "I am so sick of heart that for the first time I do not look askance at the idea of leaving my country. Surely there are more decent places where law abiding men can abide. . . . What this country needs are firing squads for people like this, firing squads that can get the same publicity that television affords murderers. Ours is not a safe country. Until we match a lot of killing with a little legal killing in our own behalf it will not be safe. I repeat that these are words of a heartbroken man. I might soften them. But I don't think so."[38]

The next day a letter from his brother in the *DD-T* pled with him not to leave. "Stay with us, my brother. I love you," John Carter wrote.

In the fall of 1965, Betty and Hodding were upset to learn that Philip was unhappy at *Newsweek* and, a little later, that he and Marcia were separating. Hodding urged him to come to Greenville, where he "could at least see the degree of happiness which Hodding and Peggy and your mother and I have discovered in a little city where there is so much to do and not a little excitement in doing it. I think just looking at the new plant is almost enough to make you forget some of your anxieties and grief. It is a lovely thing." (The *Delta Democrat-Times* was moving to larger quarters in a new, $500,000 plant with an offset press, away from the downtown area; it would no longer be where Main Street meets the levee.)

Hodding kept up his Tulane class during the academic year 1968–1969, and in July 1969 announced he would take a yearlong medical leave. He and Betty went to Maine in the summer but returned to Greenville when he became ill. Soon afterward they sold the Tenants Harbor house.

In late summer, young Hodding took his sixty-two-year-old father to St. Vincent de Paul, a New Orleans mental hospital, where he stayed six and a half months. Doctors told the family that Hodding's difficulties were caused by arteriosclerosis, but later described his illness as a combination of Alzheimer's and alcoholism.

He came home with a male attendant in early 1970. It seemed a better arrangement, but it was hard on Betty. Hodding wanted Betty, not his attendant, with him. "Bet!" he would shout. "Yes, darling," she would say, and they would go for a ride. When they came home, it was only a few minutes before he shouted again, "Bet!"

His friends pitied him and grieved to see a man they regarded as an intellectual giant acting like a babbling baby. Sometimes he would fall asleep at the dinner table, wake up and make a penetrating remark, and then go back to sleep. Sometimes he would take the gravy boat in his hands and drink the gravy. He always had been a drinker; now he was often disgracefully drunk. He set fires, called Washington to order battleships for his friends, and wrote checks for millions of dollars.[39] He called newspaper friends and offered them high-paying jobs on a newspaper he planned to start in Jackson.

One friend blamed Hodding's destruction on the outcome of the civil rights battle, which for years united white liberals and gave them a raison d'être—"us against the world." All that fell apart when the civil rights battle was won in the sixties. One of the prices of victory was the alienation of old white liberals and young black activists, many of whom Hodding found irresponsible.

Hodding's family felt that two great fears did him in after a quarter of a century. Since 1936 he had been afraid he would lose his paper, and since 1939 he had feared he would lose his eyesight. Now he had lost both, and his youngest son. It is true he had lost the paper voluntarily, by turning it over to his oldest son, but the fact remained that he was no longer in control.

If one reads through his correspondence, clippings, and newspaper files, the conclusion seems unavoidable that the persecution he suffered must have been a factor in his deterioration. The people of Mississippi literally drove him crazy. It is a miracle that this proud and sensitive man endured for as long as he did the calumny, the slurs, the insults, the abuse, and the ridicule that his neighbors poured upon him. Perhaps the bitter segregationists did not drive him out of town, as they did James Silver and Red Heffner, but their evil, malicious words helped break his spirit and his mind.

Hodding was scarcely aware that *Man and the River* appeared in 1970. "Mr. Carter has got the Mississippi River mixed up with God, but it comes out all right," wrote one reviewer. "Mr. Carter seems to write a style of 'fancy' journalese with a big lead weight in every important Pulitzer prize type poetic sentence. No matter. Everybody loves Hodding Carter and so do I. It's a lovely book. Just lovely."[40]

Ione Lundy continued to pretend to work for Hodding. "At the last, I'd go to Feliciana every morning about eleven. He liked to ride down to the newspaper and have a Coke or ride across the Mississippi River bridge and buy peaches. We still pretended he was writing a book."[41]

In 1971, Hodding was named recipient of the Columbia University Journalism Award, given annually by the alumni association for outstanding achievement during a career. When he heard he had won the award, Hodding said, "I'll have to go up to get it."

"Oh no, there's no mention of an event in connection with it," Betty told him. "They're going to mail it to you."

Betty went to accept the award for him. She was escorted by Willie Morris, the editor of *Harper's*, who had written a column for the *Delta Democrat-Times* when he was a Rhodes scholar.

On April 5, 1972, the nameplate on the front page of the *Delta Democrat-Times* was boxed in black. Hodding Carter had died. Stricken with a heart attack during a workout at the Nationwide Health Club the day before, he was taken to Greenville General Hospital, where he was pronounced dead on arrival. He was sixty-five years old.

Both of his sons wrote editorials about him. Young Hodding wrote in part:

Dad never took an editorial stand lightly or without fully realizing the consequences. Knowing them so well, each deviance from the often rigid conformity of his time was a matter of wrenching personal anguish. He didn't enjoy the hatred, the public scorn, the obscene letters and telephone calls. And yet, while he never provoked a fight, he never backed away from one either. In his code, there were values much higher than the applause of a transient majority.

But integrity enlisted in the service of man's dignity and shared humanity was not the only legacy he left to his family, his town, his state and his nation. As surely a part of Hodding Carter was abiding love of life, his feeling for place and community, and his driving curiosity about what lay over each new mountain. . . .

Death has stilled his voice. It has not, however, obliterated the call to conscience he heeded for so long. With God's help, and in the sure knowledge that the trail Dad blazed leads toward a better land for all our people, this newspaper will answer that call as long as there is a Carter to help guide it.[42]

Philip's editorial was titled "Big":

We called him Big because he was; Hodding Carter was the biggest of his clan, a legend, first of all in his own tribe. We loved him, followed him, tried to live up to him, puzzled over and debated him, swapped wild yarns and proud old fighting tales with him, and sometimes in recent days we cried. It is better now to remember.

Big cooked the biggest, richest gumbo north of Bayou Teche and could always eat most of it, usually at 2 a.m. He was the worst one-eyed, wrong-shouldered duck hunter in three states and the best hunting companion a shivering young son could have. He had an instant talent for risible nicknames we usually tried to forget and an endlessly inventive knack for family verse that only hinted at his deeper gifts as a poet. He knew his worst enemies' virtues and would recite them, and his favorite retort to the righteously angry was, "Yes, but . . ." He told great stories, full of villains and heroes and morals, stories for passing on. We will remember.

Big's tastes were simply catholic. He loved: Greenville, the Delta, Pass Christian, New Orleans, the South, the United States, his sons, his brother John and sister Corinne, his cousin Ham, Lawyer Phillips, the memory of his parents and his mother-in-law, Will Percy, the house he built and the trees he had planted, Phalange Word, nieces and nephews, the Maine coast, South Africa, Bowdoin College, Tulane, good whiskey, fresh figs, raw oysters, Doe's Eat Place, our family Christmas pageants and what they symbolized, sailboats of every description, "The Battle Hymn of the Republic," the Bill of Rights, Thomas Jefferson, Robert E. Lee, Abraham Lincoln, John F. and Robert Kennedy, new places, young reporters, old friends and old boots, wool shirts, poker, walking sticks, combative students, maybe 50 blocks and 50 people in New York, grandchildren, underdogs of all races and nations, and a good fight with the usual sonsofbitches. Most of all, he loved our mother, the wife who shared everything with him. We will remember.

Big had his portion of prejudices and other failings. He always thought Gen. Douglas MacArthur was a pompous ass and he never owned two suits that fit him, a dog that minded or a knife that would carve turkey. He loved the smell of a hardware store and wanted to buy one. Luckily he never did, for his business sense about all but newspapers was uncannily disastrous. Somehow he believed we actually lived on a farm, and for years he had the feed bills and the straying animals to prove it. He never lost an arm wrestling contest to any of his sons, which they considered unforgivable. He once tried golf and it bored him. He had read all his Bible and Shakespeare, but not two lines of the New York Review of Books, and if you cussed at him or in front of a lady he would knock you down. He spent most of his adult life ready to shoot, but was always glad no one dared press him to that. We will remember.

Big believed that the world was built from the family up, that civilization begins, as he said, with the cave. Nothing grieved him more than the death of his youngest son; nothing gave him more pride than our triumphs. He was the head of his clan, the heart of his tribe, a grandly human legend. And we will remember Big.[43]

For a while young Hodding continued to run the newspaper. Betty tried free-lance writing on her own; she published an article about mules in the Delta in *American Heritage*, and planned to write a book on the worldwide history of mules but never finished it. After Hodding's death, Ione Lundy continued to work for Betty, and later in 1972 Betty took her on a trip around the world.

Betty sold Feliciana in 1976 and rented an apartment in Greenville; she divided her time between the apartment and the house in New Orleans. After young Hodding joined the Jimmy Carter administration as assistant secretary of state for public affairs and moved to Washington in 1977, Philip commuted from New Orleans to run the paper. He was clearly not interested. Aware that neither son wanted to live in Greenville, Betty decided to sell the paper, despite young Hodding's ringing words in the editorial he wrote after his father's death: "This newspaper will answer [Hodding's call to conscience] as long as there is a Carter to help guide it."

Freedom Newspapers, a chain based in Santa Ana, California, bought the *Delta Democrat-Times* in February 1980. The price was between $14 and $16 million, at that time the largest price per subscriber ever obtained for any newspaper. (The circulation was about 17,000.)

"I sold the paper and I take full responsibility," Betty Carter said. "Young Hodding wasn't coming back. He and Peggy were divorced. Philip couldn't run it from New Orleans. John Gibson was talking about retiring, and I would have had to buy him out. And we needed a new $5 million press." Gibson sold his one-quarter interest in the paper at the same time. "I knew that I would never have the same wonderful relationship with Hodding's sons that I had had with Hodding," he said.

The *Delta Democrat-Times* is now a very conservative newspaper that calls for reducing Social Security, Aid to Families with Dependent Children, and crop subsidies and for selling all bridges, roads, and other public facilities to private operators. It does not support local civic and cultural groups the way the paper did when it was owned by Hodding Carter. And it never blasts injustice.

The sale repeated the pattern set years before in Hammond, where Hodding and Betty sold the *Courier* to the enemy, the Long machine. The Carters had turned down offers for the *DD-T* from other publishers, including the New York Times Company, the Gannett and Knight-Ridder chains, and John Emmerich, because they were not as high as the offer from Freedom Newspapers. No one seemed to remember or care that during the Depression the leading citizens of Greenville had put up the money to help Hodding get started so that their town would have a lively, worthwhile newspaper.

"Greenville was different from most Delta towns because of the leadership provided by the *Delta Democrat-Times*," said LeRoy Percy, William Alexander Percy's cousin and the Carters' good friend. "I believe that more than fifty percent of the white people in town were glad to see the Carters go. Now all of them would be glad to see them back."

Hodding Carter's newspaper is gone, and Greenville is no longer "different."

Acknowledgments

I shall be forever grateful to Betty Werlein Carter for her permission to use the Hodding and Betty Werlein Carter Papers at Mississippi State University in Starkville, Mississippi. The Carters saved everything—clippings, letters they received, carbons of letters they sent, memos, manuscripts, memorabilia, lists of tasks—and the collection in Starkville constitutes a rich lode for the researcher. I appreciate Betty Carter's help in other ways. She submitted graciously to countless interviews and innumerable questions; she gave me access to her unpublished memoir; she made valuable suggestions; and she called old friends and told them it was all right to talk to me.

Hodding Carter's relatives generously shared their memories of him. Valuable insights and recollections came from his sons, Hodding III and Philip; his sister, Corinne Carter Dyer; his cousins Mary Hall Bok, Theodore Bull, Congreve and Marilyn Carter, Tina Proctor, and Edie Congreve Carter Pryor.

Among Hodding Carter's friends, Joe Darlington answered questions and provided me with his diary and copies of the poems Hodding wrote in college; Maxine Carr Shannon shared a letter with me. Other friends from Hammond, Bowdoin, New Orleans, and Mississippi, who talked to me in person or on the telephone, or who wrote me letters, include Andrew Agnew, Harry Ashmore, Cleanth Brooks, David and Sue Brown, Mayor William Burnley, Roy Campbell, Theodosia Davis, Carolyn DeCell, Lew Dietz, Hildegarde Drott Dodson, Charles "Pie" Dufour, Shelby Foote, Mrs. J. M. Fourmy, Helen Generelly, John Gibson, Georgina Stanley Hall, Josephine

329

Acknowledgments

Haxton, Kenneth Haxton, John Herbers, Jeff Howie, Alsia Corbera Hyde, William C. Keady, Bern Keating, Julius Kohler, Albert Lake, Donovan Lancaster, Ed Lipscomb, Ione Lundy, Eva McCracken, O. C. McDavid, Vincent and Doris Maggio, Henry D. Marsh, Dr. Don Marshall, Wilson Minor, Irma Nesom, Arvid Nordstrom, Dr. Matthew Page, LeRoy Percy, Jack Potts, Senator David Pryor, Clarke Reed, James Robertshaw, Alden Sawyer, Bobby and Mary McCormick Sferruza, Margaret Shea, Father Edward Sheridan, S.J., Lydel Sims, the Honorable Frank Smith, Jake Stein, Jane Swan, Donald Webber, Don and Virginia Wetherbee, and Mrs. Tilghman Whitley.

Librarians at many institutions were extremely helpful. At the Mitchell Memorial Library, Mississippi State University, Anne Wells, Mattie Sink, and Lynne Mueller were saintly, patient, and generous. At Bowdoin College, where I had access to Hodding Carter's file, Charles Calhoun and Martha J. Adams went out of their way to assist me. I found useful files also at Southeastern Louisiana University in Hammond, at the Graduate School of Journalism of Columbia University, in the archives of the library at Tulane University, in the Mississippi State Archives in Jackson, and at the William Alexander Percy Library in Greenville, where Clint Bagley came to my aid many times.

I am grateful for a grant from the Ludwig Vogelstein Foundation, which was inordinately helpful. I would like to thank the National Endowment for the Humanities for a travel-to-collections grant.

It seems appropriate to acknowledge hospitality that made my research trips pleasant. My gratitude goes to Jim and Lib Bird, John and Celia Emmerich, Bobby and Mary McCormick Sferruza, and Forrest and Nancy Shivers.

For legal work necessary to obtain Hodding Carter's Federal Bureau of Investigation file under the Freedom of Information Act, I am eternally grateful to Kim Augustine Otis of Princeton. The Reporter's Committee on Freedom of the Press was also helpful.

Acknowledgments

Many people, at various times, read all or part of the manuscript and made valuable suggestions. I thank Ashley Brown, John Herbers, Lolly O'Brien, Michelle Preston, Robert Sherrill, and Thomas A. Underwood. Tom Underwood also suggested this project to me.

Books by W. Hodding Carter, Jr.

Lower Mississippi, 1942
Civilian Defense of the United States (with Ernest Dupuy), 1942
The Winds of Fear, 1944
Flood Crest, 1947
Southern Legacy, 1950
Gulf Coast Country (with Anthony Ragusin), 1951
Where Main Street Meets the River, 1953
John Law Wasn't So Wrong: The Story of Louisiana's Horn of Plenty, 1952
Robert E. Lee and the Road of Honor, 1955
So Great a Good: A History of the Episcopal Church in Louisiana and Christ Church Cathedral (with Betty Carter), 1955
The Marquis de Lafayette: Bright Sword for Freedom, 1958

The Angry Scar: The Story of Reconstruction, 1959
First Person Rural, 1963
Doomed Road of Empire: The Spanish Trail of Conquest (with Betty Carter), 1963
The Ballad of Catfoot Grimes and Other Verses, 1964
So the Heffners Left McComb, 1965
The Commandos of World War II, 1966
The Past as Prelude: New Orleans, 1718–1968 (editor), 1968
Their Words Were Bullets: The Southern Press in War, Reconstruction, and Peace, 1969
Man and the River: The Mississippi, 1970

Notes

A NOTE ON THE SOURCES

The primary documentary source for this biography was the Hodding and Betty Werlein Carter Papers at the Mitchell Memorial Library, Mississippi State University, Starkville, Mississippi. This collection is referred to in the notes as "Carter Papers."

Throughout the notes, an asterisk indicates an interview with the author. In addition, the following abbreviations are used:

BB	Bernice Baumgarten
BC	Betty Werlein Carter
BCOH	Betty Carter oral history, University of Southern Mississippi, volume 150 (1979)
BCUM	Betty Carter, unpublished memoirs, in Mrs. Carter's possession
DD-T	*Delta Democrat-Times*
EW	Elizabeth Werlein
HC	William Hodding Carter, Jr.
HC III	William Hodding Carter III
HDC	Hammond, Louisiana, *Daily Courier*
JDN	Jackson, Mississippi, *Daily News*
NYT	New York *Times*
NYTM	*The New York Times Magazine*
NYTBR	*The New York Times Book Review*
SEP	*The Saturday Evening Post*

Chapter I

1. HC, *First Person Rural* (Garden City, NY: Doubleday, 1963), p. 50.
2. W. D. Dunn to registrar, Bowdoin College, May 11, 1923.
3. HC to Maxine Carr, Sept. 23, 1923.
4. *Julius Kohler, Newton, MA, July 17, 1989.
5. *Mary Hall Bok, Camden, ME, July 21, 1989.
6. Ibid.
7. *Donovan Lancaster, Brunswick, ME, July 19, 1989.
8. Milton Starr to HC, May 2, 1950.
9. *Julius Kohler, Newton, MA, July 17, 1989.
10. HC, *Where Main Street Meets the River* (New York: Rinehart, 1953), p. 288.
11. The information about black students at Bowdoin and other New England colleges comes from "The

Blackman at Bowdoin," an honors thesis in history written by Kenneth Chenault at Bowdoin in 1973. Chenault concluded: "Bowdoin does not deserve its reputation as a 'friend of the Negro,' because Bowdoin had no concern whatsoever for the welfare of the Blackman."

12. *The Orient*, Bowdoin College, March 10, 1926.

13. HC, "Bowdoin College and the Bill of Rights," *Marine Digest*, Fall 1966.

14. Ibid.

15. *Donovan Lancaster, Brunswick, ME, July 19, 1989.

16. HC, "Quatrain," *The Bowdoin Quill*, December 1924.

17. HC to Carl Sandburg, Sept. 20, 1950.

18. HC to his family, June 25, 1927.

Chapter 2

1. HC to R. M. Killgore, March 8, 1965.

2. *Main Street*, p. 186.

3. R. R. Rochester, "The Louisiana Strawberry, Queen of Luscious Fruits," brochure published by Tangipahoa Parish *Daily Courier*, 1935.

4. *Main Street*, p. 9.

5. HC, *Southern Legacy* (Baton Rouge: Louisiana State University Press, 1950), p. 53.

6. *Main Street*, p. 8.

7. *Southern Legacy*, p. 53.

8. HC, unpublished autobiographical manuscript.

9. "From the Publisher's Desk," *New Orleans*, n.d., p. 5.

10. *Mrs. Tilghman Whitley, Hammond, LA, June 27, 1988.

11. *Southern Legacy*, p. 20.

12. *Main Street*, p. 6.

13. *HC III, Washington, DC, March 18, 1988.

14. *Eva McCracken, Hammond, LA, June 27, 1988.

15. *Theodore Bull, Princeton, NJ, June 14, 1989.

16. *DD-T*, Oct. 12, 1939.

17. HC to Philip Wilbanks, March 12, 1958.

18. *Southern Legacy*, p. 19.

19. Ibid., p. 21.

20. HC to Hermann Deutsch, Nov. 1, 1934.

21. *Main Street*, p. 228.

22. *Southern Legacy*, p. 38.

23. *Mrs. Tilghman Whitley, Hammond, LA, June 27, 1988.

24. *Southern Legacy*, p. 32.

25. Ibid., p. 31.

26. *Margaret Shea, Camden, ME, July 21, 1989.

27. *Hildegarde Drott Dodson, April 17, 1990 (telephone).

28. Ibid.

29. *Maxine Carr Shannon, North Salem, NY, July 27, 1988.

30. Hammond *Vindicator*, June 1, 1923.

31. James E. Robinson, "Hodding Carter: Southern Liberal 1907–1972," Ph.D. dissertation, Department of History, Mississippi State University, 1974, p. 9.

Chapter 3

1. BCUM.

2. Ibid.

3. *BC, Alexandria, VA, April 6, 1988.

4. *Corinne Carter Dyer, New Orleans, June 2, 1988.

5. *BC, Alexandria, VA, April 6, 1988.

6. Ibid.

7. *Cleanth Brooks, New Haven, CT, July 16, 1989.

8. HC, unpublished autobiographical fragment.

9. Ibid.

10. HC, address to fall convocation, Tulane University, 1948. Text in Carter Papers.

11. *Main Street*, p. 262.

12. HC, "River Plantation," in *The Ballad of Catfoot Grimes* (Garden City, NY: Doubleday, 1964).

13. *Charles "Pie" Dufour, New Orleans, May 9, 1990.

14. BCUM.

15. Ibid.

16. *BC, Alexandria, VA, April 6, 1988.

17. BCUM.

18. Ibid.

19. *BC, Alexandria, VA, April 6, 1988.

20. BC to HC, Oct. 8, 1931.

21. *Wilson Minor, Jackson, MS, January 29, 1990.

22. *BC, Alexandria, VA, April 6, 1988.

23. Copy of resolution in Carter Papers.

24. Kent Cooper to HC, June 6, 1946.

Chapter 4

1. BCOH.

2. *Main Street*, p. 1.

3. *Alsia Corbera Hyde, July 20, 1990 (telephone).

4. *Main Street*, p. 15.

5. Ibid., p. 310.

6. *Alsia Corbera Hyde, July 20, 1990 (telephone).

7. *HDC*, Feb. 5, 1935.

8. *HDC*, Oct. 12, 1932.

9. *HDC*, May 13, 1932.

10. *HDC*, Feb. 17, 1933.

11. *Main Street*, p. 20.

12. *HDC*, May 14, 1933.

13. *Main Street*, p. 188.

14. BC, manuscript. Carter Papers.

15. BC, typescript. Carter Papers.

16. HC to BC, April 9, 1935.

17. *HDC*, July 13, 1935.

18. *HDC*, July 8, 1932.

19. *HDC*, Aug. 22, 1932.

20. *HDC*, Aug. 20, 1932.

21. *BC, Alexandria, VA, April 6, 1988.

22. *HDC*, May 30, 1933.

23. *HDC*, June 15, 1933.

24. *HDC*, June 21, 1933; *HDC*, June 23, 1933.

25. *HDC*, June 29, 1933.

26. *HDC*, July 10, 1933.

27. *HDC*, July 22, 1933.

28. *HDC*, Aug. 29, 1932.

29. *HDC*, June 20, 1933.

30. *HDC*, Nov. 28, 1933.

31. Robinson, "Hodding Carter," p. 36.

32. *HDC*, Dec. 4, 1933.

33. *Alsia Corbera Hyde, July 20, 1990 (telephone).

34. Lawrence Franklin Ingram, "Hodding Carter Rebels," master's thesis, Southeastern Louisiana College, 1968, p. 78.

35. *Main Street*, p. 52.

36. Westbrook Pegler, Washington *Star*, Aug. 22, 1934.

37. Wayne Parish, "Why Senator Huey Long Rules in Louisiana," *Literary Digest*, Sept. 8, 1934.

38. Bruce Bliven to HC, Aug. 9, 1933.

39. *Main Street*, p. 313.

40. HC, "Kingfish to Crawfish," *The New Republic*, Jan. 24, 1934.

41. Bruce Bliven to HC, Sept. 14, 1934.

42. HC, "The Kingfish on His Way,"

The New Republic, Nov. 21, 1934.

43. Albert Shaw to HC, Jan. 1, 1935.

44. HC, and Gerald L. K. Smith, "How Come Huey Long?," *The New Republic*, Feb. 13, 1935.

45. T. Harry Williams, *Huey Long* (New York: Alfred A. Knopf, 1969), p. 882.

46. Edwin P. Guy, L. C. Page & Company, to HC, Aug. 9, 1935; HC to Edwin P. Guy, Aug. 15, 1935.

47. Rowe Wright to HC, March 28, 1932.

48. *The Ballad of Catfoot Grimes and Other Verses*.

49. HC, "Southern Reconstruction 1935 and 1865," *The Atlantic Monthly*, March 1935.

50. HC to Dean Paul Nixon, Nov. 7, 1935. Alumni files, Bowdoin College.

51. *The Tower*, Louisiana State University, n.d. Clipping in Carter Papers.

52. HC to Hermann Deutsch, Nov. 1, 1934. Archives and Special Collections, Center for Regional Studies, Southeastern Louisiana University.

53. *HDC*, Dec. 26, 1935.

54. Ingram, "Hodding Carter Rebels," p. 93.

55. *HDC*, May 29, 1936.

56. *Main Street*, p. 58.

Chapter 5

1. David Cohn, "Small Town Daily," unpublished manuscript. David Cohn Papers, University of Mississippi.

2. *BC, New Orleans, June 1, 1988.

3. *Main Street*, p. 74.

4. *Don Wetherbee, Chapel Hill, NC, Sept. 14, 1988.

5. *Don Wetherbee, Chapel Hill, NC, Jan. 29, 1991.

6. Arnold Rampersad, *The Life of Langston Hughes*, vol. 1: *1902–1941. I, Too, Sing America* (New York: Oxford University Press, 1986), pp. 321–322.

7. *Conversations with Shelby Foote*, ed. William C. Carter (Jackson: University Press of Mississippi, 1989), p. 207.

8. *DD-T*, June 19, 1945.

9. *BC, New Orleans, June 1, 1988.

10. BCOH.

11. HC, "The Story of the Delta Star," *Delta Star*, Nov. 28, 1937.

12. *Ed Lipscomb, Aug. 2, 1989 (telephone).

13. Bob Bowers to HC, June 17, 1947.

14. *Main Street*, p. 99.

15. *BC, New Orleans. June 1, 1988.

16. William Alexander Percy to HC, Dec. 23, 1936.

17. *Shelby Foote, Memphis, June 20, 1988.

18. *Don Wetherbee, Chapel Hill, NC, Sept. 14, 1988.

19. *Shelby Foote, Memphis, June 20, 1988.

20. BCOH.

21. Ibid.

22. *Don Wetherbee, Chapel Hill, NC, Sept. 14, 1988.

23. *Shelby Foote, Memphis, June 20, 1988.

24. *BC, New Orleans, June 1, 1988.

25. William Alexander Percy to HC, n.d.

26. *BC, New Orleans, June 1, 1988.

27. *Delta Star*, April 14, 1937.

28. *Delta Star*, June 12, 1937.

29. *Main Street*, p. 81.

30. Ibid., p. 87; *BC, New Orleans,

June 8, 1988.

31. *Delta Star,* July 16, 1937.

32. *Shelby Foote, Memphis, June 20, 1988.

33. *BC, New Orleans, June 1, 1988.

34. *Don Wetherbee, Chapel Hill, NC, Jan. 29, 1991.

35. Robinson, "Hodding Carter," p. 56.

36. HC, "Information about Delta Democrat-Times Situation," type-script, 1944.

37. HC to William Alexander Percy, Sept. 6, 1940.

38. *James Robertshaw, Greenville, MS, June 8, 1988.

39. Henry D. Marsh, unpublished typescript. Carter Papers.

40. *Don Wetherbee, Chapel Hill, NC, Sept. 14, 1988.

41. Shelby Foote, *Follow Me Down* (New York: Dial, 1950), pp. 22–24.

Chapter 6

1. *DD-T,* Sept. 29, 1938.

2. HC, unpublished typescript.

3. *Main Street,* p. 122.

4. *DD-T,* Nov. 14, 1938.

5. *DD-T,* Nov. 16, 1938.

6. *DD-T,* Nov. 22, 1938.

7. *DD-T,* Jan. 17, 1939.

8. *DD-T,* Jan. 4, 1940.

9. *Southern Legacy,* p. 11.

10. *DD-T,* Oct. 19, 1938.

11. *DD-T,* June 2, 1939.

12. *DD-T,* March 22, 1939.

13. *DD-T,* March 10, 1939.

14. *DD-T,* Oct. 28, 1938.

15. *DD-T,* Dec. 19, 1939.

16. *DD-T,* Nov. 25, 1938.

17. *DD-T,* Nov. 6, 1940.

18. *DD-T,* Nov. 21, 1938.

19. HC, printed release for National Cotton Council. Carter Papers.

20. Wesley W. Stout to HC, Jan. 16, 1939.

21. Ed Lipscomb to HC, July 3, 1939, and memorabilia, Carter Papers.

22. Joseph Darlington to the author, Jan. 18, 1990.

23. Arthur Wild to HC, telegram, n.d.

24. Jerome D. Greene to HC, April 27, 1939.

25. William Alexander Percy to BC, May 11, 1939.

26. *Don Wetherbee, Chapel Hill, NC, Jan. 29, 1991.

27. *BC, New Orleans, June 1, 1988.

28. Joseph Darlington to HC, Sept. 8, 1938.

29. *David Brown, Morehead, KY, Sept. 6–7, 1989; *Henry D. Marsh, Jackson, MS, June 10, 1988.

30. Archibald MacLeish to HC, Nov. 24, 1939.

31. Ralph Ingersoll to HC, Dec. 4, 1939.

32. Paul Mallon to HC, Oct. 21, 1940.

33. *Philip Carter, New Orleans, May 8, 1990.

34. Harold Strauss to HC, Feb. 8, 1940.

35. Harold Strauss to HC, March 7, 1940.

36. BCOH.

37. Ralph Ingersoll to HC, April 12, 1941.

38. *Don Wetherbee, Chapel Hill, NC, Sept. 14, 1988.

39. *Main Street,* p. 114.

40. Ibid., p. 115.

41. Robinson, "Hodding Carter," p. 62.

42. HC, "Showdown at Memphis," *The Nation,* July 20, 1940.

43. *Main Street*, p. 118.
44. *DD-T*, Oct. 3, 1940.
45. *DD-T*, Oct. 13, 1940.
46. *DD-T*, Nov. 18, 1940.
47. BCUM.
48. William Alexander Percy to HC, Sept. 2, 1940.
49. HC to William Alexander Percy, Sept. 6, 1940.
50. William Alexander Percy to HC, Sept. 7, 1940.
51. *DD-T*, June 15, 1945.

Chapter 7

1. *Albert Lake, Greenville, MS, June 23, 1988.
2. HC to BC, Dec. 25, 1940.
3. *DD-T*, Jan. 5, 1941.
4. HC to BC, Dec. 25, 1940.
5. HC to BC, Dec. 28, 1940.
6. HC to BC, Jan. 4, 1941.
7. HC to BC, Jan. 2, 1941.
8. HC to BC, Jan. 8, 1941.
9. HC to BC, Jan. 4, 1941.
10. Ibid.
11. BC to HC, Jan. 5, 1941.
12. HC to BC, Jan. 8, 1941.
13. Ibid.
14. *O. C. McDavid, Jackson, MS, Jan. 29, 1990.
15. BC to EW, Feb. 1, 1941.
16. John Carter to HC, Feb. 3, 1941.
17. BC to HC, n.d.
18. HC to BC, n.d.
19. Medical records, U.S. Department of Veterans' Affairs.
20. HC to BC, April 29, 1941.
21. *Main Street*, p. 139.
22. BC to HC, n.d.
23. *DD-T*, June 30, 1941.
24. John T. Kneebone, *Southern Liberal Journalists and the Issue of Race, 1920–1944* (Chapel Hill: University of North Carolina Press, 1985), p. 198.
25. BC to EW, Dec. 3, 1941.
26. BC to EW, Dec. 31, 1941.
27. BC to EW, n.d.
28. *DD-T*, Dec. 19, 1941.
29. *Main Street*, p. 140.
30. Ibid., p. 143.
31. BC to EW, Jan. 20, 1942.
32. BC to EW, Feb. 4, 1942.
33. BC to EW, Jan. 27, 1942.
34. BC to EW, Feb. 4, 1942.
35. BC to EW, March 12, 1942.
36. BC to EW, March 29, 1942.
37. BC to EW, March 21, 1942.
38. Ibid.
39. BC to EW, Sept. 25, 1942.
40. Horace Reynolds, *NYTBR*, Dec. 6, 1942.
41. BC to EW, Dec. 16, 1942.
42. BC to EW, Feb. 24, 1942.
43. William T. Wynn to HC, Feb. 24, 1942.
44. BC to EW, June 21, 1942.
45. Statement of *DD-T* financial history in Carter Papers.
46. BC to EW, Dec. 16, 1942.
47. *Main Street*, p. 191.
48. John Carter to BC, April 13, 1943.
49. Ibid.
50. John Carter to HC, June 13, 1943.
51. HC to BC, July 14, 1943.
52. HC to BC, Feb. 2, 1943.
53. *Georgina Stanley Hall, Camden, ME, July 21, 1989.
54. HC to BC, March 25, 1943.
55. HC to BC, April 16, 1943.
56. HC to BC, July 6, 1943.
57. HC to BC, July 14, 1943.
58. HC to BC, Aug. 24, 1943.

59. HC to BC, July 23, 1943.
60. Aziza Hassanein to HC, Nov. 12, 1943.
61. BC to HC, April 13, 1942.
62. BC to EW, April 24, 1942.
63. HC to BC, Aug. 24, 1943.

Chapter 8

1. *HC III, Washington, DC, Nov. 27, 1989.
2. Stanley M. Rinehart to HC, Nov. 30, 1943.
3. HC to BB, March 8, 1944.
4. HC to BB, July 26, 1944.
5. HC to BB, April 3, 1944.
6. HC to BB, May 10, 1944.
7. BCOH.
8. *Georgina Stanley Hall, Camden, ME, July 21, 1989.
9. New York *Herald Tribune*, Oct. 22, 1944; C. V. Terry, *NYTBR*, Oct. 22, 1944; Bucklin Moon, *Book Week*, Oct. 22, 1944.
10. *The New Yorker*, Oct. 22, 1944.
11. Unidentified clipping in Carter Papers.
12. HC to BB, Oct. 28, 1944.
13. HC to BB, July 26, 1944.
14. EW to HC, n.d.
15. HC to BB, Oct. 26, 1944.
16. HC to BB, Nov. 6, 1944.
17. HC to BB, Dec. 15, 1944.
18. A. R. Dillard to HC, Feb. 12, 1944.
19. Donald W. Reynolds to HC, Feb. 21, 1944.
20. *DD-T*, Sept. 14, 1944.
21. HC to Donald Smith, June 13, 1944.
22. HC to Will Carter, June 14, 1944.
23. HC to Holland Felts, June 13, 1944.
24. Holland Felts to HC, July 5, 1944.
25. John Gibson to HC, Sept. 17, 1944.
26. Holland Felts to HC, Oct. 16, 1944.
27. HC to Holland Felts, Oct. 26, 1944.
28. Holland Felts to HC, Dec. 18, 1944.
29. HC to Dean Paul Nixon, Feb. 5, 1945.
30. Milton Starr to HC, Dec. 16, 1944.
31. Donald W. Reynolds to HC, Jan. 10, 1945.
32. Medical records, U.S. Department of Veterans' Affairs.
33. HC to BB, Feb. 21, 1945.
34. HC to BB, Jan. 14, 1945.
35. John Gibson to HC, Jan. 10, 1945.
36. Holland Felts to HC, Jan. 12, 1945.
37. Donald W. Reynolds to HC, Feb. 3, 1945.
38. HC to Donald W. Reynolds, Feb. 6, 1945.
39. BCOH.
40. HC to BB, March 20, 1945.
41. HC to BB, April 23, 1945.
42. *Main Street*, p. 195.
43. *DD-T*, June 15, 1945.
44. *Ione Lundy, Greenville, MS, June 7, 1988; James Robertshaw, Greenville, June 8, 1988; Vincent and Doris Maggio, Greenville, June 21, 1988; David Brown, Morehead, KY, Sept. 6–7, 1989.

Chapter 9

1. *DD-T*, July 22, 1945.
2. *DD-T*, June 17, 1945.
3. *DD-T*, July 19, 1945.
4. *DD-T*, July 24, 1945.
5. HC to BB, June 24, 1945.
6. HC to BB, July 30, 1945.
7. *DD-T*, Aug. 13, 1945.
8. *DD-T*, Aug. 30, 1945.
9. *DD-T*, July 26, 1945.
10. *PM*, Aug. 8, 1945.

11. BCUM.
12. *Philip Carter, New Orleans, May 8, 1990.
13. *DD-T*, Jan. 22, 1946.
14. *BC, New Orleans, June 1, 1988.
15. *DD-T*, Oct. 14, 1945.
16. *Jake Stein, Greenville, MS, June 7, 1988. Stein added that Hodding was "a saint, brilliant, outspoken, fearless."
17. BCOH.
18. *LeRoy Percy, Greenville, MS, June 9, 1988.
19. *DD-T*, Oct. 11, 1945.
20. *DD-T*, Jan. 28, 1946.
21. *Dr. Matthew Page, Greenville, MS, Feb. 14, 1990.
22. HC to BB, Nov. 23, 1946.
23. Paul Flowers, Memphis *Commercial-Appeal*, March 24, 1946.
24. *DD-T*, Oct. 14, 1945.
25. HC to BB, Jan. 25, 1946.
26. HC to BB, April 19, 1946.
27. *Lew Dietz, Rockport, ME, July 22, 1989.
28. Portland, Maine, *Press-Herald*, May 8, 1946.
29. *John Gibson, Greenville, MS, Feb. 14, 1990.
30. "The Truth About the Pulitzer Prize Awards," *McCall's*, May 1966.
31. HC to Dr. Edwin Davis, May 11, 1946.
32. HC to Millard Browne, May 24, 1946.
33. Frank Smith, *Congressman from Mississippi* (New York: Pantheon, 1964), p. 66.
34. Ibid., p. 35.
35. HC, " 'The Man' from Mississippi—Bilbo," *NYTM*, June 30, 1946; *Main Street*, p. 183.
36. Jackson *Clarion-Ledger*, June 5, 1946.
37. *Main Street*, p. 183.
38. Memphis *Commercial-Appeal*, June 13, 1946.
39. *DD-T*, June 16, 1946.
40. " 'The Man.' "
41. *DD-T*, July 1, 1946.
42. *DD-T*, Jan. 7, 1947.
43. HC, "Chip on Our Shoulder Down South," *SEP*, Nov. 2, 1946.
44. *DD-T*, July 5, 1946.
45. HC, "Bilbo and the South," on Mutual Radio Network, Aug. 16, 1946. Text in Carter papers.
46. The Reverend N. Paul Arline, Jr., to HC, Aug. 17, 1946.
47. "Chip on Our Shoulder."
48. Memphis *Commercial-Appeal*, Dec. 13, 1946.
49. *DD-T*, Jan. 27, 1947.

Chapter 10

1. *Frank Smith, Jackson, MS, Jan. 29, 1990.
2. *Bern Keating, Greenville, MS, Feb. 16, 1990.
3. *James Robertshaw, Greenville, MS, June 8, 1988.
4. *John Gibson, Greenville, MS, Feb. 14, 1990.
5. *BC, Greenville, MS, Feb. 13, 1990.
6. HC to HC III, Oct. 9, 1953.
7. *Henry D. Marsh, Jackson, MS, June 10, 1988.
8. *John Gibson, Greenville, MS, Feb. 14, 1990.
9. *Southern Legacy*, p. 15.
10. S. V. Anderson to HC, Aug. 4, 1950.
11. *John Gibson, Greenville, MS, June 8, 1988.
12. *Vincent and Doris Maggio, Green-

ville, MS, June 21, 1988.

13. *Jane Swan, Opelika, AL, Feb. 11, 1989.

14. *David Brown, Morehead, KY, Sept. 6–7, 1989.

15. *Henry D. Marsh, Jackson, MS, June 10, 1988.

16. *Main Street*, p. 104.

17. *Shelby Foote, Memphis, June 20, 1988.

18. HC to "Gene," Oct. 17, 1954.

19. BC to HC, Dec. 11, 1952.

20. HC, address upon receiving William Allen White Foundation citation for journalistic merit, 1961. Reprinted as "The Editor as Citizen," in Warren K. Agee, *The Press and the Public Interest* (Washington, DC: Public Affairs Press, 1968), p. 152.

21. HC to Fred Stein, Binghamton, NY, *Press*, May 14, 1951.

22. *Main Street*, p. 318.

23. *DD-T*, Nov. 18, 1949.

24. *DD-T*, May 29, 1950.

25. HC to HC III, Jan. 17, 1950.

26. BC to Mr. and Mrs. Easton King, July 27, 1950.

27. HC to HC III, Jan. 22, 1951.

28. *Shelby Foote, May 10, 1991 (telephone).

29. For information about the Levee Press, I am indebted to a fine, unpublished study done by James Robertshaw, Jr., when he was a senior at Greenville High School.

30. Charles Poore, *NYTBR*, n.d. Clipping in Carter Papers.

31. *Main Street*, pp. 199–213.

32. Irving Howe, "The Genius as Windbag," *The Nation*, March 10, 1951.

33. HC to Mrs. R. J. Ham, July 3, 1947.

34. HC to BB, July 29, 1947.

35. Knox Burger, "Senator in the Mississippi Mud," *NYTBR*, Dec. 14, 1947. Clipping in Carter Papers.

36. David Carpenter, "Book Parade," *The Daily Worker*, Dec. 3, 1947.

37. *The New Yorker*, Dec. 13, 1947.

38. Frances Baker, "Turns with the Bookworm," *JDN*, Nov. 23, 1947.

39. HC to BB, Dec. 8, 1947.

40. HC to BB, March 18, 1947.

41. HC to BB, Aug. 18, 1947.

42. John Selby to BB, Aug. 28, 1947.

43. Paul Flowers, "Of Books and Publishers," Memphis *Commercial-Appeal*, Jan. 8, 1950. Clipping in Carter Papers.

44. Charlotte Capers. Unidentified clipping in Carter Papers.

45. Bill Skelton. Unidentified clipping in Carter Papers.

46. Lillian Smith, "The South As It Is—The Ideas That Stir Its People," *NYTBR*, May 2, 1950.

47. HC to BB, May 18, 1948.

48. HC to BB, June 17, 1948.

49. HC to BC, Oct. 28, 1952.

50. HC, "You Need Enemies," *This Week*, Nov. 14, 1948.

51. HC to Carl Brandt, May 24, 1948.

Chapter II

1. S. R. King, "An Editorial." Clipping from Unidentified source in Carter Papers.

2. *DD-T*, Jan. 26, 1947.

3. HC to Gilbert P. Buillis, July 3, 1947.

4. HC to Lucille Bass, Feb. 22, 1950.

5. *DD-T*, Feb. 3, 1948.

6. HC, address to journalism students at Washington and Lee University, as reported in the Lynchburg, Virginia, *News*, Feb. 18, 1948.

7. *DD-T*, Feb. 10, 1948.

8. HC, "A Southern Liberal Looks at Civil Rights," *NYTM*, Aug. 8, 1948.

9. *The Christian Science Monitor*, May 24, 1948.

10. "A Southern Liberal."

11. *DD-T*, Jan. 30, 1948.

12. "A Southern Liberal."

13. Ibid.

14. HC, Atlanta *Journal*, May 23, 1948.

15. Ray Sprigle, "I Was a Negro in the South for 30 Days," booklet reprinting the newspaper series. Carter Papers.

16. *DD-T*, Nov. 7, 1948.

17. Clippings from New York *Herald Tribune* in Carter Papers.

18. HC, "A Southerner Tells What's Wrong with the North," *Look*, Aug. 16, 1949.

19. James Wechsler, New York *Post*, Aug. 8, 1949.

20. Columbia Press Service release, Oct. 22, 1948. Carter Papers.

21. Lillian Smith, "A Southerner Talking," Chicago *Defender*, Feb. 5, 1949.

22. *Southern Legacy*, pp. 167–170.

23. Ibid., p. 168.

24. *DD-T*, June 6, 1949.

25. *Southern Legacy*, pp. 169–170.

26. HC to Raymond Holbrook, Feb. 12, 1948.

27. HC to Susan Myrick, Nov. 7, 1949.

28. *Main Street*, p. 257.

29. *Doris Maggio, Greenville, MS, June 21, 1988.

30. HC, "The Mote and the Beam of Bigotry," *The American Mercury*, March 1947.

31. *DD-T*, Aug. 1, 1951.

32. HC, address to fall convocation, Tulane University, 1948. Text in Carter Papers.

33. "A Southern Liberal."

34. HC to Joseph F. Ellis, Oct. 3, 1950.

35. HC, "What One Southern Town Has Done," *Atlanta Journal Magazine*, March 7, 1948.

36. "A Southern Liberal."

37. *DD-T*, Feb. 27, 1949.

38. HC, "Looking at the South." *JDN*, May 21, 1950.

39. Nicholas Lemann. *The Promised Land: The Great Black Migration and How It Changed America* (New York: Alfred A. Knopf, 1991).

40. "A Southern Liberal."

41. HC, "New Rebel Yell in Dixie," *Collier's*, July 9, 1949.

42. Walter White, "Appraising 'New Rebel Yell in Dixie,'" New York *Herald Tribune*, July 7, 1949. Clipping in Carter Papers.

43. HC, "A Community Is Outraged," *DD-T*, July 10, 1949.

44. *Main Street*, p. 228.

45. *DD-T*, June 28, 1949; *DD-T*, July 15, 1949.

46. HC, "Looking at the South," *JDN*, Sept. 11, 1949.

47. *DD-T*, June 25, 1950.

48. *DD-T*, May 28, 1950.

49. *DD-T*, Feb. 28, 1950.

50. *DD-T*, July 26, 1950.

51. *DD-T*, Nov. 27, 1949.

52. *DD-T*, Feb. 3, 1948.

53. *DD-T*, June 9, 1950.

54. HC, "Looking at the South," *JDN*, June 11, 1950.

55. *DD-T*, Oct. 11, 1950.

56. *DD-T*, Feb. 13, 1952.

57. James W. Loewen and Charles Sallis, eds., *Mississippi: Conflict and Change* (New York: Pantheon, 1974).

58. *DD-T*, June 15, 1952.
59. HC to Captain Wendell F. Kline, March 24, 1953.
60. *DD-T*, June 7, 1953.
61. Henry D. Marsh, unpublished typescript. Carter Papers.
62. Milton McKaye, "The South's Fighting Editor," *SEP*, June 14, 1947.
63. HC to Mrs. John B. Douds, March 26, 1951.
64. *DD-T*, July 27, 1950.
65. HC to Mrs. John B. Douds, March 26, 1951.
66. *DD-T*, Jan. 9, 1952.
67. HC interview with Max K. Gilstrap, *The Christian Science Monitor*, June 29, 1951.
68. Associated Press story, New Orleans *Times-Picayune*, Sept. 10, 1952. Clipping in Tulane University Library archives.
69. *DD-T*, Oct. 24, 1952.
70. BC to HC, Nov. 3, 1952.
71. BWC to HC, Nov. 15, 1952.
72. HC to BWC, Nov. 9, 1952.
73. HC, "Segregation's Way in One Southern Town," *NYTM*, April 5, 1953.
74. Walter White, letter to the editor, *NYTM*, April 26, 1953.
75. *DD-T*, April 29, 1953.
76. BCOH.
77. HC to Richard O. Arneson, Dec. 21, 1953.

Chapter 12

1. *David Brown, Morehead, KY, Sept. 6–7, 1989.
2. *Philip Carter, New Orleans, May 8, 1990.
3. *DD-T*, May 20, 1954.
4. Quoted in HC, "Racial Crisis in the Deep South," *SEP*, Dec. 17, 1954.
5. *DD-T*, Sept. 5, 1954.
6. *DD-T*, Sept. 6, 1954.
7. Quoted in Smith, *Congressman from Mississippi*, p. 10.
8. *David Brown, Morehead, KY, Sept. 6–7, 1989.
9. *DD-T*, Dec. 19, 1954.
10. "Racial Crisis."
11. *DD-T*, Dec. 19, 1954.
12. HC, "A Wave of Terror Threatens the South," *Look*, March 22, 1955.
13. Text in Carter Papers.
14. Undated clipping in Carter Papers.
15. David Halberstam, "In the Eye of the Storm: The South in 1955," in Dudley Clendinen, ed., *The Prevailing South: Life and Politics in a Changing Culture* (Atlanta: Longstreet, 1988).
16. C. L. Golightly, *The Progressive*, March 1955; Rowan quoted in Kneebone, *Southern Liberal Journalists*, p. 22.
17. Grant Reynolds, quoted in Pittsburgh *Courier*, Jan. 28, 1956.
18. *JDN*, Feb. 17, 1955.
19. HC to Ellett Lawrence and Ellett Lawrence II, Feb. 28, 1955.
20. HC to Tom Karsell, Feb. 5, 1955.
21. "A Wave of Terror."
22. *JDN*, March 9, 1955. Clipping in Carter Papers.
23. *JDN*, March 10, 1955.
24. Tom Ethridge, "Mississippi Notebook." Clipping in Carter Papers.
25. O. L. Marr, "The Farmer from Quietude" (Timmonsville, SC, n.d.). Clipping in Carter Papers.
26. *JDN*, April 1, 1955; New Orleans *Times-Picayune*, April 2, 1955. Clippings in Carter Papers.

27. HC, "The South and I," *Look*, June 28, 1955, p. 74.
28. *John Herbers, Washington, DC, March 22, 1990.
29. Mrs. Clifford J. (Virginia) Durr to HC, June 23, 1955; HC to Mrs. Clifford J. Durr, June 29, 1955.
30. "The South and I."
31. *Jack Potts, March 18, 1990 (telephone).
32. *Father Edward Sheridan, New Orleans, June 1, 1988.
33. HC to "Dear boys," May 23, 1955.
34. *Alden Sawyer, Yarmouth, MA, July 17, 1989.
35. *Roy Campbell, Greenville, MS, June 22, 1988.
36. Ibid.
37. *John Herbers, Washington, DC, March 22, 1990.
38. *John Emmerich, Greenwood, MS, January 28, 1990.
39. *Kenneth Haxton, Greenville, MS, June 22, 1988.
40. *Philip Carter, New Orleans, May 8, 1990.
41. *John Gibson, Greenville, MS, Feb. 14, 1990.
42. *Carolyn DeCell, April 3, 1990 (telephone).
43. *BC, Greenville, MS, Feb. 13, 1990.
44. *John Gibson, Greenville, MS, Feb. 14, 1990.
45. *Jake Stein, Greenville, MS, June 7, 1988.
46. Harry S. Ashmore, *Hearts and Minds: The Anatomy of Racism from Roosevelt to Reagan* (New York: McGraw-Hill, 1982), p. 27.
47. *John Gibson, Greenville, MS, Feb. 14, 1990.
48. HC, typescript of commencement address, Duke University, 1955. Robert W. Woodruff Library, Emory University.
49. Memphis *Commercial-Appeal*, May 3, 1955.
50. HC to Fred C. Berger, May 10, 1955.
51. HC to James C. Baird, Jr., May 10, 1955.
52. *Henry D. Marsh, Jackson, MS, June 10, 1988.
53. Ferd Moyse to HC, n.d.
54. HC to Marilyn Williams, Oct. 12, 1955.
55. *DD-T*, Sept. 21, 1955.
56. HC to Stanley M. Rinehart, Sept. 29, 1955.
57. *DD-T*, Nov. 10, 1955.
58. "Racial Crisis."
59. Boston *Herald*, n.d. Clipping in Carter Papers.
60. HC to Gayle Winthrop, Sept. 30, 1955.
61. Ashmore, *Hearts and Minds*.
62. *DD-T*, Dec. 9, 1955.

Chapter 13

1. HC, "Memo to Some Holmes Countians," *DD-T*, Sept. 30, 1955.
2. HC to L. A. Chase, March 13, 1956.
3. HC to Margaret Upshaw, Dec. 20, 1955.
4. HC to Anthony V. Ragusin, Dec. 5, 1955; HC to Dr. and Mrs. L. Rayford, Dec. 29, 1955.
5. *DD-T*, Feb. 3, 1956; *DD-T* Feb. 9, 1956.
6. *DD-T*, Feb. 12, 1956.
7. HC to Elia Kazan, Feb. 14, 1956.
8. Kenneth Douty to HC, Feb. 13, 1956; HC to Kenneth Douty, Feb. 20, 1956.
9. BC to Amy Tiesler, April 5, 1956.

10. Bob Brown to HC, March 13, 1956; HC to Bob Brown, March 19, 1956.

11. HC to Richard Baker, June 6, 1956.

12. *Henry D. Marsh, Jackson, MS, June 10, 1988.

13. HC to Carl Brandt, June 12, 1956.

14. HC to William Peters, May 20, 1958.

15. *Henry D. Marsh, Jackson, MS, June 10, 1988.

16. Clipping in Mississippi Department of Archives and History.

17. HC to Mark Ethridge, Feb. 5, 1957.

18. HC to Carl Brandt, May 20, 1957; HC to BB, May 20, 1957; HC to BB, June 7, 1957.

19. Boyd Ridgway to HC, Aug. 29, 1957.

20. Lewis Gannett to HC, May 12, 1954.

21. *Josephine Haxton, Jackson, MS, June 11, 1988.

22. *Time*, Oct. 7, 1957.

23. Roanoke, Virginia, *Times*, Oct. 7, 1957. Clipping in Carter Papers.

24. HC, summary of address. Carter Papers.

25. HC to Gordon Davies, Oct. 3, 1957.

26. HC to David Cohn, Oct. 3, 1957.

27. HC to BB, Oct. 3, 1957.

28. HC to Dr. William L. Giles, Nov. 8, 1957.

29. *DD-T*, Sept. 10, 1957.

30. HC to Barry Bingham, March 21, 1958.

31. John Temple Graves, Birmingham *Post-Herald*, Feb. 27, 1958.

32. Quoted in Ethridge, "Mississippi Notebook." Clipping in Carter Papers.

33. *Manufacturers Record*, March 1958.

34. HC to James M. Elliott, April 1, 1958.

35. Undated clipping in Carter Papers.

36. *DD-T*, March 17, 1958.

37. *JDN*, March 18, 1958.

38. Quoted in HC, "I'll Never Leave My Town," *SEP*, June 4, 1960.

39. R. B. Harwell, *Saturday Review*, Jan. 24, 1959.

40. *NYT*, Jan. 21, 1959. Clipping in Bowdoin College alumni files.

41. C. Vann Woodward, "Bad Times Not Forgotten," *NYTBR*, Feb. 1, 1959.

42. *The New Yorker*, Feb. 14, 1959. Clipping in Carter Papers.

43. United Press International, "Editor Brands Witness Liar After Statements to 'Subversive' Probers," *DD-T*, Nov. 19, 1959; personal statement, *DD-T*, Nov. 19, 1959.

44. *HC III, Washington, DC, Nov. 27, 1989.

45. Text in Carter Papers.

46. Quoted in Shreveport, LA, *Herald*, Jan. 29, 1960. Clipping in Carter Papers.

47. Birmingham *News*, Jan. 23, 1960.

48. HC to Mrs. H. E. Chatham, Jan. 29, 1960.

49. HC to O. W. Holmes, Feb. 15, 1960.

50. HC to Horace Lake, March 9, 1960.

Chapter 14

1. HC, "The Young Negro Is a New Negro," *NYTM*, May 1, 1960.

2. HC to Robert Sherrod, *SEP*, June 28, 1960.

3. HC to C. J. Harkrader, Jan. 29, 1960.

4. HC to "Scott and John," Oct. 24, 1963.

5. HC to Peavey Heffelfinger, July 19, 1960.

6. BCUM.

7. HC to Carol Brandt, Oct. 21, 1960.

8. HC to "Co," Jan. 9, 1961.

9. HC to Mrs. Arthur Bull, Jan. 27, 1961.

10. HC to Grace Casanova, Dec. 18, 1961.

11. Jackson *Clarion-Ledger*, Feb. 12, 1961.

12. Jackson *Clarion-Ledger*, April 24, 1961. Clipping in Mississippi Department of Archives and History.

13. *Ione Lundy, Greenville, MS, June 7, 1988.

14. Mrs. James Polk Morris, Jr., to HC, Oct. 3, 1961; HC to Mrs. James Polk Morris, Jr., Oct. 10, 1961.

15. BCOH.

16. *JDN*, Dec. 6, 1961.

17. BCUM.

18. *DD-T*, Dec. 10, 1961.

19. *JDN*, Dec. 13, 1961.

20. Statement in Carter Papers.

21. HC, "Desegregation Does Not Mean Integration," *NYTM*, Feb. 11, 1962.

22. HC to Tom Mullen, Jan. 26, 1962.

23. HC to "Dear Bo," Jan. 26, 1962.

24. HC to "Dear Anne," Feb. 2, 1962.

25. HC to Rufus Harris, Jan. 26, 1962.

26. BCUM.

27. *HC III, Washington, DC, Nov. 27, 1989.

28. BCUM.

29. HC to Carol Brandt, Nov. 14, 1961.

30. HC to John Starr, March 4, 1963.

31. *Alden Sawyer, Yarmouth, MA, July 17, 1989.

32. Jackson *Clarion-Ledger*, June 24, 1963.

33. HC, "Mississippi Now—Hate and Fear," *NYTM*, June 23, 1963.

34. HC to Mrs. Eugene Law, July 20, 1963.

35. HC to Carol Brandt, Aug. 3, 1963.

36. Jesse Burt, review of *Doomed Road of Empire, Southern Observer*, May 1964.

37. *James Robertshaw, Greenville, MS, June 8, 1988.

38. HC to Joseph R. Ator, Jan. 15, 1964.

39. HC to James S. Coles, April 29, 1963.

40. HC to "Scott and John," Oct. 24, 1963.

Chapter 15

1. HC, typescript for unpublished memoir.

2. *Josephine Haxton, Jackson, MS, June 11, 1988.

3. *DD-T*, May 3, 1964.

4. BCOH.

5. Chad Walsh, review of *The Ballad of Catfoot Grimes and Other Verses, Saturday Review*, Jan. 2, 1965.

6. HC to Carol Brandt, July 6, 1964.

7. *U.S. News & World Report*, June 29, 1964.

8. HC interview with William McCleery, *University*, 1965.

9. HC to Al Cowdrey, July 6, 1964.

10. HC to George S. Alder, Jan. 5, 1965.

11. HC, "Our Town Is Conservative," *The Virginia Quarterly Review*, Spring 1965.

12. Nicholas von Hoffman, "Mississippi Ends at Greenville," New York *Post*, Aug. 4, 1965 (originally published in Chicago *Daily News*).

13. HC to Carol Brandt, Feb. 24, 1965.

14. HC to Evelyn Spickard, Feb. 27, 1965.

15. Bruce Hilton, *The Delta Ministry* (New York: Macmillan, 1969), p. 42.

16. *Jake Stein, Greenville, MS, June 7, 1988.

17. HC to Allen E. Johnson, Jan. 6, 1966.

18. *Kenneth Haxton, Greenville, MS, June 22, 1988.

19. HC to Mrs. I. Nels Barnett, Nov. 28, 1966.

20. HC to Bill Howland, Sept. 27, 1966.

21. HC, "The Kind of Words That Make a Man a Target," *Pageant*, Sept. 1964.

22. HC to Carol Brandt, June 4, 1965.

23. HC to Albert and Malva and Heffner, April 8, 1966.

24. *DD-T*, Nov. 17, 1965.

25. HC to Norma E. Isaacs, Aug. 24, 1966.

26. HC to HC III, July 28, 1966.

27. HC to Lady Munro, Sept. 14, 1965.

28. HC, "The Old South Had Something Worth Saving," *NYTM*, Dec. 4, 1966.

29. *Jeff Howie, April 19, 1990 (telephone).

30. HC to Albert Heffner, Dec. 21, 1967.

31. HC to Dr. Politella, Dec. 29, 1967.

32. New Orleans *States-Item*, Feb. 1, 1968. Clipping in Tulane University Library archives.

33. BC to Carl Brandt, Aug. 2, 1969.

34. HC to Philip Carter, July 14, 1967.

35. HC to David Brown, July 31, 1967.

36. HC to O. A. Robinson, Jan. 23, 1968.

37. T. H. Baker, oral history interview, University of Texas Oral History Project, Nov. 8, 1968.

38. *DD-T*, June 7, 1968.

39. *Lew Dietz, Rockport, ME, July 22, 1989.

40. Richard Bissell, Philadelphia *Bulletin*, Nov. 8, 1970. Clipping in Mississippi Department of Archives and History.

41. *Ione Lundy, Greenville, MS, June 7, 1988.

42. HC III, "Hodding Carter 1907–1972," *DD-T*, April 12, 1972.

43. Philip Carter, "Big," *DD-T*, April 12, 1972.

Index

Index

Index

Index

Index

Index